From Tanqueray to the Championship
The History of Ampthill & District Rugby Club
by Mike Plant

Contents

Acknowledgements

An Introduction by Eric Webb

Chapter	1	1881 and All That!
Chapter	2	The First 10 Years
Chapter	3	The Sixties - Consolidation
Chapter	4	The Seventies – A Maturing Club
Chapter	5	The Eighties – From Friendlies to Leagues
Chapter	6	The Nineties – Silverware at Last!
Chapter	7	2000 – 2010 – The Road to Twickenham
Chapter	8	2010 – 2019 – The Race to the Championship!
Chapter	9	2019 - 2020 - The Championship & Covid-19
Chapter	10	The Mini & Youth – The Jewel in the Crown – 1971 - 2020

**Cover – Joe Bercis leads his team mates through the woods
Image – David Horn, PRIME Media Images**

Acknowledgements

I would like to thank the following for their help in compiling the information, memories, reflections, and opinions which make up this history.

Club Captains:

Norman Brown, Brian "Slim" Clark, Bob Clayton, Paul Farthing, Keith Garwood, Louis Grimoldby, John Hall, Billy Johnson, Phil Lane, Peter Nouch, Steve Peacey, Danny Phillips, Simon Spavins, Dave Tompkins, Steve Watson, John Wilkinson, Dave Williams, Graham Whitehall.

Club Members:

Phil Argent, Keith Belcher, Ellis Billington, Iain Bremner, Peter Britton, Colin Burke, Alaine & Leigh Clark, Ian Cooper, Harry Cornforth, Jonny Cresswell, Liam Duffin, Michael Dyer, Denis Hardy, Brian Hodgson, James, Justin & Simon Fletcher, Rob & Judith Fletcher, Tom Gray, Vic Kaye, Richard Mardle, Gloria Mills, Kev Miller, Paul New, James Offer, Jeff Offer, Cliff Page, Lyn Palmer, Ann & Tony Phillips, Ian Scarr, Nick Stephenson, Paul Titchener, James Wiggett, Mark Lavery, Rebecca Lane, Karen & Alex Radley, Tony Rogers, Pat Sherry, Ian Titman, Bill Warfield, Tony Willison, Martin Wythe

Others:

Richard Collins – Club Doctor, Jane Ditcham – Business Director – Rugby Journal, David Emery – Editor – The Rugby Paper, Ian Hamilton – Hon. Sec. Peterborough RUFC, Simon Hodge – Felicity Print, Bob French – ex Peterborough Telegraph Sports Ed., Jason Fox – Jersey Evening Post Sports Editor, Sam Riley – photographer Rugby World, Sarah Mockford – Ruby World, Julia Skinner – Francis Frith Collection, Nicholas Cook – Director General – The Gin Guild, Lauren Couchman – LNC Images, Chris Lishman – Newcastle Falcons, Daniele Colucciello – The Rugby Journal, David Horn – PRIME Media Images, Jo Walker – Copywriting, Editing & Proofreading.

Especially thanks to my wife Ann, who not only helped with my research in the Bedfordshire Archives, British Newspapers and Libraries but also scanned countless photographs, proof-read the script and was incredibly patient and supportive during the year and a half it took to write this history. Thanks also to my friend Norman Phillips, ex-Ampthill flanker, for his checking of the final script.

Introduction

In March 1999, Eric J. Webb a founder member of ARUFC wrote the following, as the Club approached its fiftieth year.

The idea of forming (or, as we were to find out later, re-forming) a rugby club in Ampthill originated during a "training session" in the lounge of the White Hart Hotel, Ampthill in the Spring of 1950. On that Friday evening Ken Tilston, John Churchill, Brian Staniforth and I were lubricating our tonsils with a few glasses of ale and chatting about the Bedford club's chances on the following day, when the conversation turned to the subject of having a local rugby club. Ampthill had flourishing soccer and cricket clubs and it seemed that the handling code was sadly missing. Another round (it was always my round!) and the discussion took on a more serious tone.

The first questions were, of course, who would play and where would we play? The "who" became a little clearer as we explored the matter more - apart from ourselves, who could we poach from other clubs; who could we convert from the soccer fraternity and what former players could we coax to dig out their boots and turn out for us? A quick run-down of possibilities indicated that, although it might be a struggle, we stood a fair chance of raising a fifteen by the Fall, given that we had the summer ahead of us to do a little scouting. It was evident that we would have to look further afield than just Ampthill and so we decided on the name Ampthill & District R.U.F.C.

The seed was sown! The "where" did not seem to present an insurmountable difficulty - after all, there was lots of green space around in those days. In the months that followed, we enlisted the help of (who else?) Richard Dillingham who we knew to be much involved in local sporting activity and it wasn't too long before we were granted permission to use an area in Ampthill Park, adjacent to Woburn Street and situated somewhere in the vicinity of where the cricket pavilion now is. It was the absolute antithesis of the proverbial "flat playing field" but it had grass and was accessible and (important at that time) would cost us nothing. The local builders' supply yard produced some scaffolding poles just about long enough to suffice as goal-posts and a bag of lime with which to mark out the pitch. Arrangements were made for changing facilities (and the use of a hose-pipe and a few buckets) in an outside facility somewhere down the "King's Arms" yard. After a considerable amount of leg-work and physical effort had been supplied by the "recruited" members, September came around and we were, for the most part, ready for the fray.

By that time, some basic decisions had been made. One of them was that of "colours". We assumed that everyone had something white and so, for our first game, we fielded fifteen bodies wearing a dazzling variety of dress shirts, cricket shirts and tee shirts. The colour chosen for shorts was "dark". I believe that, somewhere in the Club's records, there is an Ampthill News team photograph which attests to this fact.

Needless to say, our season was not a great one in terms of results, but we were encouraged by our ability to field a team for all of the (incomplete) fixture list. Something which also gave us a lift and spurred us go to on to "greater" things was the "Ball of the Year" (given annually to the club considered to have done most for local rugby) which was awarded to us by the Rugby Followers' Association of Bedford. Fortunately, by the time this was presented to us, we had managed to acquire jerseys in our adopted colours - maroon and gold; and looked almost presentable for the ensuing team photograph.

At this point, something should be said about the amount of effort put into the running of the Club by the members at that time. The players were well scattered around the mid-Beds. area and some of us were working away from home during the week. This made for some difficulties in organizing a team, compiling a fixture list etc- and given that only a small number of the members were available to carry out these tasks, many hours were required to be spent in order to keep things on track. Those saddled with most of this responsibility were those who lived in Ampthill and it is they who deserve much credit for what they did towards the Club's growth. Mention must also be made of the contributions made by (what we then knew as) "the girls": the wives and girl-friends who lent their support by way of catering the visitors' teas on Saturday afternoons and often dragged along to cheer us on at away games

Mention has already been made of Richard Dillingham whose help and advice has readily been given since day one. He also gave of his time to serve as our local referee for many years and I recall just how strictly he interpreted the rules of the game when the home team infringed - all in the interests of being seen to be impartial! Norman Sharpe, who became our first President, was another who gave us strong support in the Town. Our first Vice-President was Mrs. Gladys Potter of The George Inn at Maulden who made significant contributions in the early years, catering for our Annual General Meetings at a less than affordable cost and providing accommodation and refreshments for many other meetings. No funds were solicited from outside of the Club and we subsisted on the (to the best of my recollection) one-pound annual membership and half-a-crown game fee.

Our second season saw some welcome changes. Players started to come to the Club and request membership. Of great help was the acquisition of several experienced players from the Wrest Park Agricultural College in Silsoe and some very young fellows, both at school and just out of school, began to take an interest in local rugby. We also began to win some games. It was at this time that some local "Derbies" became established, notably the Biggleswade Club and Old Dunstablians. And, our fixture list was complete! Perhaps the biggest change was the move to the Station Road ground complete with its small changing hut and built in cow-flops (which were required to be moved each Saturday morning). At least it was level, even if a little damp in certain parts. The use of cold water and a few buckets which we suffered with initially in our new venue was soon deemed unacceptable and an arrangement was made with the Ampthill Towa Soccer Club to use their changing facilities in the park - a distinct improvement despite the hike across the fields to get there after the game, We were, incidentally, not the only club to lack decent changing and bathing facilities in those days - hose pipes, buckets and barns were much in evidence at some of our away games.

Things continued to go well until somewhere about half-way into the third season (1952/53). For a variety of reasons, we lost some of our more regular players, which made it difficult to field a full fifteen each week. On some occasions we were forced to "borrow" players from the opposition and on others we played a man or two short. This situation led to a feeling of some despondency amongst those who bore the responsibility of putting together a team for each match - so much so, that a special meeting of the Committee was called. The one item on the agenda was "Shall we continue to struggle like this, or shall we cancel the scheduled fixtures and disband the Club?". The meeting like many others, was held at *The George Inn" and of course, commenced with a round of Flowers' Mild & Bitter. The business of the day was then addressed and a solution to the problem sought - there were many arguments both for and against, but another round of pints conjured up a little more optimism amongst the participants. After more detailed discussion and several more rounds, the continued existence of the Club was affirmed although, by the end of the evening I am not quite sure whether any of us knew quite why. All that mattered was that we were sure that things would work out.

From that time on, I believe that the Club never looked back. Eventually enough players turned out that a second team was fielded, albeit not every week. Better fixtures were arranged and the team's performance showed a marked improvement - it became almost normal to have a handful of spectators at our home games!

At the end of the 1956/57 season I left for Canada. I will never know whether or not that was the reason, but from then on the Club went from strength to strength and began its decades of growth towards becoming the healthy organization that it is today. Author's note - Eric Webb played No. 8 in that historic first game in September 1950 and served on the Committee as Club Treasurer.

Chapter 1 - 1881 and all that!

The Bedfordshire Times And Independent for Saturday, 8th October 1881 records the following, in its Ampthill News section:

> FOOTBALL CLUB. – We have much pleasure in recording the fact that a football club has now been established for this town and neighbourhood, meetings for that purpose having been held at the King's Head Inn on the 23rd and 30th of September last. The following officers have been elected for the ensuing year:- Captain, Mr. A. H. Tanqueray; vice-captain, Mr. H. King; treasurer, Mr. G. M. Smith; Committee, Messrs. W. J. Herbert, W. Joyce, E. White, C. Crisp and --- Field; hon. Secretary, Mr. H. J. Turner. The subscription for playing members for the season was fixed at 2s 6d. The rules adopted for the government of the club were those of the Rugby Football Union.

NB Rugby clubs, in the 19th Century were referred to as rugby football clubs, as opposed to soccer clubs, who were known as association football clubs.

Kings Head Hotel in Woburn Street, where Ampthill Rugby Club was founded in September 1881

Research reveals little about Ampthill Rugby Club's first committee, except for its Captain. If the new Rugby Club was to thrive it would seem to have been heavily reliant on the redoubtable A. H. Tanqueray.

Andrew Hawkins Tanqueray (Captain)

Tanqueray was born in Tingrith, Bedfordshire, in 1864. He was the ninth son of the rector of Tingrith, Truman Tanqueray. His grandfather, Edward, was also Rector and who, at the age of 41, married a 17 year-old girl and had 14 children!

Tanqueray attended Marlborough College, a public school founded in 1843, for the sons of Church of England clergy. The Reading Mercury of 4th December 1880 reports him playing for the College 1st team against Clifton Rugby Football Club. Rugby School and other rugby playing schools, such as Marlborough College, started to spread their version of football (rugby laws) far and wide. In 1868, Marlborough Nomads Rugby Club was formed to provide rugby for Old Boys of the College living and working in London, they supplied a number of players for the sport's early international fixtures. The Marlborough Nomads Club was notable for being one of the twenty-one founding members of the Rugby Football Union in 1871. Newspaper reports of the Marlborough Nomads games in the last quarter of the nineteenth century reveal no mention of A. H. Tanqueray playing for the London team. The Marlborough Nomads were to amalgamate with the Rosslyn Park Club in 1911.

Apart from his rugby prowess, the Reading Mercury records Tanqueray playing a solo, with distinction, in a concert of the College Brass Band. He returned to Ampthill after finishing at Marlborough and in 1887, married Alice Lucy Corby (born 1861) in Kensington, London. A. H. Tanqueray would have been almost 18 years old when elected to the captaincy of Ampthill Rugby Club in September 1881. He was employed by Messrs. Morris & Co. a brewery firm with extensive premises in Bedford Street, on ground now occupied by the Waitrose Supermarket. Tanqueray became master brewer and is reported to have been highly respected and liked. He became a Lieutenant and then Captain in the Bedfordshire Volunteer Rifle Corps (a precursor to the Territorial Army, formed in 1908) which drilled in Ampthill Park and Houghton Park,

The Morris Brewery, Bedford Street in the 1930s

The Tanqueray family was well connected, Andrew's brother T.H. Tanqueray was a solicitor and Coroner for the Honour of Ampthill. His daughter, Margaret, was prominent in arts and crafts and societies for the support of local causes.

Extensive research, including contacting the Tanqueray family archivist and the Gin Guild, failed to find an image of Andrew Hawkins Tanqueray, the first captain of Ampthill Rugby Club.

Tanqueray Gin

By 1830, Andrew's Uncle Charles was distilling the famous Tanqueray gin in the Bloomsbury district of London. The retail outlet of Edward & Charles Tanqueray & Co. was established on Vine Street, London, in 1838.

Charles Tanqueray in 1890 - he and nephew Andrew were both born at Tanqueray House, Tingrith

Morris Brewery workers in the late 1880s – is the elusive A. H. Tanqueray present?

In 1888 Andrew Tanqueray was given a great send-off from Morris' Brewery, as he had taken up The Lion Brewery in faraway Totnes, Devon. The 1891 census shows that he lived in Devon with his wife and two children and gave his occupation as brewer. Within 3 years of moving to Totnes he became Mayor – this is confirmed by minutes of a Totnes Town Council meeting published in the Exeter & Plymouth Gazette on Wednesday 26th September 1894. Andrew Hawkins Tanqueray became a Freemason in Totnes in 1889.

The Totnes Weekly Times of December 1st 1888, contains a match report of Totnes versus Teignmouth with Andrew Tanqueray featuring at half-back. The Devon RFU Official Handbook shows that Andrew served on the Devon County RFU Committee from 1893-94. It also shows that Totnes Rugby Club won the Devon Junior County Cup in 1891. Having retired from playing the game, through work and civic pressures, Tanqueray became President of Totnes RFC and was presented with the County Junior Cup by Mr. A. Stuart, Honorary Secretary of Devon County RUFC, in 1891.

The 1901 census shows that the Tanqueray family had moved to Finchley, London and had a third child. Andrew Tanqueray's occupation is given as, Director Mechanical Engineering Company.

By 1911 the family had moved to 27 Landsdowne Road, Bedford and Tanqueray's occupation was Managing Director, Brewery and Mechanical Engineering. Tanqueray's elder son, Captain Andrew Alexander Trumann Tanqueray was killed in World War 1, at Ypres in 1915, aged 25.

By 1918, the family had moved to Ivy House, Clophill, Bedfordshire. A. H. Tanqueray became a magistrate and performed much voluntary work for the village. Known in Clophill as Major Tanqueray, he died in 1938, aged 73. In his will he left over £20,000 to his surviving son, David Yeo Bartholomew Tanqueray who was a Director of Baker, Perkins, Corrie, Reid, and Sharman Solicitors in Ampthill. That sum today would be worth in excess of £1,355,000.

Despite A. H. Tanqueray's impressive accomplishments and connections, there is no evidence of Ampthill Rugby Club playing any fixtures. Andrew Underwood (1934-2012), the prominent local teacher, historian and author has described the Club existence as "short-lived". An exhaustive trawl through local newspapers of the time by the present author reveals no mention of rugby football played in Ampthill i.e.

Ampthill & District News 1891-1911
Bedfordshire Mercury 1837-1912
Bedford Record 1877-1911
Bedfordshire Times & Independent 1859-1954

Ivy House, High Street, Clophill today– where Andrew Hawkins Tanqueray lived from 1918 - 1938

It seems inconceivable that rugby would have passed under the radar of the local newspapers, other sports; association football, cricket, cycling, hockey, and bowls and athletics were regularly and enthusiastically reported by the local press. A search through the archives of the various teams playing rugby football in Bedford and Olney at the time, record no fixtures with Ampthill Rugby Club. Briefly, below are the origins of other sports teams in the town?

1. Association Football Club

The Bedfordshire Times of Saturday 17th November 1888 records the following:

"Football – A meeting was held in the White Hart Hotel on Tuesday Evening for the purpose of organising a Football Club. Those present: Messrs. F.F. Stearn, G. Finding, E. White, C & H. Stapleton, C. Goff, R. Smith, E. Morris, John

Gray, and others. It was resolved to form a club to be called the Ampthill Football Club. The following were elected as members for this season: - Mr. Edward White, captain; Mr. George Finding, vice-captain; Mr. F.F. Stearn, secretary & treasurer; Messrs. H. Swaffield jun., R. Smith and E. Morris, committee. It was decided to play under Association rules. The Club ground would be Mr. Gray's field and practice commences next Tuesday afternoon at 4 o'clock. The subscription is only 1s. 6d., and it is hoped that this will be an inducement to the young men of the town to enrol themselves at once to enable the committee to select a team for playing matches with neighbouring clubs."

2. Cricket Club

The Bedfordshire Times of 23rd June 1863 reports:

"On Monday inst. The first game was played in Ampthill Park being the return match between Langford and Ampthill Clubs. The former was victorious on their own ground; but here the latter carried off all the laurels, being decided by the first innings. There was a very large attendance of spectators, the day being fine; and all would have passed off well but for the unwarrantable liberty a stripling nick-named Larky took with one of the spectators, which caused considerable annoyance in the field. We would advise this young "gentleman" to confine his larks to driving his quill in future."

In the 1840s two of the town's more prominent players were George and James Moore, whose father kept a shop at 103 Dunstable Street. The two brothers later emigrated to Australia, where they played for the new country in international games in the 1860s and 1870s.

3. Hockey Club

By 1908, reports were appearing in local newspapers of a thriving Hockey Club in Ampthill with regular fixtures, socials, and AGMs. This was a club for ladies as well as men and they played on Mr. Harry Fountaine's Field, Station Road (he also owned land near Little Farm adjacent to Woburn Road that was divined for water to supply the town – but without success). The Hockey Club, in 1908, planned to enter a league the following year, though the distance from the town centre was said to have reduced spectator numbers.

4. Cycle Club

The Club held its AGMs at the White Hart Hotel. The Ampthill & District news of 13th November 1897 records a 5th November Carnival - held by the Ampthill Social and Cycle Club:

"On Friday evening, the 5th inst., the Ampthill Social and Cycling Club organised a splendid carnival. The proceedings took the form of an illuminated Fancy Dress Cycle parade, the cyclists being attired in elaborate and picturesque costumes of the 16th Century, and the principal characters of the period contemporaneous with the historical plot against the King by Guy Fawkes and his confederates, were impersonated, as hereinafter mentioned, by about fifty members of the Club. The procession started at Cowell's Lodge, on the Woburn-Road, and proceeded through the main thoroughfare, accompanied by torch bearers on either side. The streets were lined with crowds of spectators, including a large number from the villages around."

5. Athletics – Ampthill Athletics Sports

Report in Ampthill News for Sept. 17th, 1892:

"These sports were inaugurated by Lord Ampthill and the late Captain Wingfield some three years ago, and have now become quite an annual holiday, looking forward to by the many competitors for honours with eager anticipation and interest. This year they were held in the same field as usual (Mr. Tansley) on Tuesday afternoon; the weather, which threatened rain earlier in the day, fortunately held fine and the entries were larger and better contested for generally, and the Committee are to be congratulated upon the excellent arrangements which were carried out with great success.

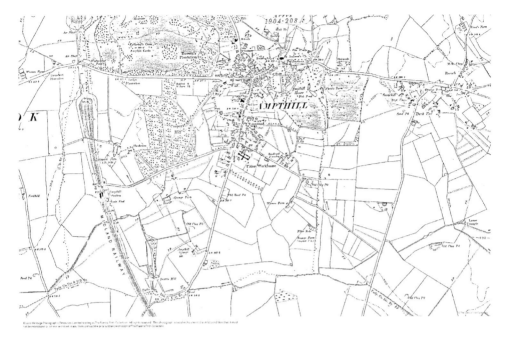

A Map of Ampthill 1882 (Copyright courtesy of The Francis Frith Collection)

6. Bowls & Tennis

The earliest public mention of Ampthill Bowls Club is in the Bedfordshire Times and Independent: Friday, 21st March 1919 edition which reported "a meeting to be held on Thursday, 27th March at The White Hart to form a Tennis and Bowls Club". On 4th. April the paper reported that "it was decided to offer the first Captaincy to Capt. A Wingfield, the Secretary and Treasurer was to be Mr. H. Swaffield, the Committee was also appointed and an announcement of playing is expected." The land that the club played on was originally leased to the club by Bedfordshire Council. The green and clubhouse is built on land originally owned by Lord Wingfield and was part of his famous 'menagerie'. He collected many exotic animals, some seen for the first time in these parts, including camels, zebras, ostrich, and llamas. Hence the llama featured on the Ampthill Bowls Club badge.

Ampthill Rugby Club in 1881

Why did the 1881 Ampthill Rugby Club flounder, when other clubs thrived in the last third of the nineteenth century? The following factors are, arguably, required in the successful launching of a sporting club, whatever the level of play or ambitions for the future.

Factors required – not necessarily in any order of importance:

1. Players
2. Leadership
3. Funding
4. Travel
5. Opponents
6. Kit and eventually posts, pitch and changing facilities
7. Collective qualities: including; adaptability, energy, fortitude, ingenuity and practicality
8. Contacts outside the Club
9. Referee

We will examine these factors in an attempt to understand why Ampthill failed to establish a rugby club in the latter stages of the nineteenth century and consider why another club, little known today, Bedford Wanderers, managed to thrive through this period.

1. Players

During the course of the nineteenth century the population of Ampthill almost doubled. Ten years after the formation of the Club, the census of 1891 gave the population of Ampthill as 2,294, consisting of 548 households living in 517 dwellings. The majority of the population were working people employed in agriculture (885), general labouring (266), building trades (150), food & lodging (141) and domestic offices (62).

The small industrial concerns of the town provided some employment; at the rear of Church Street was George Allen and Co., the manufacturing and pharmaceutical chemists employed many including women and older children. In Bedford Street were the extensive brewery works of the Morris brothers a major employer of folk, mainly men, in Ampthill. Smaller industrial concerns included the Foundry in Oliver Street which produced agricultural and domestic ironwork. The gas works, built in 1849 and run by the Ampthill Gas and Coke Company at this time, supplied light and heat to much of the town from its Maulden Road works (now Gas House Lane). Ampthill has always been a market town and extensive trade serving the surrounding villages gave employment to many, e.g. Claridge & Berwick's grocery business on the corner of Dunstable Street and Woburn Street was flourishing and had a small factory attached making candles. George Rushbrook's drapery on the Market Square employed women and girls in the shop and in dressmaking. Josiah Burgess mineral works in Oliver Street and Charles Stapleton, boot manufacturer, gave employment in Woburn Street. Other works including Dillingham Bros. wheelwrights in Arthur Street and George Hensmen, making, and repairing agricultural machinery in Park Hill. Hat-making also thrived; the town became known for its "narrow improved" version of the straw-hat.

Of the professional people: there were three doctors, two solicitors, an architect and surveyor, a bank manager, a veterinary surgeon, a superintendent of police, an Inland Revenue Officer, and other officials, including a Registrar of Marriages. The census showed there to be 26 persons engaged in general or local government and 35 in professional occupations. These were effectively the "squirearchy" of the town, the only ones likely to have had access to secondary education which, in 1881, meant independent schools. Rugby football was only available in the public schools and universities.

By the 1880's education was compulsory for children aged 5-10, there being two schools in Ampthill for that purpose; the National School in Bedford Street with an average attendance of 220 at that time and the British or Wesleyan School in Woburn Street with an average attendance of 170. There were a number of Dame Schools in the town and a small private school, in Dunstable Street – the Albion School – which prepared pupils for entry to the Bedford schools.

Secondary education for everyone awaited the Fisher Act of 1918, which made it compulsory up to the age of 14. Grammar schools have existed since the 16th Century. Locally, Dunstable Grammar School opened in 1888 and Luton Modern School in 1908, but the modern grammar school concept only dates back to the Education Act 1944. Therefore, secondary education, in the 1880s, was available locally only in the independent or public schools of Bedford, of which there were three for male scholars:

- **Bedford School**

Founded in 1552 – the school owes its existence to the generosity of Sir William and Dame Alice Harper – now The Harper Trust. This was known as Bedford Grammar School in the latter part of the nineteenth century, moving to its current campus in De Parys Avenue, in 1891.

- **Bedford Modern School**

Originally known as "the Writing School", Bedford Modern School began in what is now the old Town Hall in St. Paul's Square, before moving to Harper Square. In the late 19th. century it was known as The Modern School. In 1974, Bedford Modern School moved to Manton Lane, Bedford.

- **Bedfordshire Middle Class Public School/Bedford County School**

This purpose-built school opened in 1869, in Ampthill Road, Kempston. This was a boarding school for the sons of farmers, tradesmen and other businessmen. It was built to accommodate 300 boys in seven dormitories – but of the original entry of 105 - only 39 of the boys came from Bedfordshire. The name was changed in 1875 to the Bedford County School because as the Bedford Time reported: "The word Class grows more and more odious and its disappearance from the name of a public institution must have an advantageous effect". Although the County School was better known for cricket, its rugby football fixture list was strong and it made a positive impact on local rugby, its games reported regularly in the local press.

Bedfordshire Middle Class Public School, Ampthill Road, Kempston in 1867

Rugby Football in Bedford

The principal winter school sport of these three schools was rugby football and boarders had ample leisure time to familiarise themselves with the game and to be schooled in the finer points and laws. Public schools were greatly influenced by the example set by Rugby School and Dr. Thomas Arnold, Headmaster (1828-42). The Grammar and Modern Schools, both had a massive effect on the growth of the game in Bedford and the fortunes of the "Town Club" – Bedford RUFC - and beyond, in the British game.

The Grammar and Modern Schools had 1st XVs and "A" teams who had fixtures against the top sides of the day, including Leicester, Bedford, Blackheath, Harlequins, Rosslyn Park, Old Merchant Taylors, Oxford University & Cambridge University and the leading Public Schools. The County School, though less prominent than the other two schools, nevertheless had an impressive fixture list against other public schools and rugby clubs. Bedford Rugby Club was formed in 1886 with the merger of Bedford Rovers and Bedford Swifts and, after several changes of ground, leased the Goldington Road site from the Cricket Club. Their light and dark blue colours were chosen because of the close links with Oxford and Cambridge Universities.

There seems little doubt that the major reason for the 1881 Club's demise was a chronic lack of rugby players available locally to maintain a rugby club in Ampthill.

Bedford Wanderers RUFC 1895-98

In contrast; the Bedfordshire Times for Saturday 14th. September 1895 records the formation of Bedford Wanderers Rugby Football Club. This was formed from the old Post Office Rugby Club which was short of players/members and needed to go "open". They offered an alternative to the Town Club for old boys from the Grammar, Modern and County schools. They were to play in red shirts with a white collar. A year later, on Thursday 10th September 1896, the Wanderers held their AGM at the Embankment Hotel – 30 attended – they had played 19 matches (12 won, 6 lost and 1 drawn) during their first season. Gate money amounted to £28 6s. 7d. (about £4,000 today). They had found a rugby ground in Ampthill Road, Bedford – where Bedford Hospital stands today. In their first season they beat Northampton Saint James (now Northampton RUFC – the Saints). Below is the Wanderers' fixture list for 1896 published in the Bedfordshire Times, they were also able to run an "A" team in this second season. Games were sometimes arranged for Thursday which was a half-day holiday for Bedford. Although rivals to the Town Club, there is evidence of co-operation between the two clubs for example, player exchange and ground sharing. In 1898, Bedford Wanderers ran into financial difficulties, owing creditors £17 11s 10d. Eventually the Wanderers voted to join the Town Club - at their AGM on 27th. September 1898 – "in order to further the interests of football in Bedford". The Bedford Club paid off the Wanderers' debt having themselves made a profit of £42 9s 6d on the season 1898-99. J.R.D. Glascott had been captain of the Wanderers and he became captain of Bedford on their amalgamation.

> Mr. A. Ingram, the Wanderers secretary, has been working hard to secure a good list of fixtures for next year, and the following table will show the success of his exertions :—
>
> | | |
> |---|---|
> | Sept. 19.—Opening Match | home. |
> | ,, 26.—Rugby | away. |
> | Oct. 3. | |
> | ,, 10.—Dulwich Park (?) | home. |
> | ,, 17.—Finsbury College | home. |
> | ,, 24.—Modern School | away. |
> | ,, 31.—Leys School, Cambridge | away. |
> | Nov. 5.—Corpus College, Cambridge | home. |
> | ,, 7.—Kingston-on-Thames | home. |
> | ,, 14.—Olney | home. |
> | ,, 19.—Clare College, Cambridge | home. |
> | ,, 21.—Central Technical College | home. |
> | ,, 28.—St. Mary's Hospital | home. |
> | Dec. 2.—Grammar School | home. |
> | ,, 5.—Beckenham | away. |
> | ,, 12.—Barnes | home. |
> | ,, 19.—Hon. Artillery Company | home. |
> | ,, 26.—Kingston-on-Thames | away. |
> | Jan. 2.—Sidcup | home. |
> | ,, 9.—Nuneaton | home. |
> | ,, 14.—Cambridge Town | home. |
> | ,, 23.—Middlesex Hospital | home. |
> | ,, 30.—Grammar School | away. |
> | Feb. —.—Pembroke College, Cambridge | home. |
> | ,, 6.—Modern School | home. |
> | ,, 13.—St. Thomas's Hospital | home. |
> | ,, 18.—Cambridge Town | away. |
> | ,, 20.— | |
> | ,, 27.—Olney | away. |
> | March 6.—Beckenham | home. |
> | ,, 13.—London Scottish (A Team) | home. |
> | ,, 20.—Rosslyn Park (A Team) | home. |
> | ,, 27.—Dulwich Park (?) | home. |
> | April 3.—Nuneaton | away. |

Bedford Wanderers Fixture List 1897-98

The reason for the Wanderers success was the availability of players, thanks to the public schools in Bedford. Bedford was a hotbed of rugby and remains today one of the largest towns in England never to have had a football league club.

2. Leadership

What do we know about the personal qualities of Andrew Hawkins Tanqueray, the first Captain of Ampthill RUFC? Andrew was from a prominent and respectable local family, who would have employed servants and possessed its own horse-drawn transport. He was educated at Marlborough College, Wiltshire, which gave certain advantages and status in late nineteenth century society. Public schools organised, in great detail, the leisure time for its young, energetic and precocious young gentlemen. The various clubs, societies and sports etc would have schooled the young men into how to run these enterprises and the hierarchy of the school would have prepared young men to take their place in society. Unlike the other members of the newly formed Ampthill Rugby Club, Andrew Tanqueray was a "proper" rugby player.

Later in the century, old-boys of public schools like Marlborough, would have been the lieutenants who led the troops in the trenches of France in the First World War. Indeed, Andrew Tanqueray was to become a captain in the volunteer rifle corps. When Tanqueray was elected captain of ARUFC, at the King's Head in September 1881, he was eighteen and just down from College. Little can be found of his fellow Committee Members except for the following:

Harry J. Turner (Honorary Secretary), was born in Worcestershire in 1859 (making him 22 at the time of his election). In the 1881 census he was a border living with the Kitchener family of Farm Yard, Ampthill who were butchers. Harry was a solicitor's clerk and by 1891 he was married to Sarah Ann Lucy Kitchener, living in Buckingham, with four children. He died in 1933.

George. M. Smith (Treasurer), was born in Woburn in 1852 (he was 29 when elected). The 1881 census shows George was an auctioneer's clerk, boarding in Dunstable Street with Charles & Jane Stanbridge.

Of the others, little information survives except that Mr. E. White (Committee) was possibly a butcher's apprentice aged 18 and Mr. W. Joyce (Committee) was from Vicarage Farm, Renhold, and so, probably, in agriculture.

The future of the new Club appears to have rested heavily on the young shoulders of A. H. Tanqueray. He was to embark upon a career as Master Brewer with the flourishing Morris & Co. Brewers. Local newspapers report a celebration at the Works in Bedford Street on the occasion of his marriage. He was presented with " a handsome salad bowl, as a token of their esteem and regard for him in his profession". When Tanqueray left Ampthill in 1888 to take up his brewery in Totnes, Devon Messrs. Morris & Co. organised a lavish party to say farewell.

Considering all this; the Club would not have lacked leadership in terms of enthusiasm and, perhaps, charisma, but leadership alone would not have overcome the difficulties in other areas of the Club's development. When we contrast Tanqueray's task in 1881 with that of Ampthill captain of the 1950s, Norman Brown, the main difference is the support of men like Richard Dillingham and Norman Sharpe. Even so, as we shall see, the club almost folded through lack of players in the mid-1950s.

2. Funding

The new Club subscription was 2s. 6d. which would be worth approximately £14 today, so if the club had signed up say, 20 members, they would have an immediate income of £2.10s. (approximately £275 today). Honorary members (non-players) might be expected to contribute, but many rugby football clubs at this early stage in the development of the game would have relied on wealthy benefactors.

The club would have hoped to have borrowed a field on which to play, though many clubs started out as "Nomads" or "Wanderers". They would also have needed a rugby ball, playing kit and rudimentary washing facilities. The club would have needed to charge players for the hire of horse-drawn transport to Bedford and Olney – the only nearby towns playing rugby. However, the quality of the opposition of the rugby clubs in those places would have been truly formidable, to a fledgling Ampthill club, in the late 1880s.

Whilst this financial position appears tenuous and insecure – it might have been possible to see a future for the establishment of a rugby club if other factors were in its favour.

3. Travel

By the late nineteen /early twentieth century, road travel had improved greatly thanks to the widespread use of macadam, but was still dependent on horse-drawn vehicles, both commercial and private. The hills approaching Ampthill from Bedford and Flitwick would have made horse-drawn transport very difficult in adverse weather conditions.

In the 1880s, Ampthill's streets were dusty and the town water cart was sent out in dry spells to lay the dust. The crossing places in the centre of town were paved with cobbles and they were not macadamised until after 1902. Early in 1904, the County Council were asked to have the footpaths properly paved and kerbed. By the turn of the century "motor cars caused more interest than nuisance to the town at the time". Motor transport only became widely available in Britain from the 1920s onwards.

Local photographs show that the town used a manual fire engine in the 1890s. In 1913 Lady Ampthill christened the first steam fire engine at Park House. The Ampthill News of 18 October 1913 reported a "*capital drill with the fire escape, in which Fireman Putman ascended the escape to the top of Park House and brought down Fireman Dillingham on his shoulders with skill that raised hearty cheers from those watching ...*" Mr. Wingfield and his firemen were photographed at the inauguration of the motor fire engine on The Sands in 1928.

Two carriers went between Ampthill and Bedford twice a week and the White Hart omnibus, driven by Mr. Manton, met all trains at Ampthill Station. The railway came to Ampthill in September 1867, when the Midland Railway line opened between Bedford and London. Before the opening of Ampthill Station, passengers from the town had used the Bedford-Bletchley LNW line at Millbrook Station, which was for a time known as Ampthill (Millbrook) Station. Although the distance to the Ampthill Station was a disadvantage, the railway made local travel much more possible and even permitted daily visits to London. The platform at Ampthill station is said to be longer than any between Bedford and St. Pancras to enable troops of volunteers, arriving for training at Ampthill Great Park, to detrain efficiently.

Ampthill Railway Station

In 1881, transport would not have prevented Ampthill Rugby Club from travelling to fixtures and for opponents arriving, but such journeys would have been reliant on horse-drawn transport or the railway. The cost of such journeys may have been beyond the members' means, given that the majority of men were agricultural workers. The average farm labourer's wage rose steadily from around 9 shillings and 6 pence per week in 1824 to around 14 shillings and 5 pence in 1898. A mason might earn twenty-nine shillings a week and a carpenter twenty-five. Overall, in the middle years of the 1880s, the average annual wage for workers in England was £46/12/-. Getting time off work on Saturdays would not always have been possible for potential players in farming and other trades.

However, the state of roads was still an issue at the turn of the nineteenth century - The Bedfordshire Times of Saturday 4th January 1896 reported the following: "The approaches to the Goldington-Road ground are in shocking condition, being several inches deep in mud. It would be an easy and not very expensive way of remedying this state of things to make use of a cart load or two of cinders. The wet weather so affected the ground that it is considered advisable for the match between the Club second team and Northampton Second Fifteen this Saturday to be played on the Wanderer's ground."

In 1913 Ampthill Council felt obliged to ask the police for "protection" from traffic, particularly the corner of Bedford Street and Woburn Street. The same year, the London General Omnibus Company made an application for a license to have four motor buses each able to carry 34 passengers through the town.

By 1924, Bedford Athletic RUFC was using The National Omnibus & Transport Co. to travel to Kettering RUFC (Committee minutes show players were charged 2/-towards the cost) and in 1925, to Wellingborough RUFC (the players bore full cost).

4. Opponents

The oldest rugby clubs in Britain are:

Guys Hospital (1843), Cambridge University (1846), Marlborough College (1850), Trinity College (1854), Liverpool FC (1857), Edinburgh Academicals (1857), Blackheath (1858) and Barnes RFC (1858).

It is salutary to think that if Ampthill had succeeded in founding a functioning rugby club in 1881, it would now be among the oldest in the Rugby Football Union.

Bedford RUFC was founded in 1886 after an amalgamation between Bedford Rovers (1876) and Bedford Swifts (1882). Both parent clubs had close connections with Bedford School and Bedford Modern School, and both had fixtures with the leading teams of the period. Northampton St. James RFC (now the Saints) and Leicester RUFC (The Tigers) were both founded in 1880.

Olney Rugby Club was founded in 1877 and was a well-established club playing Bedford, Northampton and Leicester plus the Grammar and Modern Schools. Olney regularly supplied players to the East Midlands RUFC which was recognised by the Rugby Football Union in 1887. The following is an extract from an article in the Bedfordshire Times of Saturday November 10th 1894:

"The Olney Club has been in existence since 1877 and so is entering its seventeenth season. During the whole of that long period – for it is not a bad record as clubs go now – they have had fixtures with the premier Bedford Club and they have had home and away matches with the Grammar and Modern Schools. For several years past the latter have been dropped. The rugby club in Olney is decidedly popular and the club is well supported but owing to the small population (scarcely 2,500)* the "gates" are necessarily small and they have found difficulty keeping up the standards to a desirable point. Still they have been able to keep the game alive and it is a fact to their credit that at present they have forty playing members, are able to run two teams, and they boast of full membership (honorary and playing) of between 70 and 80. They have not gained in strength since last year. All the men behind the scrum are available while the places of one or two of the "old hands" in the forwards who have retired from the game have been replaced by young players from the "A" team. The greatest difficulty of the Olney Club is getting matches, due to the scarcity of rugby clubs in the neighbourhood, their funds will not permit of many matches at a distance.".

*similar to Ampthill's population in the 1891 census.

Still Olney considered themselves to be a strong team, only granting Ampthill 1st XV games against their "A" team in the 1950s. It was not until season 1972-73, that fixtures between Olney and Ampthill first teams were to begin.

Other local rugby teams were founded, as follows: Bedford Athletic (1908), Bedford Queens (1918), Luton (1931), Leighton Buzzard (1934), Stockwood Park (1947), Old Dunstablians (1948), Biggleswade (1949) and Bedford Swifts (1950). The Bedfordshire Times of October 6th 1899 reports an AGM of the Bedford & District Rugby League on 3rd October 1899 to form a league (under rugby union rules) for the minor clubs in the district, including Kempston, Clapham, Bedford Harlequins and Bedford "B" XV. Bedford Rugby Club 1st XV, Bedford Rugby Club "A" and Bedford Wanderers RUFC would be treated as "senior" clubs and therefore not eligible for the League.

It is difficult to see where the Ampthill club would have found fixtures at an appropriate level in 1881, the few available rugby teams in Bedford and Olney were too strong and well-established.

5. Kit and eventually posts, pitch and changing facilities
It is likely that other issues would have been more problematic for Andrew Tanqueray and his committee than these specifics – particularly finding players and fixtures. We will see later how these issues were tackled by the re-formed Club in the 1950-51 season, but they were not easy and probably required the collective qualities outlined below.

6. Collective qualities: including adaptability, energy, fortitude, ingenuity and practicality
These are qualities it is virtually impossible to assess at a distance of almost 140 years. However, it would seem that these factors and others were not sufficient for Andrew Tanqueray and his friends to succeed.

Rugby football clubs who managed to flourish in the late 19th Century, and there were a great many in all geographical parts of the country, were later to suffer dreadfully in the conflict of 1914-1918.

The Ampthill Club was re-founded after the Second World War, as was the case with most rugby clubs in the British Isles. As we shall see later, there are countless examples of men (and their wives, partners and families) demonstrating the "collective qualities" above. Some of these characters who established the club after WW2 are still alive and active in the life of our present, very successful, rugby club.

7. Contacts outside the Club
There were many prominent figures of the day resident in Ampthill around the turn of the nineteenth century. These included:

- Second Baron of Ampthill – Arthur Oliver Villiers Russell. A keen sportsman he rowed for Oxford in the Boat Race three times, winning twice. At Ampthill he organised annual athletics sports for the locals which were immensely popular. Lord Ampthill was closely associated with many county sporting organisations. As a politician, he was private secretary to Joseph Chamberlain and, in 1900, was Governor of Madras and also interim Viceroy of India in 1904. Apart from the House of Lords he served for many years on the County Council, becoming chairman in 1928, in succession to his cousin, the Duke of Bedford.
- The Dowager Lady Ampthill – Emily Theresa Villiers - was a close friend of Queen Victoria and a bridesmaid to Queen Alexandra. She married Lord Odo Russell, who became Ambassador to Berlin in 1871. She moved to Ampthill Park in 1884, on the death of her husband, and was very active in the cultural and social life of the community

- Doctor Henry Frederick Holland came to Ampthill in 1870 and lived in Brandreth House. During thirty-five years in practice in Ampthill, Dr. Holland held many official medical appointments – to the Guardians, Royal Sanitary Authority and Rural District Council. He worked tirelessly to overcome the town's problems with poor sanitation and water supply.
- Professor Sir Albert Richardson was an architect of considerable renown. He was President of the Royal Academy, held two chairs of architecture, honorary fellowship of St. Catherine College, Cambridge; the Gold Medal of the R.I.B.A, Gold Medal of France and Knight Commander of the Royal Victorian Order.
- Sir Anthony Wingfield came to Ampthill as a small boy in 1860, living in Ampthill House. Educated at Harrow and Christ Church, Oxford – Sir Anthony became Lord of the Manor of Maulden. He was a magistrate from 1884 to 1942 and was chairman of the Ampthill Bench for almost 20 years. In 1893 he became High Sheriff of Bedfordshire.
Ampthill House originally occupied land between where Brinsmade Road is today and to the north where the Wingfield Club is situated on Church Street. The House had been built in 1829 but was considerably enlarged by Mr. Wingfield to provide accommodation for visitors to his famous private zoo. Mr. Wingfield's Ampthill House was demolished in 1953.

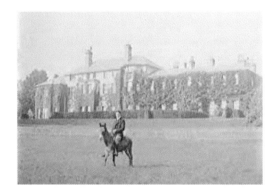

Ampthill House – home to Sir Anthony Wingfield's famous zoo – was demolished in 1953

- Less prominent individuals were employed on the great estates of the Bruce's and Ashburnham's – later owned by the Duke of Bedford – and settled in the town as stewards, lawyers, chaplains, and doctors. As Andrew Underwood has noted: these administrators "played a major role in its development giving Ampthill a benefit of experience and ability unknown in many towns of similar size". It seems, therefore, unlikely that the 1881 club foundered through lack of influential connections.

8. Referee

When the game of **rugby union** was developed at **Rugby School**, there were no official rugby referees. It was not until many years later, when the game began to spread internationally, that an official was included.

Before the creation of rugby referees, the captains from both teams would set the rules down before the game began. The two captains would arbitrate the game together as it went on. This is where the 'advantage' law comes from in rugby union. This was because a team's captain was not likely to complain or stop play if his side benefited from the other team's infringement.

Referees did not appear in matches until the mid-1890s, so appeals were heard by umpires (later known as touch judges). In 1892, the **International Rugby Board** was created as a result of a disputed try that the captains could not agree whether it had been legitimately scored. The rugby laws were changed to require one referee and two touch judges at each game to make the arbitration easier and more consistent.

On 4th December 1870, Edwin Ash of Richmond and Benjamin Burns of Blackheath published a letter in The Times suggesting that "those who play the rugby-type game should meet to form a code of practice as various clubs play to rules which differ from others, which makes the game difficult to play." On 26th January 1871, a meeting attended by representatives from 21 clubs was held in London at the Pall Mall Restaurant on Regent Street.

The Rugby Football Union was founded to standardize the rules and remove some of the more violent aspects of the Rugby School game. The 21 clubs that attended the first meeting, chaired by the club captain of the Richmond Club – E.C. Holmes, included Harlequins, Blackheath, Guy's Hospital, Civil Service, Wellington College, King's College and St. Pauls School – who are all playing today. Along with the founding of the RFU a committee was formed and three ex-Rugby School pupils, all lawyers, were invited to formulate a set of rules. Because they were lawyers they formulated "laws" not "rules"; this task was completed and approved by June 1871.

Referees Timeline:

1866   Two umpires must be provided (Rugby School Laws)

1871   "The captains of the respective sides shall be the sole arbiters of all disputes" (RFU Laws)

1875   Umpires may be appointed if desired, otherwise as in 1871 (RFU Laws)

1885   Two umpires and a referee required (RFU Laws)

1889   Two umpires or two touch-judges required (RFU Laws)

1892   A referee and two touch-judges required

1893   The referee was given the whole responsibility for running a game

1894   A try worth 3 points & a conversion 2 points, rather than the opposite

1895   Referees allowed to use a whistle and touch-judges given sticks

1886   Foundation of International Rugby Board

It does not seem likely that the Ampthill Club of 1881 reached the point where the provision of a referee or touch-judges was an issue. The 1950s Club had its own solution as we shall see!

What was the game of rugby football like in the 1880s ?

It is difficult for us today to appreciate how unstructured and informal the game of rugby football was. Originally the number of players in a game of rugby football was not limited, and there were no formal playing positions. Games at Rugby School were simply played by however many boys wanted to play in a particular game. A kind of huge rolling maul developed, moving around the field since there was a very limited amount of space on the field in which to run. See below an illustration of a rugby game at the Kensington Oval.

Scoring by points was not introduced to rugby football until the late 1880s, before that a game was won by a majority of goals: drop goals or converted tries. Penalty goals would not be introduced until more than 20 years later. Tries were of no value at all, they simply enabled teams to "try" for a goal.

The balance in value between tries and conversions has changed greatly over the years. Historically, no points at all were awarded for a try, the reward being to "try" to score a goal (to kick the ball over the cross bar and between the posts). Scoring points from tries was not introduced until the late 1880s. Until 1891, a try scored one point and a conversion two. For the next two years, tries scored two points and conversions three, until in 1893 when three points were awarded for a try and two for a kick. The number of points from a try increased to four in 1971 and five in 1992. In 1891 penalties were increased from two to three points, while drop goals were awarded four points (drop goals were subsequently reduced to three points in 1948). Before 1905 it was possible to score by kicking the ball through the posts from the ground in open play and until 1977 it was also possible to score three points by kicking a goal after taking a mark before both methods were banned in their respective years.

Rugby at Kensington Oval

Up to 1877, international games had been played between teams of 20 players a side, normally lined out with three fullbacks, a solitary three-quarter back, three half-backs and 13 forwards. Much of the game was spent in scrums and mauls comprising 26 forwards, backs would rarely see the ball and attacking movements between them would have been non-existent. If a player did manage to make a run, one of the vast number of opponents invariably corralled him. The laws of the game at that time required the tackled player to call "Down". The two packs then gathered round the player, who then placed the ball on the floor. A scrum then formed round the ball and the object was for one set of forwards to try to drive it through and break away down field, usually with a dribble. These scrums were protracted affairs, because there was no heeling or wheeling. Teams coming away with the ball left opponents lying prone in their wake.

The rugby must have appealed to the players but did little for the game as a spectacle and so the lawmakers looked to find ways of speeding up the game. In 1875 Oxford and Cambridge pioneered the 15-a-side game and just over a year later England hosted Ireland at Kennington Oval in this new form of rugby football. An observer of the game commentated, "The ball naturally made its appearance sooner from the diminished number of forwards, though the scrummages were still of formidable length owing to the methods then employed." In this match, Albert Hornby made his debut for England. He was an ex-Harrovian and it was said that the game was played in a very different style to that at Rugby School. Hornby had developed the technique of punting and it was this kicking style which made him conspicuous throughout the match. Albert's kicks were an effective innovation and caused a major change in the development of the game. As the game began to be played between different schools and clubs a fixed number of players was needed. This then allowed players to start specializing in certain positions and to develop particular skills appropriate to those positions.

Forwards and Three-quarters

It was not until the early 1880s that specialized positions began to appear, particularly among the backs, with Allen Rotherham of Oxford and England establishing the position of halfback, named for a player who took up a position between the scrum and the rest of the backs. Fullbacks, who took the farthest position from the scrum, were also common, and by this time three additional players formed the "three-quarters" line—a centre flanked by two wingers. In 1886 Wales added a second centre against Scotland. This idea became popular in New Zealand by 1889, and Jimmy Duncan of Otago and New Zealand added not only the second centre but also a second halfback.

Forward players still were not specialized by the early 1900s, and when scrums were formed, the first players to arrive usually formed the front row. By 1900 it was common to form a scrum with three men in the front, two behind, and another three behind them for a 3–2–3 formation.

In New Zealand and South Africa, innovation continued with the New Zealanders' devising of a 2–3–2 formation that freed up an additional man for the backs, who became known as a wing forward, and the South Africans' invention of the 3–4–1 formation used throughout the world today. The 2–3–2 formation created great controversy over the legality of the wing forward, and the IRB eventually banned it in 1932, requiring a minimum of three players in the front row.

November 1893 - The Roses Match – played at Bradford Park Avenue – won 8-3 by Yorkshire

The practice of showing the player's number on the shirt started in 1897 when New Zealand played Queensland in Brisbane. The idea was to enable spectators to identify players by placing numbers on their backs. Match cards were sold listing the players' names and their corresponding numbers, and these proved popular with the public. The numbers used on that tour were 1 to 15 (from full-back to the forwards) for New Zealand and 16 to 30 for the host teams. The Australians quickly adopted the practice for their Tests against New Zealand in 1903 and the British/Irish (1904), they numbered teams in reverse with the full-back wearing 15, as today. South Africa wore numbers for the first time in 1906 on their tour to the UK. The All Blacks wore numbers when they made their first official tour to Britain, and for the famous Wales Test at Cardiff in December 1905 both teams were numbered: 1 for full-back (Wales), but 15 for full-back (New Zealand).

In 1922 England played Wales in Cardiff and both teams used player numbering for the first time in a home nations championship game.

Chapter 2 – The First 10 Years

The start of the Club's journey, which would lead to its promotion to the Championship in 2019, began on 27th January 1950. At the bottom of a huge box of AGMs and Committee Minutes given to me, by a much-relieved Pat Sherry (the current Club President), was an insignificant looking file containing the following:

Minutes of the inaugural general meeting held at the Wingfield Club, Ampthill on 27th January 1950.

The meeting was arranged by Brian Staniforth and Ken Tilston and was the result of previous casual discussions on the possibility of forming a Rugby Club in the Ampthill area. Appointed Chairman of the meeting, Mr. Staniforth pointed out that the Club would be starting from scratch with no funds, no equipment and no pitch, but there was no lack of enthusiasm from those present and the decision to form the Club was unanimous.

Temporary officers and committee appointed to serve until the annual general meeting were:

Mr. W. Rogers (treasurer), Mr. K. Mobbs (secretary), Mr. R. Dillingham, Mr. B. Staniforth and Mr. K. Tilston. It was agreed that the above named should have power to appoint a Chairman.

This small note was written by K. Mobbs, on ancient notepaper with a fountain pen.

Ken Mobbs' notes taken on 27th January 1950 at the Wingfield Club

Ampthill is to have a Rugby club. An inaugural meeting was held at the Wingfield Club, and a good number of prospective players attended. Mr. Brian Staniforth has been responsible for getting the Club formed.

Sitting – Ken Tilson & Brian Staniforth

The minutes of the first decade, amazingly, survive to this day. They tell a tale of the making of a rugby club that was replicated the length and breadth of the British Isles as rugby clubs were formed, or reformed, after the second world war.

To the author, the ghost of Andrew Hawkins Tanqueray haunts these first ten years. Had he had the support of the likes of Messrs. Rogers, Mobbs, Dillingham, Staniforth and Tilston, he might have been able to succeed almost seventy years previously. However, his post-war equivalent, Norman Brown, did have their support and also that of Doug Simms, Tony "Cranky" Rogers, Barrie O'Dell, and Richard Churchill. The Club also had the constant support of wives, girlfriends and loved ones, their contribution to the life of the Club cannot be over-estimated.

Even so, the Club, after a promising opening year, was to struggle with inadequate funding, inadequate facilities, but mainly, like Tanqueray, from a chronic lack of players. It would not be until season 1957/58, that the Club would become established and secure.

It would take another 20 or so years, until rugby in the district was established in the schools.

Then the mini-youth explosion took place, and the Club began to produce its own players. The population increase of Ampthill, Flitwick, and mid-Bedfordshire from the 1970s onwards was also a factor in bringing rugby players into the Club.

The First Season 1950-51 - (Captain – Eddie McDonald)

Officers

President	N.F. Sharpe
Chairman	R. Dillingham
Hon. Secretary	K. Mobbs
Hon. Treasurer	W. Rogers
Committee	K. Tilson

I am indebted to the memories and records of Tony Rogers (who played in the first ever game in the Park) and Norman Brown (who was to go on to captain the team for almost 10 years and to become Club Chairman and President) for these insights into the early history of the Club. During the summer of 1950 much time was spent in planning for the coming season. Permission was obtained from the Town Council (who had recently negotiated the purchase of Ampthill Great Park from the Duke of Bedford) to rent some land for the modest sum of five shillings per annum. The pitch was situated between the present Cricket Club clubhouse and West Car Park, and parallel with Woburn Road. Mike Henderson, the County PE organiser acquired some posts, a line-marker was borrowed, and the pitch prepared. Some training sessions took place on the cricket grounds outfield supervised by Mike Henderson.

The new Ampthill Rugby Union Football Club had been keeping abreast of all the necessary preparations throughout the summer and had secured about fourteen fixtures for this season.

Arrangements to mark and lay-out their pitch in Ampthill Park were in hand, and it was intended that they would open the season there on September 16th, meeting Bedford Lions "A" XV.

One of the difficulties encountered in arranging a fixture list was that most of the established clubs were already fixed up for two years ahead. However, Ampthill felt that more than a dozen games during the first season will be sufficient to "put them on the map" as an established club and attract more members.

The adoption of colours was a matter still under consideration. Members were anxious to play in colours with some local significance and which really mean something, rather than to "turn out in any old colour."

Richard Dillingham was the person responsible for the maroon and gold colours that were chosen. These colours were found on the crest of Nigel d'Albini of Cainhoe who, at Domesday, held Ampthill for William the Conqueror (see also page 37).

The captain of Ampthill Rugby Club in the first season was Eddie McDonald. Tony Rogers remembers that not all players had that much experience of rugby: "I was 17 years old, six- foot tall and 12 stone wringing wet – I was told to play lock and was too young to go into the pub after the game". Doug Simms, who was to become a stalwart prop for the Club for many years, played on the wing. Ampthill had no kit, so the team played in white shirts and "dark" shorts – "I wore a dress shirt", said Tony Rogers. Richard Dillingham marked out the pitch on 28 August and refereed the first ever match on 16th September 1950 against Bedford Lions "A", a club based at Bedford Park. The Ampthill News reported:

"The newly formed Ampthill Rugby Club played their first match on Saturday against Bedford Lions "A" in Ampthill Park. They lost by 1 goal, 2 tries (11 points) to 1 try, 1 penalty goal (6 points).

Though beaten, the home team were far from disgraced. Their comparatively fast and light pack were out-weighted in the set scrums but were superior in the loose and lines-out. D. Young at scrum half and D. Pulley, fly, showed promise of establishing a good partnership when they have played together more.

An early forward rush by the home side was checked on the line and play swept to the other end where Rideout broke through and scored. P. Wooding converted.

Ampthill pressed hard for 15 minutes and were seldom out of the visitor's half. They were unable to finish off, however, and the Lions broke through after a neat movement and P. Wooding went over for an unconverted try. Shortly before half-time K. Tilston kicked a penalty-goal for Ampthill.

Much of the play in the second half was again in at the visitors' end of the field. Pulley took a quick pass from Young on the 25-yard line and found an opening to score Ampthill's try. Tilston failed with the kick. The home forwards made another vigorous rush and there was a touch-down over the goal-line, but they were called back for a knock-on. Ten minutes from time Wardley scored an unconverted try for the Lions."

After the game players were able to wash and have tea in premises down the Kings Arms Yard. Tony Rogers remembers the subscription being £1 and the match fee 2s 6d. The rest of the season's home games took place in the Park, Richard Dillingham recalls that on one notable occasion the match was halted in a blizzard, the players taking shelter behind trees near Woburn Road.

Ampthill Team on September 16th 1950 in Ampthill Park

back-row   R. Dillingham, (referee), E. Webb, W. Rogers, A. Webster, J. Churchill, B .Abraham, T. Rogers; middle-row W. Thompson, B. Gilbert, D. Simms, K. Tilston, D. Pulley and J. Lawson (touch-judge); front-row D. Young, R. McDonald (captain), B. Staniforth and K. Mobbs

Ampthill Park – September 16th 1950 – Ampthill RUFC's First-Ever Game

Abraham is tackled with Staniforth and McDonald in support

J. Ridout, the Bedford Lion's right-winger, makes a determined run, but Ampthill players Roger Thompson and Brian Staniforth cut him off

On Friday 18th May 1951, the first AGM was held at the Wingfield Club at 7.30pm. The following is the retiring Secretary, Ken Mobbs' Annual Report:

This our first year, has been as of course it should be, one of rapid progress and achievement. Our success as a Club – if not necessarily as a team – should be a great source of encouragement to us in the year ahead.

We began as a bunch of fellows who just wanted to play rugby, but we have developed into a firmly established club with a pitch and colours of our own and we are now affiliated to the East Midlands Rugby Football Union.

At the beginning of the season we had only about a dozen fixtures, but we were able to add to it as we went along and there were few Saturdays on which we did not have a game.

The Urban Council granted us the use of a pitch in the Park but unfortunately it needed considerable attention to make it safely playable. The headmasters of the schools very kindly co-operated, however, and we were permitted the use of an alternative pitch which overlapped theirs. Only with the greatest stretch of the imagination could it be described as level, but it has provided us and our visitors with many an enjoyable game and at least it provides a source of conversation at the tea table after matches. Reference to tea table brings us to a point which we would be very remiss to overlook. That is the splendid co-operation and support we have received from wives and girlfriends of some of our members. Their interest and help were a great encouragement from the very start and I'm sure we would all readily acknowledge that most of the credit for our position today should go to them. We are indebted too, to Mid. Beds. Conservative Association for the use of their hall for entertaining visiting teams.

For our flying start at the beginning of the season the mysterious appearance of goalposts and a host of other things, not to mention coaching and encouragement and a helping hand behind the scenes, we owe much to our father-confessor, Mike Henderson. But for his infectious enthusiasm we might never have started.

At this stage I would like to mention that before our first match calamity overtook us when two well-meaning gentlemen broke one of the posts when taking them down to clear away. At a few hours' notice, Mr. Jan Botsford supplied and erected another post in time for the match to be played and I believe there are some players today who knew nothing about the incident. Mr. Botsford also supplied all flag posts.

Last, but not least, of our benefactors is Mr. Richard Dillingham our referee and critic. We were lucky to have such a good referee available for all our home games and we look forward to seeing him again next season.

From our point of view the outstanding feature of the year was that we were awarded the Ball of the Year for junior clubs by the Rugby Followers Association of Bedford. This was presented by Capt. Percy Burke at our first dinner.

Socially, this was a great success and among the guests were the Secretary & President of EMRFU and the President of Bedford Club.

Our other social venture was a dance at the Drill Hall from which we made a substantial profit. We played Unilever at New Eltham on the date of the Calcutta Cup and went along to see the international match in the afternoon. We were the hosts of Unilever on Easter Monday and after the game spent a pleasant evening at The George, in Maulden.

Our special aim for next season is to secure a better pitch in the Park and to add to the inadequate changing and washing conditions and, of course, to improve our play. If we progress at the same rate then, as we have done this season, we need have nothing to fear."

Richard Dillingham was elected Chairman, Norman Brown – Captain and W. Rogers -Treasurer.

Capt. Percy Burke presents the Ball of the Year Award to Brian Staniforth at the first Club Dinner held on Friday 9th March 1952 at The White Hart

The decision to make an award of a "Ball of the Year" by Rugby Followers of Bedford to ARUFC was a major boost to the Club. There was no rugby school in the district and most players had no experience of the game until taken in hand by Mike Henderson, the Scottish international and former Bedford player. The club had a pitch but no other facilities apart from a small hut to change in. To provide showers for visitors, the players carried water over a quarter of a mile to the ground. Funds were so low that everyone had to buy their own jersey and the Club had only one ball. Players paid a match-fee of 3/6 for home games and paid all their expenses for away games. The club had a very up and down existence in the early days, both on and off the pitch, as one of the founding members remembers, "There were never any players left over, if you could walk you could play, you didn't let a little thing like flu stop you turning out". For many years Richard Dillingham ran regular jumble-sales to raise funds for the Club. Richard was also captain of the Town Cricket Club and in these early years the rugby club trained on the cricket field supervised by Mike Henderson.

On 2nd December 1950 the game against Bedford Swifts was notable for two reasons, the team played in their new strip of maroon and gold and Norman Brown made his first appearance for Ampthill Rugby Club at tight-head prop. This is how the Ampthill News reported the game:

Ampthill Show Best Form

"Resplendent in new maroon and gold jerseys and stockings, Ampthill were in good fettle for their home match against Bedford Swifts, whom they beat by 1 goal and 3 tries (14 pts.) to nil. Although their captain had elected to play against the slope, they pressed hard at the onset and only a long kick into touch by the Swift's full-back, Martin, relieved pressure.

The Swifts forwards swarmed downfield, but Ampthill beat off these foot rushes, the steady Tilston kicking soundly. The home pack retaliated and, holding their own in the tight and loose, dominated the lines-out, where Brown shone. Well served by a smooth-working pair of halves, Young and Taylor, Ampthill's back division handled cleanly, but it was a forward, Webster, who got over after 30 minutes. Tilston converted with a perfect kick from a difficult angle.

The Best Move

Ampthill could not be stopped in the second half. Webster quickly scored from a forward rush. The best move of the match came when Young, from a loose scrum, gave to the nimble-footed Mobbs who made ground and passed to Taylor, who cross-kicked for Pulley, following up smartly to gather the ball at speed leaving his opposite winger standing and sprint over wide out on the left for an unconverted try.

With their scrum-half doing the work of two men the Swifts rallied, but attacks broke down against dour resistance. Ampthill forwards, led by Webster, came back in a series of short-passing movements. From a line-out W. Rogers dived over the line near the corner flag."

R. Dillingham, H.C. Taylor, W. Rogers, E. J. Webb, N.J. Brown, A. Sibley, A. Rogers
K. Tilston, A. Webster, E. McDonald (Capt.), K. Mobbs, D. Young, J. Lawson
W. Thompson, B. Staniforth, D. Simms, J. Churchill.

Ampthill XV 1950-51 – in their new kit at Station Road – Little Park Farm is in the background

Results – Season 1950-51

	date	venue	opposition	points for	points against	result
Sept.	16	H	Bedford Lions "A"	6	11	L
	23	H	Leighton Buzzard	3	19	L
	30	H	Bedford Colts	13	9	W
Oct.	7	H	Vauxhall Works	5	19	L
	14	A	Lynton Works	9	8	W
	21	H	Leighton Buzzard "A"	5	5	D
Nov.	4	A	70th Heavy Ack. Ack. Regt.	0	6	L
	11	A	Vauxhall Works "A"	3	19	L
	18	H	Biggleswade	3	9	L
Dec.	2	H	Bedford Swifts	14	0	W
	9	H	Bedford Lions "A"	5	13	L
	23	A	Igranic	0	8	L
Jan.	13	H	Bedford Athletic Extra "A"	16	0	W
	20	A	Leighton Buzzard "A"	6	0	W
	27	A	Bedford Swifts	6	8	L
Feb.	10	H	Bedford Athletic "B"	9	6	W
	17	H	Lynton Works	3	0	W
	24	H	Biggleswade "A"	9	6	W
March	3	H	Old Lutonians Extra "A"	3	0	W
	10	A	Igranic "A"	8	3	W
	17	A	Unilever Sports	0	23	L
	24	A	Old Dunstablians	0	13	L
	31	H	Bedford Athletic Extra "A"	14	6	W
April	21	H	Old Lutonians Extra "A"	3	6	L
	28	A	Biggleswade	0	22	L

1950 - 51

played	won	draw	lost	points for	points against
25	11	1	13	143	219

Season 1951-52 - (Captain – Norman Brown)

Officers

President	N.F. Sharpe
Chairman	R. Dillingham
Hon. Secretary	K. Tilson
Hon. Treasurer	E.J. Webb
Committee	B. Staniforth
	J. Churchill

This season the Club played all its home games at the bottom of Station Road, on land generously loaned by Mr. Lionel Burgoyne. The pitch was situated near the railway line (behind the Station House) and not far from Little Park Farm. In 1951, there was no bypass (opened 1983) and Ampthill Station was fully-functioning (closed 1959).

The land was flat, but very damp – a stream ran down one side. Horses and cattle roamed over the ground during the week. Brian Hodgson (now 93), who played for Ampthill at this time, recalls having to clear cow pats from the ground before games – an old pram was used to carry away the unwanted detritus! An old wartime Radar Hut was donated by LW. Vass and served as a shelter for kit, marking equipment and flags. However, the ground was generally better than the previous pitch in the Park and helped promote the Club's status in the eyes of other clubs. Some stirring encounters took place at Station Road, for the nine seasons it was the Club's home, and old players speak of those years with nostalgia and affection.

Tony Rogers recalls that players, particularly visitors, had the use of washing/changing facilities at the Town Football Club, on Woburn Road. However, there was often friction with the soccer players, if the muddy rugby players used the tin-baths first! Norman Brown, the Club Captain, recalls that home team players washed the worst of the mud off in the stream and then changed at home. After games the Club would entertain visiting teams at the White Hart in Dunstable Street, run by the redoubtable Mrs. Bray. In this second season there was a rapid turn-over of players and post-Christmas, a spate of injuries, that led to some heavy losses.

Station Road rugby ground 1951-1960 – pitch situated as Norman Brown remembered

1952 AGM

Ken Tilston reported to the AGM that the Club's finances were in a parlous state and only unexpected grants of £20 from the East Midlands RUFC and £10 from The Rugby Followers of Bedford kept the Club afloat. Loans paid back to players left the Club with £9 17s 6d in the bank.

During the season, the club lost the services of several key players, including Geoff Mobbs, Harry Taylor and Dave Pulley and were occasionally forced to turn out short. The Club was invited to play in the Aylesbury Sevens – their first ever taste of the abbreviated form of the game. The fixture list had improved markedly: to include Bedford Athletic, Biggleswade, Bedford Swifts, Olney "A", Unilever (London), Luton "A" and Leighton Buzzard "A", Queen's Works "A" and Bedford Lions 1st XV.

The next few seasons at Station Road were a period of consolidation. The main problems were, considerable changeover in membership and injury to players. Four founder members were unavailable for season 1952-53. Tony Rogers was posted to Germany for two years on National Service, John Churchill emigrated to New Zealand, Henry Taylor to Canada and Ken Hobbs retired after a broken ankle. Centre three-quarters, Holman, and King, who the previous season were stationed at Kempston Barracks, doing National Service, were no longer available. Among a number of new players welcomed to the Club was the legendary Barrie O'Dell – of whom, more later. Another famous character, Richard Churchill played his first game for Ampthill at outside-half against Lynton Works (Bedford) on the 22nd December 1951.

Depleted Ampthill Hold Lynton

Ampthill's clash with Lynton Works at the Polo Ground Bedford, on Saturday, was marred by an unfortunate accident, for the Work's right-wing, Bill Shepherd, fractured a leg in the last few minutes and was taken to hospital.

The game itself, which resulted in a draw of no score, took a heavy toll in injuries on both sides, although play was cleanly fought. Six men left the field at various times, but four were fit enough to return after a few minutes' absence.

Ampthill, who played two-short throughout, were hard pressed in the early stages, but were beginning to dominate towards the end.

Team: forwards - A. Webster, K. Tilson, N. Brown, S. Fossey, W. Rogers, E. Webb

backs – G. Mobbs, R. Churchill, K. Mobbs, E. Devine, D. Simms, A. Briggs & E. McDonald

New fixtures included Old Dunstablians, Aylesbury, Huntingdon, Bletchley, and Rushden & Higham. However, recruitment of players remained the major concern.

The biggest win of the season was against Bedford Athletic Extra "A" by 29-6 and the heaviest defeat was by the Athletic 1st XV by 40-0 – the latter marked the opening of the Club's new ground at Station Road – 8th September 1951. Centre three-quarter Michael Holman was the top scorer with 42 points, including 13 tries.

Eric Webb made the most appearances, 23 out of a possible 25. Norman Brown and Tony Rogers appeared in 22 games, McDonald & Tilson 21, Webster 20, Fossey, D. Brown and Wallis 18 each, Churchill 17 and Mobbs 16.

The Station Road ground in 1952. Next to the Radar Hut is Harry Taylor, Norman Brown (Captain) John Wallace and Eddie McDonald (Mac) – captain 1950-51.

1951-52	played	won	drawn	lost	pts. for	pts. against
	25	11	3	11	148	223

Season 1952-53 - (Captain – Norman Brown)

President	N.F. Sharpe
Chairman	R. Dillingham
Hon. Secretary	K. Tilson
Hon. Treasurer	E.J. Webb
Captain	N. Brown
Committee	B. Staniforth
	J. Churchill

This was a disappointing season, mainly due to a shortage of experienced players. Though, in his report to the AGM, on 21st May 1953, Roger Arnold (Hon. Secretary) was fairly upbeat:

"Viewing the 12 months in retrospect, it can be said that it has been a year of consolidation. Considerable changes have taken place in membership and in the team itself due to injury.

Ground: Once again, we are very grateful to Mr. Burgoine for the use of his field, without which we should have been in difficulty. The small hut on the ground has been purchased by the club and certain improvements have been made to it.

Changing and Washing Facilities: These have remained as the previous year and the arrangement has, in general, proved satisfactory. A move is in hand whereby the football club become the "governing body" of the Pavilion and the Rugby Club pay a rent for it each time it is used, subject to certain conditions. This, however, has not been finalised.

Players: Several new players turned out on different occasions. These included David Allen from Wrest Park and Barrie O'Dell from Houghton Conquest, John Lawson, Roy Burrows and Pete Stevens have now played for a complete season. We hope to have the services of all these players again next season in even greater form. We lost a good friend and founder-member in John Churchill due to his emigration to New Zealand. Whether this is only a temporary loss or not, only time will tell though he wrote to me recently saying that he has started to play "down under". Neither Stan Fossy, nor Paddy Devine was able to turn out while at the end of the season, a broken ankle deprived us of another founder-member – Ken Hobbs. Reliable reports indicate that Ken has joined the Hon. Sec. in hanging up his boots. Derek Browne gave up during the season, but Tony Rogers is now demobilised and we hope he will be playing next season. Injury has again taken a heavy toll and difficulty was often experienced in fielding a full side every week. Great work has been done by the skipper - Norman Brown - in raising a side each week in very trying circumstances.

Social Activities: A Grand National Sweepstake, was organised by the Hon. Treasurers and details will be given to you in their report. The theatre outing was not organised this year, but it has been whispered that an informal dinner or supper – for mixed company – might be held before the start of the season.

Future Activities: Increasing the number of playing members should be the prime consideration, as at the moment it is very much below strength! Further improvements can be made to the small hut on the ground and a more determined attitude towards the raising of money must be adopted.

Teas: I feel that the sincere appreciation of all Club members must be extended to the ladies of the Club for organising the teas last season. The arrangements proved highly satisfactory and we thank them for their fine work."

1952-53	played	won	drawn	lost	Pts. for	Pts. against
	19	4	2	13	79	238

Season 1953-54 - (Captain – Norman Brown)

Officers
President   N.F. Sharpe
Chairman   R. Dillingham
Hon. Secretary   R.E. Arnold
Hon. Treasurer   E.J. Webb
Hon. Match Secretary R. Burrows
Captain 1st XV   N. Brown
Vice- Captain 1st XV E.J. Webb

Another disappointing season ensued – the usual problem – finding and retaining players.

The Club started this season with only 20 playing members – John Lawson, Keith Fishes, Roy Wignall and Dougie Simms having been called up by HM Forces and this quickly dwindled to 17. At this point the Club was facing a crisis, captain Norman Brown was barely able to raise 15 players on match days. However, the return of John Churchill and the arrival of Roger Thompson and the redoubtable prop-forward, Fred Thistlethwaite (Fylde and Bedford) relieved the pressure. Fred (in 2020) is 95, and a regular supporter of the Club's home fixtures. Notable wins were recorded against Lynton Works (Bedford), Huntingdon and Kettering. Eric Webb became the first player to reach 100 appearances for the Club in March 1954, in the 8-0 defeat by Kettering "B" at Station Road.

The weakness of the team this season lay in the threequarters. Loss of players and injury meant there was little continuity.

Reporting to the AGM in May 1954, Roger Arnold gave this summary:

"The final assessment of the season's activities must be a highly satisfactory one and reflects great credit on all those most concerned with the work of organisation. One can say without fear of contradiction that every game has been thoroughly enjoyable and the spirit of the team beyond criticism.

No members of the Club have contributed more to the good feeling that has prevailed this season than Mr. N.F. Sharpe himself who, apart from filling the role of President, has been a most welcome figure on the touch line at all our home games. It is equally true to say that for the ceaseless hard work of the Captain we would be without a team. Norman Brown has succeeded every week in getting the right number of players to the scene of operations after overcoming several difficulties on the way.

After-match arrangements have worked very well. The arrangements with the Football Club has been successful as has the provision of teas for which the Club and visitors alike have been very grateful to Mrs. Brown, Mrs. Rogers, Mrs McDonald, and Mrs. Simms.

We are grateful to Mr. Staines for his interest in the dinner, the revival of which proved so successful. We were particularly glad to see present Mr. Henderson who played such an important part in the Club's formation, Mr. Blake, President of the EMRU and Mr. Burke Chairman of the Bedford Rugby Followers who brought with him a cheque for £10 on which to base the foundation of a successful next season."

RUGBY CLUBS' FINAL RECORDS

	W	D	L	F	A
Ampthill	19	1	13	362	311
Wanderers	11	2	17	237	374
Athletic	22	1	7	355	184
Athletic Extra 1st	22	1	7	514	117
Athletic "A"	9	1	13	215	271
Ampthill	7	2	11	119	191
Hawks	7	3	5	157	82
Lions	16	5	12	356	327
Swifts	13	5	14	219	187
Biggleswade	17	1	11	325	220
Biggleswade "A"	6	5	12	150	240
Lynton Works	13	3	5	209	132
Queen's Works	12	1	13	201	225
Queen's "A"	5	0	16	77	280

Bedfordshire Times, Friday 30 April 1954

1953-54	played	won	drawn	lost	pts. for	pts. against
	20	7	2	11	119	191

Season 1954-55 - (Captain – Norman Brown)

Officers

President	N.F. Sharpe
Chairman	R. Dillingham
Hon. Secretary	R.E. Arnold
Hon. Treasurer	E.J. Webb
Hon. Fixture Secretary	B. O'Dell
Captain 1st XV	N. Brown
Vice- Captain 1st XV	P.J. Lawton
Committee:	E. McDonald, D. Young & W. Rogers

1954-55 season was a very difficult season for Norman Brown and his team. Archie Webster was lost to the Merchant Navy and Derick Browne was badly injured. The redoubtable Doug Simms who "apparently came off second best after attempting to tackle a lorry somewhere near Aylesbury on his motor-cycle", was side-lined for a time.

Members met one Friday night at the George Inn, Maulden to consider disbanding the Club. The following day, with a much-weakened team, they beat Old Dunstablians by 22-6 and the pessimistic thoughts of finishing were brushed to one side. Even so, several games had to be cancelled, as a team could not be raised. The team suffered three heavy defeats in September to Biggleswade, Rushden & Higham and Bedford Lions.

The fortunes of the Club improved in October and November but fell away again in the New Year when cold/poor weather did not seem to suit the Club. After Christmas, Bedford Swifts were beaten by a 13 - man Ampthill team. Lynton Works was defeated, and a creditable draw recorded against Bedford Swifts. Fifty players, including 25 "outsiders", were used during the season. 19 games were played with 6 wins, 1 draw and 12 losses. Norman Brown and Barrie O'Dell played in 17 of these games; Tony Rogers and Roy Burrows appeared in 16 and McDonald in 15.

The minutes of the Club AGM, held at the Park Pavilion on May 6th 1955, show that the problem of playing strength was raised by the Chairman Richard Dillingham – "but the fact that the dearth of players in the Ampthill district placed the club in a precarious position was generally appreciated".

It was clearly essential that more players be recruited, and Richard Dillingham invited suggestions as to how to set about this. Eddie McDonald suggested amalgamating with the Bedford Hawks. However, Doug Simms pointed out that that even if the school to which most of them belonged would allow it, they were rather young to join in the type of play which the Club normally indulged. The President then suggested a "press-campaign" and this was endorsed by the meeting. Someone present, suggested a general "keenness campaign" to run throughout the summer and include large amounts of PT. But this latter suggestion was not approved and the Secretary, "particularly thought the summer a suitable time for relaxation."

Bedford Hawks was a junior club whose players were generally ex-Bedford Modern scholars and retained close links to that school. They were having reasonably good results at this time, although their forwards were considered lightweight in comparison with many clubs. Interestingly, Norman Brown has a clear recollection of several Hawks players subsequently joining Ampthill. Throughout this early and difficult period of the Club's development it was indebted to the support, goodwill and sheer hard work of its President, Norman Sharpe and Chairman, Richard Dillingham.

At the Club's Annual Dinner held at the White Hart Hotel on Friday 7 May 1955, a brief review of the club's fortunes since it was formed four years ago was given by the captain, Norman Brown, replying to the toast.

He recalled that after a flourishing first season, there had been a period of gradual deterioration until the club reached a low ebb in its third season.

This was expected, he said, as the initial enthusiasm had been dampened. But the club had weathered that storm and, during the season just ended, had grown from strength to strength.

Match records showed 21 games played, 7 won, 12 lost, and two drawn, with 119 points for and 127 against. The club had been pleased to welcome some new members and to have the services of a number of visitors from neighbouring clubs during the season, Mr. Brown went on, but had lost four members to the Services.

The club looked forward confidently to the coming season, he said, and was prepared to play the game in the right spirit with any club which had the same approach to rugby.

1954-55	played	won	drawn	lost	Pts. for	Pts. against
	21	7	2	12	119	127

Season 1955-56 - (Captain - Norman Brown)

Officers

President	N.F. Sharpe
Chairman	R. Dillingham
Hon. Secretary	R.E. Arnold
Hon. Treasurer	B.S. O'Dell
Hon. Fixture Secretary	R. Burrows
Captain 1st XV	N. Brown
Vice- Captain 1st XV	A. Rogers
Committee	D. Simms, E. McDonald
	B. Hodgeson

The resilience of the Club is reflected in Roger Arnold's (Hon. Sec.) annual report to the AGM at the end of the following season - 1955-56 - which I now record in part:

"During the past season, the Club has fielded a team on 22 occasions. In 9 of these it was victorious and on 10 suffered defeat, three games reaching no decisive end. This statement of bare facts and figures gives a true indication of a much-improved state of things, especially compared with last year, when you may remember we won but seven out of a similar total of games. This improvement is by no means attributable to chance but is due almost entirely to the satisfactory result of the campaign suggested by the President at the last AGM and conducted by the Captain and several members of the committee, to ensure more playing members. We now have about 32 names from which to draw which has made the task of team secretary a very much easier one, but even now, the problem cannot be considered fully solved because there have been occasions when it has proved impossible to field a full-side and it is highly significant that only on such occasions has the team suffered heavy defeat. On only four occasions when at full-strength did we fail to score and were only once heavily defeated by Rushden, the score 19-0 against us.

Among our more outstanding wins was the game against Old Dunstablians when the score was 22-6 and those against Biggleswade and Vauxhall when it was 23-8 and 22-0 respectively. The team spirit has been good and while this must take much of the credit for the Club's success it is good to see that some members have proved their ability to score large numbers of points. In particular mention must be made of John Hall with no less than 36 points to his personal credit, to John Comerford with 19 and to Terry Comerford, Don Palmer, Eddie MacDonald, and Brian Hodgeson with 12 each.

The work of the committee stands out as highly satisfactory and relatively smooth working. We have had eight meetings and have dealt with a wide variety of topics ranging from playing strength and team selection to money raising schemes and visits abroad. A great deal of attention has been paid to provide all the facilities necessary out of annual subscriptions, match fees and donations from V.Ps and other well-wishing patrons of the Club and the Committee has been hard put to think of ways of ensuring solvency. The Dance yielded £10 10s and the raffle on the Grand National a further £16. The topic which has particularly occupied most of the Committee's time has been the search for a suitable piece of land on which to build a pitch and Club H.Q. But we must report very little success. A vast number of suggestions have been made and a very considerable number of fields have been explored but nothing worthy has been found. All hope has not been abandoned and now that we have more members perhaps fresh incentive has been provided. In the meantime, our thanks are once again to due to Mr. Burgoyne.

In conclusion, mention must be made of the Club's most recent "other activity" involving a trip to France where, among other things, several members and their friends watched England suffer defeat at the hands of France. This show of opulent enthusiasm provided a fitting curtain to a successful season."

At an extraordinary meeting held at the Park Pavilion on June 10th, 1955 the treasurer Eric Webb announced that the Club had £16 in hand of which about £10 10s was needed to settle outstanding accounts. He reported that collection of match fees "was still an awkward problem and there were still some annual subscriptions still outstanding."

At a subsequent Committee meeting held on 7th August 1955 the Chairman, Richard Dillingham, "informed all present, with ill-concealed pride, that he had devoted some of his leisure time, when not playing cricket, to the invention and construction of a novel and ingenious machine to make the task of removing cow-manure from the pitch a simpler and less messy task. This brought grunts of approval from the floor and several suggestions concerning other possible uses for the machine."

New opponents in 1955-56 included RAF Henlow, BB Old Boys, St. Albans, Bedford Hawks and Shuttleworth.

1955-56	played	won	drawn	lost	pts. for	pts. against
	22	9	3	10	160	194

Season 1956-57 - (Captain - Norman Brown)

Officers

President	N.F. Sharpe
Chairman	R. Dillingham
Hon. Secretary	M.P. Turvey
Hon. Treasurer	E.J. Webb
Hon. Fixture Secretary	B. S. O'Dell
Captain 1st XV	N. Brown
Vice- Captain 1st XV	J. Hall
Committee	J. Lawson, A. Rogers, D. Simms, A. Stevens & F. Thistlethwaite

1956-57 saw the Ampthill Club play 28 matches there being only a few cancellations due to inclement weather and petrol restrictions (*see below). 10 matches were won, 17 lost and 1 drawn. The first 10 matches of the season were lost mainly due to an inability to field a complete team because of player shortage and the petrol crisis. The second half of the season was an improvement with new players becoming familiar with the team's structure under the strong leadership of their experienced captain, Norman Brown. The fine form of John Hall and the Comerford brothers was again a feature of this improvement, they being responsible for 149 of the 235 points scored for the Club that season. M.P.Turvey (Hon. Sec.) in his report on the season to the AGM made the following interesting comment: "It would seem though that much success is obtained from the kick and rush tactics evolved by the forwards and not the orthodox methods of a strong three-quarter attack".

On the social front, a successful Dance was held before Christmas and a Jumble Sale in the New Year brought in income, as did the by now well-established Annual Grand National Draw; these events earning £45 profit. Sadly, the Club lost the services of Eddie McDonald and Eric Webb (who was emigrating to Canada) as playing members at the end of the season.

At a meeting held at 4, Dukes Road on 4th November 1955, the Committee considered for the first time the design of a Club badge. The Chairman, Richard Dillingham "produced from his pockets two designs reputedly used to ornament the headgear of some other club and asked if they would be suitable for us. Approval was forthcoming, but not whole-hearted, as it was felt that a ball – an oval one – should figure somewhere in the design, and discussion flourished for several minutes as to just how this and possibly a set of posts, could best be incorporated.

We were asked to draw what we felt the finished article should look like but this, on the whole, was not a success because the only member present professing some ability in that direction was Mr. Hodgson and he could not remember what a ball looked like and said posts were hard things to have anyway since they were bound to be mistaken for TV aerials! However, some measure of agreement was finally reached, and it was decided that the badge should simply consist of a rampant lion with the letters ARUFC underneath, in archaic gold lettering. Mr. Dillingham would obtain an example of such a badge and show it to members so that they would be able to place firm orders for them and the Club would not be left with large numbers of them on their hands."

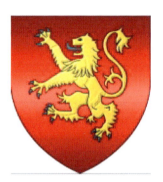

The rampant lion was the crest of Nigel d'Albini of Cainhoe who, at Domesday, held Ampthill for William the Conqueror.

At the next meeting held at The George Inn, Maulden, on December 2nd 1955, the matter of the Club Badge was raised again: "It appeared that members were not very enthusiastic on this score – especially when told that the price quoted did not include a blazer! It was decided to leave the matter open and raise it again in the presence of the Chairman."

Tony Rogers' records show that the Club had £15 10s in the bank in 1956. That season, players' annual subs. were 10/6 or 5/- for non-players and match fees were 2/6.

A remarkable feature of the season was the recovery made by the 1st XV in the second half of 1956-57. The first ten games were all lost and only two games were won by Christmas, this being mainly due to fielding incomplete XVs. From January, with full teams, eight games were won, one drawn and only three lost.

* In 1956 the Suez Crisis caused petrol supplies from the Middle East to be practically cut off. In November 1956, the government announced that petrol rationing would be introduced in December and continue until April 1957.

1956-57	played	won	drawn	lost	pts. for	pts. against
	28	10	1	17	235	275

Season 1957-58 (Captain – Norman Brown)

President	N.F. Sharpe
Chairman	R. Dillingham
Hon. General Secretary	G.W. Burrows
Hon. Treasurer	E.J. Webb
Hon. Fixture Secretary	B. S. O'Dell
Captain 1st XV	N. Brown
Vice- Captain 1st XV	J. B. Hall
Committee	J. Lawson, A. Rogers, D. Simms, E. McDonald, D. Simms & F. Thistlethwaite

This season was a turning point in the Club's fortunes. I reproduce M. P. Turvey's report to the AGM as it seems to capture the atmosphere of this period in the Club's development:

"This past season should be divided into two parts, the beginning of which was engulfed by disappointments, and the latter three-quarters where spirits rose and success was experienced. The season began quite early in the summer with the painting and erection of new posts and thanks to a small band of workers, the pitch was ready only just in time for the first match on October 5th against Wellingborough. The first five matches were all lost, several heavy defeats being received due to lack of fitness and the overwhelming strength of our opponents. This period of the season was noted for lack of support from club members, more of which is stated later.

November 16th was a turning point, for on that day we lost to Igranic at home, the only game lost at home during the season, and the following Saturday we won our first, to remain victorious into the New Year. In fact, only two matches were lost since November. As a result of these games, we completed the season having won 12, drawn 3 and lost 9; scoring 182 points against a total of 222 scored by the opposition. In all these matches the leadership of Norman Brown was inspiring and invaluable and vice-captain, John Hall, for the third successive season showed his worth by being top scorer with 55 points. Furthermore, we also encountered new opponents in the form of B.T.H., who visited from Rugby, and Nottingham Nomads - both of whom gave us valuable experience as well as encouraging victories. No matches were seriously affected by shortage of players as teams have been easier to raise. Affiliation to the EMRS, came into operation during the season and we have received a regular supply of referees, Mr. Dillingham, our Chairman retiring to the touchline to give his support and advice.

The provision of after match teas by a committee of ladies has been reintroduced with the generosity of the proprietess of the White Hart who permits the use of this room and kitchen facilities at no charge consequently relieving considerably the burden on the Club's exchequer, to such an extent that upon unique occasion the total cost of teas amounted to 13/10 against the average cot of two guineas as previously paid.

Changing facilities in the Park have caused some unhappiness and, after discussion with the Football Club and Youth Club, who were asked to co-operate, the Committee decided the matter should be taken to the Council who are now in the process of considering what should be done.

The Committee has served the Club faithfully and has met on six occasions, each having a constitutional quorum and averaging an 80% attendance. A sub-committee has been elected and have organised two dances during the season.

Four money ventures have helped the funds, the Jumble Sale was poorly supported but resulted in a profit of £11 15s 0d, the Annual Draw and first Dance were better supported and resulted in a profit of £29 11s 0d. Another Dance has been organised for Whit Monday.

To sum up this season has been one of the most successful in the Club's history, from a poor beginning we have gradually grown in prestige and must endeavour to carry this into the future. This future has promise, for the great event of the season has been the purchasing of a new pitch about more will be heard during the meeting."

The AGM adopted the Club's first formal constitution and Eric Webb was made a Life Member.

Purchase of a New Ground on Woburn Road

The minutes of a Committee Meeting held at the White Hart on Friday March 21st 1958 contained a reference to Mr. A. J. Woodward who had agreed to lease part of his field in Woburn Road to the Club. At the next Committee Meeting, on Friday April 11, it was reported that Mr. Woodward was willing to sell three acres of his land to the Club at a cost of £100 per acre. The Committee agreed to purchase the land but, "as yet were uncertain of sources of payment."

At the 1958 AGM held at the White Hart on 16th May under "Provision of New Field", the following was recorded:

"The situation was outlined by the Chairman who stated that at present everything was in safe hands and we were waiting for planning permission to use the ground. Thanks, were expressed to Mr. O'Dell for all his work."

In July 1958, the Treasurer reported that Club Funds stood at £170. Mr. O'Dell, the Treasurer, proposed £140 should be put into a deposit account and £10 of premium bonds be purchased for the Club.

The minutes of the Committee meeting of August 8th 1958 record that, "Notice has been received that the hoped-for grant from the Ministry of Education would not be available and the Secretary was therefore requested to contact the Rugby Union as to the possibility of a loan."

At the next Committee Meeting of September 19th, the following is recorded:

"During the period between Committee Meetings much had been done by the representatives authorised to be responsible for work on the pitch. Briefly summarised the following had been done. The pitch had been levelled, not to complete satisfaction, but nevertheless improved. The RFU had been approached with a view to a loan and application, together with valuation, plans and EMRU backing had been made. The Agriculture Advisory Service had provided details of seed and fertiliser. Mr. Butterworth Senior, had agreed to supply the same after testing soil for correct fertilisation and was requested to supply these as soon as possible to Mr. A.J. Woodward, who had agreed to do all that was required to sow the field."

The Chairman, Richard Dillingham – "stated that the record should be made of the enormous amount of work done by club members in order to prepare the Station Road pitch for this season."

The next Committee Meeting occurred on 17th October – the following are the main points covered as regards the new pitch; "The RFU had agreed to loan £400 at 2% per annum for 15 years. The National Playing Field Association had granted £120. The Agreement and Contract with Mr. Woodward was signed, and £30 deposit paid. Mr. Hall was authorised to obtain posts, wire, and gates at an approximate cost of £130. Mr. O'Dell pointed out the Council's interest in the possibility of a loan towards providing changing accommodation. He was authorised to sound-out the Council further, though it was agreed the Club was not in a position to borrow any more money at the moment."

Barrie O'Dell dealt with the legal agreement, some levelling of the pitch was required, and equipment was loaned from Bedfordshire County Council for this purpose, thanks to Mike Henderson. Norman Brown obtained grass seed and Mr. Woodward ploughed, harrowed and then sowed the seed. Unfortunately, an indigenous weed, corn spurry, grew amongst the grass, but this was treated, and the pitch flourished.

New Pitch Expenses

Cost		Monies	
Field	£300	County Playing Fields	£100-0-0
Seed	£40–13s-0d	National Playing Fields	£120-0-0
Fertiliser	£24-17s-6d	RFU	£400-0-0
Levelling	£24-17s-6d	East Midlands RFU	£ 20-0-0
Fencing	£25-10s-10d		
Total	£527-15s-4d		£640-0-0

The loans were to be repaid at a rate of £81-6s-8d for 3 years and £48 for 7 years

A little later, Ted Lawrence, the local bookmaker, was to buy some ground at the far end of the Woburn Road field for the Queensmen Football Club, which was to become known as Lawrence Park.

At this time, the Club was sharing changing and bathing accommodation in the Park with the Football Club and Youth Club – the committee minutes record the unhappiness of the players with the upkeep of the Pavilion by the Council and the frustration of trying to get co-operation of other clubs. With a new ground in the offing it was time to look for a better solution for the Club's accommodation.

1957-58	played	won	drawn	lost	pts. for	pts. against
	24	12	3	9	182	222

Season 1958-59 - (Norman Brown)

President	N.F. Sharpe
Chairman	R. Dillingham
Hon. Secretary-Treasurer	M.P. Turvey
Hon. Fixture Secretary	W.N.G.L. Whiskin
Hon. Team Secretary	J.W. Lawson
Captain 1st XV	N. Brown
Vice- Captain 1st XV	J. B. Hall
Committee	J.W. Butterworth, D.L. Simms
	T.M. Comerford, B.S. O'Dell

This was a momentous season for the Club. Firstly, because of the outstanding performance of the 1st XV. Of the 32 games played; 27 were won, 4 drawn and only 1 lost – the second game of the season 12-14 to Bedford Igranic played on 20 October 1958.

Ampthill 12 pts. Igranic 14 pts. – September 20th, 1958

Although Ampthill Rugby Club lost their first game of the season at Station Road on Saturday to Bedford Igranic by 14 points (1 goal, 1 penalty goal, 2 tries) to 12 points (2 penalty goals, 2 tries) the honours were as evenly divided as the score suggests. Indeed, it was only a slowing down ten minutes from the end, at which stage they were leading 12-8 that cost Ampthill the game.

Ampthill attacked from the onset and skipper Brown (who rallied and led the forwards well throughout) was almost over from a foot-rush. A long run from centre Eric Arnold took play to the other end, but Turvey beat him to the ball to prevent a score. However, when Ampthill were penalised for handling in a loose scrum in front of their own posts, Arnold converted an easy kick.

Ampthill almost equalised when Harry Arnold was robbed of a try by a defender kicking the ball over the dead ball line. A penalty resulted from the five-yard scrum, but Bassett (a newcomer with plenty of weight) missed the kick.

The Works went further ahead when poor tackling by Ampthill left a man over and winger Hull scored in the corner. Arnold converted the difficult shot.

This rather took the wind out of Ampthill's sails but with Barry Parker winning most of the set scrums and Hall well served by Bean, using the touch line intelligently, they gradually gained confidence again. After a good run by Terry Comerford and Moore which took the ball over the line, Norman Brown backing up, took the ball between the posts for the touchdown.

The second half opened with John Hall just missing a penalty. Then a fine run down the touchline by Harry Arnold, in which he beat several defenders brought a try. His conversion attempt was just wide.

Mervyn Turvey had a good run and then Nigel Whiskin was all but over from a line-out in the corner. A dummy and break through by Terry Comerford put Phil Bean over, but a try was not allowed. An infringement in the following five-yard scrum cost Igranic a penalty. Harry Arnold kicking a good goal.

Terry Comerford made another dash down the centre to force a touchdown. Barry Parker charged down the 25 kick and Igranic's Arnold was penalised for laying on the ball. Harry Arnold again kicked a good goal. Eric Arnold then took play to Ampthill's line and almost scored, but a five-yard scrum was given. The ball went out to the other wing and Ivan Young scored in the corner – taking the corner flag with him. Arnold missed the conversion that would have put Igranic in the lead, but the winning try came almost immediately. Ampthill were caught on the wrong foot, all their players expecting a place-kick when a penalty was given against them. Instead, Igranic's second row forward Page merely tapped the ball and ran over for a try.

John Hall, who played at fly-half that day – though equally home in the centre or wing – recalls that the 1st XV then went 40+ games unbeaten before losing to Brush Sports, Loughborough, on 2 January 1959

Their strength in defence is illustrated by a points-against total of only 56 while the points scored – 453– shows there was nothing wrong with their attack either, especially as 72 of the 108 tries were scored by the backs. Ampthill's line was crossed 10 times, the other points conceded being made up of 6 penalty goals, 2 dropped goals and 1 conversion. In only one game – their last against Vauxhall – did Ampthill fail to score. Three matches had to be cancelled in January because of the weather and it was perfectly possible that 500 points could have been scored that season. Top scorer for the fourth season was vice-captain John Hall, who also captained the team (17 times), after an injury side-lined Norman Brown from December. John scored 15 tries, 7 penalty goals and 21 conversions (108 points). Winger, Harry Bassett bagged 60 points, John Comerford 51 points, Mervyn Turvey 36 points and fly-half Richard Churchill 30 points. Richard Churchill, who joined from Bedford Rugby Club, was to have a long and distinguished association with the Club. Apparently, Richard played one game for Ampthill on 21 December 1951 when still at Bedford Modern School – but without their knowledge or approval!

It was fitting that after such a season, to hold a celebration dinner – this took place the White Hart on May 8th 1959 with 60 members, their wives and guests attending.

The new pitch in Woburn Street was levelled and seeded but various problems included a poor growing season meant that the 1959-60 season would again begin at the Station Road ground. During this period the Club was proactive in approaching Mr. Woodford to purchase land to create a second pitch and a sub-committee looked into procuring a clubhouse of sorts. Fund-raising was important, as there was now a mortgage to pay for the new pitch. The usual Grand National Draw was held, a Watch Swindle, two Jumble Sales and with the assistance of the ladies a Christmas Bazaar – these brought in £150. It was estimated that the ladies "provided something like 1800 sandwiches, over 200 cups of tea and 900 cakes". Doug Simms "supplied gratis over 120 pints of milk."

In 1959 Ampthill & District Community Rugby Football Club was incorporated as a company limited by guarantee. At a Special General Meeting held at the White Hart Hotel on March 13th, 1959, Barrie O'Dell proposed, "That on the recommendation of the Committee the club be formed into a Limited Company". This was seconded by Doug Simms.

The minutes state that; "After some discussion covering such points as the actual value of this move, the query if the club could afford to do this and if the RFU had any views on the subject, which were all adequately covered by Mr. O'Dell, the proposition was put to the vote and passed by 13 votes to none."

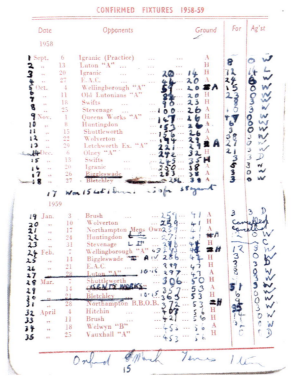

Norman Brown's Fixture Card 1958-59

In March 1999, Eric Webb, who had emigrated to Quebec, was in touch with Richard Dillingham about the possibility of a fiftieth-year celebration in Ampthill the following year. In response to Richard, Eric provided the following list of club members from 1950 to 1957:

Roger Arnold*	Brian Hodgson*	Bill Rogers*	Mervyn Turvey
Norman Brown*	David Hempsall	Tony Sibley*	John Wallis
Roy Burrows	John Huckle	Doug Simms*	Eric Webb*
John Churchill*	John Lawson	Brian Staniforth*	Archie Webster
Richard Churchill*	Peter Lawton	Alan Stevens	Nigel Whiskin
John Comerford	Eddie MacDonald*	Harry Taylor*	Mike Waldren
Terry Comerford	Ken Mobbs*	Fred Thistlethwaite	Geoff White
Taffy Evans	Barrie O'Dell	Roger Thompson	Chalky White
Stan Fossey	Dave Pully*	Bill Thompson*	Doug Young*
John Hall	Tony Rogers*	Ken Tilston*	

* earliest members of the Club – season 1950-51

1958-59	played	won	drawn	lost	pts. for	pts. against
	32	27	4	1	453	56

Season 1959-60 - (Captain - **Norman Brown**)

President	N.F. Sharpe
Chairman	R. Dillingham
Hon. Secretary	M.P. Turvey
Ho. Treasurer	B.S. O'Dell
Hon. Fixture Secretary	R.G. Churchill
Hon. Team Secretary	E.W. Billington
Captain 1st XV	N. Brown
Vice- Captain 1st XV	J. B. Hall
Committee	D.L. Simms, M.G. Bassett
	M. Houston, F. Thistlethwaite & H.S. Arnold

The 1959-60 was notable for three reasons; the new pitch was officially opened, Norman Brown stood down as captain after 9 years at the helm, and the Exiles XV was founded. Considering all the difficulties associated with the development of the Club; scarcity of players, pitches, clubhouse and a hundred and more issues, this was an astonishing achievement.

Norman Brown

Norman Brown was educated at Haberdashers Askes Public School in Elstree, Hertfordshire and served as a rear gunner in Lancaster bombers during the war. Norman started his senior rugby career in 1946 playing prop for the Old Haberdashers Rugby Club, when London Old Boys' Clubs were a force in club rugby. Haberdashers, played teams such as Plymouth Albion, Saracens and London Irish.

He married and moved to Ampthill in 1949, taking up a position at Wrest Park, the home to the National Institute of Agricultural Engineering, later the Silsoe Research Institute. Norman played rugby for Bedford, where he played in the Wanderers with Fred Thistlethwaite, and was friendly with a youthful Richard Churchill, then fly-half in the 1st XV. He was invited to join the new Ampthill Rugby Club and played in the first season, first appearing at tight-head prop against Bedford Swifts on 2nd December 1950, the eighth game of that first season (a win for Ampthill by 14pts. to nil). Norman elected as Club Captain in his second season a position he retained for a further eight years.

Norman Brown was Club Chairman from 1962-1970, and President from 2002-2004. He was made a Life Member in May 1960. In 1985, he was elected as the Bedfordshire representative to the East Midlands Rugby Union. For many years he was responsible for the coaching set-up at East Midlands. Norman was East Midland's President in 1993-94 and was made a Life-Member the following year. He served on the Mobbs Memorial Organising Committee for eight years and also became the Press and PR Officer for East Midlands RFU.

Following the success of the Mini Rugby and to provide continuity for the young players, Norman was asked to form a Youth Section in 1980. Starting at under 13 level and expanding year on year by 1983 the Ampthill Club were able to offer teams, coaching and matches at every level from under 7 to under 17 age groups.

Norman's memories and memorabilia were enormously influential in the writing of this history.

At the AGM at the end of this season M.P. Turvey, then Honorary Secretary stated: "There are many details missing from this report that probably deserve mention, but one which cannot be forgotten is the retirement of Norman Brown, our Captain, who has seen this Club through its apprenticeship and now feels he must hang up his boots. It is not proposed to write an obituary, but I feel that it should be recorded here, in the report of his last season playing with the club, that the name of Norman Brown will be remembered with reverence as long as rugby union football is played in Ampthill."

Sadly, Norman passed away in September 2020, never having seen the completed book to which he had contributed so much.

Player numbers increased and the Club approached A.J. Woodward again for some more land for a second pitch. He agreed in principal, to lease or to sell the remaining ground (approximately 2 acres), but this would not happen until 1968. Over time, the Club has sought more playing capacity and matches have been played at Hunting Engineers, Alameda and Redborne Schools. An agreement was thought to have been made with Fergusons to use the field at the bottom of Hazlewood Lane Hill, but it fell through, on the advice their solicitors. A pitch in the Park near to Katherine's Cross was used during the 1980s - with its hazards of wind, cattle and rabbit holes.

John Hall broke all previous records with his total of 153 points made up of 11 tries, 20 penalties and 30 conversions. Mervyn Turvey was top try scorer with 16 tries (he also scored tries for the Exiles). Several big victories were recorded in the season, 43 points being scored in one game against Wellingborough "A" and 20 points or more in nine other matches.

At the AGM, last-season's vice-Captain, John Gough, was elected as Club Captain. Mervyn Turvey, Treasurer, announced that the Club had an income of £950. Of this sum, however, £400 was on a mortgage to the Rugby Football Union and £120 a grant from the Playing Fields Association. Expenditure was £735 19s. 8d, and this included £270 to complete the purchase of the Woburn Road ground.

The meeting felt that the Club was sufficiently financed to pay off the loan from the Playing Field Association at once, even though payment was not due until the next season.

One of the highlights of the season was reported in the Ampthill News in May 3rd, 1960:

Ampthill end season scoring ten tries, all unconverted

Ten tries and not one of them converted! That was how Ampthill Rugby Club finished the season, when they beat Bedford Athletic Extra 1st at Station Road – probably the last time they will play on that field – by 30 points to nil. Seven different kickers were tried, and besides the conversions attempts, an easy penalty shot was also missed.

Athletic arrived with only 13 men, but Alan Stevens and Tim Moore, the Ampthill reserves, turned out for them. The forward exchanges were pretty even, Ampthill having no experienced hooker in the team, but outside the scrum the Athletic had few ideas.

It took a while for the game to settle to a pattern, but then from a short penalty the ball went along the Ampthill line for Young to put Turvey over in the corner. Hall was close with a long kick and then missed an easier penalty shot.

Lloyd, a promising youngster, went over from Comerford's break, but was called back, touch being given, but Lloyd got a legitimate try shortly after when he rounded the opposing winger. Young, Churchill and Houseman combined in a move which lead to another, Greaves, grabbing a loose ball to dive over.

Skipper Brown made a great side-stepping run at the start of the second half, getting right to the posts before giving a forward pass. Brown then initiated a scoring move, putting the ball back for a passing movement out to winger Turvey, who went over for his second try.

Turvey got a third, and then a brilliant change of direction by Churchill put Whiskin through, but he was tackled on the line. An Athletic penalty was fielded by Hall who ran right through for a brilliant try, and inter-passing by Simms and Rogers put Brown over.

A break by Churchill followed for a try, and finally Doug Simms got two fine bustling tries in the corner. Of the players who did not score, Comerford deserves mention for strong running, and at forward Williams was outstanding in the loose.

Another impressive season produced almost 500 points scored by the Club – something unthinkable a mere five seasons before. More than 200 points were scored by the three-quarters including 15 tries by John Hall, John Comerford "the artful dodger" scored 16 tries and Turvey 12.

Ampthill Town Rugby Club circa 1950
Standing: R.Dillingham (referee), R. Arnold, S. Fossey, E. McDonald, R. Burrows,
T. Rogers, P. Mears, J. Rose, A. Webster and N. Sharpe (President)
Seated: D. Simms, E. Webb, N. Brown (Captain), B. Hodgson and J. Huckle
Seated on ground: B. Lowings and B O'Dell

Source: Brian Hodgson in March, 2018 (aged 90)

Norman Brown's 1st XV photographed at the Station Road ground in the early 1950s

For the first season the Club fielded a 2nd XV - The "Exiles" led by the inimitable Barrie O'Dell. The Exile's skipper offered constant encouragement to his new side and a number of experienced players helped out, most notably Turvey, Arnold, Parker, and Ellis Billington. The Exiles pack was a lively unit but they needed more experience in the backs to pose a more potent threat. They played 27 games, won 6 and lost 21 scoring 173 pts. and conceding 468pts. Sometimes, when light permitted, the Exiles played after the first team with some players involved in both matches and with Richard Dillingham refereeing both games!

In this last season of the decade, sixty-two games were played arranged by Richard Churchill, now fixture secretary. Ellis Billington was the Honorary Team Secretary that season. At the AGM of 1959-60, it was estimated that Ellis must have written and posted 1,000 postcards and made countless numbers of telephone calls to ensure the teams were organised in those pre-internet times and few people had a telephone installed. Off the field, the Club received valuable support from the Ladies Committee in the matter of post-match refreshments, but they also raised £60 in their bazaar and jumble sales. Further monies were raised in a Vital Statistics Competition, a Whit Monday Fete and the Annual Dinner at the White Hart.

1959-60	played	won	drawn	lost	pts. for	pts. against
1st XV	35	27	3	5	485	122
Exiles	27	6	0	21	173	468

In the Club Membership Card for 1959-60, Rule 17 concerned subscriptions:

Annual Subscription 10s. 6d., Non-playing Members 5s. 0d., are due for the coming season and should be paid to the Treasurer as soon as possible.

The match Fee is 2s. 6d. and every effort should be made by players to help the Vice-Captain in collecting it. A fee of 6d. per week will be charged for the use of Club Shirts.

Results of the First Decade

season	played	won	drawn	lost	Pts. for	Pts. against
1950-51	25	11	1	13	143	219
1951-52	25	11	3	11	148	223
1952-53	19	4	2	13	79	238
1953-54	20	7	2	11	119	191
1954-55	**21**	**7**	**2**	**12**	**91**	**127**
1955-56	22	9	3	10	160	194
1956-57	28	10	1	17	234	275
1957-58	24	12	3	9	182	222
1958-59	**32**	**27**	**4**	**1**	**453**	**56**
1959-60	**35**	**27**	**3**	**5**	**485**	**122**
Exiles	**27**	**6**	**0**	**21**	**173**	**469**

There is a stark contrast between season 1954-55 when the Club nearly folded through chronic lack of players and the final two seasons of the decade which record excellent results and the formation of the Exiles under Barrie O'Dell.

I am indebted to Tony Rogers' meticulous record keeping throughout this first decade of the Clubs re-formation after the War.

10 Year Fixture Comparison (1st XV) 1950-1960

Sept.	1950/51 Bedford Lions "A" Leighton Buzzard "A" Bedford Town Colts	Sept.	1960 Northampton Men's Own English Electric Stevenage E.A.C. St. Albans Bedford Swifts
Oct.	Vauxhall Works "A" Lynton Works, Bedford Leighton Buzzard "A"	Oct.	Rushden & Higham Ex. 1st Stevenage Igranic Queens Works
Nov.	70th. Heavy Ack Ack Regiment Vauxhall Works "A" Biggleswade	Nov.	Worcester College Oxford Brush Sports, Loughborough Bletchley Northampton Men's Own
Dec.	Bedford Swifts Bedford Lions "A" Igranic "A"	Dec.	Queens Works Huntingdon Igranic Wellingborough Biggleswade Brush Sports, Loughborough
Jan.	Bedford Athletic Extra "A" Leighton Buzzard "A" Bedford Swifts	Jan.	De Havilland Igranic Rushden & Higham Ext. 1st Bletchley
Feb.	Bedford Athletic "B" Lynton Works, Bedford Biggleswade "A"	Feb.	Stevenage English Electric, Stevenage Buckingham A.E.I . Rugby
Mar.	Old Lutonians Extra "A" Igranic Works "A" Unilever Sports Old Dunstablians Unilever Sports Bedford Athletic Extra "A"	Mar.	Shuttleworth College Old Dunstablians Vauxhall Old Lutonians Ext. 1st Wellingborough Old Grammarians "A"
Apr.	Vauxhall 7-a-side Tournament Old Lutonians Extra "A" Biggleswade	Apr.	Northampton B.B.O.B. "A" Biggleswade Huntingdon Bedford Athletic Extra 1st

Chapter 3: The Sixties - Consolidation

Season 1960-61 - (Captain - John Hall)

Officers

President	N.F. Sharpe
Chairman	R. Dillingham
Hon. Secretary	M.P. Turvey
Hon. Treasurer	A.T.J. Hobley
Fixture Secretary	R.G. Churchill
Team Secretary	Messrs Young & Lake
Committee	M.G. Bassett, A.T. Rogers, D.L. Simms, A.T. Williams

Playing

Captain 1st XV	J.B. Hall
Vice-Captain 1st XV	F. Thistlethwaite
Captain of Exiles	J. Course
Vice-Captain of Exiles	B.S. O'Dell
3rd XV	F. Thistlethwaite

During the sixties, the Club consolidated its playing standards and its fixtures gradually improved. By the end of the decade the Club would be running 4 XVs. For season 1960-61, the Club ran a 3rd XV for the first time, captained by Fred Thistlethwaite, the Exiles were again captained by Barrie O'Dell. The Thirds played 8 games that season, winning 4, losing 3 and drawing 1 (one other match was cancelled). This "experiment" was dropped for the following season and it was 1965-66 before the Thirds were revived and they then flourished through to the end of the decade.

On September 3rd 1960, the new pitch on Woburn Road was officially opened with a match between a Norman Brown's XV and a team raised by the new captain, John Hall. The match was refereed by former England & RAF Captain, Squadron-leader Bob Sterling; Richard Dillingham and Bill Rogers were the touch-judges.

Norman Brown XV (in hoops) v. John Hall's XV at the new pitch at Woburn Road – September 3rd 1960

Earlier in July, a committee meeting was held at the White Hart, but members present also went to the Great Park to inspect the Park Gate House as a prospective clubhouse. The Committee decided "to lease the complete site". It was agreed that the back of the Lodge should be used for changing accommodation and the front as a club room. The Pavilion in the Park was known locally as John Gunn's Lodge, named after a local character who had resided there. The Lodge was situated at the entrance to what is now the West Carpark at the end of Woburn Road.

A sub-committee was formed under Doug Simms to plan the refurbishment of the Lodge with a sum of £100 to be spent during season 1960-61. Tony Rogers and Doug Simms were charged with overseeing the refurbishing of the Lodge and creating changing, washing facilities and a clubroom. The water heater and light were powered by Calor Gas and water for the baths came from the reservoir at the top of the Park, the water arriving as a trickle. When the water was being heated, the lights would dim so the door was left open and passers-by were treated to the sight of naked rugby players! The Lodge was divided into two rooms, one for changing and washing (a tin bath approx. 5'x5'), the other for entertaining the away team.

This would remain the club's home until the move to the Pavilion behind Parkside Hall in September 1969. Controversially, the eighteenth-century Lodge (said to be part of Capability Brown's development of the Great Park) was demolished by the urban council in 1972.

Highlights of the season for the 1st XV were a 50-8 win against Wolverton, 34-0 versus Tring and 19-0 over Huntingdon. The Exiles XV captained by Dougie Simms enjoyed good victories over Hitchin 42-5 and Bletchley 16-9. The thirds skippered by Fred Thistlethwaite, had a good season including a win away at Stockwood Park 12-0 and a victory over Bedford Swifts 12-3.

John Gunn's **Lodge in the Park, the rugby Club's first clubhouse - 1960**

1960-61	played	won	lost	drawn	pts. for	pts. against
1st XV	32	17	11	4	387	341
Exiles XV	26	6	18	2	173	288
3rd XV	8	4	3	1		

Season 1961-62 - (Captain - John Hall, Nigel Whiskin and F. Thistlethwaite)

Officers

President	N.F. Sharpe
Chairman	R. Dillingham
Hon. Secretary	R.A.D. Williams
Hon. Treasurer	A.T.J. Hobley
Fixture Secretary	R.G. Churchill
Team Secretary	Messrs Holder & O'Donnell
Committee	B.S. O'Dell, A.T. Rogers, D.L. Simms, F. Thistlethwaite

Playing

Captain 1st XV	J.B. Hall
Vice-Captain 1st XV	W.N.G.L. Whiskin
Captain of Exiles	M.R. Brooker
Vice-Captain of Exiles	H.S Arnold

In season 1961-62, John Hall's spell as captain did not last long, as he was forced to resign through injury. The election of a new captain took place at the Club trial match on 2nd September: present was the President, Chairman and thirty-three members. Nigel Whiskin was proposed and seconded by Messrs. Churchill and Bean and was elected Captain by a majority vote. John Hall was co-opted onto the Committee.

However, in January 1962, Nigel Whiskin resigned in writing – the committee meeting minutes do not provide a reason for this – and an extra-ordinary general meeting was called to elect his successor on 26th January. Richard Churchill and Fred Thistlethwaite both got through to a second ballot and Fred was elected by 12 to 11. Richard Churchill agreed to serve as vice-captain.

This was not the only loss sustained by the Club this season, as members sadly learned of the death of their President, Norman Sharpe. Norman had been a tireless worker both for the Club and sport in Ampthill in general. He served as President from 1950 to 1961 and left the Club a legacy of £100 (worth £2,250 today).

At the AGM in 1962, Richard Dillingham was justly elected to fill the vacant presidency, a post he held until his death in 2001.

Despite the loss of John Hall, a fine player, the 1st XV record is an enviable one.

1961-62	played	won	lost	drawn	pts. for	pts. against
1st XV	32	26	1	5	428	174
Exiles	29	2	24	3	120	528

Tony Parrott scored 174 points – a Club record at that time. For the unhappy Exiles, Harry Arnold was top scorer with 36 points. In his Hon. Secretary's report to the 1962 AGM, R.A. Williams said:

"They (Exiles) are a very young side and have stuck to their guns in a manner which promises very well in the coming season, when the experience they have gained will be invaluable to them. It is not so long ago that the 1st XV were in just the same situation. But it is not on the playing record alone that the Club must be judged; it is also on the conduct of its members. We are fortunate in having a bunch who will always play the game as it should be played, and who are not averse to getting together afterwards. It is this spirit which makes Ampthill one of the most popular matches for opposing sides, and we should try and keep it that way.

The Gatehouse has been in use all season and has provided excellent service. Some of the Exiles have a theory that a full gas-cylinder is only provided for the 1st XV, but then the 1st XV is a much dirtier team after their matches!"

Season 1962-63 - (Captain - Fred Thistlethwaite)

Officers

President	R. Dillingham
Chairman	N.J. Brown
Hon. Secretary	R.A.D. Williams
Hon. Treasurer	H.S. Arnold
Fixture Secretary	R.G. Churchill
Team Secretary	S.M. Holder & R.S. Deller
Committee	J.P. Mears, A.T. Rogers, D.L. Simms, M.P. Turvey

Playing

Captain 1st XV	F. Thistlethwaite
Vice-Captain 1st XV	R.G. Churchill
Captain of Exiles	B.S. O'Dell
Vice-Captain of Exiles	H.S. Arnold

The winter of 1962-63 was not as severe in Bedfordshire as for most of the rest of the country, but the weather prevented any rugby between December 22nd 1962 and March 9th 1963. The playing record for the 1st XV was very evenly balanced with 13 out of 29 matches won, 13 lost and 3 drawn.

The one notable aspect of the season was Steve Holder's goal-kicking, he made 19 conversions, 1 dropped goal and 19 penalties. Other leading scorers were Tony Parrott with 48, John Comerford with 27 and John Huckle with 18 points. Most tries were scored by Tony Parrott with nine, John Comerford scored eight and John Huckle six. Their last game brought their biggest win by 29-0 against Royston. The worst defeat was 0-31 to Wellingborough. A number of young players were introduced, and Dellar and Greenley became regular first teamers. Injuries accounted for the loss of some top players. Hall, Churchill, and Parrott all missed a significant number of games, disrupting the attack in vital mid-field positions.

Barrie O'Dell's Exiles doubled their number of victories – winning 4, losing 14 and with 1 game drawn with 66 points scored and 250 against. Encouragingly, they found it easier that season to field a full team. Several heavy defeats were suffered, the worst being 0-44 to Queens Works "A". Victories were Olney "B" 8-5, Wolverton 5-0 and Northampton Casuals "A" 3-0 and 9-3 against Huntingdon "A".

Socially, it was a successful season and the Club looked forward to attaining a second pitch and pavilion. In November 1964 one of Richard Dillingham's regular series of raffles raised £17 6s 6d.

At the AGM on 31st May 1963 the Treasurer, A.S. Arnold, announced that the Club had made a loss for the first time in its history - £43 – this was "mainly due to lack of fund-raising events." R.S. Deller, (Hon. Sec.) commented: "as well as being enjoyable this season has also been a very encouraging one. As the Club now boasts more members than ever before, a third team seems inevitable. Together with this the purchase of a second pitch has become almost essential, and the possibility of building a Clubhouse has caused a lot of serious thought among members, and it is upon these two points that the future advancement of this Club seems to rest."

1962-63	played	won	lost	drawn	Pts. for	Pts. against
1st XV	29	13	13	3	280	213
Exiles XV	19	4	14	1	66	250

Season 1963-64 - (Captain - Fred Thistlethwaite)
Officers

President	N.J. Brown
Chairman	R. Dillingham
Hon. Secretary	R.G. Churchill
Hon. Treasurer	H.S. Arnold
Fixture Secretary	A. Parrot
Team Secretary	S.M. Holder & B.S. O'Dell
Committee	J.B. Hall, F.J. Comerford, D.L. Simms, C. Goodwin, A.T. Rogers & M.P. Turvey

Playing

Captain 1st XV	F. Thistlethwaite
Vice-Captain 1st XV	R.G. Churchill
Captain of Exiles	B.S. O'Dell
Vice-Captain of Exiles	J. Hobley
Coach	N. Brown

Norman Brown became the Club's first ever coach. Fred Thistlethwaite led the 1st XV for the second successive season and his pack formed the basis of a strong team. Steve Holder scored 98 points, Tony Parrott 48, Richard Churchill 42 and John Comerford 27. Success was essentially a team effort but perhaps the brilliance of Len Simm, who's last try of the season against Hitchin was considered one of the best individual tries seen at Woburn Road.

Perseverance, more experience and an excellent team-spirit enabled the Exiles to become a good team. Harry Arnold top-scored with 21 points.

Dave Williams

Joining the Club this season was Dave Williams, who had moved from the Rhondda Valley to take up a position with Hunting Engineering. Dave would be a fixture as hooker for many seasons, captaining in 1965-66 & 1969-70. He was a fast, ball-handling forward in the modern mode. A fine reader of the game and astute judge of playing talent, Dave Williams would be a major contributor to the success of the Club on and off the field. A popular and highly respected Club member within the Bedfordshire and East Midlands RFU, he was instrumental in founding the mini & youth section which has been an enduring achievement in the Club's history. He would become Chairman and President.

In 1964, a Whit Monday Fete raised £50 and a further £75 from Whist Drives, Grand National Draw and Jumble Sales. Tony Rogers continued to maintain the Lodge changing facilities and Club President, Richard Dillingham continued the refereeing of home games.

During this decade, Ampthill continued to change and bathe at the Lodge in the Park, but it was cramped, and sanitary arrangements were inadequate for the developing needs of the Club. A war-time wooden building was considered to replace it, but it was thought that those that were inspected would not withstand removal and erection at the ground.

At the AGM in May 1964 annual subscriptions were revised to:

	£	s.	d.
members 18 & over	1	5	0
if paid before 1st October	1	1	0
members under 18 in full-time education		12	6
if paid before 1st October		10	6

And match fees were revised to:

members 18 & over	3s 6d.
members under 18 in full-time education	2s 0d.

Both Ampthill teams had performed well:

1963-64	played	won	lost	drawn	Pts. for	Pts. against
1st XV	32	24	1	7	554	202
Exiles XV	30	16	1	13	380	265

Season 1964-65 - (Captain - Peter Mears)

Officers
President   R. Dillingham
Chairman   N.J. Brown
Hon. Secretary   E.J. Milton
Hon. Treasurer   R. Babb
Fixture Secretary   F. Thistlethwaite
Team Secretary   S.M. Holder & B.S. O'Dell
Committee   F.J. Comerford, D.L. Simms, R. Deller, A.T. Rogers & M.P. Turvey
Playing
Captain 1st XV   P.J. Mears
Vice-Captain 1st XV S. Holder
Captain of Exiles   B.S. O'Dell
Vice-Captain of Exiles I. Owen
Coach   N. Brown

New opponents for 1964/65 were Cambridge 2nd XV, NCAE Silsoe and Stamford 1st XV. The Exiles too, had improved fixtures; with Stockwood Park, Shuttleworth College, EAC St. Albans and Towcestrians featuring.

In December 1964, Peter Mears reported, on behalf of the Selection Committee, that some players would have to be left out of both sides in order to give every member a game. The Committee agreed that a reserve should be selected for each team and should travel. Barrie O'Dell captained the Exiles during this season.

At the AGM held in May 1965, a motion was passed regarding the Selection Committee. This was to consist of the Captain & Vice-Captain of each XV, with others appointed each season, (Brian Hodgson and Richard Dillingham were appointed for a trial period). Norman Brown continued as coach this season.

Highlights of the season for the first XV were impressive wins against Igranic 29-3, Buckingham 24-3 and Leighton Buzzard 31-6. The worst defeats were a 3-23 loss at AEI Rugby and 10-24 to Huntingdon, other matches lost were by very small margins.

In July 1964 Mr. L.F. Burgoine, the owner of the Station Road pitch, had died and a letter of sympathy was sent to his widow and a donation to the Freedom from Hunger Campaign. That year the Club Membership Card contained the following:

Subscription

The Annual Subscription is now £ 1 5s 0d (Under 18 or in full time education on 1st September 12s. 6d.) or £1 1s. 0d (Under 18 or in full time education on 1st September 10s 6d.) if paid *before* 1st October each year. IT PAYS YOU TO PAY THE CLUB.

The Match Fee is now 3/6d. (2/6d. if under 18 or in full-time education). Please pay your Vice-Captain every game.

1964-65	played	won	lost	drawn	Pts. for	Pts. against
1st XV	30	13	17	0	302	332
Exiles XV	20	6	14	0	158	300

Season 1965-66 - (Captain - Dave Williams)
Officers

President	R. Dillingham
Chairman	N.J. Brown
Hon. Secretary	E.J. Milton
Hon. Treasurer	R. Babb
Fixture Secretary	F. Thistlethwaite
Team Secretary	R. Deller & B.S. O'Dell
Committee	J.P. Mears, A. Owen, I. Owen, D.L. Simms & A.T. Rogers

Playing

Captain 1st XV	D. Williams
Vice-Captain 1st XV	I. Gough
Captain of Exiles	B.S. O'Dell
Vice-Captain of Exiles	H.S. Arnold
Captain 3rd XV	F. Thistlethwaite

This season it was noticeable how under Fred Thistlethwaite's auspices the fixture list was growing stronger. The Club now played the full Stockwood Park team, Wellingborough Old Grammarians, Rushden & Higham and Old Perseans (Cambridge) appeared on the fixture list for the first time.

In December 1965, the Club decided to trial a 3rd XV under Fred Thistlethwaite (ex-1st team captain and Fixture Secretary). Fixtures were arranged included, Huntingdon, Kettering, Bletchley and Old Dunstablians. Redborne School pitch was unavailable, so various ground options were to be explored for the 3rd XV. Richard Dillingham was to approach the East Midlands for a set of shirts. By the following season the 3rd XV had a full set of fixtures – thanks to Fred Thistlethwaite.

The 1st XV were in the black for the season with notable wins against Wellingborough 37-0, Stockwood Park 13-3, Cambridge 2nds 15-9, Stevenage 21-11, Bedford Swifts 18-6, Huntingdon 15-3, Buckingham 13-9, Wolverton 16-12, and Stevenage 22-11.

Barrie O'Dell's Exiles also finished in credit with useful performances versus Luton 22-4, Stevenage "A" 16-5, Bedford Athletic 4th XV, 21-0 and Vauxhall "A" 28-0. The 3rd XV played four games this season, no scores can be found, but in October 1965, the team enjoyed a good win over Bletchley.

The annual subscription was £1 5s. 0d and match fees were 3 shillings and sixpence

Life Members

R.E. Arnold	F. Thistlethwaite
N.J. Brown	M.P. Turvey
E. McDonald	R.J. Webb

1965-66	played	won	lost	drawn	pts. for	pts. against
1st XV	32	16	14	2	308	253
Exiles XV	32	18	13	1	250	271
3rd XV	4					

Season 1966-67 - (Captain - John Gough)

Officers

President	R. Dillingham
Chairman	N.J. Brown
Hon. Secretary	E. J. Milton
Hon. Treasurer	R. Babb
Fixture Secretary	F. Thistlethwaite
Team Secretary	R. Deller & B.S. O'Dell
Committee	J.P. Mears, R. Howitt, A. Owen, B. Clarke, V. Kaye, N. Yarolositis

Playing

Captain 1st XV	J. Gough
Vice-Captain 1st XV	D.L. Simms
Captain of Exiles	B.S. O'Dell
Vice-Captain of Exiles	E. Billington
3rd XV Captain	F. Thistlethwaite
3rd XV Vice-Captain	P. Waller

Dave Williams stood down as Club Captain as he contemplated a work-related move back to South Wales. Thankfully, from the Club's perspective, this did not occur, and Dave remains an active Club member to this present day.

Claridge's Lane – ARP Hut

In September, Barrie O'Dell reported that an Ex-Air Raid Precaution (ARP) Hut was available in Claridge's Lane, in Ampthill, which might be used for teas and social gatherings whilst the proposed Pavilion was unavailable. Members of the committee visited the ARP Hut and it was agreed to undertake a programme of refurbishment. Ellis Billington agreed to supervise and organise working operations with a budget limit of £30. Barrie O'Dell would submit a planning application to the local authority for a change of use. By the end of September, Ellis reported the building was ready for use and the owners had agreed to sell the ARP Hut to the Club. The only problem seemed to be a lack of suitable toilets – these being required to obtain a drinks licence. Ivor Owen was asked to prepare an estimate of the costs required to make these suitable. In the meantime, the Hut began to be used for committee meetings and other Club matters.

However, in August the hut was broken into and vandalised. Therefore, in view of the work still to be done, objections to the planned toilets by the authorities and the advancement of the Pavilion project, the committee decided to vacate the Claridge's Lane site. The Club subsequently sold the ex-ARP Hut to the Post Office.

On the playing side, the first XV under John Gough enjoyed a successful season winning 22 matches. A 50-8 win in October over Wolverton and a 34-0 beating of Tring were notable victories as was the Easter Monday 16-3 defeat of Old Yardlians.

The Exiles under Barrie O'Dell won 70% of their games, including 36-3 win over Wolverton "A" a 42-5 demolition of Hitchin "A" and a 21-8 defeat of Cambridge 4th XV.

3rd XV Established

This season was the first that the Club fielded an "official" 3rd XV and the team captained by Fred Thistlethwaite had a very encouraging playing record. Hard fought victories over Aylesbury 6-0, Leighton Buzzard 6-3, Stockwood Park 11-8, Old Northamptonians 22-3 and Luton "B" 14-3 were, perhaps, the highlights.

1966-67	played	won	lost	drawn	Pts. for	Pts. against
1st XV	34	22	11	1	403	244
Exiles XV	29	20	8	1	370	186
3rd XV	29	23	6	0	162	152

Season 1967-68 (Captain – Colin Cresswell)

Officers

President	R. Dillingham
Chairman	N.J. Brown
Hon. Secretary	H.T. Robinson
Hon. Treasurer	H.S. Arnold
Fixture Secretary	F. Thistlethwaite
Main Committee	B.S. O'Dell, R. Wood, J.G. Aynsley
General Committee	W. Edwards, I. Owen, A. Owen, M. Akerman, R. Wood, V. Kaye

Playing

Captain 1st XV	C.L. Cresswell
Vice-Captain 1st XV	D. Williams
Captain of Exiles	E.W. Billington
Vice-Captain of Exiles	R. Babb
3rd XV Captain	B.S. O'Dell
3rd XV Vice-Captain	R. Howitt
4th XV	R. Williams

This season was a successful one for the Club both playing and social.

Colin Cresswell, captain, was a stickler for physical fitness and insisted on regular training. An ex-Army PT instructor, he had represented the Army in the Hong-Kong Sevens. Regular training was not entirely popular with some of the senior players, and there were mutterings of disquiet. However, the Committee supported their captain and issued the following statement:

"All team skippers should make it known that the Committee fully support team training, and every encouragement should be given to training schemes, but the teams will be selected on the basis of merit, taking into account, fitness and ability."

The first team enjoyed a very successful season, the insistence on mid-week training had the desired effect. The forwards, well-led by Dave Williams, paved the way for many of the team's victories. The backs had some glorious games. Mention must be made of Brian Clark's accurate kicking, which on occasions demoralised the opposition. "Slim" Clark was a traditional front on toe-kicking place kicker in the Don Clarke mode.

The Exiles also enjoyed a good season, winning almost 70% of their games. It was only a few years ago that they were pleased to get any victory. However, under the captaincy of Ellis Billington they had developed into a well-disciplined unit. Any member chosen to go into the first team could now be relied upon to play the part well. Ellis Billington is one of the stalwarts of Ampthill Rugby Club. An excellent front-row player, Ellis has given freely of his time and his generous patronage of the Club has been greatly appreciated. Today, Ellis is a supporter of the first team at all home and away games.

The 3rd team too, had a very successful season under the leadership of Barrie O'Dell. Significant results were 16-0 victory over Bletchley, 22-0 over Bedford Swifts 15-3 over Wellingborough and 16-0 at home to Olney. What they may have lacked in skill, they made up for in enthusiasm and team spirit. The feeling was that some of these players would be representing the first team in the future.

For the 1st XV, the two playing highlights of the year were the 9-6 defeat of Old Yardlians (Colin Cresswell's old club) on Easter Monday and the 20-9 defeat of the Jersey 1st XV in March, whilst on tour.

During this season John Woodward and Clive Lewis represented Bedfordshire County team and Bill Edwards was a travelling reserve.

4th XV Emerges

The success of the Exiles under Ellis Billington, and the 3rd XV under Barrie O'Dell was the cause of great Club satisfaction. A 4th XV, under Roger Williams, won 4 of its 12 games in its first season, including Peterborough 5-3 and Old Lutonians 16-8.

The Club organised a trip to Twickenham to see the Wales match, after beating Stevenage in the morning en route. Socially, there was a Tramps Ball at the Greyhound in Haynes, a Dance at the Wingfield Hall, a Wine Evening at the White Hart, a New Year's Eve Ball at Haynes, a Car Treasure Hunt, and the Annual Dinner at Maulden Village Hall.

Chairman, Norman Brown, reported to the 1968 AGM that membership stood at 130.

A Second pitch at Woburn Road (1969 – 70)

In August 1967, Barrie O'Dell met with Mr. Woodward who, at first, agreed to lease the two acres of land (between the rugby pitch and the Queensmens' pitch) to the Club over a five-year period at a rent of £50 per annum. Mr. Woodward would also level and seed the land. The aim was to have the pitch ready for season 1968-69. However, in October 1968 the Committee was informed that Mr. Woodward now wished to sell the land to the Club at £500 per acre. The Committee agreed to buy the land but asked Norman Brown to negotiate a reduced cost.

Applications for loans were made to East Midlands RFU, the RFU and the Club's bank was approached for a bridging loan. The Club paid Mr. Woodward the full price of £1,000 in December 1968. The Club approached the Ministry of Education for a grant of £500 towards the cost of the new pitch. As the Club was now running four teams, it would continue to lease the pitch at Hunting Engineering, for the following season (Richard Dillingham to mark out the pitch.). The second pitch at Woburn Road was eventually ready for the 1969-70 season.

In August 1968, the Club were informed by the East Midlands Referees Society had agreed to provide referees for Exiles' games.

A New Rugby Pavilion at Parkside

At a Committee meeting held back in October 1963, a sub-committee of Messrs. Churchill, Comerford, Mears, O'Dell and Simms were appointed to "investigate the whole aspect of a club hut and make recommendations to the full committee in due course." However, it would take until 1969 for the project to near completion. In April, Barrie O'Dell reported on progress in funding the Pavilion: The Department of Education & Science would grant £2,700, The Rugby Football Union had promised a loan for £1,500 and Green King had offered a loan of £1,000 at reasonable interest and agreed to equip the Bar free of charge. The land on which the Pavilion would be erected would be leased from Parkside Hall.

The lease would be for 28 years with an option to renew at the end of that period. Rental to be agreed between the Trustees of Parkside Hall and the Committee of Ampthill Rugby Club and reviewed every seven years. The Rugby Pavilion to be sited separately and be self-contained and its position agreed between the two organisations. The Rugby Pavilion was to be decorated simultaneously with Parkside Hall. Car parking was to be limited to an area to be agreed between the Committees. Barrie O'Dell was delegated to deal with the negotiations with the trustees of Parkside Hall.

By this time Richard Churchill had been elected as Treasurer – a position he would hold until 1997. In August 1968, three estimates were considered for the new Pavilion and the Committee accepted the quote of Stanford and Clark for £5,450.

Monies available were as follows:

£2,700	Grant from Ministry
£1,000	Loan from Ampthill Urban District Council (approx. 7%)
£1,500	Loan from the Rugby Union (0-5% in 5 years, then 5% for next 5 years)
£1.500	Loan from Brewery
£1,000	Loan from The National Playing Fields Association
£1,100	Approximate capital of the Club
£8,800	Total

In February 1969, the Pavilion was erected, however, there were no funds for decorating, laying of floor, architects' fees, furniture etc, so a great deal of completion work would be undertaken by the Club members in three phases.

In Phase I, Brian Clark was to be asked to take charge of painting and decoration of the Pavilion, this was to start almost immediately. In Phase II, Ivor Owen was to be asked to supervise and advise on the laying of flooring. In Phase III, Alan Owen was to be asked to organise the bar, including shuttering. Colin Creswell was to ask his wife to consult the Ladies Committee on curtaining, Bert Robinson was to purchase furniture. Gregory Harris was to be asked to run the Bar. It was agreed to ask Ellis Billington to act as Pavilion Committee Chairman.

Chairman, Norman Brown commenting on the new Club premises to the AGM said,

"The dream has become a reality. After many years of talk and planning, we now have a Pavilion of which we can be proud. I must record how deeply indebted we are to Barrie O'Dell for nursing the project through all its difficulties and for the skilful way in which he has presented our case to the various organisations that have subsequently provided us with the grants and loans needed to finance the enterprise. Our thanks are also due to those willing hands who have helped to put the final touches to the building during the past months."

Barrie O'Dell was undoubtedly a character! A local solicitor, he was full of mischief and fun - there are a legion of stories which cannot be told here! He was not a great rugby player himself, but few have enjoyed the playing of the game as much as Barrie. As we have heard he was the mainstay, as captain, of the Exiles and 3rd XV. He gave his time and legal expertise freely and generously to the Club.

Barrie was an excellent chairman from 1976-1987, introducing the Covenants Scheme and overseeing the fund-raising for and building of the present clubhouse in Woburn Road. During his time as chairman the Club moved forward on the playing side, fielding five senior sides and with an outstanding mini and youth organisation. His leadership was crucial to the building of the Club's first two clubhouses.

Richard Churchill was the prime mover in discussing the budget for 1969-70, which was a difficult task since there was no precedent, as such. Richard estimated the expenditure on the Pavilion to be £600 per annum and the expenditure on the Club was an additional £140 per annum, including teas. Income amounted to £350 per annum, so that the Club must realise a profit on beer etc. of about £12 per week to break even. Richard subsequently recommended increasing subscriptions rather than match fees.

Colin Cresswell's 1st XV – 1967-68

R. Garratt	B. Robinson	D. Williamson	R. Day	J. Wilkinson	J. Woodward	R. Duffin	B. Clark
	B. Pearson	P. Lewis	C. Lewis	C.L. Cresswell	D. Williams	A. Jones	A. Bancroft

The tour to Jersey was a great fillip for Ampthill rugby, as The Jersey Evening Post ruefully reported on 25 March 1968 – *reproduced here with the kind permission of Jason Fox, Sports Editor – Jersey Evening Post:*

WEEKEND RUGBY

A black day for Jersey's 1st XV

ELEMENTARY MISTAKES COST VITAL POINTS

The blackest day of the season. That is how Sunday, March 24 will go down in the Jersey rugby calendar this year. The 1st XV with four wins and a draw out of their last five games, lost their form, their heads, the faith of their supporters and the match with a woefully weak display of rugby against what was, after all, very ordinary opposition.

It was a day when nothing went right for the Jersey side. Elementary mistakes cost them at least 12 points and as it turned out 12 points would have been enough for victory.

But all credit to the visitors. They played to their strength – they had eight grafting forwards and at outside half they had Stephen Holder a player who might well have scored six drop goals. As it was, he was successful with two, hit the post with another, and was only inches wide with the three other attempts. Holder did not make one single break throughout the afternoon. His educated right boot was enough to demoralize and finally destroy the island side.

FURNESS MISSED

No one was missed more from the Jersey side than Bobby Furness, the vice-captain and outside-half. His covering would have been invaluable yesterday. In his absence the back division was reshuffled – without success.

Brian Screen, the regular scrumhalf played at stand-off for the first half and then was forced to move out onto the wing after the interval suffering from a sudden attack of migraine. As a result, Langois came into the centre and Hanley moved to outside half.

Of the Jersey pack only Hudson, playing out of position in the second row and Burger, played to their true form. Ampthill tore great gaps in the Jersey pack in the loose, harrying the Islanders into all sorts of elementary mistakes.

The visiting fly-half, Holder, showed his dangerous potential with his very first kick of the game – a swirling drop-kick from nearly 40 yards which hit the top of an upright. And after five minutes they led through a Howitt try when the open-side flanker forced his way over in the corner.

Head-high token tackling led to Ampthill's next score when left wing Butterworth was allowed to grab a soft one in the corner, beautifully converted by hefty second-row Clark.

It was Clark who put Ampthill further in front from a penalty after a foot-up was given against the Jersey hooker from just outside the home 25.

Peter Burger missed a great chance of reducing the arrears with a penalty from a relatively simple position before the interval.

CLARK AGAIN

Five minutes after the interval the visitors made it 14-0 when Clark stormed over from a loose ruck near the Jersey line. Jersey at last began to open up and regain some of their lost form when Burger lofted a great up-and-under into the Ampthill 25. Andrew gathered cleanly and passed to Langois who went over near the flag.

But Ampthill countered and the peerless Holder popped over the first of two dropped goals to restore the visitors' 14-point lead.

Andrews slit the Ampthill defence wide open with a tremendous burst from half-way before his final pass to Screen went astray, but three minutes later Ampthill heeled against the head and Jersey were through onto the ball in great style for Neil Hartley, Hanley and Andrew to link up for the latter to score Jersey's second try. But from an innocuous-looking position way out on the edge of the field near the Jersey 25 Holder again went for the drop goal and banged the ball well and truly between the posts to make the score 20-6.

Langois cut through for Jersey but threw out a wild pass when it seemed easier to cross on his own after Maltman had given a half-chance a yard from the Ampthill line, but was not strong enough to force his way over for the try. Jersey final try was scored by Bill Hudson, who crashed through in the corner. But the island side had woken up too late and Ampthill were home and dry 20-9.

Ampthill – G. Harding, J. Butterworth, J. Woodward, C. Cresswell (capt.), R. Osborne, S. Holder, R. Radcliffe, E. Billington, D. Williams, R. Duffin, R. Day, B. Clark, J. Williamson, J. Day, B. Howitt

Jersey A XV 6 pts v. Ampthill A XV 0 pts.

Jersey just about deserved to win this very keen, hard fought encounter at St. Peter on Saturday afternoon. There was never much really much between the two teams, but the island XV got the vital points through two good tries – one by Jim Waites and the other by Beeches Old Boy Len Stevens, playing his first match for the A XV.

Jersey really won the game in the forwards, where Barrie Steed dominated the lineouts and Martin Sheridan was supreme in the hooking duels.

The score was 0-0 at half-time and it was increasingly obvious that the team which adjusted itself to the near gale force wind would win. Ampthill missed five reasonable kicks at goal because of the strength of the wind.

John Murphy, Jersey's scrumhalf again played an outstanding part in his team's win.

Ampthill A XV – A. Arnold, R. Hunter, G. Hawkins, J. Butterworth, M. Barnett, S. Holder, T. Ludlow, R. Williams, T. Smith, J. Hobley, P. Eversley, T. Rogers, D. Williamson, A. Owen, B. O'Dell (capt.)

	played	won	lost	drawn	pts. for	pts. against
1967-68						
1st XV	34	22	11	1	403	244
Exiles XV	29	20	8	1	370	186
3rd XV	23	17	6	0	259	141
4th XV	12	4	8	0	74	151

Season 1968-69 - (Captain Colin Cresswell)

Officers

President	R. Dillingham
Chairman	N.J. Brown
Hon. Secretary	H.T. Robinson
Hon. Treasurer	R. G. Churchill
Fixture Secretary	R. Duffin
Main Committee	B.S. O'Dell, F. Thistlethwaite, R. Wood
General Committee	B. Clarke, V. Kaye, I. Owen, L. Higgs, R.J. Day, R. Wood

Playing

Captain 1st XV	C.L. Cresswell
Vice-Captain 1st XV	D. Williams
Captain of Exiles	A. Owen
Vice-Captain of Exiles	R.G. Churchill
3rd XV Captain	B.S. O'Dell
3rd XV Vice-Captain	H.S. Arnold
4th XV Captain	R. Williams
4th XV Vice-Captain	J. Course

In January 1969, work began on the new Pavilion and on March 29th the changing facilities were first used. Further, the additional two acres of land were levelled and seeded ready for the following season. The rugby pitch at Hunting Engineering was again leased and this was essential to the running of four teams. The National College of Agricultural Engineering at Silsoe was extremely generous with the provision of special equipment and technical assistance.

Ampthill 25 pts. Wolverton 16 pts. – 14 September 1968

The opening of the rugby season is usually accompanied by an Indian summer and rock-hard grounds. But on the first Saturday of the season there was rain with the ball like a bit of wet soap. Ampthill's make-up showed a marked resemblance to last year's team with the notable exception of a new player, Dave Leigh. His baptism was sharpened by the fact that he had to take over as hooker after 20 minutes following a back injury to Dave Williams.

The adverse conditions naturally brought a feeling of frustration as everyone had looked forward to an open game. Both teams did their best in this direction, but the slippery ball was the master and it was left to the forwards to do all the bursting through.

At half-time with score 17-5 in Ampthill's favour, it seemed they would end up with a cricket score. But now they conceded points that could and should have been avoided. The forwards ran out of steam (playing one short) but eventually established themselves again and the final score was a good measure of the game as a whole.

Woodward, on the wing showed real strength in his running. Besides scoring a good try on his own account he was instrumental in giving Wilkinson a chance to go over in the second period. Duffin and Day were rewarded for their hard work with tries and Clark, combining brains with brawn kicked three good penalties and two conversions.

Once the defence is tightened and the team got used to the tactics to employ with the new rule* they should prove formidable opposition to any local club.

Ampthill Exiles drew 3-3 with Wolverton "A" while a young fourth side, with several new members being bloodied, did very well against heavier and older opposition, Letchworth 4th losing 3-19. Their try was scored by Thompson.

(*law change discouraged kicking directly into touch from outside your 25-metre line)

At the AGM, H.T. Robinson (Honorary Secretary) reported:

"This is, once again, a very good record and, undoubtedly the training sessions held under the auspices of Colin Cresswell have contributed largely to this success. Two sessions were also held on Sundays under the guidance of George Cullen. These were very valuable to the few who turned up.

Our new pitch should be ready to use next season and I am sure you are all looking forward to playing on it. However, it may be that our existing pitch will be out of action due to the re-levelling project. Consequently, we may be faced with another season using the pitch at Huntings.

The highlight of the season was, once again, the trip to Jersey. We could not repeat last year's performance, however, and were beaten by 6 points to 3 in one game and 52 points to 3 in the other. However, I gather that the tour was again, very enjoyable. On Easter Monday an Ampthill team visited Old Yardlieans and lost the Cup game by 5 points to 3. However, our team was rather depleted, and the result was a brave effort.

Trips were organised to Twickenham and to the East Midlands versus Warwickshire game at Northampton. Several social occasions were organised through Len Higgs (Social Secretary), these include a New Years Dance at Haynes and a Black Magic Evening at Silsoe Village Hall.

No matter what the results of the remaining games we can say again we have had a great season. We can look back and say that we have at last got somewhere to change and somewhere to go for a drink. We can look back and say that we have two pitches which are on our own property and we can look forward to some vocal support at our matches next season, and to making the Club some profit from the Pavilion." At the AGM in May 1969 Barrie O'Dell was made a Life Member of the Club. Annual subscriptions were increased to £3 per annum, but match fees remained at 3/6d."

1968-69	Played	Won	Drawn	Lost	For	Against
1st XV	32	21	3	8	590	294
Exiles XV	27	16	3	8	412	122
3rd XV	22	16	1	5	336	196
4th XV	16	6	1	9	85	183

Season 1969-70 - (Captain Dave Williams)

President	R. Dillingham
Chairman	N.J. Brown
Hon. Secretary	H.T. Robinson
Hon. Treasurer	R. G. Churchill
Fixture Secretary	R. Duffin
Main Committee	B.S. O'Dell, F. Thistlethwaite, R. Wood
General Committee	E. Billington, F. Pitkin, D. Hartup, R. Day, J. Day, R.G. Churchill

Playing

Captain 1st XV	D. Williams
Vice-Captain 1st XV	J. Woodward
Captain of Exiles	A.T. Robinson
Vice-Captain of Exiles	W.E. Edwards
3rd XV Captain	D.L. Simms
3rd XV Vice-Captain	D. Cheeseman
4th XV Captain	L. Higgs
4th XV Vice-Captain	R. Williams

The season was dominated by the Pavilion Project of course, but playing results were good. For Dave Williams, the Clubhouse opening game was always to be the highlight of the season. However, there were fine wins over Corby 30-8, Stevenage 22-3, Bedford Swifts 27-15, Towcester "A" 24-0, Queens Works 34-3 and Luton 25-16. However, in 1969-70 there was only one team in town – the Ampthill Exiles!

The Unbeaten Exiles

Their final tally for the 1969/70 season reads like an unblemished entry in an accountant's book – played 26, won 26, points for 410, against 113.

It is hard to believe that, when the Exiles were first formed some 12 years ago, they went a few seasons without hardly winning a game. Undoubtedly the man behind the team's success has been the skipper, Bert Robinson, a second row forward, who managed to keep together a good team spirit – despite the fact that he could not field the same team on any one occasion. With Churchill, the Owen brothers, Bob Hartop, Dicky Babb, Tony Ludlow, Roger Ratcliffe, Ellis Billington and John Butterworth, he had a fine basis on which to work. And it is a tribute to the team, that of the 410 points scored, 276 came from tries and a further 15 from dropped-goals. Robinson proved to be an accurate kicker with 97 points to his credit, 88 from kicking goals. Only 10 penalty kicks were kicked against them in 26 matches.

The main strength of the side lay in the pack, where a very strong front row of Alan Owen, Dicky Babb, and Ellis Billington, so often gained the upper hand in demoralising the opposing three. Robinson gained good possession in the lines-out, but it was perhaps in the loose, with the ball on the move, that the pack was at its best. An outstanding effort both collectively and individually – yet to be bettered!

Bert Robinson's undefeated Exiles XV- 1969-70

Back: V. Kaye   R. Churchill   A. Owen   R. Hartop   A. Carr   P. Light   I. Owen
      A. Roffe   H. Arnold

Front: A. Ludlow   A. Burgoyne   W. Edwards   H. Robinson   R. Babb   R. Ratcliffe   E. Billington

Bedfordshire RFU

In February 1969, a steering committee was set-up to form a Bedfordshire County Rugby Union, consisting of the following representatives:

Ampthill RFC	Mr. R. Dillingham
Bedford Athletic RFC	Mr. M. Robinson
Bedford Swifts RFC	Mr. J. Dickson
Luton RFC	Mr. D.A. Tattam
N.C.A.E RFC	Mr. G. King
Old Dunstablians RFC	Mr. B. Tompkins
Stockwood Park	Mr. L.C. Carr

Richard Dillingham became the first Chairman of Bedfordshire RFU and he was charged with finding out what were the appropriate county colours. The county side was to play in gold shirts with white collars.

Several social occasions were organised including a New Year's Eve. Dance at Haynes and a Black Magic Evening at Silsoe Village Hall.

The Opening of the New Clubhouse

Ampthill 0pts. Bedford 32pts. – Tuesday 9th September 1969

Ampthill celebrated the opening of the new Clubhouse and extension to the ground, with an evening match against Bedford captained by Budge Rogers. Ampthill were captained by Dave Williams and played on their new pitch for the first time.

Although Ampthill's 1st XV were outclassed by Bedford to the tune of 32pts. to nil, they shared in a thoroughly rousing match and afterwards members right royally entertained a wide circle of well-wishers in their spanking new clubhouse. "This is the fulfilment of a dream", said their President, Mr. Richard Dillingham, when asking Budge Rogers, the most capped England rugby player of all time, to cut the tape to the clubhouse. And in doing so Budge congratulated the Ampthill team on "a darn sight harder game than Saturday" (when Bedford beat Leicester 39-5). The new clubhouse was about four pitch lengths away from the ground, but this was the limit of water and electricity services and it tucked in well behind Parkside Hall. It was very compact with the changing rooms separated from the bar by a sliding partition which soon slid to accommodate the great press of folk who stayed until midnight.

The former Northampton and England prop forward, Ron Jacobs, represented the Rugby Union and Mr. Les Carr, President of East Midlands, kicked off the match. Ten local rugby clubs were represented and other organisations like the Playing Fields and Central Council of Physical Recreation.

Mike Nurton lodged an uneasy penalty goal, but for a quarter of an hour Bedford had nothing else to show and Ampthill might have scored twice. Steve Holder smacked the crossbar with an enormous drop at goal and only fast backtracking by "Tod" Slaughter stopped a try by John Woodward on the wing. Woodward was to impress with his hard tackling on Neil Boult, the prolific Bedford scorer did not add to his tally that evening. But Ampthill's tackling was good all round and tireless covering checked a complete rout when the Bedford team start to turn on their quick slip-passing game. Walters at fly-half was always quick to pounce on any Bedford slip and set his own backs going, while Day at second row proved altogether a big handful.

Inevitably, however, the well-practised Bedford side steadily built up the points, through 16-0 at half-time to a final tally of four goals, three tries and a penalty goal. Slaughter, Else and Janion each had two tries and Davies one, and Nurton converted four and a penalty. Among the few home chances, Walters was just wide with a drop-goal as was Holder with a penalty and Woodward lost out on another try-scoring chance.

The referee that day was Geoff Aynsley, a prominent Secondary Headteacher in Bedfordshire and Ampthill resident and Club member. Geoff was a fine referee and good friend to the Ampthill Club – he was widely liked and respected. The teams:

Bedford: M. Nurton; N. Boult, J. Janion, G. Davies, A. Towersey; P.D. Briggs, A. Lake, B. Arthur, N. Barker, S. Onyett, A. Else, J. Wilkinson, D. Rogers (capt.), R. Landon, R. Slaughter

Ampthill: S. Holder; A. Jones, R. Garret, C. Lewis, J. Woodward, P. Walters, P. Lewis, E. Billington, D. Williams (capt.), R. Duffin, B. Clark, R. Day, B. Tuckett, J. Wilkinson, B. Cooper

Referee: G. Aynsley (East Midlands Society), Touch-Judges: J.P. Mears & F. Thistlethwaite

Budge Rogers OBE - was also the holder of the England record of 34 caps (subsequently overtaken), British Lion and Barbarian many times over. He was captain of England on seven occasions and the first English player to be honoured by the Queen for his services to rugby football.

Pat Briggs was a final England trialist and also played cricket for Cambridge University, Cheshire and Bedfordshire.

Jeremy Janion was to go on to represent England twelve times between 1971 and 1975.

Neil Boult was a final England trialist

Dave Williams' 1st XV – 1969-70

Standing: J. Butterworth, E. Billington, R. Day, A. Roffe, J. Day, B. Clark, R. Duffin, S. Jones

Sitting: P. Lewis, C. Lewis, T. Walters, D. Williams, J. Woodward, R. Hewitt, C. Tuckett

Only four days later Ampthill were, disappointingly, to lose on the same pitch to Bedford Rovers (the Town's Third XV) by 3–18. Mike Lord converted a first half try by Alan Towersey, and though Ampthill replied with a penalty after the interval, Lord also obliged with a penalty and then converted tries by Russell and Stapleton.

Jack Wilkinson and Reg Wood painting the new Pavilion behind Parkside Hall

Jack was a hard-nosed number eight, almost impossible to stop from the base of a scrum and near the goal-line. He was quick for such a big man, possessed good hands, and loved to surprise opponents with deft chips ahead.

During his playing days he also maintained the Club pitches and when his playing days were over Jack made a massive contribution to the development of the Youth Section. When he passed away in August 2018, it seemed the whole membership turned out to celebrate his life and contribution to the Club.

Jack Wilkinson

The Ampthill News reported: "Two Ampthill players have been selected for the county junior side: Terry Waters, an experienced man who has played for Maesteg and Staffordshire, and prop Brian Clark who joined Ampthill five years ago with no previous rugby experience."

Brian "Slim" Clark is a legend at the Club – first XV Captain from 1974 to 1977 and Club Chairman from 1988 to 1998. "Slim" was a fearsome forward – mostly at second row forward - for Club and County. He was the "enforcer" with a heart as big as his massive frame. Brian was of an uncompromising temperament but, if you are fortunate to be a friend, he was as loyal as the day was long. Ampthill Rugby Club meant everything to Slim and together with his great friend, Jack Wilkinson, he was the heartbeat of the club – they both worked tirelessly for the cause.

Brian "Slim" Clark – "Your Club Needs You!" (photo by the author - 1998)

The Pavilion was to be extended in the next few years, to the rear, the south side and eventually Parkside Committee agreed to an extension to the front. Dave Williams remembers the front extension being built at weekends by a couple of Irish labourers employed building the new Sainsburys in Kempston. They literally were paid in pints! However, by season 1971-72 with the founding of the Extras, the Club was running five teams and the changing facilities were inadequate for 3 home games. By the end of the decade the 1st XV were using the new joint Alameda School/Town Sports Hall for changing and showering.

As the decade closed there were changes in the way rugby was approached by the Club. Colin Cresswell and Dave Williams were responsible for an emphasis on fitness and coaching. Norman Brown and Richard Dillingham attended games to advise on selection and Roy Duffin attended selection meetings in his capacity as Fixture Secretary. Thanks to Roy Duffin, and earlier Richard Churchill and Fred Thistlethwaite, fixtures were improving. The minutes of a Committee held in July 1969 record a request from Roy that selection ought not to take place on Saturdays, as this meant captains travelling back from away games at an early hour, and this was not in the right spirit, especially if we were expecting visiting teams to stay fairly late ourselves.

1969-70	Played	Won	Drawn	Lost	For	Against
1st XV	30	18	1	11	490	397
Exiles XV	28	28	0	0	429	119
3rd XV						
4th XV						

10 Year Fixture Comparison (1st XV) 1960-1970

	1960/61		1969/70
Sept.	Igranic Bletchley Wellingborough O.G.	Sept.	Bedford Rovers Corby Stevenage
Oct.	Old Towcestrians Extra 1st Wolverton Buckingham Huntingdon Bedford Athletic Extra 1st	Oct.	Wellingborough Leighton Buzzard Rushden & Higham Bedford Swifts
Nov.	Bedford Swifts Wellingborough Hitchin Biggleswade	Nov.	Towcestrians Extra 1st Huntingdon Queens Works Westminster College, Oxford Bedford Athletic Extra 1st
Dec.	Stockwood Park Extra 1st Queens Works Old Dunstablians Tring Biggleswade Cambridge 2nd	Dec.	NCAE - Silsoe Stamford Stevenage Biggleswade St. Neots
Jan.	Wolverton Bedford Swifts Stamford Stevenage	Jan.	Luton Queens Works Bedford Swifts Wellingborough Biggleswade
Feb.	Wellingborough O.G. Igranic Bletchley EAC St. Albans	Feb.	Rushden & Higham EAC St. Albans Cheylesmore Old Boys EAC St. Albans
Mar.	Queens Works Shuttleworth College Rushden Aylesbury	Mar.	Old Askeans Old Dunstablians NCAE Silsoe Slough
Apr.	Leighton Buzzard St. Neots Old Towcestrians Ex. 1st Huntingdon Vauxhall Silsoe College	Apr.	Leighton Buzzard Bedford Rovers Huntingdon Vauxhall Motors

Chapter 4 – The Seventies – A Maturing Club

Season 1970-71 - Club's 20th Anniversary - (Captain - Bill Edwards)

Officers
President   R. Dillingham
Chairman   H.S. Arnold
Hon. Secretary   H.T. Robinson
Hon. Treasurer   R. G. Churchill
Fixture Secretary   R. Duffin
Main Committee   A. Carr, D. Williams, N.J. Brown
General Committee   I. Owen, A. Owen, J. Wilkinson
Playing
1st XV Captain   W.E. Edwards
1st XV Vice-Captain   P. Lewis
Exiles XV Captain   A. Carr
Exiles XV   J. Wilkinson
3rd XV Captain   A.T. Rogers
3rd XV Vice-Captain   R.G. Churchill
4th XV Captain   M. Larby
4th XV Vice-Captain   E. Cameron
Extra 4th XV Captain   V. Kaye

At the end of the previous season, Norman Brown stood down as Chairman and was succeeded by Harry Arnold. Richard Dillingham was unanimously created a Life Member. This season the Club fielded 5 XVs for the first time, Vic Kaye leading the Extra 4th XV.

This season's captain, Bill Edwards, was not only an outstanding player, he was also widely respected within the Club and the East Midlands rugby community. After the successful 1969-70 season for the first XV and Exiles; hopes were high for the seventies. For Bill Edwards, these hopes were dashed with the news that the whole back division from the First XV, bar two, were moving from the area and would not be available for the season ahead. This was a bitter pill, as the main strength of Ampthill was shifting from the forwards to the backs and the loss of players like the Clive and Phil Lewis, Bob Garrett Richard Hewitt, Richard Tuckett and John Woodward would leave huge gaps to fill.

There was Bob Demming, of course, and Colin Tuckett, a talented wing-forward, moved into the centre and was joined by Bob Hartup. Stan Jones, last year's winger dropped back to full-back and Mick Valentine was to have a steady season at scrum half, while Terry Walters outside him was selected for the County. The forwards led by Bill Edwards had a great deal of experience, with Peter Liptrott, Dave Williams, and Doug Simms, in the front row, having over 70 years of rugby between them. Brian Clark and Mick Murray (a sergeant from USAF Chicksands) made up the second row. The back row of Brian Cooper, Bill Edwards and Tim McNeil were a very effective unit in attack and defence.

The Exiles led by Adrian Carr, had several players with first XV experience in Dave Leigh, Jack Wilkinson, Richard Churchill, Roy Duffin, Peter Phillips and there were younger players like Steve Dennis (County Colts winger), Alan Roffe and Dave Newbury who were holding their own in a team, despite keen competition. The 3rd XV was led by Tony Rogers and contained players of note such as Terry Comerford, John Butterworth and Ellis Billington.

Bert Robinson, Secretary, summarised the season thus:

"The season started with the new Committee facing a great deal of work. Many functions had to be organised, tours and outings had to be arranged, press coverage had to be looked into, and of course, a lot of work had to be done on the Pavilion. This report will give an outline of all this work.

The nerve centre of the Club, the Pavilion, has seen many functions, most of which have made money for our funds. We have held Xmas parties for the kids, Xmas Dances, Stag Nights, a number of Club Dances, and a highly successful VP Evening. On top of this we held a most memorable 21st Birthday Dance in the Parkside Hall – the highlight of the season, not forgetting an entertaining Annual Dinner. Other than these functions, our facilities are used by the Pre-school Playgroup, a Dancing Class, The Inner Wheel, Rotary functions, various private parties and Discotheques, all of which help to swell our funds. As a result of this we are now able to raise our standards. Already we have achieved success in an improved bar and décor. Very shortly we expect to commence work on our extensions. One bay extension on the rear, and two bays on the front.

As to some of the highlights of the season, the ones that readily come to mind are the annual outing to Twickenham and the traditional festivities after the game. The most entertaining Easter Tour of the North country, where despite a few heavy defeats, the morale of the Club was maintained and everybody enjoyed the Northern hospitality – some, perhaps, more than others. The 1st XV's highlights came with 4 great results. The wins over Leicester Vipers (8-6), Stockwood 2nd XV (6-0), and Luton (11-3), and the draw with Henry Mellish (3-3). The 2nd XV can congratulate themselves with wins over Kibworth (21-0), Royston (8-3), and Yardlieans (8-6), and the 3rd XV had memorable victories over Hitchin 1st XV (11-8), and Towcestrians (6-0). The 4th XV can be congratulated on achieving 8 victories. A newly -formed Extra 4th XV, achieved 6 victories. The latter include a 12-6 win over Bedford Athletic Avengers by 12-6, a 14-11 victory over Buckingham 3rd XV and a 15-5 toppling of Luton 5th XV. "

Robert Oliver Demming

In 1970, the Club was using Redborne South School for fitness training at a cost of £22 per term. However, the school insisted that a qualified member of the PE Department should take the training. The Club agreed to pay the additional charge and turned up on the first Tuesday to find that a certain Bob Demming was their fitness trainer. At the end of the training Dave Williams invited Bob Demming to play rugby for the Club. Bob had no experience of rugby, but he was phenomenally fast, powerful, and elusive. The following Saturday, Bob scored 5 tries for the Fifths! He progressed via the Fourths, Thirds and Extras to the 1st XV in successive Saturdays.

Bill Edwards' 1970-71- 1st XV featuring: Mike Murray, Bob Hartop, Bob Demming, Brian "Slim" Clark, Doug Simms (20th season in the 1st XV) & Roy Duffin

Bob Demming's first game in the 1st XV

Ampthill 24 pts. v. Old Askeans Princes 13pts. – 19th September 1970

The Ampthill pack dominated right from the kick-off. Instead of a 30-point lead they were able to boast only a slight advantage 9-6 at half-time.

The points came from a "Slim" Clark penalty and a try which Stan Jones converted. Yet they had won the tight heads 8-1 and the lines by a 75-25 margin. That they did not score more points will rank as one of the mysteries of the season.

In the second half it was slightly better. Clark bustled over from a line-out, but he was unable to convert.

The high spot came when Dave Williams took a kick ahead on his own ten-yard line and set off up the wing. With a number of forwards in support he dummied his way into the home 25 and slipped the ball to Bob Demming who charged into top gear and outstripped his opposite number for a beautiful try which Clark converted.

Demming, a physical education instructor was a fine all-rounder with Luton Cricket Club and was top marksman with Ampthill Queensmen Football Club the previous season. He was very raw when he joined Ampthill, but he had then attended a Rugby Football Union coaching course and it paid dividends. His speed was alarming, and it certainly impressed the selectors in the County trials.

Bob was selected for Bedfordshire to face Norfolk in October. Sadly, he was to miss the game through injury, but returned for the next match against Cambridgeshire. Bob was again selected for the County versus Northants in November, which was played at Ampthill, and he scored a try in a 27-7 defeat.

Bob scored regularly for Ampthill that season, startling the opposition with his scorching pace.

Bob Demming's Future Sporting Career

Obviously, the Ampthill Club had discovered a player of exceptional talent and it was Roy Duffin, ex-Askeans, and Club Fixture Secretary, who persuaded Bob to try his luck with Bedford Rugby Club. Bob became a prolific try scorer for Bedford on the right wing.

For Bedford, Bob Demming scored 73 tries, including seven hat-tricks, in 147 appearances. He represented England 'B' as well as having a final England trial. He scored two tries in Bedford's 28-12 victory over Rosslyn Park in the RFU John Player Knockout Cup final in 1975. The game was played at Twickenham in front of almost 18,000 spectators.

Bob Demming – The Cricketer

Robert Oliver Demming (born 5 May 1947, in Trinidad) was a right-handed batsman who bowled right-arm fast-medium. Bob made his debut for Bedfordshire against Shropshire in the 1972 Minor Counties Championship. He played Minor counties cricket for Bedfordshire from 1972 to 1977, making 38 Minor Counties Championship appearances. Bob made his List A debut, against Lancashire in the 1973 Gillette Cup.

Bob Demming - "the finest wing three-quarter in the world"

Bedford's Bob Demming in full flight, on the way to his second try against Rosslyn Park.

In the 1986 Bedford RUFC Centenary Season Brochure Derek Wyatt – the Bedford and England winger had this to say of Bob:

"Then, there was Bob Demming. On his day (which somehow implies that a derogatory statement is about to follow) he was the finest wing three-quarter in the world. In 1977 and 1978 his play reached a quite remarkable pitch and had the England selectors had the guts he would have played for his adopted country and dominated international rugby………..an endearing personality………his silky, sinuous running was a joy to watch.

Pavilion Extension

During 1970-71, Parkside Hall was approached seeking permission to extend the Pavilion to the rear and front. No objection was made by Parkside and the planning authorities to a rear extension. Parkside did, however, object to the front extension due to losing parking space. In September the Committee agreed to the go-ahead with the rear extension at a cost not exceeding £1,454 – this to be undertaken by Ivor Owen. However, one winter morning a heavy wind blew over the brick wall that had been finished only the previous afternoon to form part of the extension to the clubhouse. Foreman, Ivor Owen said it was a major setback as it had been hoped to get all the bricklaying done before frosts set in and it could cost the club a lot more money than had been bargained for. Players were dragged out of their beds in the early hours to try and salvage as many of the bricks as possible but, despite working all day, as darkness fell there was still a considerable amount of work to do. Ivor Owen said ,"The wind blew the wall over just as the bricklayers were arriving and one was able to witness the whole scene. The wall just fell from the damp-course and hit the clubhouse, bowing in the back wall."

Treasurer Richard Churchill said that it might be possible to raise a bank overdraft to cover the extra cost, but obviously it will not be possible to estimate the extra money needed until later when Ivor Owen has been able to assess the damage properly. By the end of February 1972, the rear extension to the Pavilion was structurally complete.

1970 -71	played	won	drawn	lost	pts. for	pts. against
1st XV	32	20	3	9	390	304
Exiles XV	29	19	1	9	463	285
3rd XV	30	20	2	8	432	207
4th XV	24	8	1	15	256	359
Extras XV	15	6	0	9	142	263

Season 1971-72 - (Captain - Peter Liptrott)

Officers

President	R. Dillingham
Chairman	D. Williams
Hon. Secretary	H.T. Robinson
Hon. Treasurer	R. G. Churchill
Fixture Secretary	R. Duffin
Main Committee	W. Edwards, J. Wilkinson, R. Duffin
General Committee	V. Kaye, M. Kaye, I. Owen, P. Phillips
Playing	
1st XV Captain	P. Liptrott
1st XV Vice-Captain	T. Walters
Exiles XV Captain	D. Leigh
Exiles XV Vice-Captain	B. Hartup
3rd XV Captain	P. Light
3rd XV Vice-Captain	E. Billington
4th XV Captain	
4th XV Vice-Captain	R. Foxwell
Extras XV Captain	V. Kaye
Extras XV Vice-Captain	J. Daniels

From this season, a try was worth four points. Until 1891, a try scored one point, a conversion two. For the next two years, tries scored two points and conversion three. In 1893, the modern pattern of tries scoring more began, with three points awarded for a try, two for a kick. The number of points from a try increased to four in 1971 and five in 1992.

In his Chairman's statement for the season, Dave Williams pointed out the improvement in the Club's fixtures made since 1967. New opponents since that date were Fairburn House, Old Askeans, Kibworth, Northampton Men's Own, Henry Mellish Old Boys, Old Yardlieans, Rushden & Higham, Oxford Old Boys, Leicester Vipers, Royston, Cheylesmore Old Boys, Corby, Colworth House.

The loss of so many talented threequarters the previous season had made selection throughout the Club, very difficult, and Dave felt the results were excellent considering that fact. He reported that the Club intended to appoint a coach – Barry Parker - but asked members not to think that "coach" is some sort of magic which will cure all our playing problems. Barry had played hooker for the 1st XV.

A domestic 7s tournament was to be played in October – with a limit of one 1st XV player per team.

He concluded by saying that the challenge for the approaching season would be greater than ever and it can only be met in one of two ways:

1) An influx of new 1st XV players
2) A much greater effort on the part of players; last season's training attendances were appalling.

Dave Williams retired at the end of the season having been the ever-present 1st XV team hooker for many years. He had been Club Captain, Committee member and, of course, Club Chairman and was to become President.

In 1971, for the first time, the 1st XV would be turning out in jerseys provided by the Club and would switch to all maroon socks. The reader will have noted the lack of consistent club kit in the photographs in this and previous chapters. Among the highlights of the season for the 1st XV were a 44-3 win against Aylesbury, 19-6 versus Old Askeans, 45-8 defeat of Stevenage, 44-6 win over Cheylesmore Old Boys and a 40-3 demolition of Corby. However, Ampthill were edged out of the Bedfordshire Cup, beaten by old rivals, Biggleswade 15-13 in the first round.

Mike Murray's Last Match

The ambitions of Ampthill lock forward Mike Murray to play for Bedfordshire were finally doused by the news that he was to return to the United States. In a few weeks he would fly back to the States for intensive training before being posted to Vietnam. Murray, from the American air base at Chicksands, played his last match for Ampthill against Wellingborough in October after a year of regular first-team appearances – when he has been fit. Unfortunately, Murray, one of the fittest members of the club, had been hounded by injury all that season. He began by playing in the first county trial and was selected for the final trial only to break two toes in the County KO Cup with Biggleswade. When he regained fitness, an accident at work injured his hand and kept him out of the game for a further month. Mike and his wife Alice had devoted a lot of their time to the Club and one of the highlights of last season was a match organised by Mike at the Chicksands base. (see below).

An Ampthill Invitation XV v. Keith Lawrence's XV at RAF Chicksands - Sunday 13 December 1972

Back row:	Geoff Bailey	Pete Naylor	Stuart Coeshall	Slim Clark	Jack Wilkinson
	John Humphries	Mike Murray	Roy Duffin		
Front row:	Bernard Jackson	Colin Tuckett	Terry Walters	Bill Edwards	Richard Butt
	Dave Williams			(captain)	

Guests: John Humphries (Stockwood Park & Beds. County), Bernard Jackson (Luton & Beds. County), Richard Butt (Bedford & Bucks. County)

Roy Duffin's Ampthill Extras

In October 1970, the committee minutes show that Harry Arnold had written to USAF Chicksands following the interest by the base in our code of rugby. *"This may lead to the formation of the Ampthill Americans, who could use our facilities, and operate under the affiliation of the Ampthill and District R.U.F.C."* The airbase operated at Chicksands from 1950, serving as the base for the 6,940th Radio Squadron, responsible for continued communications and SIGINT operation through the Cold War. The RAF continued to act as a host unit for the resident USAF units, including over time the 6950th United States Air Force Security Squadron, later becoming the 6,950th Electronic Security Group and the 7,274th Air Base Group, until it reverted to British control in 1997.

In 1972, Roy Duffin had formed the Extras XV. In the next few years, he began to develop strong links with the American airbase at Chicksands – near Shefford. In the 20 years of its existence under Roy, the Extras introduced the game to our American cousins and 463 US servicemen were to play for the Extras. There was a very good rugby pitch at Chicksands and the Rod & Gun Clubhouse was very popular with non - American Extras players and Americans alike. Games were sometimes videoed, and it was a novelty to sip American beer in the bar and watch yourself play! In the latter days the Extras rarely played at home, and would meet up at the Flying Horse, at Clophill, before departing for their fixtures. The Americans were wonderful athletes and brought a physical enthusiasm to the team which was a mix of "old-heads" – experienced players from the Club – and their friends from the Chicksands Base. No penalties were ever kicked – Roy insisted on running rugby, which suited the Americans and terrorised the opposition!

The Extras eventually played in "flashy" red shirts with a blue stripe containing white stars and had letters on the back (A-O) instead of numbers. Quite what the opposition thought of this is hard to imagine! Ampthill was introduced to the American way of barbeques – huge steaks, ice-filled dustbins full of Budweiser and Strawberry Hill Wine, with Betty Crocker cakes for dessert.

For the Extras' 20th Birthday – 28th October 1995 – Roy wrote the following:

"Well it only seems like yesterday that I led a band of 12 players to Watford for the first ever Extras, game – in fact it was 20 years ago, and I've been lumbered with the team ever since, and to be honest I'm glad I have. I've had a great deal of pleasure, and not inconsiderable pain I might add, running the side, playing in some memorable games, and having some wonderful nights that I only wish I could remember better. But most of all the pleasure has been in knowing some really great people and been proud to call them friends. This in itself, has been a mixed blessing as the one certainty has always been that with the international make-up of the team we will be constantly saying "goodbye" sometimes for good, sometimes just really "adieu" until they return again. The current players, very nearly exclusively Brits, for the first ever season, are cast in the same mould as previous players, always together until thrown out of the Rugby Club, still at the Three Fyshes at Turvey or the Cock at Broom and, eventually, at the White Hart in Ampthill."

There are some instances of Americans coming through the ranks of the Club up to 1st XV status at the instigation of Roy Duffin. The first, as we have seen, was Mick Murray a super-fit second row for Ampthill and grid-iron player for Chicksands. He played in the 1st XV with Brian Clark and Bob Demming in 1971-72 before being posted back to the USA. Later in the 1980s Don Malik and Ralph Norton were outstanding wingers for the successful 1st XV under Bob Clayton. Randy Livingood, at loose-head prop, and Neil Townsend, a terrific winger, later featured in the Club's 1st XV from the Chicksands base.

Roy Duffin (pictured below) was a wonderful character, an ex-Askeans 1st XV prop, an editor of Hansard and, latterly, a shop steward for the Printers Union. Roy was immensely popular and did sterling work for the Committee acting as Fixture Secretary from 1970-1980 and again from 1986-90. His Friday nights and Saturday mornings were spent on the telephone communicating with captains, club members and officials. He attended every selection committee meeting and his opinions were welcomed and valued.

Ampthill Rugby Club's connection to the Americans through Roy, is unique in world rugby, we should all be proud of what this remarkable man achieved. Roy's influence went beyond the leadership of the Extras and his Committee work, his calmness, wisdom, and good humour helped many a club member in difficult situations. His son, Liam Duffin now manages the Extras – who, today, are a highly successful Ampthill 4th XV.

Extras line-up on the Dillingham Park grid iron

Quarter-back skipper Roy Duffin (with the ball) - is the only Englishman in the line-up

back-row: K. Kanizar P. Plant R. Duffin D. Hollister R. Fulton

front-row: H. Bretton R. Rinaldi D. Perry J. Madden M. Ross B. Skoubo L. Warren

Looking to the future, and playing policy, Jack Wilkinson proposed to the Committee (Feb. 25th 1972) that a team of young, promising players be formed, to play at 3rd XV level; that the team be kept together for at least half a season regardless of their performance, and of the effect on the other teams in the club. The Club Captain, Peter Liptrott and the selection committee considered Jack's proposal, "and in spite of the difficulties had decided to go ahead with the scheme, but by utilising the 4th XV instead of the 3rd XV."

1971-72	played	won	drawn	lost	pts. for	pts. against
1st XV	31	15	1	15	455	552
Exiles XV	29	15	0	14	465	365
3rd XV	26	14	3	9	408	302
4th XV	28	12	1	15	353	391
Extras XV	13	3	1	9	96	248

Season 1972-73 - (Captain - Alan Jones)

Officers

President	R. Dillingham
Chairman	D. Williams
Hon. Secretary	B. Hall
Hon. Treasurer	R. G. Churchill
Fixture Secretary	R. Duffin
Main Committee	R. Duffin, I. Owen, H. Robinson
Playing	
1st XV Captain	A. Jones
1st XV Vice-Captain	B. Clarke
Exiles Captain	R. Ratcliffe
Vice-Captain of Exiles	A. Owen
3rd XV Captain	H. Robinson
4th XV Captain	
4th XV Vice-Captain	P. Waller
Extras XV Captain	B.S. O'Dell
Extras XV Vice-Captain	J.H. Arnold
Coach	B. Parker

The Chairman, Dave Williams presented this assessment for the season 1972-73:

"You may recall that I concluded my last season's review by saying "the problems or shall we say the challenge to the club next season lies, where it always should lie, on the rugby field". Examination of the 1st XV records show how accurate this statement proved to be. We would be foolish to try to consider this a successful season but at the same time I would remind members, that the 1st XV fixture list is now some 60% stronger than it was five years ago, and certainly next season will be no easier.

When our 1st XV is having a poor season, it is even more important that our 2nd, 3rd and 4th XVs win the corresponding matches, if we are to maintain fixtures with stronger sides. I am very pleased to report that our 2nd XV under Roger Ratcliffe won 60% of its fixtures while the 3rd and 4th teams generally held their own. While it is some source of satisfaction to report the successes of the lower sides, may I again say that it is the 1st XV that really carries the flag as far as the club is concerned, and if the club is to make further progress on the rugby field, it is the 1st XV that must do it.

Your club captain last season, Alan Jones, made tremendous efforts to produce a winning XV unfortunately he did not get the support he deserved from more than six or seven players, when we really needed a squad of about 20 potential 1st XV players to succeed.

We introduced a club coach this season, Barry Parker who, in my opinion did a first-class job, again all our members have not really accepted or understood the concept of coaching. If you don't do anything else during the summer, I would ask you how you would coach a side, with the emphasis on the coaching of a 1st XV rather than the training, and when you've understood all the problems I'm sure we will all get more out of our coaching sessions.

The highlight of the season was undoubtedly to see one of the club members – Bob Demming playing regularly for the Bedford 1st XV. I believe this to be the first time Ampthill has produced a "Blue", and while we can claim no credit for Bob's playing ability, it's all natural, we did introduce him to the game, and this is a great credit to the club.

To introduce players to the game is of course one of the primary objects of a junior club, and perhaps while on this subject I should define the objects of our Saturday morning training sessions for the 7 to 13-year olds. The object is simply to introduce young lads to the game at an early stage, it is not our intention to produce a squad of heavily coached rugby robots."

The reader will sense (I hope!) at least three aspects to this assessment. The first, is Dave William's far-sightedness and philosophy of how coaching can help develop individual and unit skills. The second, is his frustration with the response of the playing members to these early attempts at organising coaching. The third, is an over-riding love for the game – shades of his Rhondda background perhaps.

Dave was responsible for introducing the mini & youth section when he was asked by the local scout master to prepare scouts for their sports badges. This developed into regular Saturday morning sessions led by Dave. Saturdays were chosen to provide non - Harper Trust pupils the chance to experience rugby and to avoid a clash with Sunday morning church services. This was before mini-rugby was codified into a nine-aside game. Dave coached the game he knew - boys played sevens rugby, with tackling. When the East Midlands RFU asked Ron Jacobs to come up with a plan to develop mini rugby, he called Dave Williams to lead a meeting with other interested East Midlands coaches at Rushden, and the rest is history. The East Midlands can justifiably claim to have played a leadership role in the development of mini & youth rugby in this country.

However, since the 1970s Ampthill's Mini & Youth section for boys and girls has gained a national reputation. As the strength of the Club increased steadily from this time it is a matter of record of how many first XV players were home-grown through the mini & youth and, of course, through local schools and the Bedfordshire Schools RFU. When we look at the outstanding 1st XVs of the 1990s this will become apparent.

At the AGM held at the Pavilion on 23rd. June 1972; Life Membership was unanimously bestowed on Doug Simms and Tony Rogers. These were two outstanding players and club-men, Doug has sadly passed on, but Tony keeps in touch with old friends and occasionally attends Club functions.

Match fees were raised to 25p (under 18s to pay 10p) and annual subscriptions were raised to £3.50.

1972-73	played	won	lost	drawn	pts. for	pts. against
1st XV	32	8	23	1	251	504
Exiles XV	30	18	11	1	400	346
3rd XV	29	13	15	1	297	289
4th XV	26	7	19	0	252	347
Extras XV	14	1	12	1		

Season 1973-74 - (Captain - Ian Messer)
Officers

President	R. Dillingham
Chairman	D. Williams
Hon. Secretary	M. Kaye
Hon. Treasurer	R. G. Churchill
Fixture Secretary	R. Duffin
Main Committee	R. Duffin, I. Owen, H. Robinson

Playing

1st XV Captain	I. Messer
Vice-Captain 1st XV	T. Foot
Exiles XV Captain	J. Wilkinson
Exiles XV Vice-Captain	R. Ratcliffe
3rd XV Captain	W. Edwards
3rd XV Vice-Captain	P. Eversley
4th XV Captain	J. Sidney
5th XV Captain	n/a
Coach	B. Parker

In his Chairman's report for 1973-74 Dave Williams wrote:

"The season started on rather a frightening note, the groundsman knocked the posts over with £60 of damage, the Club was broken into with a subsequent bill for £50, and we found that the Club needed re-roofing at an estimated cost of £400. Fortunately, our insurance covered the damaged posts, while Ivor Owen again repaired the damage to the club at a nominal cost. He also negotiated the re-roofing of the Club, how he did it I don't know, and our bill was nothing.

The 1st XV made a big improvement on last year's record and Ian Messer and Terry Foot are to be congratulated on producing such a fine result, which would have been even more impressive if we had not lost a few key players."

However, the records themselves did not tell the whole story. During the season, Messrs. Troiano, King, Clark, Bancroft, and Argent appeared together in the 1st XV – this was home-grown talent. In particular, Phil Argent, went on to become one of the best prop-forwards the Club has ever seen. Phil was a Bedfordshire County regular and during his career had a successful series of games for Bedford's 1st XV. It is clear that the Club's greater emphasis on fitness and the coaching of individual and unit skills was paying off.

On the social side, the Club had its most successful season for some time thanks to Bert Sheard and Brian Clark, ably assisted by the ladies. The Ladies Night at Henlow Grange and the Annual Dinner were enjoyable and profitable.

Bert Sheard

Bert Sheard was the 1st XV full-back for many seasons. Hailing from Cleckheaton near Leeds, Bert was an absolute rock in defence – a safe pair of hands, shuddering tackler, and sound kicker. He was an electrical engineer and was gave his time and expertise unselfishly to the Club. Like Jack Wilkinson and Brian "Slim" Clark he produced a son - Richard Sheard - who would go on to star and captain an outstanding Ampthill team in the 1990s with James, Justin and Simon Fletcher sons of Rob Fletcher, the former Bedford player and coach of Ampthill in the 1980s. Bob Campbell, line-out ace also provided two sons to the 1st XV, Ian and Robert – both three-quarters.

Ian Messer, this season's Club skipper, was a good ball-playing eight; he was quick in attack and resolute in defence. He joined the Club in 1972, having previously played in Reading.

The addition of Stan Jones and Graham Steen to the back-division had made Ampthill look a better team. However, Jones was soon to sail for the West Indies, so the outside half problem would again become acute.

Steen, a new acquisition, had been plagued by injuries, but happily looked to be rid of them now and his experience in the centre allowed the younger players to improve their play.

Stan Jones's brother Alan, 1st team captain the previous year, had sadly broken his leg in the last training session before the season started. However, he was to return and had lost none of his old skills and timing.

The pack was still relying on the vast wealth of age and experience, although an injury to prop Roy Duffin resulting in the inclusion of Phil Argent had greatly reduced the average age. Slim Clark, one of the club's most faithful servants, was still grafting away in the second row, where he was been joined by Colin Hitchcock, who, although reasonably new to the club had more years' experience than he liked to admit to with clubs of the calibre of Oxford and Blackheath.

With Hitchcock and Clark originally prop-forwards, this made Ampthill a bit short in the height stakes, but with tame giant Geoff Bailey getting fitter every week it seemed as if this deficiency would not last for long.

Matt King now seemed to have found his true position on the wing, while on the other flank Raff Troiano was benefitting from the revitalised back division and had again started to appear on the score sheet.

The back row was having most trouble settling down. Ian Messer, the captain, has moved to the number 8 position, and Alan Bancroft, Norman Phillips, Stuart Barclay, Bob Jackson, Tim McNeill, and Steve Richardson were all fighting for the wing forward positions.

1973-74	played	won	lost	drawn	pts. for	pts. against
1st XV	35	19	15	1	414	463
Exiles XV	29	13	13	3	402	389
3rd XV	27	19	8	0	427	346
4th XV	23	11	11	1	348	404
5th XV	7	3	4	0	48	85

Season 1974-75 – 25th Anniversary - (Captain - Brian Clark)

Officers

President	R. Dillingham
Chairman	D. Williams
Hon. Secretary	M. Kaye
Hon. Treasurer	R. G. Churchill
Fixture Secretary	R. Duffin
Main Committee	B. Bartram, H. Robinson, H. Sheard

Playing

1st XV Captain	B. Clarke
1st XV Vice-Captain	I. Messer
Exiles XV Captain	R. Duffin
3rd XV Captain	P. Eversley
3rd XV Vice-Captain	I. Tennant
4th XV Captain	R. Hamer
4th XV Vice-Captain	R. Burgess
Coach	B. Parker

In his Chairman's Report Dave Williams said:

"This season the Club is 25 years old, and while it may seem appropriate to review the history of the Club, I think it is more relevant to remind members what a large organisation we have become. The Club membership, at this time, is as follows:

Playing Members	98
Non-Playing Members	25
Vice Presidents/Life Members	78
Mini-Rugby Players	61
	262

Your Treasurer will present the detailed financial position but, as a guide to the season's costs, we need approximately £1,400 to run the club at the present level. The larger the club, the more effort there is required to support it. The AGM is your opportunity to criticise our efforts for last season, and at the same time your committee is entitled to request some additional effort for next year.

The 1st XV had a very good season, winning nearly two thirds of their games which was the best record for a number of seasons and included a victory over the Welsh touring side, Girling Brakes. The season ended on a high note with the 1st XV winning the Cresswell Cup for the first time ever, beating Old Yardlians."

Dave Parker

During this season Dave Williams heard that a rugby player had moved into Oliver Street. He called on the said player and invited him to train with the club at Redborne School the following Tuesday. Thus, recruited was one of the finest rugby players ever to represent the Club – Dave Parker.

Ampthill 11 pts., Bedford Rovers 4pts. – 22nd December 1973

Ampthill took heed of last week's poor performance and were determined not to be caught out again. They attacked the Rovers from the word go and their strong pack denied their free-scoring opponents any of the possession so vital to their game. Slim Clark gave Ampthill the lead with his third penalty attempt and this was a lead his side were determined to keep. They did this with an all-out team effort and a special effort from their forwards which slowly allowed Dave Parker playing his first game in the first XV – and only his second for the club – to dominate the game.

In the second half the Rovers were still strangely off-form but managed a try by Fensome for a 4-3 lead. But this was short-lived. A loose maul saw the ball come out and Dave Parker made the break and slipped the ball to Raff Troiano who slipped under three defenders for a try near the corner flag.

Ampthill's second try came near the end. The forwards won the ball and Parker again opened up the play and scissored with Stan Jones. Jones caught a number of Rovers players on the wrong foot with some neat side-stepping and scored near the touch line.

Continuing with Dave Williams' AGM report –

"The Exiles XV, under Roy Duffin, had a rather erratic season, at one time you needed to keep count of points they scored, while a few months later you needed the same machine to count the points against. Still, they too, finished on a high note by defeating Old Yardlians.

The 3rd XV was probably the most consistent side in the Club and retiring Captain Peter Eversley could be well pleased with his efforts. The 4th XV did not quite make a 50% record but again played a major part in introducing new players to the Club.

Some of these new players came from the USAF base at Chicksands and the base did turn out a full XV to play against Ampthill on three occasions. On two of these occasions the team from the base was successful, and it was a strange experience to see so many Ampthill members genuinely pleased to see their own team beaten, it was indeed a pleasure and we look forward to many of airmen joining the club.

For the first time I include the record of the Mini-Rugby sides you will note that the under 11 side won all four games and gave away only one try. The other sides were, apparently, unfortunate in that in some cases the opposing clubs had different age limits………Suffice it to say that we have over sixty very young men very interested in our game.

Social Events

If you ask the question, when did you last attend an unsuccessful social event, most members will reply: "I can't remember." This is partly due to Bill Mills and Bert Sheard's efforts this year and Brian Clark and Bert Sheard last season, but common to both years has been the tremendous effort by the ladies committee. The equation is quite simple, a good financial year – come from good bar profits – comes from successful social events – comes from hard-working Social Secretary/Ladies Committee.

The Future

We shall start the forward extension to the Club in about eight weeks. The position is that Vic Hallam will erect the structure once we have laid the base at a cost of £1,968, we believe we can raise £2,000 at this time. We shall need effort to lay the base, we shall have to provide fixtures and fittings and we will have to furnish the extension which will take the form of a lounge bar. We estimate that we will need an additional £1,300 to complete the extension so we will be asking for additional financial effort for our "silver" season but we hope to arrange a couple of celebration games and events, and again bring a first-class team to visit Ampthill.

The problems ahead are many and varied but with the same effort your committee put in last season and a little extra effort from some members and a little bit of luck, there is nothing ahead that we cannot cope with!"

1974-75	played	won	drawn	lost	pts. for	pts. against
1st XV	36	21	4	11	478	351
Exiles XV	31	14	2	15	455	452
3rd XV	31	18	2	11	373	276
4th XV	19	8	0	11	180	204
Mini-Rugby						
Under 9	1	1	0	0	24	4
Under 10	1	0	0	1	0	4
Under 11	4	4	0	0	40	4
Under 12	3	0	0	3	10	56
Under 13	6	1	0	5	36	106

Season 1975-76 Club's 25th Anniversary - (Captain - Brian Clark)
Officers

President	R. Dillingham
Chairman	D. Williams
Hon. Secretary	H. Sheard
Hon. Treasurer	R. G. Churchill
Fixture Secretary	R. Duffin
Main Committee	P. Britton, I. Messer, P. Argent, M. King

Playing

1st XV Captain	B. Clarke
1st XV Vice-Captain	D. Parker
Exiles XV Captain	G. Steen
Exiles XV Vice-Captain	D. Denyer
3rd XV Captain	I. Tennant
3rd XV Vice-Captain	R. Burgess
4th XV Captain	B. O'Dell
4th XV Vice-Captain	B. Keefer
Extras XV	R. Duffin
Coach	B. Parker

In his final Chairman's report to the AGM Dave Williams emphasised the following:

"The Club's 25th season is now over, and I think it is fair to say that we have celebrated it in the appropriate fashion. The Club has had one of its best playing records for a number of years, we have successfully completed phase one of the Club extension and your treasurer will report that we have succeeded in making a profit this season.

The Club was most unfortunate in losing two of its most hard-working members, Bill Mills and Bert Robinson. Bill has been involved on the social side for a number of years, while Bert was the Club Secretary for a number of seasons, and of course has been the organiser of the mini rugby section; I can assure you that both of them will be difficult to replace.

The extension is complete and we, as members, have had nothing to do in the way of labouring, no concreting, no off-loading of bricks, it was all done by Brian Bartram and Company ably assisted by Bert Sheard who spent days up here wiring out the place. The Club is deeply grateful to those two, without them there would be no extension, but they will need a great deal more assistance when we start phase two of the extension.

The Silver Jubilee Raffle was an outstanding success, it was the most rewarding activity of any sort that the Club has been involved with, it was conceived and organised by Peter Britton and without it the Club would have made a loss. (Author's note: - Peter Britton was a very effective first XV wing-three-quarter).

Pete Eversley, ably assisted by Bill Dickinson, has done an excellent job in running the Pavilion but I do wish members would consider how much time and effort the two have put in this year, when they are asked to do their two duties a year.

The 1st XV had one of its best ever seasons defeating the President's XV and giving Stockwood Park a nasty fright in the Cup, and I believe that in this period December to April this side was as good as any XV that Ampthill has ever fielded."

Notable 1st XV victories included Bedford Rovers 18-0, St. Neots 20-0, St. Albans 51-3, Bicester 22-3, and Olney 19-7.

March 6th 1976 - Ampthill 1st XV which beat Bicester 22-3 (by Alameda Sports Hall, Woburn Road)

front row: Duncan Brown (mascot), Pete Monday, Alan Jones, Stan Jones, Raf Troiano, Dave Parker, Mike Magin, Roger Holmes & Phil Argent **back row**: Brian "Slim" Clark (capt.), Peter Britton, Geoff Bailey, Terry Foot, Dave Chapman, Malcolm Truman, Brian Hartley, Bob Campbell and Barry Parker (coach)

"The Exiles were the most improved side in the Club and a number of Vice Presidents and former players have commented to me on the attractive rugby they have played this year."

Exiles wins included Wellingborough 32-8, St. Neots 41-0, Datchworth 53-0 and Tring 38-0

"The 3rd XV was disappointing, but this side has had a good record for a number of years, and this season things levelled up somewhat. The 4th XV had a good season with even Barrie O'Dell getting a few tries, and this is the real measure of their success. The Extra 4th XV functioned regularly this season and had a number of very good wins, the important thing is that we do run a fifth side in Ampthill, but it really is a one man show and without Roy Duffin's effort this team would not exist.

The mini rugby section continues to grow in organisation and ability, and I have included it on your agenda as a separate item. There are now over fifty boys playing rugby, they scored hundreds of points against a very smart Cambridge Club, beat St. Neots handsomely and when we took three sides to the Mini Rugby Festival they played 13 matches; winning 9, losing 3 and drawing 1; which was the best overall club performance there."

1975-76	played	won	drawn	lost	pts. for	pts. against
1st XV	34	22	3	9	505	274
Exiles XV	32	23	1	8	563	210
3rd XV	31	13	1	17	328	524
4th XV	29	16	0	13	432	455
Extras XV	18	8	1	9	277	204

Dave Williams stood down as Chairman, a position he had held with distinction for five years, he was succeeded by Barrie O'Dell.

Season 1976-77 - (Captain - Brian Clark)

Officers

President	R. Dillingham
Chairman	B.S. O'Dell
Hon. Secretary	H. Sheard
Hon. Treasurer	R. G. Churchill
Fixture Secretary	R. Duffin
Main Committee	S. Brown, R. Campbell, I. Messer

Playing

1st XV Captain	B. Clarke
1st XV Vice-Captain	P. Britton
Exiles XV Captain	G. Steen
Exiles Vice-Captain	P. Jellis
3rd XV Captain	A. Owen
3rd XV Vice-Captain	R. Ratcliffe
4th XV Captain	B. O'Dell
4th XV Vice-Captain	J. Davies
Extras XV Captain	R. Duffin
Extras XV Vice-Captain	D. Wright
Bionics	B. O'Dell
Coach	B. Parker

This was Slim Clark's final season as captain, but he would continue to terrorise opponents through to the 1980s. The 1st XV had a modest season, in contrast with the Exiles, but could still call on significant players such as Ian Messer, Phil Argent, Brian Clark, Malcolm Truman, Peter Britton, Bill Mills, Terry Foot and Bert Sheard. Dave Parker and newcomer Neil Thompson (from Luton RUFC) were making an immediate impact at half-back.

In October, Ampthill lost in the first round of the Bedfordshire Knockout Cup to Bedford Athletic 6-7. In November, there were good results against Huntingdon 26-3 and St. Neots 40-0. Poor weather in December meant all games were cancelled. In the New Year, there were victories over Olney, Buckingham and Stevenage. In February, St. Albans was defeated by 52-0 – the 1st XV biggest win of the season.

Near the end of his final season, Brian Clark broke an ankle and was forced to see out the rest of the season from the side lines. In April, Ampthill enjoyed victories over local rivals Biggleswade and Dunstablians but lost, again, to Bedford Athletic 7-28 and narrowly 17-19 to Cambridge.

It is worth noting how large the playing membership had become, the Club was now running six teams. 60% of the 151 games played by the 6 teams were won – this would have been astonishing to the men of the 1950s. Much of this was due to the population expansion of mid-Beds. and especially Flitwick at the time.

It also was due to the contribution of members like Norman Brown, Richard Dillingham, Barrie O'Dell, Richard Churchill, Dave Williams, Tony Rogers, Dougie Simms, Ellis Billington, Brian Clark, Roy Duffin, Jack Wilkinson, Ivor and Alan Owen, George Jenkins, Bert Sheard, Mike Marsden, Mike Larby, John Groom, Joe King-Johnson, Peter Britton, Vic Kaye and others, too numerous to mention. The Club was well-managed and thriving by the mid-70s and was ready to move forward on the playing side.

1976-77	played	won	drawn	lost	pts. for	pts. against
1st XV	33	19	2	12	522	279
Exiles XV	30	24	1	5	573	178
3rd XV	29	15	2	12	444	408
4th XV	28	18	0	10	384	170
Extras XV	22	10	0	12	300	237
Bionics XV	9	7	0	2	165	68

A very rare photo of the Ampthill Tour 1st XV v. Guernsey - February 1977 – Ampthill won 12-6

Back row: **Steve Watson, Ian Messer, Richard Butt, Dave Chapman, Steve Holder, Malcolm Truman, Phil Argent, George Randall, Ian Harlow** Front row: **Dave Parker, Dicky Babb, Andy Huckle, Neil Thompson, Peter Britton, Don Malik**

This would have been a formidable touring side, there are some very good players on display. Don Malik (pictured front right) was from the US Airforce base at Chicksands. Don and fellow American Ralph Norton forced their way into the 1st XV through their unique blend of speed, power and un-orthodoxy. Richard Butt had played for Bedford and East Midlands. The deeds of Dave Parker, Neil Thompson, Steve Watson, Phil Argent, Andy Huckle, Malcolm Truman, Dicky Babb, and Ian Messer are well chronicled in this history. Steve Holder (now sadly deceased) was one of the best kickers of a rugby ball ever seen at the Club. Peter Britton, now living in Harrogate, is a frequent supporter of the team in the Championship.

Season 1977-78 - (Captain - Bob Clayton)

Officers

President	R. Dillingham
Chairman	B.S. O'Dell
Hon. Secretary	N. Thompson
Hon. Treasurer	R. G. Churchill
Fixture Secretary	R. Duffin
Main Committee	S. Brown, I. Messer, H. Sheard
Playing	
1st. Captain 1st XV	R. Clayton
1st XV Vice-Captain	D. Parker
Exiles XV Captain	P. Jellis
Exiles Vice-Captain	N. Macklin
3rd XV Captain	D. Williams
3rd XV Vice-Captain	R. Ratcliffe
4th XV Captain	M. Gonse
4th XV Vice-Captain	D. Hook
Extras XV Captain	R. Duffin
Extras XV Vice-Captain	D. Wright
Bionics XV Captain	B.S. O'Dell
Coach	B. Parker

An outstanding captain, Bob Clayton accelerated the development of the Club, generally, but he was determined to improve the performance of the 1st XV. He achieved this through force of personality, determination and organisational ability. As Club Captain, Bob worked closely with Roy Duffin to improve fixtures at a time when leagues were only a distant possibility. Bob was later to take over as Fixture Secretary from 1980-1986.

In the late 1970s the Club experienced an influx of ready-made 1st XV players. These included Bob Clayton (Bedford), Malcolm Davies, (Shrewsbury & Shropshire), Bob Campbell (Luton), Neil Thompson (Luton), Dave Sprigg (Ruislip), Mike Plant (Aylesbury & Bucks.), Don Malik & Ralph Norton (USAF) and later, Peter Cadigan (St. Lukes) Steve Peacey (Bedford), Dennis Hardy (Leighton Buzzard), Martin Nolan (Dunstablians) and Howard Summers (Pontypool). These joined established stalwarts – such as Dave Parker, Brian Clark, Phil Argent, Malcolm Truman, Terry Foot, Ian Messer, Terry Rust, Peter Britton, Bill Mills, Andy Huckle, Nigel Fletcher, and Cameron Sedman.

Ampthill's First Bedfordshire Knockout Cup Final – 11th December 1977

In the quarter finals on October 30, the 1st XV narrowly defeated Luton 9-6, away from home.

On 20 November 1977, Ampthill overcame Leighton Buzzard 15-7 at home to reach the final of the Bedfordshire Cup for the first time.

On Sunday 11 December 1977, Ampthill played Stockwood Park, away, in the Cup Final. Several first-choice players were absent from the Ampthill team due to injury and a number of the side played out of their normal position. Nonetheless the players were very determined, because at that time Stockwood Park refused to give the Ampthill a Saturday fixture.

Stockwood Park 20 pts. Ampthill 4 pts.

In the first half of this close, hard-fought Beds. KO Cup Final, Ampthill were in a generous mood, giving Stockwood an easy ten points. First of these came when a kick-ahead by Park was badly fumbled on the Ampthill line, and the ensuing scrum was won against the head and the Stockwood scrum-half scored.

The same player added two penalty goals as Ampthill were in trouble at nearly every maul, and as the half drew to a close this 10-point lead looked reasonably secure. In the 39th minute, however, Ampthill won a strike against the head and the ball was chipped ahead. Terry Foot and Don Malic chased and hacked on, and Dave Parker appeared from "nowhere" to pick up and score. Only six points down, Ampthill's second half task assisted by the wind didn't appear impossible. Much of the game was dictated by kicking, but with fifteen minutes to go Ampthill were really pressing, being stopped on the line four times in as many minutes. What seemed like a certain try by Mike Plant was disallowed by the referee.

Then, in the last five minutes, Stockwood doubled their score with a try and a goal, giving the game a score-line it really didn't deserve, and one which must be especially disappointing to the Ampthill pack who played exceptionally well against the more fancied Stockwood forwards, Bob Campbell especially in the line outs.

Bob Clayton – Captain - "Laying down the law". Left to right: Howard Summers, Malcolm Truman, Dave Day, Bob Clayton, Phil Argent and Denis Hardy

Team: Mike Plant, Don Malic, Terry Foot, C. Sedman, Malcolm Truman, Neil Thompson, Dave Parker, Malcolm Davies, Bob Clayton (capt.), Brian Clark, Bob Campbell, Terry Rust, Dave Sprigg & Ian Messer

There were a number of outstanding players in Bob Clayton's team, but the star was undoubtedly the scrum-half Dave Parker. He was the complete package; quick, brave, unselfish, an excellent tackler, and possessed a great passing and kicking game.

Later in his career Dave Parker switched to fly-half and continued to represent Bedfordshire. On 9th October 1982 Dave became the first Ampthill player to be selected for the East Midlands in the game against Leicestershire at Stoneygate RUFC.

In a successful season for the 1st XV there were victories over; St. Albans 44-0, Datchworth 4—6, Olney 50-3, Buckingham 34-0, Aylesbury 12-0 and Bacavians 32-9.

Standing: Bill Beaumont, Brian Clark, Simon Brown

Front: Bert Sheard, Dave Parker, Tony Phillips & Dave Williams (internal Club 7s)

In 1977-78, the Player of the Year was Neil Thompson, a talented rugby player, equally at home at 9 or 10 - he partnered Dave Parker wonderfully well and was top points score with 118 points. Top try scorer was Malcolm Truman, a tireless and swift open side. Young player of the year was the versatile Laurie Barlow.

Bob Clayton, Mike Plant, Malcolm Davies, Brian Clark, Bob Campbell, and Dave Parker were Bedfordshire regulars. Don Malic (from USAF Chicksands) and Simon Brown (son of Norman Brown) both represented Bedfordshire U.23. Full-back Simon Brown also represented the East Midlands U.23.

Barrie O'Dell's – Bionics

During this season the famous, or infamous, Bionics XV got properly underway. Barrie O'Dell persuaded a group of old friends out of retirement to form a team of veterans As you might expect with a team led by Barrie O'Dell, the Bionics became well-known for their high-jinx and enormous post-match celebrations At half time, instead of oranges, the players would imbibe gin and orange! Often the team was short of players on a Saturday morning and Barrie would trawl the town streets and local hostelries seeking anyone willing to play. The Bionics were the very embodiment of the "Art of Coarse Rugby" – except for Barrie's Rolls-Royce!

Jack	Doug	Steve	Richard	Ian	Roger	A.N.	A.N.	Paul
Wilkinson	Simms	Holder	Churchill	Tennant	Phillips	Other	Other	Titchener
Terry Comerford		Dave Williams	Barrie O'Dell		Mick O'Donnell	Pete Eversley		Johnny Groom

1977-78	played	won	drawn	lost	pts. for	pts. against
1st XV	34	26	0	8	591	204
Exiles XV						
3rd XV	23	15	1	7	486	206
4th XV						
Extras XV						

Season 1978-79 - (Captain - Bob Clayton)

Officers

President	R. Dillingham
Chairman	B.S. O'Dell
Hon. Secretary	N. Thompson
Hon. Treasurer	R. G. Churchill
Fixture Secretary	R. Duffin
Main Committee	S. Brown, I. Messer, H. Sheard

Playing

1st XV Captain	R. Clayton
1st XV Vice-Captain	D. Parker
Exiles Captain	T. Edwards
Exiles Vice-Captain	N. Macklin
3rd XV Captain	A. Owen
3rd XV Vice-Captain	H. Sheard
4th XV Captain	M. Gonse
4t XV Vice-Captain	D. Hook
Extras XV Captain	R. Duffin
Extras XV Vice-Captain	T. Hartline
Bionics XV Captain	B.S. O'Dell
Coach	B. Parker

This was to prove one of the best seasons to date for Ampthill 1st XV. 25 games were won, 2 drawn and only 3 lost, to Tabard, Leighton Buzzard and Luton. The side was unbeaten through September to November before a shock loss in the semi-final of the Cup to Leighton Buzzard.

Bedfordshire Knockout Cup

In the first round of the Bedfordshire Cup, Ampthill beat Luton by 24-0 at home.

Ampthill served notice that they were now a force to be reckoned with in Bedfordshire rugby. The team who the previous season were the surprise runners-up in the Bedfordshire Knock-out Cup, proved it was no flash in the pan when they started the new campaign with a conclusive 24-0 win over Luton.

"It was a case of experience beating youth," said Ampthill skipper Bob Clayton, "it was our biggest win over Luton for years and perhaps now we will start getting the recognition we deserve."

Bob Clayton and his Ampthill team-mates clearly had sights on the final again. On the evidence of the Luton game their pack would take some stopping. They were bigger and more powerful than their opposition and as a result snuffed them out almost completely.

Ampthill's fixtures, thanks to Bob Clayton and Roy Duffin had greatly improved and notable wins this season included Stamford 12-7, Chiltern 27-12, Huntingdon 15-4, Mill Hill 17-6 and Wellingborough 29-3. There were two notable draws 9-9 away to Bedford Athletic and 9-9 at home to Mansfield.

Dunstablians were beaten 19-12 away in the next round of the Bedfordshire Cup, on October 29. Ampthill was slow to get into the game, and at one stage they were trailing 9-0 after a sluggish start which must have caused some anxious moments among their supporters. In the end, however, they remained strong contenders for the title after a deserved 19-12 victory. Skipper and hooker Bob Clayton admitted afterwards: "I was never worried. We were so much on top in the scrums I knew it would come right in the end."

On Sunday 19 November, Ampthill travelled to Leighton Buzzard in the semi-final of the Knockout Cup. Leighton Buzzard produced the shock of this season's competition by ending Ampthill's unbeaten record with a 9-7 win. It was a case of unlucky 13 for Ampthill who had gone the first 13 games of the season without defeat.

"The better side won on the day," admitted Ampthill skipper Bob Clayton. "They rose to the occasion better than we did."

Yet Ampthill had only themselves to blame. At half time they were leading 7-0 thanks to a Simon Brown try and a Terry Foot penalty – and it should have been so much more. They had camped on the Leighton line throughout but had been unable to turn their territorial advantage into points.

After the break it was a different story with Leighton Buzzard turning on the pressure. And in the end the only difference between the sides was a conversion. Leighton's try was scored by their second row following a line out close to the try line.

In the other semi-final Stockwood gave their supporters a few scares before clinching a deserved victory over Bedford Athletic.

Leighton Buzzard were to defeat Stockwood in the 1978 Cup Final. In the following February Ampthill had the satisfaction of beating Leighton Buzzard narrowly 7-6 at home.

Ampthill, under Bob Clayton won 25 games, drew 2 and lost just three games: 7-9 to Leighton Buzzard in the Cup semi-final, 3-6 away to Tabard and 6-9 away to Luton.

Alan Lovell Memorial Match

In September 1975 the first Alan Lovell memorial match was played between Bedford Rugby Club and the Bedfordshire County XV. Alan Lovell, a great servant of the Bedford Club, had an untimely death at the age of 39. He had made 320 appearances for the 1st XV and played for the East Midlands 21 times, twice against the Barbarians.

Bedfordshire lost this first game by 74-6, but beat Bedford in 1976, by 25-29. The third Allan Memorial game was won by Bedford by 46-3 in 1977. In the Allan Lovell Memorial game on September 27, 1978, Ampthill had five players in the Bedfordshire team to play the Bedford Blues, Bob Clayton, Malcolm Davies, Brian Clarke, Malcolm Truman, and Mike Plant.

Last-kick Misery for Bedfordshire

Bedfordshire junior clubs were robbed of a shock win over Bedford last night with the last kick of the match. Fly-half Martyn Humberstone, who on Saturday kicked a last-minute penalty to beat Richmond, did it again this time to earn them a fortunate 20-19 win over the junior clubs' side.

Inspired by an impressive performance from their pack the Beds team led throughout the second half. Their only try came when Ampthill back-row forward Malcolm Truman capitalised on a mistake by the Bedford backs.

Dunstablians scrum-half Micky Flecknell kicked three long range penalties and fly-half "Digger" Timothy dropped two goals to make up the Bedfordshire points.

Gordon Ascroft Cup

Ampthill Rugby Club were well represented in the County XV throughout the late 1970 and early 1980s when Bedfordshire won the Gordon Ascroft Cup for five consecutive seasons.

This was a competition played between the four regions of the East Midlands RFU (Bedfordshire, Northampton Alliance, East Northants. & Huntingdon & Peterborough.).

Ampthill 1st XV 1978-79

back-row: **Steve Watson, Malcolm Davies, Ian Messer, Brian Clark, Bob Campbell, Dave Sprigg, Terry Foot, Randy Livingood, Phil Argent**

front-row: **Malcolm Truman, Neil Thompson, Dave Parker, Bob Clayton, Mike Plant, Les Craggs, Micky Jupp, Barry Parker**

Barry Parker, pictured above, was Ampthill's longest serving coach at that time, an ex-1st XV hooker and an astute reader of the game.

1978-79	played	won	drawn	lost	pts. for	pts. against
1st XV	31	2 6	2	3	599	177
Exiles XV						
3rd XV	25	15	2	8	492	190
4th XV						
Extras XV						

Season 1979-80 - (Captain - Bob Clayton)

Officers

President	R. Dillingham
Chairman	B.S. O'Dell
Hon. Secretary	N. Thompson & Ian Messer
Hon. Treasurer	R. G. Churchill
Fixture Secretary	R. Duffin
Main Committee	D. Williams, P. Tookey, H. Sheard

Playing

1st XV Captain	R. Clayton
1st XV Vice-Captain	M. Plant
Exiles XV	T. Rust
Exiles Vice-Captain	S. Brown
3rd XV Captain	A. Owen
3rd XV Vice-Captain	H. Sheard
4th XV Captain	D. Jenkins
4th XV Vice-Captain	J. Groom
Extras XV Captain	R. Duffin
Coach	B. Parker

After the success of the previous season 1979-80 was something of an anti-climax. After beating Dunstablians comfortably by 32-0 in the first round of Bedfordshire Cup, they were beaten in the next round away at Bedford Athletic. It was some comfort when, a week later at home, the Bedford side were beaten 9-6 by Ampthill.

However, the mid-season was blighted by serious injuries to Mike Plant, Dave Parker, and Neil Thompson. This put a great deal of pressure on the three-quarters and players were forced to play out of position for much of this period. Fortunately, the versatile Terry Foot took over at outside-half and Simon Brown had a richly deserved run at full-back in the 1st XV.

The debut of former Bedford flanker Steve Peacey saw him score the first two tries in a 50-4 dismantling of Cheylsmore Old Boys. A young Steve Watson was forcing his way into the side and scoring regularly from the backrow. Both Steve Peacey and Steve Watson were to go on to have highly successful playing careers with Ampthill and both were to captain the Club.

Problems at the Dunstablians club meant that the talented centre, Martin Nolan joined Ampthill and this was a major coup. However, the team drew heavily on its traditional strength - the forward pack.

The front-row of Malcolm "Dad" Davies, Bob Clayton and Phil Argent were highly experienced, skilled, and intelligent (though Phil did his best to hide this – but no one was fooled!). This trio was briefly threatened by the arrival of the massive presence of Tim Lane, a tight-head prop, who joined from Luton RUFC (he was the father of Phil Lane – a future star player and captain). However, the skipper, Bob Clayton found it impossible to bind with Tim and he reluctantly returned to Luton. "Slim" Clark's graft and aggression were perfectly complimented by the superb line-out skill of Bob Campbell, in those pre-lifting days. In the back row the evergreen Dave Sprigg, a destructive presence at No.6, was partnered by the metronomic Malcolm Truman and the youthful Steve Watson.

As their injured players returned, there were notable victories over Leighton Buzzard 35-9, Chiltern 27-12, Bicester 31-6, and Kibworth 36-0, in the Spring of 1979.

Ampthill 35 pts. Leighton Buzzard 9 pts. – 2nd February 1980

Bedfordshire cup finalists Leighton Buzzard suffered one of their worst defeats for a long time at the hands of close rivals Ampthill.

Playing against the slope, Ampthill's forwards powered their way to the first try in the opening minutes that was scored by Steve Peacey with Terry Foot converting. This determined start by Ampthill stirred Leighton and they responded with a converted try.

This stalemate soon changed when Terry Foot scored two penalties and Steve Watson capped a brilliant forward link-up with Terry Foot to score near the posts. Leighton Buzzard responded with a single penalty that left the half time score at 18-7.

They failed to improve their first half score, whereas Ampthill went on to score three tries by Mike Plant, Scott Goodson and, once again, Steve Watson. Mike Plant added a further nail to the coffin with a brilliantly executed drop goal. With an additional conversion by Terry Foot the final score resulted in an impressive 35-9 win for Ampthill.

However, behind the scenes Barrie O'Dell (Chairman), Richard Churchill (Treasurer) and the Committee : Ian Messer, & Neil Thomson (Hon. Secs.), Roy Duffin (Fixture Sec.), Bert Sheard, Phil Tookey and Dave Williams – were pre-occupied with the next great step forward in the Club's history – the present clubhouse.

Mini & Youth

For the first time Mini & Youth fixtures were published in the Members Card

FIXTURES

Date	Opponent	H/A
28 Oct.	Dunstable	H
11 Nov.	Stockwood Park	A
25 Nov.	Leighton Buzzard	H
16 Dec	Bedford	H
20 Jan	Biggleswade	A
3 Feb.	Milton Keynes	H
24 Feb.	Stockwood Park	H
23 Mar.	South Beds. Festival	A
30 Mar.	St. Neots	A
20 Apr.	St. Neots Festival	A

1979-80	played	won	drawn	lost	pts. for	pts. against
1st XV	31	21	1	9	510	203
Exiles XV						
3rd XV						
4th XV						
Extras XV	26	14	0	12	330	285

10 Year Fixture Comparison (1st XV) 1970–1980

Sept.	1970/71 Bedford Rovers Old Askean Princes Stevenage	Sept.	1980/81 Bedford Rovers Oxford Old Boys Tring Stewart & Lloyds
Oct.	Wellingborough Leighton Buzzard Bedford Swifts Ilkeston Biggleswade	Oct.	Wellingborough Bedford Athletic Mill Hill
Nov.	Fairbairn House Huntingdon Queens Works Corby	Nov.	Cheylesmore Old Boys Huntingdon St. Neots Tabard
Dec.	Rushden & Higham Royston Stevenage Biggleswade	Dec.	Milton Keynes Fullerians Colworth Stevenage
Jan.	Luton Queens Works Shuttleworth College Wellingborough Westminster College	Jan.	Olney Buckingham Bletchley Norwich Crusaders
Feb.	Rushden & Higham Stockwood Park Extra 1st XV St. Neots St. Albans	Feb.	Leighton Buzzard Letchworth Kibworth Chiltern
Mar.	Kibworth Colworth House Leighton Buzzard Leicester Vipers	Mar.	Stamford Jersey Old Cantabridgians Bacavians Luton
Apr.	Bedford Swifts Horsham Henry Mellish Old Boys Royston Luton	Apr.	Biggleswade Cambridge Dunstablians Old Yardlians
May	Old Yardlians		

Chapter 5 – The Eighties -From Friendlies to Leagues

Season 1980-81 – 30th Anniversary - (Captain – Steve Peacey)

Officers

President	R. Dillingham
Chairman	B.S. O'Dell
Hon. Secretary	N. Thompson & Ian Messer
Hon. Treasurer	R. G. Churchill
Fixture Secretary	R. Clayton
Hon. Team Secretary	B. Clark
Main Committee	G. Myler, P. Tookey, D. Williams

Playing

1st XV Captain	S. Peacey
1st XV Vice-Captain	M. Nolan
Exiles XV Captain	A. Bailey
Exiles XV Vice-Captain	P. Britton
3rd XV Captain	T. Huckle
4th XV Captain	P. New
4th XV Vice-Captain	G. Mapp
5th XV Captain	
Bionics XV Captain	J. Wilkinson
Extras XV Captain	R. Duffin
Coach	B. Parker

The new skipper, Steve Peacey, had joined the Club from Bedford the previous season. An excellent backrow forward, Steve was quick, uncompromising and a good footballer. He proved to be an able leader, possessing a wry sense of humour and a firm, but fair, way of dealing with the strong characters at the Club. Like Bob Clayton, he continued the tradition of being Club Captain, as well as leading the 1st XV.

Significant arrivals included Peter Cadigan, an ex-St. Luke's College scrum half. In the forwards, Tony Willison made the first of many 1st XV appearances. Fred Haines at No.8 and Bill Beaumont at lock, were both to make an important contribution to the season.

Young players such as Kevin Moore, Leigh Clarke (son of Slim), Nigel Rendle, Peter Ogilvie, Paul Day, Bob Wagstaff, Chris Hopgood and Andy Huckle were coming through from the Club's Youth and Colts systems and would become first teamers.

In its 30th year of existence, senior section members from Ampthill, Flitwick and the surrounding villages now numbered about 300 – and nearly 150 of these were playing members. Speaking to the local press, Chairman Barrie O'Dell said, "The club membership has grown rapidly over the last couple of years. This is a result of the expansion of Flitwick and more rugby being played at local schools. The idea of a new club building has been in our minds for about 18 months and it will be double the size of the old one."

The Present Clubhouse on Woburn Road

The Rugby Pavilion behind Parkside Hall went up for sale in January 1980 – the club needing the cash from the sale to help finance their new, larger premises next to the two pitches on Woburn Road. The agent, Stonebanks said the asking price was in the region of £30,000.

The cost of the new clubhouse was estimated at £85,000, providing changing for 6 teams.

Through loans (two major breweries) and a grant (Sports Council) and the sale of the old Pavilion it was anticipated that £45,000 would be raised leaving a balance of £40,000 to be financed. During the next 12 months a series of fund-raising activities would include; a sponsored walk, lottery and a Gala Ball. However, the majority of the necessary funds were to be raised from club contribution through deeds of covenant. A seven-year plan to raise £25,000 via deeds of covenant was proposed. Two advantages were claimed for this proposal;

1. A donor was able to give substantially more by spreading contributions over seven years.
2. Covenanted gifts would enable loans for the total value to be negotiated, in order to make an early start to building.

Building was due to commence in mid-Summer 1980, so the club issued a new clubhouse appeal – "but we are dependent upon widespread support from both club members and the local community to ensure that the necessary finance is available and for the completion of the clubhouse during our 30th Anniversary Season (1980-81)" - Barrie O'Dell.

The Committee men driving this appeal were Barrie O'Dell, Club Chairman, Richard Churchill Treasurer and Gerry Myler, Chairman of the Building Committee. Barrie was personally pro-active, making many phone calls to club members to ensure that the maximum number joined the deed of covenant scheme. In the event, 60 members became covenanters in this first wave.

Marking out of the footings for the new Clubhouse - May 1980. (front - Mike Plant (Alameda School), Brian Clark (Committee), Barrie O'Dell (Chairman), Frank Porthouse (Architect – Project Dunstable), Gerry Myler & Dave Williams (Committee) behind – rugby players from Alameda Middle School, Ampthill, and Phil Tookey (Grounds). Richard Horton is holding the shovel.

NB sixth schoolboy from the left is Ian McGregor who went on to captain the Club from fly-half

In the event, the new clubhouse was completed and opening games were played on Sunday 14th December - a Day of Rugby:

Mini: versus Leighton Buzzard - 10.30am kick-off

Youth: versus Leighton Buzzard & St. Neots - 10.00am kick-off

1st XV: versus   Bedfordshire County XV

Ampthill: M.Plant, S.Goodson, M. Nolan, B. Taylor, P. Ogilvie, P. Day, D. Parker, A. Owen, B. Clayton, P. Argent, B. Clark, T. Rust, M. Truman, S. Peacey (capt.), S. Watson, Rep.: W. Beaumont & P. Cadigan

Bedfordshire: M. Holton (LB), D. Budge (SP), R. Eglington (L), B. Jackson (L), P. Swain (SP), R. Timothy (capt.) (BA), J. Humphries (SP), S. Spring (BA), M. Cooper (BA), G. Mansell (SP), K. Healey (LB), J. Fraser (LB), R. Keating (LB), R. Poulter (SP), S. Moore (SP) Rep.: G. Griffiths (BA)

The game, closely fought, resulted in a win for Ampthill by 10-3.

The Official Opening of the new clubhouse took place on April 5, 1981 with a game between the 1st XV and the Public-School Wanderers.

Opening of The New Clubhouse – Sunday 5th April 1981

Ampthill, having beaten the Bedford Wanderers 13-0 last Wednesday, confirmed their improving status in rugby by playing a full part in a Barbarian style match of exciting running in front of a full house at Dillingham Park on Sunday. The match marked the official opening by Budge Rogers of their new clubhouse. They eventually lost by 3 goals and 3 tries to a penalty and 2 tries to a scratch Public School Wanderers side.

But they never gave up and though 14-0 down at half-time they fought back strongly to take a 15-14 lead just 10 minutes into the second half.

Five minutes from the end, they were down by only 15-20 before Rossborough (Coventry) on the end of a marvellous service from Peck (Rosslyn Park) sent Malic (Coventry) in for the try of the match which Peck converted. And then two minutes from the end Peck and Wilkinson (Bedford) combined to send the former England lock over for a try which really exaggerated the score for the visitors.

McGuckian (Northampton), Rossborough (Coventry) and Cheesesman (Bedford) got the early tries before Ampthill staged their great revival inspired by skipper Peacey and wingers Hindmarch and Ogilvie.

Just four minutes into the second half, Ampthill full back Mike Plant burst into the line for Ogilvie to make the break and for Plant to be on hand from Peacey's pass to get the try. Parker converted and was on target again a minute later after Ogilvie and Peacey had sent in Truman for Ampthill's second try. It looked at this stage as though Ampthill might take charge of the game through Parker's teasing kicks down the slope. They got their fair share of loose ball but Wilkinson and Kidner (Coventry), dominated the lineout. Parker was able to test the visitors' defence with a hoisted Garryowen and then slot home a penalty from the ensuing ruck infringement. But the game was really about running and playing to the crowd and McGuckian put the Wanderers back in the lead when he charged through from 20 yards with two men on his back. And even then, it took the visitors another 20 minutes to secure the game with some scintillating running from Rossborough and Peck.

P.S.W. Skipper Bob Wilkinson said, "It was a thoroughly entertaining game and full credit to Ampthill for coming back when they could so easily have gone under." Ampthill's Steve Peacey added, "All our players played up to form for the occasion and on behalf of the club I should like to thank everyone who turned up and made it such a memorable day."

Ampthill: M. Plant, J. Hindmarch, P. Day, M. Nolan, P. Ogilvie, D. Parker, P. Cadigan, A. Owen, B. Clayton, P. Argent, B. Clark, G. Bailey, M. Truman, S. Peacey, S. Watson

Public School Wanderers: Rossborough (Coventry), Griffiths (Bedford Athletic), Moore, McGuckian (Northampton), Peck (Rosslyn Park), Fox (Northampton), Raphael; (Northampton), Hobley (Coventry), Kidner (Coventry), Malic (Coventry), Wilkinson (Bedford), Wilson (Northampton).

Referee: Clive Leake (EMRURS) Touch-Judges: Ivor Owen & Paul Johnson (EMRURS)

The opening of the Dillingham Park Clubhouse by Budge Rogers, OBE

Ampthill 1st XV versus Public School Wanderers

Back row: **P. Johnson, S. Moore, P. McGuckian, E. Hyde, M. Hobley, B. Kidner, N. Fox, C. Leeke (ref.) M. Truman, S. Watson, P. Argent, M. Nolan, B. Clark, G. Bailey, B. Clayton, K. Betts, S. Barker, I. Owen** Middle-row: **R. Cheesman, T. Buttimoore, J. Raphael, M. Malic, R. Wilkinson, R. James, D. Rogers, D. Dillingham, B. O'Dell, S. Peacey (capt.), P.Day, J. Hindmarch, P. Cadigan, B. Hart** Front row: **G. Wilson, P. Rossborough, I. Peck, G. Griffiths, A. Owen, D. Parker, P. Ogilvie, M. Plant** Mini-rugby boys

Liam Duffin, Adrian Downing, Russell Hart, Mark Bishop, Stewart Pegg, Michael Tanner, Justin Fletcher, John Wilkinson, Nigel Vicary, Steven Marsden, Richard Holmes, Graham Baston.

Mini-Rugby Boys
Liam Duffin, Michael Tanner, Justin Fletcher, John Wilkinson and Steve Marden were all to play senior rugby for the Club.
Liam Duffin played for Ampthill senior teams and now is the Manager of the Extras
Michael Tanner: Ampthill, Bedfordshire, England Students, England U/21, Richmond, Royal Navy, Combined Services
Justin Fletcher: Ampthill, Midlands Colts, England Colts trials, Bedfordshire
John Wilkinson: Ampthill, Bedfordshire, East Midlands, Bedford
Steve Marsden: Ampthill senior teams
Ampthill lost narrowly, 9-11 to Stockwood Park at home in the County Knockout Cup. In other games, Bedford Wanderers were beaten 13-0 away, Stamford 8-0, Cambridge 34-8, and Towcester 27-0. Under Steve Peacey, the first team played 34, winning 22 games, drawing 2 and losing 11.

7 Club XVs

The Club was now running seven senior teams, with Roy Duffin's Extras and the Bionics, under Jack Wilkinson. The Extras scored over 700 points this season including 141 tries and 61 conversions – they never kicked penalties!

Brothers in Arms – Terry Foot & Dave Sprigg (centre) in action against Luton – 31 January 1981 - (12-9 to Ampthill)

1980-81	played	won	drawn	lost	pts. for	pts. against
1st XV	36	23	2	11	468	251
Exiles XV	30	14	2	14	357	337
3rd XV	25	15	1	9	283	158
4th XV	27	16	2	9	406	258
5th XV	27	16	2	9	459	207
Extras XV	30	24	2	4	702	272
Bionics XV						

Richard Dillingham

The opening of the new clubhouse was a massive achievement by the Club. When the Club's new name was unveiled it read – **Dillingham Park**. Richard Dillingham thoroughly deserved this honour and the Club, as a whole, was delighted for him.

Richard was born in Flitwick in 1914, and attended Luton Modern School from 1926, travelling by steam train each day. He obtained his school certificate and London Matriculation, but his main interest at school was sport. Richard gained 1st XI cricket, football and rugby XV colours and was Victor Ludorum in athletics. He entered St. Paul's College, Cheltenham to train as a teacher, gaining his Teacher's Certificate in 1935. Richard was a member of the College 1st XV but excelled in athletics – being unbeaten in the 440 yards and was elected Secretary of the athletics section.

Richard Dillingham was appointed Assistant Master at Stotfold Boys' School in 1935 on a salary of £168, teaching a class of 58, 7 to 9-year-olds. He played rugby for Luton & Bedford Nondescripts and was Bedfordshire County Captain in athletics from 1936, whilst also playing cricket for Flitwick CC. In 1937 Richard competed at the White City Stadium and won the Midlands triple jump title.

At the outbreak of war in 1939, Richard was posted to France and Belgium where he rose through the ranks to sergeant in charge of chemical warfare protection in addition to gunnery duties. Whilst on leave he married his sweetheart, Mary, returning to France after the honeymoon. Back in England in 1940, Richard applied for a commission and became a gunnery officer.

After the war, he returned to athletics, rugby and cricket but was plagued by hamstring problems. He became captain of Ampthill Cricket Club from 1947-57 and then Chairman until 1962 when he became President. In 1950, Richard became Head of the "National" School in Toddington, a post he held until his retirement in 1977. Richard and Mary had two daughters, both of whom won scholarships to Bedford High School.

In 1950, Richard became the first Chairman of Ampthill Rugby Club and in 1962, the President. On its formation Richard became Chairman of the Bedfordshire County Rugby Union and for thirty years he was a member of the East Midlands RFU, becoming its President in 1972. He was a founder member of the Ampthill Rotary Club and was elected President in 1978. In 1972 he was made President of the Bedfordshire Head Teachers Association.

After his retirement, Richard Dillingham was instrumental in the formation of the Ampthill Festival and became its first chairman.

In the 1994 New Year's Honours List, Richard Dillingham was awarded the MBE for – Services to Sport in Bedfordshire. Richard passed away in 2001, aged 86. Writing about his life in 1987, Richard had this to say:

"Looking back on my life, I may not have been too successful financially but I have riches in my wife Mary, my children and grandchildren."

It is no exaggeration to say that without Richard Dillingham there would be no Ampthill Rugby Club today.

Tony Rogers & Richard Dillingham at Dillingham Park – Founder Members of ARUFC & player & referee in the first ever game – September 16th, 1950 versus Bedford Lions in Ampthill Great Park

Season 1981-82 (Captain – Steve Peacey)

Officers

President	R. Dillingham
Chairman	B.S. O'Dell
Hon. Secretary	N. Thompson & Ian Messer
Hon. Treasurer	R. G. Churchill
Fixture Secretary	R. Clayton
Hon. Team Secretary	B. Clark
Main Committee	Peter Britton, P. Tookey, D. Williams

Playing

1st XV Captain	S. Peacey
1st XV Vice-Captain	M. Nolan
Exiles XV Captain	D. Sprigg
Exiles XV Vice-Captain	T. Foot
3rd XV Captain	M. Jupp
3rd XV Vice-Captain	I. Cosgrove
4th XV Captain	H. Sheard
5th XV Captain	
Bionics XV Captain	I. Tennant & Jan Mazgaj
Extras XV Captain	R. Duffin
Coach	B. Parker

This first full season in the new clubhouse was a frustrating one for Steve Peacey's first XV. Of the 16 games lost, a number were by 3 points or less. However, the loss at home to Stockwood Park by 31 points to nil, in the Bedfordshire Knock-out Cup, was a major reversal.

It was not a great season for any of the Club teams except Roy Duffin's Extras, who won 18 of their 26 matches, scoring 463 points against 152.

There were, however, some good 1st XV results against strong opposition notably the 35-7 defeat of Old Hamptonians, Harrow 32-3, 31-0 against Harpenden, 24-0 over Dunstablians and a convincing 31-3 demolition of Wellingborough Old Grammarians.

At the end of the season, Steve Peacey left to teach in Indiana, USA, on a Fullbright Exchange Programme. He coached and played for the Northwest Indiana Rugby Club. In the autumn of 1983, to celebrate their 10th year anniversary, the Northwest Indiana Club came to England playing Ampthill, Bedford Athletic and Bedford rugby clubs.

Eric Webb's Reunion Lunch at Dillingham Park, 1982

As the 30th Anniversary approached Eric Webb wrote to the Club from Canada, enquiring about any plans for celebrating this event. Eric had been Treasurer in the 1950s and was one of the earliest Life Members. No doubt the Club was preoccupied with the new clubhouse and the rapid expansion of the membership. However, this was too good a chance to miss and Eric flew over for a reunion lunch with founder members and fellow players from the 1950s.

Back	John Churchill	Alan Stevens	John Wallis	Stan Fossey	
Upper Middle	J.P. Mears	John Huckle	Richard Churchill	Fred Thistlethwaite	John Inskip
	Bill Rogers	Archie Webster	Terry Comerford		
Lower Middle	Bill Thompson	Norman Brown	Eric Webb	Richard Dillingham	Tony Rogers
	Ken Tilston				
Front	Doug Simms	Nigel Whiskin	Dave Pulley	John Comerford	

1981-82	played	won	drawn	lost	pts. for	pts. against
1st XV	29	13	0	16	354	306
Exiles XV	27	13	2	12	323	495
3rd XV	24	15	1	8	238	147
4th XV	24	16	2	6	266	148
5th XV	27	16	2	9	302	134
Extras XV	26	18	1	7	463	152

Season 1982-83 - (Captain - Bob Clayton)

Officers

President	R. Dillingham
Chairman	B.S. O'Dell
Hon. Secretary	N. Thompson & Ian Messer
Hon. Treasurer	R. G. Churchill
Fixture Secretary	R. Clayton
Hon. Team Secretary	B. Clark
Chairman of Selectors	M. Plant
Assist. Team Secretary	S. Watson
Main Committee	P. Britton, P. Tookey, D. Williams

Playing

1st XV Captain	R. Clayton
1st XV Vice-Captain	D. Parker
Exiles XV Captain	D. Sprigg
Exiles XV Vice-Captain	T. Foot
3rd XV Captain	M. Jupp
3rd XV Vice-Captain	M. Rose
4th XV Captain	N. Kelliher
5th XV Captain	M. Greene
Extras XV Captain	R. Duffin
Bionics XV Captain	J. Wilkinson
Coach	B. Parker

This was to prove a highly successful season for the Club as a whole. Not only did the 1st XV reach its second ever Bedfordshire Knockout Cup Final, but the Club won an unprecedented 65% of its games that season. The Club owed a huge debt to the team captains; Bob Clayton, Dave Sprigg, Mike Jupp, Neil Kelliher, Matt Greene, Roy Duffin and Jack Wilkinson.

Of the nearly 200 games played by the Club's seven teams: 128 were won, 10 drawn and 60 lost with 3,222 points scored and 1,601 points conceded. The 1st XV was to suffer persistent injury problems to key personnel throughout the season and this undoubtedly affected what promised to be an outstanding campaign.

Denis Hardy arrived from Leighton Buzzard, and he was to be highly influential as a player, administrator, coach and Director of Rugby. Kevin Moore at No.8 was a real find, going on to play for the County and then Bedford. John Hindmarch (ex-Tynedale RUFC) – a speedy winger – was a welcome arrival from Stockwood Park.

A new star entered the stage – John Little - a scrum half from Cheltenham studying at Cranfield University. He got his chance, through injuries to key players, in November against Huntingdon, and kept his place against strong competition from Pete Cadigan. His presence allowed Dave Parker to switch permanently to fly-half and gave the Ampthill threequarters real attacking options.

Undoubtedly, the club's fixture list had become stronger, thanks to Bob Clayton. For the first team the season's opening game was away against Saracens Crusaders (2nd XV). Neil Townsend, a winger from the Chicksands base scored on his debut against Saracens in a creditable 4-25 result.

Cup Campaign

Ampthill, began its Knockout Cup Campaign against Bedfordshire Police lacking a number of first choice players. A cobbled together side, had no trouble disposing of the Police by 54-3.

Ampthill drew the holders and much-fancied Leighton Buzzard at home in the quarter final.

Because of numerous injuries, a side put together by skipper Bob Clayton, virtually at the kick off, thrilled a packed Dillingham Park. Their victory by a try and a penalty to two penalties earned them a semi-final tie against Luton.

Clayton had became a father earlier in the week and in an inspired front row performance with Phil Argent and Digger Day took upteen strikes against the head. Centre Dennis Hardy celebrated against his old club with a stellar performance.

Ampthill had the worst possible start when the visitors kicked a first minute penalty, but came back strongly and started to put their game together, centres Hardy and Wagstaff combining well in the attack. Fred Haines twice went close before great work by Plant and Hardy sent full-back Huckle over for a superb try.

By now the Ampthill pack were dominating all phases of play and Bob Clayton and the front-row took the first of their incredible strikes against the head.

A Kevin Moore penalty opened the second half to put Ampthill further ahead but Leighton Buzzard came back strongly and a penalty narrowed the margin. With Ampthill defending well and some timely clearing kicks from fly-half Mike Plant and full-back Andy Huckle, Leighton's time ran out and a final Ampthill surge safeguarded a tremendous victory.

Ampthill: T. Huckle, P. Britton, R. Wagstaff, D. Hardy, N. Townsend, M. Plant, P. Cadigan, D. Day, R. Clayton, P. Argent, A. Burnage, P. Lees, S. Watson, K. Moore, F. Haines.

Playing that day for Leighton Buzzard at loose-head was Malcolm "Dad" Davies, an ex-Ampthill stalwart. Malcolm, a proud man, would not have enjoyed this experience. Thankfully, he was welcomed back to the Club the following season.

Ampthill were again the underdogs for their Beds Cup semi-final against Luton at Wood Meadow on Sunday 28 November. Clayton's side qualified with the final against the Ath. by holding Luton to a 0-0 draw on a muddy pitch and going through as the away team. Athletic beat Vauxhall 14-0 with three second half tries at Putnoe Wood.

"We took it to them from the start", said Clayton. "We had tremendous support from the touchline and by keeping our cool and our discipline we made it through a tough but clean match that had all the ingredients. We were magnificently served at half back by Dave Parker and John Little but the truth is we had 16 heroes. Ampthill lost Tony Willison with an injury just after the interval. Because of the occasion he was reluctant to go off, but the experienced Malcom Truman was on hand to maintain the momentum. Against expectations Ampthill, in fact, had the clearer chances to win. Clayton himself was stopped just short of the line. John Little and Kevin Moore were just wide with penalties. Luton had a last minute chance to grab the match with a penalty, but failed to take it.

The price of a magnificent performance would be an enforced rest for a number of players who were carrying injuries into the match.

Ampthill: T.Huckle, P. Smith, P. Ogilvie, D. Hardy, R. Wagstaff, D. Parker, J. Little, D. Day, B. Clayton, P. Argent, T. Willison, P. Lees, S. Watson, F. Haines, K. Moore, replacement M. Truman.

Ampthill's Second Bedfordshire Cup Final – December 19th 1983

Ampthill 3 pts. Bedford Athletic 9 pts.

A brave Ampthill team failed in their bid for glory in a penalty dominated Bedfordshire Cup final, played in atrocious conditions at Dillingham Park.

The season's giant killers went down by 9-3 to the favourites Bedford Athletic. .They took the title for the fourth time, with three penalties from Paul Evans, two of them coming in the last five minutes. In a dour match Bob Clayton's men went down fighting.

Evans, a former captain of the Swifts, kept his cool at the end of a match in which Ampthill gave away too many penalties and started to panic with time running out.

Clayton's crew had a clear advantage in the backs, but their forwards on the day came off second best to a side that went on the rampage right from the start. The victory gives the Athletic the right to go into the last four of the East Midlands championship with the eventual winner going into the first round of next year's John Player.

If the Ampthill plan was to run at the Athletic midfield, then the Ath's was always to play a tight nine man game keeping the ball as far away as possible from John Little and Dave Parker and co.

With Saturday's perfect conditions for the running game turning into a torrential downpour and a gale force wind by Sunday, the battle up front was always to be decisive and Athletic won it hands down.

They won a critical toss played into the wind in the first session and looked home and dry when they changed round at three all after Evans and scrum half Little exchanged penalties.

Little was probably the outstanding player on the field and while he was darting around at the base of the scrum Ampthill were still in with a shout. Towards the end of the first half he looked a good bet for a try with a put in on the Athletic's goal line that ricocheted off a prop and came out the wrong side for the first of a handful of strikes against the head.

15 minutes into the second half, he had the chance to put his team ahead for the first time but missed a difficult shot under intense pressure. The penalty was won by a counterattack via Paul Smith and Andy Huckle. But with the Ath. needing only a draw to win, the Ampthill moves became more desperate as the whistle drew nearer. In the end they played the ultimate penalty close to their line and Evans kept his cool, with the wind behind him and nothing to lose, he added 75 and 80 minute penalties.

Ampthill: A. Huckle, P. Smith, D. Hardy, H. Summers, D. Parker, J. Little, D.Day, B. Clayton (capt.), P. Argent, P. Lees, M. Haville, M. Truman, F. Haynes, K. Moore. Replacements: S. Watson, R. Wagstaff

Bedford Athletic: P. Evans, T. Calloway, N. Mears, P. Clarke, S. Brown, R. Timothy, G. Griffiths (capt.), J. McCreadie, M. Thomas, S. Spring, G. Coomb, C. Liptrot, P. Dawes, M. Norman, N. Proudman

Bedford Athletic went on to win the East Midlands Cup and enter the first round of the John Player Cup the following season.

This was a serious set-back to the Club's ambitions and, in particular to its captain, Bob Clayton. He was truly a Club Captain, present at all Committee and selection meetings, he was also Fixture Secretary (seven teams and Colts) and was fully involved in the planning process for the new Clubhouse.

Today a 1st XV captain is just that, he has a Director of Rugby, a coach, medical team and Team Manager to support him and he does not have to pick the team. Bob would continue to play, but after two stints as Club Captain and having a young family he gave up the captaincy.

Phil Argent

Left to right: Phil Argent, Bob Clayton and Dave "Digger" Day

In April 1983, Phil Argent joined Bedford Rugby Club for the last three games of the season.

Following his first team debut at Waterloo and a fine appearance against Gosforth, Phil Argent was one of the stars against the best team in England, Bath. Bath eventually won by scoring four second half tries and they took their win total for the season to 38 with 1,278 points and 205 tries in an unbeaten run of 25 games. The Bedford side raised its game and hooker Don Henderson took three strikes against the head, "I put them down to Phil," said Henderson. "he told me about some tricks he'd learned with Bob Clayton at Ampthill." Happily, from Ampthill's point of view, Phil returned to Ampthill, playing in a 19-22 loss to Bletchley, in November 1983.

Wife orders the skipper to carry on

Bob Clayton was standing down from the captaincy at Ampthill Rugby Club. However, he would not be hanging up his boots yet – because his wife refused to let him. Clayton told the members of wife Lesley's decision at the annual dinner at the end of the season. He had just completed his fourth year as captain and had it in mind to call it a day after one of the most successful campaigns in the Club's 30 year history. His wife, he said, had just started getting used to being a rugby widow and was beginning to like it…….

Clayton himself was awarded the Geoff Ainsley Cup for the Player of the Year, Teenage centre Bob Wagstaff won the Barrie O'Dell Cup for the Young Player of the Year and the Slim Clark Trophy for Perseverance went to gutsy flanker Paul Stokes.

1982-83	played	won	drawn	lost	pts. for	pts. against
1st XV	37	20	3	14	486	368
Exiles XV	33	17	4	12	518	276
3rd XV	32	24	0	8	511	255
4th XV	33	24	1	8	613	257
5th XV	27	18	1	8	533	169

Extras XV	32	21	1	10	616	321
Bionics XV	16	7	6	3	113	90

Mike Marsden - Trouble Brewing with the Club's Finances

I am endebted to Dave Williams for the details of this difficult time in the Club's history. On the surface all seemed fine, a new clubhouse and a successful season for all teams. However, there was real drama over the Club's coffers that was exercising the Committee. The financing of the new club had included, apart from covenants and grants, loans from two major breweries of £20,000 each. These loans depended on the Club being able to sell an agreed quota of beer. In the event, members greatly preferred the products from one brewery to that of the other.

The committee was horrified to learn that the less well-favoured brewery required a £4,000 penalty payment, to which it was entitled under the terms of the loan. Today, this sum may seem comparatively small, but nearly 40 years ago this was a major blow to the club's finances. In Richard Churchill (Treasurer), Barrie O'Dell (Chairman) and Richard Dillingham (President) the club possessed great experience and resourcefulness. The money was found and repaid to the brewery.

Not long later, however, the same brewery informed the Club that it now required the return of the full amount of the loan - £20,000 – as it was clear that the required volume of sales would never be met.

Dave Williams remembered the feeling that this would mean the end of the Club – since it simply did not have that kind of money available. However, "cometh the hour cometh the man!" Sitting quietly listening to the discussion of this seemingly intractable issue was Mike Marsden. Few members of the committee knew that Mike Marsden was on the board of a major national bank. Mike said, "Leave this with me" and within a short period of time he had arranged an overdraft facility that covered the debt.

Outside the Committee very few members were aware of this extremely perilous moment in the club's comparatively short life. (£20,000 in 1983 would be the equivalent of £108,700 today.)

Season 1983-84 - (Captain - Steve Watson)

Officers

President	R. Dillingham
Chairman	B.S. O'Dell
Hon. Secretary & Chairman of Selectors	M. Plant
Hon. Treasurer	R. G. Churchill
Fixture Secretary	R. Clayton
Hon. Team Secretary	B. Clark
Main Committee	P. Britton, P. Tookey, D. Williams, L. Clark

Playing

1st XV Captain	S. Watson
1st XV Vice-Captain	D. Hardy
Exiles XV Captain	D. Sprigg
Exiles XV Vice-Captain	T. Foot
3rd XV Captain	M. Jupp
4th XV Captain	N. Kelliher
5th XV Captain	
Extras XV Captain	R. Duffin
Bionics XV	J. Wilkinson
Coach	B. Parker

New opponents this season included; Old Northamptonians, London New Zealand and Ruislip.

For season 1983-84, there was intense speculation about the Club's back-row options where the was competition was extraordinary. Malcom Truman, Steve Peacey, Kevin Moore, Fred Haynes, Phil Wright and Steve Watson were all worthy of a first team place, and in some cases a County place, in the back-row. Fred Haynes had been voted Club captain which narrowed down the options. Then Kevin Moore, regular County No.8, announced he was trying his luck with first-class rugby at Bedford, as Phil Argent had done previously.

Sadly, after his election in April 1983, Fred Haynes was involved in a serious car crash that was to end his playing career. An emergency meeting was held in July and Steve Watson was elected captain.

A young Steve Watson first appeared in the first XV in season 1976-77, he was to go on to become captain of Bedfordshire under-23 XV and to represent the senior County team. Match reports note his enthusiasm, try scoring frequency and his love of harrasing half-backs from No.8. He was also inclined to appear in the three-quarter line with great regularity! Steve possessed a great sense of humour and he became a very popular Club captain.

Steve Watson's first game as skipper produced a useful 11-9 win over Old Northamptonians at Dillingham Park. The following Saturday was a "plum" fixture against London Welsh Druids – arranged through Tony Phillips' connections at Old Deer Park.

Druids turn on Welsh magic

In the first fixture between the clubs Ampthill held out in the early stages and won the second half of a memorable match.

But a 36 point blitz, 20 minutes before half-time by a side that switched on the magic, condemned Steve Watson's men to a 48-13 defeat.

The Druids contained backs of the class of Andrew Yeandle, Cardiff and Wales B, Howard Evans formerly of Newbridge and Bob Avery a full-back from Newport. In the end their superior class and fitness told when they raised the pace of the game with breathtaking support play. For a while Ampthill seemed totally demoralised but, after turning round at 36-0, they showed their mettle with a gutsy second half fightback.

With a couple of minutes to gather their thoughts, Ampthill started the second half with renewed enthusiasm. From a set piece penalty move Watson made a break, passed the ball to Steve Peacey, who put prop Dave Day over in the corner. Ampthill took heart from the try and despite a swift reply from the Druids, they followed up with a blind side move which included Dave Parker and Bob Wagstaff and was completed by Bob Clayton. Dave Parker landed the conversion and kicked a penalty to complete the scoring. Bob Wagstaff, Dennis Hardy, Duncan Bathe, John Hindmarsh and Mike Plant, in the Ampthill back line, acquitted themselves well against opposition backs who had all played first class rugby.

Dave Parker and Pete Cadigan were, once again, Ampthill's heroes and the home forwards, although considerably smaller, never slackened from their task in the second half, when they won more than their share of scrummage and ruck ball in particular against the best team they are likely to meet all season."

Making his debut in the Exiles that day was Phil Wright, scoring two tries in the loss to St. Albans 1st XV. Phil Wright was studying at Cranfield University with tough-guy centre Duncan Bathe and after graduation he joined Hunting Engineering, in Ampthill. He was to play with distinction in the back row for the 1st XV from 1983-88, after which he returned to Manchester, playing for Sale.

On the Cup Trail

Ampthill met Dunstablians in the first round of the County Cup in September, winning 17-3. Bedford Athletic beat Potton by 28-12, having gone down by 18-9 to Vipers at Leicester in the John Player first round. Ironically, Ampthill were drawn at home to Bedford Athletic in the quarter-final.

In the next game Malcolm "Dad" Davies returned to Ampthill for the match against Wellingborough, the 1st XV managed to lose a game they always looked like winning, 9-7. The 38 year-old Davies helped Bob Clayton to take four strikes against the head and scored a try.

Leigh Clark

Leigh Clark stepped out of the shadow of his famous father and scored all Ampthill's points in a 15-13 home win over Harrow. Son of the Ampthill legend, Brian "Slim" Clark, young Leigh had had the "promising" tag around his neck since his childhood. Called up at the eleventh hour out of his fly-half apprenticeship in the second-team, Clark landed three penalties and converted his own match-winning try.

Quarter-Final of the Bedfordshire Cup versus Bedford Athletic

At the end of October, Ampthill played their much-awaited quarter-final against old-rivals Bedford Athletic. The Ampthill forwards delivered the goods in their 9-0 county cup win over Bedford Athletic on 23 October. They earned sweet revenge for their 9-3 defeat in last year's final and booked a home date against Stockwood Park in the semi-final. Beaten badly up front in rough conditions last year they marched on in the cup through an interception try by scrum half Peter Cadigan, a conversion by winger Leigh Clark and a dropped goal by Dave Parker.

Geoff Bailey, recalled to the engine room, had a monumental game for Ampthill. He dominated the front of the line while Peter Lees looked after the middle. The front row of Bob Clayton, Dave Day and Dad Davies were well on top and the back row of Steve Watson, Steve Peacey and Phil Wright won the loose.

For the Athletic it was another sorry story in a miserable season. Stand-in skipper, Paul Evans, hero of last year's final, missed five kicks at goal and lock Gary Woods was sent for an early bath after hitting Ampthill's Duncan Bathe. Woods was earlier cautioned by referee Chris Harrison.

From the resulting penalty, drop goal ace Parker slotted the ball between the posts. Earlier his half-back partner Cadigan intercepted an Ath back row move after reading it like a book. He sped half the length of the pitch for a brilliant try.

Semi-Final Bedfordshire Cup versus Stockwood Park

In late September Ampthill were drawn at home against Stockwood Park in the semi-final of the knock-out Cup. Again the team was ravaged by injury. In the event Stockwood's 10 man game plan, based on their dominant pack and the kicking of John Humphreys, succeeded and Ampthill were well beaten.

John Humphreys turned the clock back at Dillingham Park on Sunday with a masterly performance as Stockwood Park beat Ampthill 32-9 in a Beds. Cup semi-final. Humphreys, 36, boss of a tractor firm and chairman of the county selectors, directed operations from fly-half for a side that was seriously threatened only at the start of each half.

His legendary left foot created havoc in the Ampthill defence. And with his pack always in command, he was the perfect pivot between forwards and backs, youth and experience.

"We were a well beaten side", said Ampthill skipper Steve Watson. "We knew the way they would attack us, but we could do little about it. We have never beaten them. They are obviously a jinx, but we'll be back for another go next year."

"We have a simple game plan," said Stockwood captain Mark Lovell who represents the youthful section of a team with five men around the 35 mark and 10 under 25. "We are a forward orientated team with enough experience in the backs to know when and where to attack."

Red hot favourites Stockwood earned the right to stage county final on December 18 against neighbours Luton who brushed aside Queens of Bedford by 44-6.

The prize for the winners of the Beds Cup was a home tie against Towcestrians, champions of the Northampton Alliance in an East Midlands semi-final. The winners of the East Midlands Cup would go into next season's John Player first round.

Overall, this was a disappointing season for Steve Watson, numerous games were narrowly lost, with injuries being a contributing factor. Good wins over Huntingdon 32-14, Mill Hill 16-13, Bedford Athletic 9-0, Luton 9-0 were the season's highlights. However, the welcome return of Phil Argent and Kevin Moore and the debuts of Sos Randall and Graham Whitehall were reasons for optimism, as was the outstanding form of the captain.

Leigh Clark in scrum-half action against Bedford Athletic

1983-84	played	won	drawn	lost	pts. for	pts. against
1st XV	35	15	1	19	409	455
Exiles XV	32	23	0	9	669	293
3rd XV	31	17	2	11	503	305
4th XV	29	20	1	8	532	348
5th XV						
Extras XV	30	26	1	3	620	210
Bionics XV						

Tony Philips

Tony Phillips was an outstanding flanker with London Welsh, at a time when they were considered the best club team in the world. Tony played with Welsh internationals, John Dawes (now London Welsh president), JPR Williams, Gerald Davies, Mervyn Davies, John Taylor, Mike Roberts, and Geoff Evans.

Probably the best Welsh flanker never to win an international cap, Tony was a stellar member of the London Welsh teams that won the Middlesex Sevens, in 1971, 1972 & 1973. In his younger days Tony was an outstanding athlete (440 yards) and soccer player. He was to go on to coach Ampthill Rugby Club whose players had enormous respect for his coaching ability. In addition, many referees were grateful for his helpful advice from the touchline!

Dave Sprigg

Dave Sprigg retired from playing at the end of this season, having captained the Exiles for three years. The Exiles enjoyed a tremendous season winning over 70% of their games and scoring almost 700 points in the process. A Club stalwart, Dave Sprigg went on to have a successful coaching career with the Colts.

Season 1984-85 - (Captain - Steve Watson)

Officers

President	R. Dillingham
Chairman	B.S. O'Dell
Hon. Secretary	M. Plant
Hon. Treasurer	R. G. Churchill
Fixture Secretary	R. Clayton
Hon. Team Secretary	B. Clark
Main Committee	R. Clayton, P. Tookey, J. Wilkinson, P. Cadigan, S. Peacey, A. Plant

Playing

1st XV Captain	S. Watson
1st XV Vice-Captain	D. Bathe
Exiles XV Captain	A. Bailey
3rd XV Captain	N. Thompson
4th XV Captain	N. Kelliher
4th XV Vice-Captain	J. Mulhern
5th XV Captain	D. Griffiths
5th XV Vice-Captain	C. Simpson
Extras XV Captain	R. Duffin
Bionics XV	J. Wilkinson
Coach	R. Fletcher

Heart of England Merit Table

With Bedford Wanderers, London Welsh Druids and John Player hopefuls Oxford Old Boys starting the season, skipper Steve Watson was determined his players would be ready to play good adventurous rugby to overcome such tough opposition.

Watson was looking forward to the involvement in the "Heart of England Merit Table" in which he hoped to do well. This competition helped bring in more "plum" fixtures including Leicester Vipers and Barkers Butts from Coventry.

Training had been particularly well attended on the Tuesday and Thursday evenings, with a number of "new faces" turning up; players had been put through their paces by ex-Bedford three-quarter, Rob Fletcher. Rob was pleased with the response from the lads and was planning a "new style" Ampthill this season.

Rob Fletcher had played in Budge Rogers' outstanding team from 1964-69. Rob recognised that Ampthill's traditional dominant front-five no longer existed. Its strength now lay in the back row, half backs and three quarters. This made Ampthill vulnerable against strong forward packs and Rob developed innovative strategies aimed at playing to the team's strengths. These included rapid completion of scrummages and shortened lines-out. It is probably fair to say these were only partially successful, given the strength of the opposition the Club faced game by game. However, the team had tactics and a game plan they could apply to the best of their ability.

The team still contained Phil Argent at tight-head, young Paul Litchfield at loose-head and Nigel Rendle had switched to hooker. Graham Whitehall and Tony Willison combined as stalwarts in the pack. Back-rowers Steve Peacey and Steve Watson were potent weapons. The peerless Dave Parker was partnered at fly-half by Bob Wagstaff, a product of the mini-youth conveyor belt. The youth of Leigh Clark was balanced by the experience of Dennis Hardy, Duncan Bathe and Scott Goodson. Chris Hopgood's reliability at fullback was another strength of the side.

In the first game of the season what the local press regarded as a "light-weight" team put in a creditable performance in an away victory over Old Cryptians (Steve Peacey's old team) in Gloucestershire.

They were to lose their next game at home to a very good Bedford Wanderers team by 13 points to 30, where an eight containing six back-rowers was exposed.

The following Saturday Ampthill entertained the powerful London Welsh Druids knowing that their new approach would face a stern test. This was Ampthill's second meeting with London Welsh Druids and despite the final score of 7-28 they put up a creditable performance. The home team scored the only try of the first 30 minutes and Druids could only reply with penalties. However, at the end of the half Druids scored an unconverted try making the score 16-7. There was no more scoring until the final ten minutes of the game when Ampthill forwards, who had given all, tired and allowed two converted tries to make the scoreline seem very one sided.

Ampthill scrummaged well and won more than their share of second phase ball. However, their line-out could not match their prowess in other areas. The backs were in fine form and their hard running and solid tackling posed many problems for the Welsh. Half-backs Parker and Wagstaff played intelligently throughout the game and it was a kick from Wagstaff, cleared by Bathe and Peacey, that led to the break where Parker scored the try

Heart of England Merit Table

This season the Sunday Telegraph Merit Tables, the precursor competitions to leagues, were introduced. Ampthill were placed in the Heart of England Merit Table, the results were as follows:

date	opponent	venue	score	result
Sept. 22	Wigston	away	3-17	lost
Nov. 3	Barkers Butts	home	4-12	lost
Dec. 29	Bedford Athletic	home	7-8	lost
Feb. 16	Old Northamptonians	home	cancelled	
Feb. 23	Long Buckby	away	10-16	lost
Mar. 2	Stamford	home	12-15	lost
Mar. 16	Towcester	home	10-12	lost
Apr. 13	Leicester Vipers	away	16-56	lost

This was a tough Merit Table – the results would indicate a clear relegation had this been a league.

In the Alan Lovell Memorial Match played on September 19th 1984, Ampthill had 4 players in the County squad. Dave Parker played at scrum-half and Steve Watson at No.8. Steve Peacey and Duncan Bathe were replacements. Bedfordshire were narrowly beaten 10-6 by the Blues. This was the tenth match in the series, Bedfordshire's sole victory was still the 29-25 success in in 1975-76 season. Bob Wagstaff and Sos Randall would represent Bedfordshire under 23 this season.

The Club's pursuit of the Bedfordshire Knockout Cup followed a predictable path. Biggleswade were despatched 15-7 in the first round and Colworth House demolished 52-3 in the quarter - final. In the semi-final Ampthill were convincingly beaten by Leighton Buzzard, 6 points to 20.

In October, Steve Watson's men put four straight wins together over Wellingborough OGs, Wellingborough, Harrow and Banbury. In December they met Rushen & Higham the previous season's East Northamptonshire Cup winners.

This was a stylish Ampthill performance - a 25-6 thrashing of Rushden & Highams. Right from the kick-off Bob Wagstaff dictated the whole course of the game with a brilliant individual try after the forwards had won a scrum just outside the Rushden 22. He continued to cause all sorts of problems for the Rushden defence with clever running, deft handling and some nice inter-play with Duncan Bathe in the centre.

The smaller Ampthill pack completely dominated the second phase with a good display of rucking, providing scrum-half Dave Parker with quick clean possession. The second try came when Wagstaff and Bathe engineered a break in the middle of the field resulting in a score for John Hindmarch in the corner. A penalty by Wagstaff and one for Rushden made it 11-3 at half-time.

The second half started with a more determined effort by Rushden, but some excellent defensive kicking by Parker relieved the pressure and eventually, a scrum in the Rushden 22 allowed Parker to score. Further pressure resulted in another scrum in the Rushden 22 and a clever back-row move saw Graham Whitehall cross the line. Rushden kicked another penalty 10 minutes from time, but a try by Ampthill captain Steve Watson completed the scoring.

In strictly games lost, as opposed to games won, this would seem to have been a poor season. In particular the Heart of England Merit Table results were disappointing. However, a glance at the points for and against shows how easily the season could have been so different. Whenever their pack could get a toe-hold in the game, Ampthill produced some terrific running rugby. Steve Watson and coach Rob Fletcher, both sensible characters, would not have been happy with the results, but they could be quietly pleased with the performances of the team.

1984-85	played	won	drawn	lost	pts. for	pts. against
1st XV	35	13	2	20	453	496
Exiles XV	30	15	2	13	305	331
3rd XV	29	17	0	12	363	277
4th XV	30	16	2	12	395	321
5th XV	24	14	0	10	346	262
Extras XV	29	22	0	7	720	219
Bionics XV						

The Extras scored over 700 again this season, including 146 tries, 62 conversions and 4 drop goals – but no penalties!

Season 1985-86 - (Captain - Graham Whitehall)

Officers

President	R. Dillingham
Chairman	B.S. O'Dell
Hon. Secretary	M. Plant
Hon. Treasurer	R. G. Churchill
Fixture Secretary	R. Clayton
Membership Secretary	D. Hardy
Hon. Team Secretary	B. Clark
Main Committee	R. Middleton, P. Tookey, N. Brown, M. Davies, D. Hardy, D. Williams, A. Plant & P. Litchfield

Playing

1st XV Captain	G. Whitehall
1st XV Vice-Captain	D. Parker
Exiles XV Captain	P. Stokes
Exiles XV Vice-Captain	M. Jupp
3rd XV Captain	K. Collins
4th XV Captain	T. Huckle
4th XV Vice-Captain	C. Simpson
5th XV Captain	D. Griffiths
5th XV Vice-Captain	P. Britton
Extras XV Captain	R. Duffin
Coach	R. Fletcher

The Club was in its 35th year and it was clear that the first-team was in transition. Anno domini meant the old guard from the early 1980s had either retired or were playing down the Club teams. There were some very promising youngsters – products of the club's mini & youth system – coming through. However, there was no influx of experienced players that could shear up Graham Whitehall's team. As a result, for the first time in its history, the 1st XV lost 25 of the 33 games played - almost 80%.

In the team's defence, only against Bedford Wanderers 9-40, Mill Hill 0-64, Old Albanians 0-30, Leighton Buzzard 6-37, Wasps 3rds 3-27, Cheshunt 0-37 was it dismantled.

The majority of losses were by a few points; but they were losses, and Graham Whitehall showed enormous courage, resilience and leadership to keep the team together. He was to captain the team for a further two seasons, continue playing at that level and then to coach the first team. Graham had no choice but to blood youngsters like Andy Teague, Leigh Clarke, Paul Ludlow, Gavin Griffiths, Richard Beasley, John Wilkinson, Ian Burgess and Bob Smallshaw. This policy would pay-off long-term, but it was an agonising time for the skipper.

As usual, Ampthill reached the semi-final of the Bedfordshire Cup; beating Bedfordshire Police 28-0 in the first round, Dunstablians 13-4, in the next before losing to Luton 4-14 in the quarter-fnal.

Graham Whitehalls 1985-86 1st XV

back row: M. Truman, C. Hopgood, N. McKenzie, A. Bailey, P. Litchfield, P. Wright, T. Willison, L. Clark, I. Williamson
front Row: P. Day, J.Hindmarch, I. Burgess, S. Randall, G. Whitehall (capt.), D. Parker, N. Thompson, P. Argent

Heart of England Merit Table

date	opponent	venue	score	result
Sept. 28	Wigston	home	7-17	lost
Nov. 2	Barkers Butts	away	0-26	lost
Nov. 16	Bletchley	home	4-14	lost
Nov. 30	Bedford Athletic	away	6-6	draw
Feb. 15	Old Northamptonians	away	cancelled	
Feb. 22	Long Buckby	home	cancelled	
Mar. 1	Stamford	away	cancelled	
Mar. 15	Towcestrians	away	0-31	lost
Apr. 12	Leicester Vipers	home	11-39	lost
May 3	Banbury	away	no record	lost

Vic Kaye

Vic Kaye became the Club Steward, at a very perilous time as far as the functioning of the bar and, therefore the Club, was concerned. He was to serve the Club, honestly and faithfully, as Bar Steward for 24 years, standing down finally, in 2009. It is impossible to overstate the value of Vic's commitment to the Club. He also served on the main Committee from 1966-1972. Today, Vic still works tirelessly on matchdays to ensure that players, officials and visiting supporters can park satisfactorily at our small ground. He continues to tackle many tasks that others prefer not to – as a player, member and official, his contribution has been exemplary.

1985-86	played	won	drawn	lost	pts. for	pts. against
1st XV	32	7	1	24	285	725
Exiles XV	29	13	2	14	302	320
3rd XV	32	17	1	14	472	303
4th XV	27	11	1	15	318	388
5th XV	20	11	0	9	364	277
Extras XV	28	18	1	9	578	289

Season 1986-87 - (Captain - Graham Whitehall)

Officers

President	R. Dillingham
Chairman	B.S. O'Dell
Hon. Secretary	M. Plant
Hon. Treasurer	R. G. Churchill
Fixture Secretary	R. Duffin
Assis. Fixture Secretary	P. New
Hon. Team Secretary	B. Clark
Membership Secretary	D. Hardy
Main Committee	F. Henry, T. Willison, P. Litchfield, R. Phillips, M. Larby, N. Brown, M. Davies

Playing

1st XV Captain	G. Whitehall
Exiles XV Captain	P. Stokes
Exiles XV Vice-Captain	R. Middleton
3rd XV Captain	K. Collins
4th XV Captain	C. Simpson
5th XV Captain	D. Griffiths
Extras XV	R. Duffin
Bionics XV	J. Wilkinson
Coach	D. Williams, G. McIlroy

The second season of Graham's stewardship is a testimony to his persistence and resolve – the results were ground out steadily and consistently. The infallibility of hindsight allows us to see this as the development of a very powerful time in the Club's history – the best until very recent times. Then, those of us supporting the team, could not see it and found it trying, to say the least! There were, however, young players slowly finding their feet, who were to serve the Club well in the coming, more successful, seasons.

In February 1988, Ampthill won four of the weekend's six games against Leighton Buzzard.

The 1st XV finally emerged 14-12 victors at Leighton Buzzard after losing their concentration in the last 20 minutes when 14-0 ahead. Leigh Clark was prominent in both Ampthill tries before the break. First, Leigh chipped ahead into the arms of Andy Teague who scored in the left corner, and later accelerated through Leighton's back row to feed outside half Nick Reagan who went over for a try with a jink and a hand-off. Reagan converted to give Ampthill a 10-0 half-time advantage.

Ampthill continued to press after the interval and increased their lead when Teague chased down a kick to score his second try.

Leighton capitalised on some jittery play by Ampthill in their own 22 to score a try which was converted. They became more positive and inventive and put considerable pressure on Ampthill particularly when they shortened their line-outs. A deserved second try, also converted, took the home side within two points of Ampthill.

Leigh Clark could play anywhere in the three-quarters, but was now a shoe-in at scrum-half and in Nick Regan he had a half-back partner of real ability and reliability. Andy Teague had pace and a rare instinct for try-scoring. All three represented Bedfordshire with distinction, as did the skipper, Graham Whitehall.

Other notable wins that season included 33-14 away at Wigston and 22-10 away at Olney. The firsts were knocked out of the Bedfordshire Knockout Cup by Bedford Athletic 6-20.

Heart of England Merit Table

date	opponent	venue	score	result
Sept. 27	Wigston	away	33-14	won
Nov. 1	Barkers Butts	home	0-19	lost
Nov. 15	Bletchley	away	8-6	won
Nov. 29	Bedford Athletic	home	4-13	lost
Feb. 21	Old Northamptonians	home	9-9	draw
Feb. 28	Long Buckby	away	12-22	lost
Mar. 21	Towcestrians	home	no record	
Apr. 11	Leicester Vipers	away	no record	
May 2	Banbury	home	no record	

1986-87	played	won	drawn	lost	pts. for	pts. against
1st XV	32	12	2	18	346	451
Exiles XV	33	14	17	2	487	419
3rd XV						
4th XV						
5th XV						
Extras XV	34	27	2	5	652	232

Season 1987-88 - (Captain - Graham Whitehall)

Officers

President	R. Dillingham
Chairman	M. Plant
Hon. Secretary	P. Cadigan
Hon. Treasurer	R. G. Churchill
Fixture Secretary	R. Duffin
Assist. Fixture Secretary	P. New
Membership Secretary	D. Hardy
Hon. Team Secretary	B. Clark
Main Committee	F. Henry, R. Phillips, P. Litchfield, N. Brown, M. Larby, T. Willison

Playing

1st XV Captain	G. Whitehall
1st XV Vice-Captain	N. Regan
Exiles XV Captain	P. Stokes
Exiles XV Vice-Captain	M. Wells
3rd XV Captain	K. Collins
4th XV Captain	N. Kelliher
5th XV Captain	D. Griffiths
Coaches	D. Williams & G. McIlroy

During the close season major work was undertaken to improve the playing surface of the Club's two pitches. £8,000 was spent on the project, which saw heavier soil brought in from Sawford Mill. During the work, Redborne School allowed the Club the use of a pitch. In October the pitches were re-opened when Ampthill hosted Biggleswade – the visitors winning the match by nine points to six.

In Graham's third season, a sense of stability was achieved. The coaching was paying-off and the youngsters were delivering. Eighteen matches were lost, but the same number were won. In Nick Regan, vice-captain, the 1st XV had a fly-half of real class, who could control a game and put his forwards in good places. Nick was to serve the Club and County with distinction. John Wilkinson was an emerging talent at full-back, quick, strong and excellent in attack and defence – he was to go on to play for Bedford and the East Midlands.

This season Alex Radley and Ian Titman joined the Club as players; Alex in the backs and Ian in the front row. It is doubtful if the Club realised at the time how influential these two would become in the course of time. Both were to go on to become Club chairman.

League Rugby - East Midlands League 1

For the first time Ampthill played league rugby - in the East Midlands League 1, finishing comfortably in mid-table, Dunstablians were relegated that season.

In January 1988, the 1st XV played Stewarts & Lloyds. Ampthill surprised even themselves with a shock win over League supremoes Stewart and Lloyds at Dillingham Park Hot favourites S and L were riding high at the top of the East Midlands/Leicester League, one division above Ampthill. They had lost only one of nine League matches. Underdogs Ampthill pulled out all the stops to run riot over the Corby side, winning 27-13.

The clash brought joy for new number eight Andy Szymanski who scored his first try for the side in only his second appearance. Ampthill had the confidence to take the game to Stewart and Lloyds. Their back division was back to full strength and the arrival of Andy Hawke and Gavin Griffith bolstered the pack. Throwing caution to the wind, Ampthill attacked from the onset. They were quickly rewarded when left-winger Andy Teague outpaced his opposite man to score in the corner.

The pack took the initiative Hawke, Szymanski and Whitehall won second phase ball and played off the hard work of the front five. Warning bells rang when S and L scored, but scrum-half Leigh Clark replied with two tries. Nick Regan matched an earlier S and L penalty soon after the turnaround, 15-7.

Simon Jarvis was awarded a penalty try after he was held up short of the line and the steel men from Corby replied with their second try. Szymanski got this debut try from a five-metre scrum to restore the Clubs pride after the previous weeks league drubbing.

Ampthill: Litchfield, Randall, Middleton, Nouch, Griffith, Hawke, Szymanski, Whitehall, Clark, Regan, Beasley, Price, Hardy, Teague, Jarvis.

Richard Middleton had joined the Club from Bedford Swifts and joined local boys Sos Randall and Peter Litchfield in the front row. Gavin Griffiths (son of 5th team captain Doug Griffiths) joined Nouch and Whitehall at the heart of the pack. The three-quarters had the class of centre Denis Hardy and Nick Regan and there was genuine pace with Leigh Clark, Andy Teague and Richard Beasley.

Also, in January Graham Whitehall's team took on Wasps Wanderers (Wasps' second-string):

Ampthill 10 pts. Wasps Wanderers 13 pts. – 16th January 1988

A bruising battle between two aggressive packs ended with Ampthill going down to a 13-10 defeat against 14-man Wasps' Wanderers.

Hopes were high after last week's excellent triumph over high-flying Stewart and Lloyds. But the pack could not gain the upper hand, despite a Wasps' lock being sent off after half an hour for stamping.

Ampthill fielded the triumphant team that notched up the best win of the season so far. And they started confidently with try from Nick Regan after only eight minutes.

Wasps came back with a penalty, which inspired them, and bad defending by the home side gifted Wasps a try with a flowing move from their own 22.

Ampthill pulled back to 7-7 with a Leigh Clark penalty just before the controversial sending-off. But the dismissal only served to incite Wasp's efforts. The visitors piled forward and went into half-time with a 10-7 lead.

Both front rows were warned by the referee after the break as the match turned into a battle. And the pressure on Ampthill finally told when they conceded another penalty which the Wasps kicked.

Ampthill supporters were roaring with ten minutes to go as Andy Teague broke from his own half, kicked over the Wasps defence and seemed away and clear for a try. He was floored by a cynical shove from a beaten Wasps player, Leigh Clark kicked the penalty, but it was not enough to bring Ampthill back into the game.

Despite the defeat, the whole side and particularly the backs, could take pride in their display against a strong and experienced side.

Bizarrely, in March, Ampthill were beaten at Towcestrians by 73-0 after losing three players to nasty injuries.

Heart of England Merit Table

date	opponent	venue	score	result
Sept. 26	Wigston	home	no record	
Nov. 14	Bletchley	home	no record	
Feb. 20	Old Northamptonians	away	29-21	won
Feb. 27	Long Buckby	home	20-19	won
Mar. 5	Stamford	away	8-29	lost
Mar. 19	Towcestrians	away	0-73	lost
Apr. 16	Banbury	home	10-42	lost
April 23	Bedford Athletic	away	14-9	won

1987-88	played	won	drawn	lost	pts. for	pts. against
1st XV	36	18	0	18	512	569
Exiles XV						
3rd XV						
4th XV						
5th XV						
Extras XV	34	28	2	4	640	218

Season 1988-89 - (Captain - Peter Nouch)

Officers

President	R. Dillingham
Chairman	B. Clark
Hon. Treasurer & Hon. Sec.	R. G. Churchill
Assist. Hon. Secretary	M. Marsden
Fixture Secretary	R. Duffin
Assis. Fixture Secretary	P. New
Hon. Team Secretary	B. Clark
Membership Secretary	D. Hardy
Main Committee	F. Henry, G. Lasham, H. Cornforth, J.Wilkinson & M. Davies

Playing

1st XV Captain	P. Nouch
1st XV Vice-Captain	N. Regan
Exiles Captain	L. Arnold
3rd XV Captain	D. Shepherd
4th XV Captain	N. Kelliher
5th XV Captain	D. Griffiths
Extras	R. Duffin
Coach	D. Williams, G. McIlroy

Peter Nouch took over as Club Captain, Graham Whitehall having stood down after three years in charge. The first XV enjoyed a fine season with 23 games won and two drawn from 34. Pete Nouch was a terrific player and a deep thinker about the game. He formed an excellent relationship with the coaching staff, particularly with George McIlroy, and tried to move the Club away from its traditional forward-oriented game plan. The Club, through Graham Whitehall and Pete Nouch, were moving forward steadily and purposefully. The 1st XV were runners up in the league to the winners, Biggleswade.

The Club had unearthed a real try machine in Andy Teague – Pete Nouch recalls that Andy scored 30 tries that season, which is a remarkable achievement.

East Midlands League 1 – Runners-up

In the league, the Club were runners up, achieving the following record:

played	won	lost	draw	pts. for	pts. against
10	7	2	1	192	99

In January 1989, the 1st XV played a League match against Old Northamptonians:

Ampthill clocked up their twelfth successive win, taking league points from Old Northamptonians. The Ampthill forwards dominated from the start and after 15 minutes spectators were treated to one of the best tries ever seen at Dillingham Park.

From a penalty Leigh Clark slipped the ball to skipper Pete Nouch and then it went through several pairs of hands before being released along the backline for winger Andy Teague to score.

Two Nick Regan penalties and a penalty reply from ONs left the half-time score at 10-3. Another penalty from Regan put Ampthill in what appeared to be a safe position however, as the home side began to relax, a rare ONs foray into the Ampthill 22 led to a try for their No.8 which was converted.

It was hoped that this win would bolster Ampthill's confidence further as they prepared for a "giant killing" act in the semi-final of the Bedfordshire Cup against Stockwood Park on January 29 at Dillingham Park.

Bedfordshire Knockout Cup Semi-Final- 29th January 1989

In the event Ampthill narrowly lost the Beds. Cup semi-final 12-14 to Stockwood.

Brave Ampthill failed by a whisker to pull off a rugby cup miracle when the top team in the East Midlands denied them with two sensational injury time scores.

A full-house at Dillingham Park cheered on their on their heroes as little Ampthill built up a 12-0 lead to champions Stockwood Park.

However, their cheers would turn to groans as the Park, famous for their escape acts, clawed themselves back from the dead to win 14-12 and earn the right to stage the 1989 Bedfordshire Cup Final.

Going into injury time few of the bumper crowd could have foreseen any other result than an Ampthill win. However, as bodies tired and panic set in, the Park pulled it off with the last act of a pulsating game, just as they had at the same stage of the competition back in 1981.

Two penalties from the boot of Tesco executive Nick Regan gave Ampthill, playing up the hill in the first half, a 6-0 lead at half-time.

Seven minutes into the second session they were 12-0 up after scrum-half Leigh Clark passed blindside to replacement winger Stephan Biloux, who beat his man and touched down for Regan to convert to a cheer that must have been heard in Biggleswade where the hosts lost to Leighton, in similar style, 9-7 in the other semi. Biloux, became the toast of the town.

At that stage it looked all over. Cleaned up in the line-out and, for the most part out-scrummaged, Ampthill played their hearts out with skipper Pete Nouch and flanker Graham Whitehall never out of the action.

But the Park, East Midlands champions, piled on the pressure as they came back like masters and a series of clearance kicks that failed to find touch showed them the lifeline.

With 20 minutes left centre Scott Wade crashed over for a try – 12-4. The Matt Hignall, out of touch earlier, kicked a penalty – 12-7.

Just on time, Park number eight Wynne Davies, hat trick hero in the previous round against Dunstablians, touched down next to the posts. Hignall could not convert, but it was then 12-11. Then it happened. Home fans turned away as Hignall was given a chance to make amends in the fifth minute of injury time. He made no mistake with his toughest kick of the day.

Stockwood Park Sevens

However, on 23 April, Ampthill won the Stockwood Park Sevens Tournament:

Ampthill were in seventh heaven after avenging their earlier County Cup semi-final at the hands of Stockwood Park. Ampthill flattened the hosts on the way to winning the coveted Stockwood Park Sevens tournament.

Starting as underdogs, Ampthill began with a convincing 34-0 victory over Vauxhall.

Then came the clash with Stockwood Park. Park tried delaying tactics that gave themselves an hour to recover from their first match, but it was to no avail. Ampthill poured on the pressure and they emerged as 18-4 winners.

Next came Letchworth, potentially their toughest game. But Ampthill started to play some of their best flowing rugby and by half-time were 18-0 ahead. This acted as a spur to Letchworth, who responded with three tries.

Andy Teague then chose this moment to produce his slick check move to go over for a try. Their opponents ran in a late try, but Ampthill went through to the final.

In the final they faced a Welwyn side containing two quicksilver players. Justin Fletcher gave Ampthill the crucial first try, however, from a brilliant 50-yard burst. Welwyn replied but Teague, chipping on and handing off two players went through for the score to make it 10-4 at half-time.

The second half followed the pattern of the first with James Fletcher and Richard Beasley running in fine tries.

The winning team consisted of Richard Beasley, Sos Randall, James and Justin Fletcher, Ian McGregor, captain Leigh Clark and Andy Teague.

East Midlands League 1 – Runners-up

A win over Northampton Men's Own by 29-3, secured a runner-up spot in the League.

Huntingdon	home	10-10	draw
Northampton Old Scouts	home	9-17	lost
Northampton BBOB	away	15-7	won
Biggleswade	home	18-19	lost
St. Neots	away	22-6	won
Daventry	home	42-12	won
Rushden	away	12-10	won
Old Northamptonians	home	19-9	won
Brackley	away	22-10	won
Northampton Men's Own	home	29-3	won

The Club now had an abundance of talent at its disposal – most of it a product of the Alameda School production line and the burgeoning Mini & Youth section. James and Justin Fletcher and Richard Sheard had returned to Ampthill after playing for Bedford and East Midlands, and James Fletcher - the full Midlands side versus the North at Burton. The future looked very bright indeed after the dark times of the mid-1980s.

Rob Fletcher who coached Ampthill with eldest son James (Bedford, East Midland & Midlands centre)

Heart of England Merit Table

This was the final year of the Merit Table – the more serious business of league rugby was to replace it.

date	opponent	venue	score	result
Nov. 5	Bletchley	away	4-7	lost
Jan.14	Old Northamptonians	home	13-9	won
Feb. 11	Bedford Athletic	away	20-9	won
Feb. 18	Wigston	away	14-14	draw
Feb. 25	Long Buckby	away	20-19	won
Mar. 4	Stamford	home	63-3	won
Mar. 18	Towcestrians	home	cancelled	

1988-89

	played	won	drawn	lost	pts. for	pts. against
1st XV	34	23	2	9	674	478
Exiles XV	32	23	0	9	492	346
3rd XV						
4th XV						
5th XV						
Extras XV	31	17	0	14	405	340

Barrie O'Dell - 1937-1990

Barrie had played for the Club since the earliest days, captaining the Exiles and then forming the famous Bionics team. He was chairman of the Club from 1976-86 and was influential in the building of the Rugby Pavilion behind Parkside Hall and the establishment of our current facilities on Woburn Road. Barrie's legal expertise, his love of all things to do with Ampthill Rugby, but most of all his sense of fun were to be greatly missed. Like Richard Dillingham, Norman Brown, David Williams, Richard Churchill, Jack Wilkinson and Brian Clark – Barrie O'Dell was fundamental to the establishment of Ampthill Rugby Club.

At the Club's Vice-Presidents' Evening Richard Dillingham paid the following tribute to Barrie O'Dell who sadly passed away in 1990, aged 53, after a long battle with motor neurone disease:

> Sadly during last year one of our loyal members died. Barrie O'dell played for the club as a schoolboy soon after the club was re-formed in 1959. He continued to play in various teams and started the "Bionics" team in the 1970s. He became chairman of the club and his legal expertise was a great asset. He was a familiar figure in all aspects of club life and bore his illness with great courage. He loved Ampthill Rugby Club and it was his wish that his ashes should be scattered on the pitch. His wish was carried out one evening attended by relatives and many club members.

Barrie O'Dell with some of his beloved Bionics

Back Row: Paul New, Dave Cheeseman, Pete Eversley, Pete Sayer, Brian Todd, A.N.Other.

Front Row: Tony Ludlow, Mark Ellis, A.N. Other, Barrie O'Dell, Vic Kaye, Doug Simms

Season 1989-90 - (Captain - Richard Sheard)

Officers

President	R. Dillingham
Chairman	B. Clark
Hon. Treasurer & Hon. Sec.	R. G. Churchill
Assist. Hon. Secretary	M. Marsden
Fixture Secretary	R. Duffin
Assis. Fixture Secretary	P. New
Hon. Team Secretary	B. Clark
Membership Secretary	D. Hardy
Main Committee	F. Henry, G. Lasham, H. Cornforth, J.Wilkinson A. Teague, N. Brown & M. Davies

Playing

1st XV Captain	R. Sheard
1st XV Vice-Captain	P. Argent
Exiles XV Captain	L. Arnold
Exiles XV Vice-Captain	T. Willison
3rd XV Captain	C. Drea
4th XV Captain	N. Kelliher
5th XV Captain	G. Cunnif
Extras	R. Duffin
Coach	D. Williams, G. McIlroy, T. Phillips

The Captain, Richard Sheard is the son of former 1st XV full-back and Club stalwart, Bert Sheard. Richard had come through the Alameda and mini-youth conveyor belts and then went on to play for Bedford Colts with his friends James, Justin and Simon Fletcher, Tommy Gray and Ian MacGregor. Richard Sheard and James Fletcher had gained 1st team status at Bedford, so it was a major coup for the Club when they returned. In Richard's first season as captain, the Club won promotion to East Midland & Leicestershire League from East Midlands 1. Richard lead a young, talented and quickly maturing group of players. The first game of the season – a 39-9 dismissal of St. Albans - saw John Wilkinson making his debut. John Wilkinson and Michael Tanner were two of the best local players the Club has ever produced – both would go on to have stellar rugby careers. Michael and his elder brother, David (another outstanding forward) were the sons of the local scoutmaster who had persuaded Dave Williams to give rugby coaching to the boy-scouts. This, of course, was the beginning of the much-acclaimed Ampthill Mini & Youth section.

East Midlands League 1 - Winners

Promotion from East Midlands/Leicestershire Division 1 was clinched with a fine away win at Northampton Men's Own . Half time saw the score at 9-6 to the home side. However, drop goals by Sheard and Clark, a penalty from Wilkinson and a fine try from Gavin Griffith sealed a 9-19 win.

Huntingdon	home	13-9	won
Northampton BBOB	away	4-12	lost
Corby	away	30-16	won
Wellingborough O.Gs	home	30-3	won
Daventry	away	10-6	won
Rushden	home	19-3	won
Wellingborough	away	17-10	won
Old Northamptonians	away	19-9	won
Brackley	home	16-6	won
Northampton Men's Own	away	19-9	won

This season, the team's league record in the East Midlands League 1 was:

played	won	lost	draw	pts. for	pts. against
11	10	1	0	192	98

The sole loss was at home to Northampton BBOBs 4-12. Missing five injured players, Ampthill just about held their own in the first half. They went ahead early in the second half when Andy Teague scored after collecting a long pass from Leigh Clark. But BBOBs came back strongly, scoring a try in the corner which was converted. The game was then nicely poised until Paul Ludlow had to leave the field injured. The Ampthill forwards looked the worse for wear in the closing stages and a concerted effort from the visitors was rewarded with another converted try.

However, the 1st XV was promoted into East Midlands/Leicestershire Alliance League.

Notable victories in the league included; Wellingborough O.Gs 30-3, Corby away 30-16 and Northampton Old Scouts away 21-17 and away to Northampton Men's Own 19-9. In friendly games London Welsh Druids were beaten 10-9, a President's XV 46-37, Seven Rivers, on tour from the USA, 21-18.

Bedfordshire Knockout Cup

In the first round of the Bedfordshire Knockout Cup, the Club beat Potton by 102-11, a record score! 20 tries were scored, including 5 for Andy Teague; Ian MacGregor converting 11 of them. Ampthill were to lose in the Beds Cup semi-final to Leighton Buzzard 10-21, but gave the visitors, from 3 leagues above, a real fright when they lead 7-0 early on. Leighton lost to Stockwood 6-16 in the final.

In January 1990 George McIlroy was in charge of his last game as coach and manager when the 1st XV beat Old Northamptonians 17-7 away. As well as playing in the first team at Ampthill; George had played at a high level in Ireland and in the forces. He was a strong and mobile loose-head prop. A popular Club member, George was a deep thinker about the game and was a good manager of players.

In the author's opinion, Richard Sheard's side were to go on to become the second "great" team in the Club's history, better even than Bob Clayton's team in the late 1970s and early 1980s. It is fair to say that a number of the players would not have been out of place in the team playing Championship rugby today.

The 1st XV lost only 5 games this season. They lost to Leighton Buzzard in the Beds. Knockout Cup by 10-21. They also lost to Nuneaton Extra 1sts by 20-23, to Syston 6-7, to Long Buckby 16-28 and BBOB 9-32 in the League. James Fletcher, Justin Fletcher, Ian MacGregor, John Wilkinson, Paul Ludlow, and Tom Gray played for Bedfordshire and Justin Fletcher and John Wilkinson for the East Midlands Under 21 XV.

Brigadier Michael Tanner OBE RM

Michael Tanner who performed outstandingly for the Club in the last two seasons left to join the Royal Marines. He was capped by England under 21 against Ireland and played for Richmond, England Students, Royal Navy, Combined Services, as well as Bedfordshire.

A serving officer, Mike joined the Royal Marines in 1989. His Lieutenant Colonel appointments include EA to the Second Sea Lord, Commanding Officer of Commando Training and author of the Royal Marines 2010 SDSR communications strategy. He is currently Chief of Staff Navy Command (HQ). He took command of 45 Commando Group in January 2012 and deployed the Commando soon after on HMS Illustrious. He holds a Masters (MA) degree in Defence Studies (Kings College). He was awarded a Presidential citation and the US Bronze Star with Combat Valour decoration for his part in the assault into An Nasiriyah in 2003, and a Queen's Commendation for Valuable Service for his time in Iraq in 2005.

He is a former professional rugby player with Richmond RFC, with international caps at England U21 and the Combined Services. Previously he was Captain of the Base Portsmouth and in 2016 appointed as Commandant of the Commando Training Centre Lympstone.

Mike Tanner, OBE RM

Ampthill 10 pts. London Welsh Druids 9 pts. - Sunday 3rd September 1989

A penalty in the last minute gave Ampthill a dramatic 10-9 victory in a hard game at Dillingham Park.

However, a narrow victory was no more than Ampthill deserved for a determined effort against their illustrious opponents. Their intentions were shown early on when full-back John Wilkinson pulled off a thundering tackle. And the constant pressure brought its reward when Welsh dropped the ball in the centre. Mel Seacome gathered and drew the defence before sending skipper Richard Sheard on a thirty-yard gallop to the line. Just before the break the lead was increased to 7-0 when Ian MacGregor kicked a penalty. Welsh hit back with a penalty of their own. They then put Ampthill under intense pressure for 15 minutes and eventually scored from a scrum. The conversion gave the London Welsh Druids a 9-7 lead. But Ampthill were not finished and drove upfield. The charge was halted illegally and MacGregor calmly slotted the ball over the bar.

Ampthill: J. Wilkinson, A. Teague, Mel Seacome, S. Biloum, I. Burgess, R. Sheard, J. Fletcher, L. Clark, S. Voysey, T. Gray, I. MacGregor, G. Whitehall, P. Ludlow, S. Peacey, P. Dobson, G. Griffiths, M. Rose, S. Randall, P. Litchfield, I. Titman

1989-90	played	won	drawn	lost	pts. for	pts. against
1st XV	34	29	0	5	902	392
Exiles XV	20	10	1	9	280	309
3rd XV	18	15	1	2	426	130
4th XV	17	12	0	5	388	206
5th XV	12	5	1	6	28	65
Extras XV	31	21	0	10	668	293

Paul Dobson and Tommy Gray in action against London Welsh

Leading by example – Ampthill skipper Richard Sheard scoring the important try against London Welsh

10 Year Fixture Comparison (1st XV) 1980-1990

Sept.	1980/81	Sept.	1990/91
	St. Neots		St. Albans
	Ruislip		Huntingdon *
	Oxford Old Boyd		
	Wigston		Northampton Old Scouts *
	Stockwood Park		Luton
Oct.		Oct.	
	Wellingborough		Milton Keynes
	Harrow		Northampton BBOB *
	Tottonians		Stewarts & Lloyds
	Mill Hill		Corby *
Nov.		Nov.	
	Wasps		Bletchley
	Huntingdon		Wellingborough O.G. *
	Bletchley		Daventry *
	Tabard		Rushden *
	Harpenden		
Dec.		Dec.	
	Old Cryptians		Esher
	Rushden		Barnet
	Opening Game v. Beds.		Royston
	Colworth		
Jan.		Jan.	
	Olney		Wellingborough *
	Buckingham		Old Northamptonians *
	Old Albanians		
	Wellingborough O.G.		Saffron Waldon
	Luton		
Feb.		Feb.	
	Leighton Buzzard		Leighton Buzzard
	Bedford Athletic		Bedford Athletic
	Kibworth		Wigston
	Stevenage		Long Buckby
Mar.		Mar.	
	Stamford		Stamford
	Bishop Stortford		Hitchin
	Towcester		Towcestrians
	Bacavians		Cheshunt
			Brackley *
Apr.		Apr.	
	Bedford Wanderers (Wed.)		Olney
	Biggleswade		
	Cambridge		
	Club Official Opening v. Public School W.		Northampton Men's Own *
	Dunstablians		
	Old Yardlians		*League Matches

Chapter 6 – The Nineties – Silverware at Last!

Season 1990-91 – 40th Anniversary – (Captain – Richard Sheard)

Officers

President	R. Dillingham
Chairman	B. Clark
Hon. Treasurer & Hon. Sec.	R. G. Churchill
Assist. Hon. Secretary	M. Marsden
Fixture Secretary	R. Duffin
Assis. Fixture Secretary	P. New
Hon. Team Secretary	B. Clark
Membership Secretary	D. Hardy
Committee	G. Lasham, C. Hopgood, A. Teague, M. Gonse

Playing

1st XV Captain	R. Sheard
1st XV Vice-Captain	T. Gray
Exiles XV Captain	I. Burgess
Exiles XV Vice-Captain	J. Wood
3rd XV Captain	C. Drea
3rd XV Vice-Captain	S. Stanbridge
4th XV Captain	N. Kelliher
4th XV Vice-Captain	M. Desquesnes
5th XV Captain	F. Dimmock
Extras XV Captain	R. Duffin
Coach	D. Williams, T. Phillips, S. Peacey

East Midlands/Leicestershire Alliance League

In its fortieth season, the Club's 1st XV played in the East Midlands/ Leicestershire Alliance League, with Lutterworth, Long Buckby, Bedford Athletic, Aylestone St. James, Belgrave, Northampton Trinity, Luton, Coalville, Wellingborough and Stoneygate.

The league campaign saw Bedford Athletic achieve promotion, with Ampthill finishing third.

League results this season were:

Lutterworth	home	22-10
Long Buckby	away	26-6
Bedford Athletic	home	3-13
Northampton Trinity	away	45-8
Luton	home	9-3
Coalville	away	6-16
Wellingborough	home	27-14
Stoneygate	away	19-10

Other notable victories for the 1st XV included: Shelford 26-15, Royston 58-0, Leighton Buzzard 20-10. London Welsh Druids won the, by now, regular "friendly" by 19-9.

John Wilkinson, Andy Teague, Ian Marshall, Ian McGregor, Leigh Clark, Tommy Gray and Graham Whitehall all represented Bedfordshire, in the Gordon Ascroft Cup this season.

Bedfordshire Knockout Cup

The Bedfordshire Cup campaign had a distressingly predictable outcome for Ampthill. They were defeated 7-13 away at Stockwood Park - their regular nemesis. Ampthill were confident of gaining revenge for the defeat two years earlier when they were beaten in injury time by Stockwood. However, league form held-up in the quarter-final as they were beaten in the Luton mud.

Commenting afterwards, Jack Wilkinson said, "It was a question of their big forwards against our backs, who are the best in the county. We had 75 per cent of the territorial advantage but our three-quarters were denied the possession which would have won it for us. When they gave the ball to the backs it never got further than their fly-half."

Ian MacGregor kicked Ampthill's penalty and Tommy Gray scored a try against Stockwood Park.

Justin Fletcher on the charge against Stockwood Park in the mud, supported by Leigh Clark & Paul Farthing – 18th November 1990

Until the arrival of the Tongans, Justin Fletcher and Tommy Gray were, arguably, the most abrasive forwards Ampthill had ever produced (Slim Clark might disagree!).

Led by the youthful Ian Burgess, the Exiles enjoyed a very successful and high-scoring season, amassing nearly a thousand points. Lutterworth were beaten 52-0, Gosford 46-0, Aylestone St. James 51-4, Bletchley 58-0 and Royston 90-0.

1990-91	played	won	drawn	lost	pts. for	pts. against
1st XV	32	24	0	8	718	357
Exiles XV	33	25	0	8	929	281
3rd XV						
4th XV						
5th XV						
Extras XV	32	20	2	10	691	311

The Extras scored 83 tries this season, converting 38, no penalties kicks were attempted.

Season 1991-92 – (Captain – Richard Sheard)

This season floodlights were erected and this transformed training nights, under the guidance of Tony Phillips and Dave Williams. The 1st XV continued to play in the East Midlands/ Leicestershire League.

Officers

President	R. Dillingham
Chairman	B. Clark
Hon. Treasurer & Hon. Sec.	R. G. Churchill
Assist. Hon. Secretary	M. Marsden
Fixture Secretary	R. Duffin
Hon. Team Secretary	B. Clark
Membership Secretary	D. Hardy
Committee	J. Wilkinson, J. Johnson, S. Powell, A. Teague, T. West

Playing

1st XV Captain	R. Sheard
1st XV Vice-Captain	T. Gray
Exiles XV Captain	I. Burgess
Exiles XV Vice-Captain	N. Watson
3rd XV Captain	C. Drea
3rd XV Vice-Captain	L. Barlow
4th XV Captain	N. Kelliher
4th XV Vice-Captain	M. Desquesnes
5th XV Captain	F. Dimmock
Extras XV Captain	R. Duffin
Coach	D. Williams, T. Phillips

Bedfordshire Knockout Cup

Biggleswade were nudged aside 10-9 in the quarter-final, and Bedford Athletic 12-6 in the semi-final.

The search for a first ever Bedfordshire Knockout Cup title continued. With home advantage Ampthill were confident of lifting the cup against Leighton Buzzard on February 16, their first final for 10 years.

Having disposed of holders Biggleswade in the second round, they showed in the shock 12-6 semi-final win at Bedford Athletic on Sunday that they have a back division to terrify anyone.

Skipper Richard Sheard said, "Everyone wanted to be in their first ever final. Bedford Athletic had a very good pack on paper, but they just didn't play!"

Ampthill were outgunned in the scrum by a powerful Bedford Athletic pack that had former Blues Gerald Bygraves and Andy Walne at prop and County hooker Kevin Ward took four against the head. But the lineouts gave Ampthill surprisingly amounts of possession and their forwards were much quicker in the loose play.

The real difference was in the backs with Gavin Burger, James Fletcher and Andy Teague threatening every time they were given a yard of space. Both sides missed early penalties before Steve Turner opened the scoring for Athletic from in front of the posts after 10 minutes.

Concerted Ampthill pressure came to nothing with Burger pulled down just a yard short after a storming run. And, midway through the half Turner landed an identical penalty for 6-0. Ampthill were indebted to full back John Wilkinson who showed his defensive qualities to save a certain try.

Athletic would have been mightily relieved to turn around in front but, in injury time, they were pegged back in dramatic fashion. A missed tackle in midfield allowed James Fletcher a run and created a two-man overlap. His pass to Teague was deliberately punched clear by home winger Robin Robinson and referee Ian Bullerwell awarded the penalty try which MacGregor converted. Six minutes into the second half Ampthill led for the first time thanks to a MacGregor penalty, in off the left post. Turner missed a couple he would normally expect to get before, in the last minute, MacGregor made sure with another penalty, this time in off the right post.

Win or lose in the final, Ampthill were guaranteed a place in the East Midlands Cup. The winners of that go into next season's Pilkington Cup first round.

In the other semi-final Leighton Buzzard, who reached last year's final as well, were too strong for Stockwood Park. The sides were locked at 3-3 when the half-time whistle went.

Nick Watkins added a drop-goal and a penalty before Leighton wrapped up victory with late tries by Jimmy Goodier and Adrian Carne.

Ampthill were the surprise package of the competition having already shocked two teams from further up the league pyramid. Richard Sheard had this to say before the Final:

"We're going to give it our best shot. We are aware of the opposition and their strengths but we don't underestimate ourselves. If we put our minds to it and play together on the day, we can win. Nobody expected us to beat Biggleswade and the no-one expected us to beat Bedford Athletic. We've been the underdogs all the way and we will be underdogs again. That suits us because there will be no pressure."

Back row: **Richard Middleton, Pete Nouch, Tom Gray, Gavin Griffiths, Tony Willison, , Paul Ludlow, John Wilkinson, Graham Whitehall, Mark Lavery**

Front Row: **Pete Litchfield, Leigh Clark, James Fletcher, Richard Sheard (capt.), Ian MacGregor, Dave Tomkins, Gavin Burger, Andy Teague**

Ampthill's Third Bedfordshire Cup Final – February 16th 1992

Ampthill 13pts. Leighton Buzzard 15pts.

Ampthill's fly-half Ian MacGregor missed a late penalty, as his side was denied a famous victory in the closing stages of the cup final. Having seen favourites Leighton Buzzard claw their way back from a 13-0 deficit to lead 15-13, MacGregor hooked his 25-yard chance wide, from in front of the posts.

It was cruel luck on the home side who had looked set to continue their giant killing feats, but they found the power of the Midlands Division One side just too strong to resist.

MacGregor had opened the scoring with a seventh minute penalty and after Leighton's Nick Watkins saw his penalty hit the post. The home side produced some sterling defensive work.

MacGregor had also missed with two further efforts, but Ampthill, playing down the slope, were always the more willing to give their backs the ball, and it was no surprise when full-back John Wilkinson raced over to put his side 7-0 in front after 34 minutes. MacGregor converted from the touchline, and just four minutes later it was James Fletcher who crashed his way through to the delight of the packed crowd.

But at 13-0 down Leighton managed two vital scores either side of the interval, with a Jimmy Goodier penalty and Watkins added another drop goal to reduce the deficit to 13-9.

Fletcher was forced off by injury, but the Ampthill defence held firm until just seven minutes from time, when Leighton Buzzard hooker Ben Irvine pounced on a loose ball to score. Goodier converted for a 15-13 lead, but with four minutes remaining MacGregor had his chance to regain the lead.

Sadly, the penalty went wide, and despite six minutes of injury time, Ampthill could not find another opening. But they could be justifiably proud of their first final appearance for 10 years.

East Midlands Cup

In March, Ampthill were away to Huntingdon in the East Midlands Cup quarter-finals – their reward for reaching the Bedfordshire Cup Final.

Against Huntingdon, Ampthill struggled in the first half, before running out 23-9 winners. They drew mighty Towcestrians, the holders, from 3 leagues higher in National 4 North. Not surprisingly Ampthill lost by 3-29.

Skipper Richard Sheard said, "We were not disgraced . They are one of the best 55 teams in the country …… it took us 25 minutes to adjust to the pace they were playing at." At half-time Ampthill trailed 15-3 but, after James Fletcher left the field with concussion, the team lost its most influential player of the season and never really troubled the visitors.

East Midlands/Leicestershire League

Results

Lutterworth	away	11-7	won
Hinkley	home	12-26	lost
Kettering	away	16-15	won
Aylestone St. James	home	30-10	won
Belgrave	away	0-18	lost
Northampton BBOB	home	26-3	won
Luton	away	14-17	lost
Coalville	home	19-9	won
Wellingborough	away	16-12	won
Stoneygate	home	21-38	lost

Not a great league campaign, but the 1st XV moved into Midlands East League Division 1 for 1992/93, as the leagues were re-structured. The new league was an amalgamation of East Midlands, Leicester, and Notts. Lincs. & Derbyshire, which meant travel as far as Chesterfield, Hinkley and Scunthorpe.

Ampthill Colts

Clearly, the establishment of the Colts was a major step forward and their captain Robert Campbell was fortunate indeed to have Denis Hardy and Dave Sprigg – two of the best players to have worn the maroon & amber – to lead the coaching and organisation. Getting a Colts XV established – even on the back of a thriving mini & youth section – was no walk in the park. The Colts were to exceed everyone's expectations in the seasons to come.

1991-92	played	won	drawn	lost	pts. for	pts. against
1st XV	30	20	0	10	810	720
Exiles XV						
3rd XV						
4th XV	28	19	1	8	710	244
5th XV						
Extras XV	32	20	2	10	691	311
Colts XV	17	11	1	5	313	253

Season 1992-93 – (Captain – David Tompkins)

Officers

President	R. Dillingham
Chairman	B. Clark
Hon. Treasurer & Hon. Sec.	R. G. Churchill
Assist. Hon. Secretary	M. Marsden
Fixture Secretary	R. Duffin
Hon. Team Secretary	B. Clark
Membership Secretary	D. Hardy
Committee	J. Wilkinson, R. Golder, S. Powell, A. Teague, T. West

Playing

1st XV Captain	D. Tomkins
1st XV Vice-Captain	J. Fletcher
Exiles XV Captain	I. Burgess
Exiles XV Vice-Captain	R. Mortimer & A. Dadley
3rd XV Captain	C. Hopgood
3rd Xv Vice-Captain	T. Willison
4th XV Captain	N. Anderson
4th XV Vice-Captain	S. McCrindle
5th XV Captain	L. Mogridge
Extras XV Captain	R. Duffin
Colts XV	Robert Campbell (Capt.) Denis Hardy & Dave Sprigg (coaches)
Coach	Graham Whitehall

This season the 1st XV played in Midlands East League Division 1, finishing third, with Amber Valley, Belgrave, Chesterfield, Dronfield, Hinkley, Luton, Mellish, Scunthorpe, Spalding, Stewart & Lloyds, Stoneygate and West Bridgford.

In December 1992, the 1st XV won a notable victory over Rosslyn Park 2nd XV by 22 points to 15.

Bedfordshire Knockout Cup

For the followers of Ampthill in the Championship today, it may be difficult to appreciate how winning the Bedfordshire Cup had become the holy grail for the Club. Bob Clayton's teams lost the 1977/78 final away to Stockwood Park by 4-20 and at home to Bedford Athletic by 3-9, in season 1982-83. In 1991-92 Richard Sheard's side narrowly lost to Leighton Buzzard 13-15. These were bitter pills to swallow for a proud Club, which had come to measure its progress and success by its yearning for a Bedfordshire Knockout Cup win. However, Dave Tomkins led a team that was a blend of youth and experience and possessed real pace.

Ampthill reached the final by beating Colworth House in round one, Luton in round two 23-12 and Bedford Athletic in the semi-final. Scrum-half Leigh Clark scored both tries in the 17-14 defeat of Bedford Athletic, to secure a second successive County Final.

Queens RUFC were the first unseeded club ever to reach the final. Under the guiding hand of coach and captain, ex-Blue's player Richard Millard, they had beaten teams five and four leagues above them – Leighton Buzzard 12-11 and Biggleswade 10-0, respectively. Bedford Queens were undoubtedly the underdogs. The irony of this was not lost on the Ampthill club, usually cast in that rôle themselves in the Bedfordshire Cup.

Round 2 of Beds. Cup: Ampthill beat Luton – 23-12 on 29th February 1992

From the left: Richard Beasley, Danny Phillips, Paul Talling, Graham Whitehall, Gavin Griffiths (on floor), Tom Gray & Leigh Clark

From the left: Gavin Griffiths, Tom Gray, Danny Phillips, Graham Whitehall on the charge

Ampthill's Fourth Bedfordshire Cup Final – Queens v. Ampthill – February 7th 1993

Bedford Queens 9pts. - Ampthill 21pts.

Bedford Queen's giant-killing exploits came to an end, as Ampthill lifted the Beds County Cup at Allen Park.

Queen's dream of victory in their first cup final appearance in a 75-year history was very much alive un the opening stages of the match, as they took a 9-3 lead, with three Andy Moffat penalties to one kick from Ampthill's Ian MacGregor.

But Ampthill were determined not to go the same way as Leighton Buzzard and Biggleswade, Queen's victims in the previous rounds.

Ampthill hit back with 18 unanswered points to erase the memory of last season's cup final defeat by Leighton. MacGregor added a further penalty, Danny Phillips raced over for a try, converted by MacGregor, with the latter then kicking his third penalty for a 16-9 half-time lead.

Pete Bailey's second half try sealed the game. Both Queens and Ampthill would now line up in the East Midlands Cup.

Ampthill: P. Talling, S. Gilbert, P. Litchfield, G. Whitehall, G. Griffiths, R. Beasley, T. Gray, D. Phillips, L. Clarke, I. MacGregor, D. Tomkins (capt.), R. Sheard, J. Fletcher, P. Bailey, J. Wilkinson

subs: A. Dadley, A. Szymanski

Queens: T. Hewitt, D. Stapleton, S. Lousada, A. Radnor, S. Pierce-Roberts, B. Aceto, Richard Millard (capt.), D. Fayle, J. Cunningham, T. Durak, T. Iaciofano, C. Holloway, D. Twigden, S. Smith, A. Moffat

Subs: K. McMillan, Ian Seagar

A week after this historic victory, Ampthill were drawn away at Scunthorpe in the league. In their worst performance of the season they were mauled by the strong home pack and were comprehensively beaten by 39-0. Ampthill's cloak of invincibility was to be severely tested the next week when the club met Kettering, a team a league below, in the quarter-final stage of the East Midlands Cup – a game they were expected to win.

East Midlands Cup Quarter Final

Ampthill 6pts. Kettering 27pts. – Sunday, February 21st 1993

There was no joy for the Beds County Cup winners in the quarter-finals. Newly crowned county champions Ampthill lost 27-6 at home to Kettering. Trailing 13-6 at the interval, Amps were unable to take advantage of the elements in the second period. Meanwhile an injury-hit Bedford Queens went out 42-0 at Peterborough.

Midlands East League – Division 1

Results

Amber Valley	home	28-9	won
Chesterfield	home	14-13	won
Dronfield	away	11-10	won
Hinkley	home	15-22	lost
Luton	away	23-12	won
Mellish	home	8-0	won
Scunthorpe	away	0-39	lost
Spalding	home	31-18	won
Stewart & Lloyds	away	15-18	lost
Stoneygate	home	26-14	won
West Bridgford	away	31-22	won

Ampthill finished in third place in Midlands East Division 1. The following players represented Bedfordshire this season; Leigh Clark, Richard Sheard, James Fletcher, John Wilkinson, Gavin Griffiths, Paul Talling, Danny Phillips. Additionally, John Wilkinson and James Fletcher played for the East Midlands.

John Wilkinson

John is the son of Ampthill legend Jack Wilkinson, so it was inevitable that he would take up the game. Whilst Jack was a number eight, John was clearly destined to play in the three-quarters. With the pace of a winger and the skills of a fly-half, John became the complete full-back in attack and defence.

He played in an outstanding Ampthill back-line including Leigh Clark, Ian MacGregor, James Fletcher, Richard Sheard, Andy Teague and Gavin Burger. On their day, they were a devastating unit that would not have disgraced the Championship today. They had all come up through local schools and the Club's mini and youth system and most had attended the Blue's finishing school – the Bedford Colts.

John Wilkinson, having represented Bedfordshire, was called into the East Midlands squad for season 1992-93 – together with James Fletcher. Against Staffordshire, East Midlands recorded their first win in the ADT County Championship for three-years. John scored a try and created another, as East Midlands fought back to win 26-22.

John's performances earned him a place in the East Midland team to play the Barbarians in the Mobbs Memorial Match at Franklin's Gardens on Wednesday March 10, 1993. The Mobbs Memorial Match in the amateur era, was an outstanding day in the annual calendar – in 1993 it was 72 years since the first Mobbs game was played at the Gardens in memory of Edgar Mobbs. Mobbs was the Northampton and England captain who had died at the Battle of Passchendaele during the First World War.

At that time, John Wilkinson and James Fletcher were only the third Ampthill players to be selected for the East Midlands, following Dave Parker. However, no other player had been selected for such a prestigious game and the Club was extremely proud of John's achievement. He received letters of congratulations from both Richard Churchill and Brian Clark (Ampthill Committee) and also John Humphreys (East Midlands Committee).

In the event John Wilkinson, the only player from a junior club, was to score a brilliant 70 metre try against a very strong Barbarians side who won by 77 points to 55 in front of a crowd of 4,000 at Franklins Gardens.

The clash with the Barbarians was a family affair for former Ampthill No.8 Jack Wilkinson. Jack's grandson, Paul Gilroy, is John's nephew, and he was in the under 12 team that met Northampton Old Scouts in the curtain-raiser before the Mobbs showdown. It is only played at under 10 and under 12 – always before the clash with the Barbarians – but the Ampthill club achieved the amazing feat of reaching the final at both age-groups. At this time, Jack Wilkinson was also the Bedfordshire County Team Secretary and the Bedfordshire representative on the East Midlands Cup Committee.

Mobbs Memorial Match – Wed. 10th March 1993 at Franklins Gardens

John Wilkinson's famous try

East Midlands 59 pts. Barbarians 70 pts.

In a game that would have given a defence coach of today nightmares, twenty-two tries were scored at Franklin's Gardens.

The Barbarians won by six goals and seven tries to seven goals and two tries to the hosts. Simon Geoghegan, the Irish international winger, ran in four tries.

Undoubtedly, the most memorable try was scored by Ampthill's John Wilkinson, who ran 70 metres for East Midlands fifth try.

East Midlands: J. Wilkinson (Ampthill), J. Chandler (Bedford), R. MacNaughton (Northampton), R. Glover (Rugby), B. Ward, S. Tubb, D. Elkington, (Northampton), L. Mansell, M. Howe (Bedford), C. Allen (Northampton), P. Alston (Bedford), G. Webster, J. Etheridge, P. Pask (capt..), W. Shelford (Northampton).

Barbarians: I. Hunter (Northampton & England), S. Geoghegan (London Irish & Ireland), F. Packman (Northampton), H. Woodland (Neath), R. Wallace (Garryowen & Ireland), A. Davies (Cardiff & Wales), Richard Moon (Rosslyn Park), Rupert Moon (Llanelli capt.), M. Linnett (Moseley & England), N. Meek (Pontypool & Wales), H. Williams-Jones (S. Wales Police & Wales), T. Rodber (Northampton & England), S. Lloyd (Moseley), N. Back (Leicester), G. Weir (Melrose & Scotland,). Referee: F. Howard -(Liverpool) Attendance 3,500

Mobbs Curtain Raiser under 12 v. Northampton Old Scouts

Ampthill Under 12s on the charge at Northampton, under the watchful eye of coach Jack Wilkinson

Ampthill Colts – Rugby World's - "Youth Team of the Month"

In its first full season the Colt's record was a remarkable:

played	won	drew	lost	pts. for	pts. against
22	20	0	2	709	194

The Colts lost only 2 games, both to Stockwood Park; 5 – 14 in the Bedfordshire Cup Final and 5 – 24, in the final of the East Midlands Cup. In December 1992 the Rugby World publication made Ampthill Colts "Youth Team of the Month". Robert Campbell, Simon Spavins, Paul Smedley, Jonathan Bugg, Mark Cheeseman, Mark Green, Johnny Sprigg and Steve Gyau-Awuah played for Bedfordshire Colts against the Army.

In the East Midlands Cup, the Colts beat Men's Own 51-0, Old Scouts 22-21, Wellingborough 86-0, Kettering 25-8, before losing to Stockwood Park in the final.

East Midlands Colts Cup Final

An injury-hit Ampthill Colts side lost 24-5 to Luton's Stockwood Park in the East Midlands Cup Final, at Dillingham Park. But they could look back on a fine campaign, with just two defeats in 22 games this season – ironically both to Stockwood. The visitors led 7-0 at half-time and added another try soon after, before Ampthill's hopes were raised by a try from Robert Campbell. However, Stockwood added two more tries and a conversion to secure their victory.

1992-93	played	won	drawn	lost	pts. for	pts. against
1st XV	30	20	2	8	551	502
Exiles XV						
3rd XV						
4th XV						
5th XV						
Extras XV	30	23	0	7	671	371
Colts XV	22	20	0	2	709	194

Ampthill Colts

Changes at the breakdown – the law of unintended consequences.

In 1992, the laws were changed at the breakdown – having a profound effect on rugby union, particularly the ruck. Until then, if a ruck ended indeterminately, a scrum was awarded to the team moving forward. The new laws were meant to speed up the game and to have fewer dead balls. Arguably it had the opposite effect. Overnight, instead of the stirring sight of two sets of forwards hunting as a pack, the teams disengaged and stood in two lines across the field, as in rugby league. Indeed, international and club teams came to employ ex-rugby league players such as Sean Edwards and Andy Farrell to coach the defensive duties.

Whilst many forwards today will have welcomed this "freedom", many older observers will rue the lack of room for three-quarter play, because of a field littered with forwards. Other unwanted consequences including the dominance of defence, concussions from high tackles and the increase in tactical kicking – arguably – stem from this law change.

Paradoxically these changes coincided with a dominant phase in Ampthill's history, but in truth the club had traditionally relied on a strong set-piece and first phase possession.

Season 1993-94 – (Captain – Ian MacGregor)
Officials

President	R. Dillingham
Chairman	B. Clark
Hon. Treasurer & Hon. Sec.	R. G. Churchill
Assist. Hon. Secretary	M. Marsden
Fixture Secretary	R. Duffin
Hon. Team Secretary	B. Clark
Membership Secretary	H. Cornforth
Committee	P. Sherry, S. Powell, A. Teague, T. West, J. Wilkinson

Playing

1st XV Captain	I. MacGregor
1st XV Manager	I. Owen
Exiles XV Captain	Kevin Anderson
Exiles XV Manager	S. Marsden
3rd XV Captain	C. Hopgood
4th XV Captain	L. Mogridge
5th XV Captain	A. Barnard
Extras XV Captain	R. Duffin
Main Committee	P. Sherry, S. Powell, A. Teague
Colts XV	L. Matthews (Capt.) Denis Hardy & Dave Sprigg (coaches)
Coach	Graham Whitehall, T. Phillips, G. McIlroy

Norman Brown was President of the East Midlands Rugby Union for 1993/94 – a great honour for the Club and a fitting tribute to Norman's contribution to rugby in the region.

All the talk, for the first few weeks of the new season, was over how the first-team would cope without John Wilkinson (Bedford), Tom Gray (London Scottish) and Danny Phillips (Saracens). In the event the 1st XV won their first six games; Old Laurentians, Dunstablians, Huntingdon, Bedford Athletic and Rushden fell by the wayside before Colworth House were thrashed in the Bedfordshire Cup 45-16 a score that flattered the Sharnbrook side. Newcomer Dave Robertson made a promising start in the 15 shirt and Justin Fletcher and Richard Beasley grabbed their chance of a regular place in the side.

The last game of October saw Ampthill notch its best win for a few years when Wigston were dispatched by 71-7. Numerous scorers included, two tries for Bobby Parker making his first team debut, a pair for Andy Teague and Dave Robertson's first touchdown for the Club.

Harry Cornforth

Harry Cornforth became Chairman of the Bedfordshire Rugby Football Union; he was to serve from 1993-95. Some years later, having moved back to the North East, Harry served on the Committee of Tyndale Rugby Club and is currently an independent non-executive director of the Northumberland Rugby Union.

The Club continued to play in Midlands East League Division 1. This was the first season in the Club's history that the 1st XV had a manager, but it was a significant step. However, the manager's role was to take a while to become firmly established at the Club.

Ian MacGregor, Club Captain, was a local product of the Alameda School whose PE master, Will Hunt, was an inspirational teacher of rugby, but he also came up through the Club's mini & youth section. Ian was an excellent fly-half, quick, inventive, and complemented a fine back-line – the best the Club had seen. He was also a prolific goal-kicker, one of the very best in the Club's history.

Ivor Owen

The 1st XV manager, Ivor Owen had been a player and loyal servant of the Club using his experience of the construction industry to great benefit. He was a key element in the construction of the Pavilion behind Parkside Hall.

An eminently practical man, Ivor worked closely with Ian MacGregor to ease the load and to establish the importance of the new role.

Bedfordshire Knockout Cup

In the Bedfordshire Cup Ampthill reached the semi-final but lost 8-13 to Bedford Athletic. In the East Midlands Cup, Ampthill went out in the quarter final, losing 6-7 to Kettering at Dillingham Park.

Disaster: Kettering pile over for their first try at Dillingham Park. Ampthill players (left to right); John Wilkinson, Peter Litchfield, James Fletcher, Leigh Clark and Richard Sheard

In the new year John Wilkinson, a Bedfordshire County and East Midlands regular, joined Bedford to experience first-class rugby. His loss was a blow to the 1st XV, but he went with the best wishes of the Club.

John made his debut for Bedford 1st XV in the 27-12 Courage League win against Havant, at Goldington Road on February 12th 1994. He scored a maiden try in the second half.

Thankfully, John returned to the fold the following season and gave outstanding service to the 1st XV and the Club generally.

SLIMLINES – an extract from Chairman, Brian Slim Clark's Newsletter January 1994

Happy New Year

!Congratulations to our President for the award of his MBE in the New Year Honours List.

Good luck to Graham Whitehall who is preparing to run in this year's London Marathon. Last year it was Denis Hardy who ran the Marathon, next year Slim?

Congratulations to Steward, Vic Kaye for persisting with his new colour coded hair – it only needs an amber strip to be club colours!

First XV

The 1st XV ended their recent sequence of drawn games when they beat Stewart & Lloyds in a see-saw East Midlands Division 1 match on Saturday. Their tremendous home form stood them in good stead against the Corby unit and a good second half recovery earned Amps the points.

It was the visitors who took the lead when two penalties put them 6-0 ahead. But we hit back when Leigh Clark kicked a penalty, and then Derek Welton took advantage of a defensive error after a five- metre scrum to get the first try.

Stewarts & Lloyds took the lead again before Justin Fletcher tiptoed over after a 30-yard run to make it 13-13. Leigh Clark again kicked a penalty before Andy Dadley brought gasps from the crowd with a tremendous 30-yard drop goal. Whilst the success continued our 100% record on our own ground this season, it was not a performance to get Tony Phillips and Graham Whitehall too excited.

The much-improved league form really started with a very lucky win at home to Luton in December. A late conversion by skipper Ian MacGregor from way out, added to a Richard Sheard try which rescued Ampthill with a 13-12 win. Earlier Ian had kicked two penalties to help us win a game which we frankly deserved to lose. After the Christmas break Amps. ran off the plum pudding and put their away form behind them when they returned from Nottingham with a 20-10 win over Moderns. A 17-5 lead was built up in the first-half: MacGregor converting tries by Gavin Burger and Justin Fletcher. The skipper scored a drop goal in the second half to make sure of the win. Slim's hair was just the same as it was before the game and 1994 opened with that elusive away victory.

Semi-final weekend in the County Cup, and after our first away win we were geared up for a crack at Bedford Athletic, leaders of the league above – but disaster struck. We went out 13-8 on a real mud heap. After Ath. got an early try from a line-out near our line, a MacGregor penalty made it 5-3. The Ath's. forward dominance led to a back row try but with time running out a consolation try by Leigh Clark raised spectators' hopes. But it was not to be our day and the feeling was that on a different pitch the score would have been much changed.

This newsletter has dealt with some highs and lows in form, but the win over Scunthorpe 13-7 was a great fighting performance under forward pressure. The boys gave Harry Cornforth something to smile about in that his uncle is chairman of Scunthorpe and last season Harry had travelled all the way to Scunthorpe with the Amps. to see them hammered by "Scunny". A draw at Spalding on February 12th further helped our position in the league. In total, 4 wins from the last six games has done wonders for our East Midlands prospects since December. Who would bet against Richard Beasley for player of the year on current form? Opposing stand-offs are cursing him."

Richard Bearsley harasses the Kettering No. 10 in the East Midlands Quarter Final

George Jenkins

Sadly, George Jenkins died on 10 April 1994. George was a great benefactor to the Club; he particularly supported the mini & youth section including sponsoring their sevens tournament. He loved the atmosphere at The Club on Sunday mornings – his only day off from his business in Dunstable Street.

Midlands East League Division 1

Notable victories in the league included a 71-3 demolition of Wigston, 22-10 against Biggleswade, a 24-0 victory over Kettering, a 20-10 beating of Moderns and a 26-14 result against Stoneygate. As it was, Ampthill finished in mid-table

Ampthill 26pts. Stoneygate 14pts. – March 26 1994

Ampthill Rugby Club ended their home programme in Midlands East One with a tremendous victory over high-riding Stoneygate and showed their home supporters the kind of thrilling rugby they can produce when they are at their best. Ampthill had slumped to defeat at Stewarts & Lloyds in their previous league clash a week earlier, but they were back to form with a vengeance against the Leicester side who were left chasing shadows in the second half as the Dillingham Park side turned on the style.

The visitors were third and gunning for promotion from Division One but their hopes were dashed in no uncertain fashion as Ampthill served up a feast of top-class rugby.

Leigh Clark opened the scoring for Ampthill, breaking away on the blind side from 25 metres to score in the corner. Ian MacGregor notched a penalty before Stoneygate hit back with a converted try for an 8-7 score at the interval. At the start of the second-half, Tom Gray capped an outstanding performance with the second try when he ran the ball in from the ten-metre line after a short kick from MacGregor whose conversion put Ampthill eight points ahead.

Ampthill now began to step on the accelerator and produced some tremendous stuff which left Stoneygate trailing in their wake as they produced a string of super team movements. From one well-worked sequence Graham Whitehall scored a rare vital try, the move starting when the ball was kicked out of defence. James Fletcher then played a big part when he beat two men to pass to Paul Talling who touched down in the corner.

The try was unconverted, but Ampthill's pressure led to mistakes by Stoneygate and penalties from MacGregor stretched the lead to 20-7 before the visitors fought back for some consolation points near the end. The team were geared up for the game since they have not done themselves justice since their County Cup win, a 20-minute spell in the second half was as good as anything they have shown for some time.

Paul Teague racing past his Stoneygate opposite-number – April 1993. Mike Larby, Mike Plant and Tony Phillips look on approvingly

Season 1994-95 – (Captain Ian MacGregor)

Officers

President	R. Dillingham
Chairman	B. Clark
Hon. Treasurer & Hon. Sec.	R. G. Churchill
Assist. Hon. Secretary	M. Marsden
Fixture Secretary	R. Duffin
Membership Secretary	H. Cornforth
Committee	P. Sherry, S. Powell, A. Teague, J. Wilkinson, T. West, S. Powell

Playing

1st XV Captain	I. MacGregor
1st XV Manager	A. Teague
Exiles XV Captain	R. Redman
Exiles XV Vice-Captain	I. Burgess
3rd XV Captain	C. Hopgood
3rd VX Vice-Captain	K. Anderson
4th XV Captain	L. Barlow
4th XV Vice-Captain	L. Adams
5th XV Captain	R. Troiano
Extras XV Captain	R. Duffin
Colts XV	P. Smedley(Capt.) Denis Hardy & Dave Sprigg (coaches)
Coach	Graham Whitehall, T. Phillips, G. McIlroy

1994-95 Midlands East Division 1

	Won	Drawn	Lost	F	A	Points
Scunthorpe	11	0	1	366	86	22
Long Buckby	11	0	1	285	83	22
Spalding	7	1	4	137	185	15
Kettering	7	0	5	172	99	14
Ampthill	**7**	**0**	**5**	**189**	**141**	**14**
Stoneygate	6	1	5	163	125	13
Stewart & Lloyds	5	1	6	124	146	11
Biggleswade	5	1	6	131	165	11
Leicester Vipers	5	0	7	135	152	10
Amber Valley	4	1	7	72	121	9
Wellingborough	4	0	8	133	141	8
Northampton Boys' Brigade	2	0	10	85	207	4
Chesterfield	1	1	10	66	407	3

The 1st XV finished comfortably in the top half of Midlands East 1, as usual away form in the league was the key to success. Ironically the 1st XV won both away games after long trips to Amber Valley and Chesterfield that season.

Other notable results for the 1st XV included a 48-0 victory over Dunstablians, a 60-12 beating of Stevenage, a 20-9 win over Leighton Buzzard and 26-10 triumph over Stoneygate

As can often be the case, the Colts found the going tougher in their second season but recorded outstanding victories against Kettering 43-8, Towcestrians 53-6 and Northampton Casuals 26-0.

1st XV 1994-95

rear: J. Wilkinson, I. Marshall, J. Fletcher, G. Griffiths, I. Burgess, B. Baber, D. Welton, R. Campbell, G. Whitehall. K. Smith, B. Clark, J. Bishop - front: G. Burger, R. Beasley, P. Litchfield, J. Fletcher, I. MacGregor, D. Tompkins, P. Farthing, L. Clark, S. Fletcher

Bedfordshire Knock-Out Cup

League status counted for nothing as Bedford Swifts gave Ampthill a fright in the County Cup clash at Newnham Avenue. Swifts led briefly and were always in contention but eventually slipped out by 12-19. Ampthill could point to three tries to none by Swifts as justification for the result and also to the real difference – the backs.

Swifts more than matched their guests in the forwards, but Ampthill used the ball better with Leigh Clark, Ian MacGregor and John Wilkinson making breaks and skipper MacGregor peppering the touchline with superb kicks. Tries by brothers Simon and James Fletcher and finally prop Bob Baber put the visitors into to the semi-final.

"Super Mac" - Ian MacGregor – in the 74-5 trouncing of Colworth House in April 1995

However, they were to lose to Stockwood Park, who themselves were beaten by Leighton Buzzard 9-6 in the final.

	played	won	drawn	lost	pts. for	pts. against
1994-95						
1st XV	32	22	0	10	574	257
Extras XV	27	19	1	7	655	340
Colts XV	26	13	1	12	364	350

*No records for Exiles, 3rd, 4th or 5th XV this season

Season 1995-96 – (Captain – David Tompkins)

Officers

President	R. Dillingham
Chairman	B. Clark
Hon. Treasurer & Hon. Sec.	R. G. Churchill
Assist. Hon. Secretary	H. Cornforth
Fixture Secretary	G. Whitehall
Membership Secretary	H. Cornforth
Director of Rugby	T. Phillips
Committee	A. Teague, S. Templeman, A. Clark, J. Wilkinson

Playing

1st XV Captain	D. Tompkins
1st XV Vice-Captain	J. Wilkinson
Exiles XV Captain	R. Campbell
3rd XV Captain	C. Hopgood
4th XV Captain	R. Troiano
5th XV Captain	
Extras XV	R. Duffin
Colts	Denis Hardy & Dave Sprigg (coaches)
Coach	G. McIlroy

Tony Phillips became Ampthill's first Director of Rugby, a role he was to undertake with distinction for the next four seasons.

Rugby Union Goes Open

In 1995 rugby union turned professional after the South Africa World Cup tournament. Fired by the success of the 1995 World Cup, media moguls threw money at the sport and the IRB declared rugby union professional. The change came halfway through the northern hemisphere 1995-96 season. In September, Sir John Hall became involved with Newcastle Falcons bringing in Rob Andrew, Inga Tuigamala, Jonny Wilkinson and Tony Underwood, among others. The Heineken Cup Champions League was launched, but no English or Scottish teams took part.

In the southern hemisphere Super 10 evolved into Super 12 and became fully professional with Auckland Blues taking the title. Back in the northern hemisphere Richmond backed by Ashley Levett turned pro, while Saracens were bought by Nigel Wray. England were thrown out of the Five Nations after an £87.5m deal with BSkyB. English clubs threatened to quit RFU competitions in a spat over the structure of the game, while in Ireland the first player contracts were signed. Rugby league giants Wigan and leading union side Bath played the first cross-code encounter with each side winning their own code with ease. Toulouse beat Cardiff, in front of 22,000 at the Arms Park, to claim the first Heineken Cup title.

In 1997, a restructured Four Nations was announced without England's inclusion because of the dispute over its contract with Sky. England were eventually allowed back into the tournament following lengthy talks.

The Club made the decision not to pay its players and some of Ampthill's best players were lured away to other local clubs as a consequence. Within 10 years Ampthill was running just 3 senior teams. For three seasons, 2005 to 2008 only the firsts, seconds and Extras fifteens were put onto the field.

Dave Tompkins

This was Dave Tompkins' second spell as Club Captain, he was to inspire the 1st XV to its best ever season. The Club became East Midlands champions for the first time ever, narrowly beating Kettering 15-14. This momentous win also ensured a place in the next season's Pilkington Cup.

Ampthill also won the Bedfordshire Cup for the second time, defeating Bedford Athletic by 31 points to 20. The 1st XV finished third in Midlands East 1 League and were promoted as the leagues were re-structured and four clubs went up to Midland League 2.

League Results – Midlands East 1

Amber Valley	16-15	A	won
Biggleswade	39-14	H	won
Huntingdon	22-25	A	lost
Kettering	17-21	H	lost
Long Buckby	17-26	A	lost
Vipers	17-0	H	won
Ilkeston	15-10	A	won
Newark	30-3	H	won
Spalding	11-12	A	lost
Stewarts & Lloyds	15-11	H	won
Stoneygate	8-7	A	won
Peterborough	34-6	H	won

Fifth Bedfordshire Knockout Cup Final 1996

In the semi-final, in January, Ampthill were drawn away, but defeated Leighton Buzzard by 19 points to 9. Playing against the slope and the elements, Ampthill were down 9-0 at one stage, but bounced back scoring a crucial Ian MacGregor penalty just before the break to make it 9-3. Fired up, the visitors hit back with another penalty through MacGregor. The game then turned, when a long kick from Ampthill was fumbled by the Leighton Buzzard full-back, allowing Richard Sheard to run in a score which MacGregor converted. The boot of MacGregor then sealed it with two more kicks which not only guaranteed a final spot, but also a place in the quarter-finals of the East Midlands Cup.

The weather for the final was uncertain but the game promised to be a cracker. High flying Ampthill would have home advantage against a Bedford Athletic side who were struggling in the league above, so the sides looked pretty evenly matched.

Bedford Athletic may have had the edge in the pack with experienced old campaigners such as Gerald Bygraves, Paul McGuckian, and skipper Neil Patterson. Lock Chris Homan showed his class in the semi-final against Luton, as he gave away several inches to his opposite number but still dominated the lineouts.

However, the outcome was likely to be decided behind the scrum and, with both sides having some real speedsters. Ath. have Tommy Cassidy and Alf Bartlett on the wings and Chris Eldridge at full-back who can cause problems for any defence.

However, Ampthill could point to players such as Richard Sheard, James Fletcher, Gavin Burger and Andy Teague to do the same for them. Sadly, Ampthill full-back John Wilkinson would miss the game – and probably the rest of the season – because of knee ligament damage.

Ampthill had won the cup for the first time three years before when they beat Queens at Allen Park. It was a long time since Athletic last won it and their only recent appearance in the final in 1994 saw them throw away the lead to lose to a late score by Stockwood Park.

The teams had some tremendous battles in the County Cup in recent years and actually met in the semi-finals for three years in a row, Ampthill claiming two wins to Ath's one.

Whatever the result, both would qualify for the East Midlands Cup, along with the finalists from Huntingdonshire, East Northants. and the Northampton Alliance. The winners would go into the first round of the Pilkington Cup.

The Club's Fifth Bedfordshire Knockout Cup Final – Sunday, 4 February 1996

Ampthill 31 pts. Bedford Athletic 20 pts.

Ampthill were crowned champions following a thrilling 31-20 Beds Cup win at Dillingham Park.

The County Cup was a fitting reward for an Ampthill side who, despite being underdogs on a number of occasions, had risen to the task in hand.

It was Bedford Athletic, playing with the wind at their backs in the first half, who took the initiative. A penalty and an unconverted try saw them go 8-0 up, and although Ampthill hit back with a score from Ian Marshall, Athletic looked to be getting away when they made it 17-7, with just half an hour gone.

The game was to turn in the spell leading up to the break, however, as Ampthill tracked their opponents before taking a vital half-time lead. Tommy Gray was a try scorer, making it 17-12, while two penalty chances were eagerly taken by Ian MacGregor, as the Ampthill took a crucial lead at 18-17. With the wind, there was to be only one winner - and so it proved, both Gray and Gavin Burger adding to the lead with unconverted scores. A further penalty from MacGregor put the icing on the cake, and although Ath. did manage to add three more points just before the death, Ampthill already had their hands on the silverware and were ready for the well-earned celebrations to commence.

The East Midlands Cup Final – April 21st 1996

On the way to the final Ampthill beat Long Buckby 27-21 at the quarter-final stage and Wellingborough 39-19 in the semi-finals.

Kettering 14 pts. Ampthill 15 pts.

Ampthill saw their dreams become reality as they claimed the East Midlands Cup. Victory in the competition, which ensured Ampthill a berth in the National Cup had come at the end of a campaign in which nearly everything had gone right.

In a tense final, played at Kettering, Ampthill fell behind 6-0 at the interval, but hit back and took a lead they were never to lose. Tommy Gray crashed over for a converted score before MacGregor made it 10-6 with a penalty.

Kettering did pull to within a point thanks to a penalty, but the lead opened up to 15-9 when Richard Sheard robbed Steven Dawkins in midfield and fed fellow centre James Fletcher to score. However, they lost possession from the restart as referee Chris Harrison awarded Kettering a scrum under the "use it or lose it" maul law and No.8, Parker, eventually crashed over for Kettering.

Franklin's conversion sailed wide to leave the score at 14-15 with eleven minutes and any injury time – 3 minutes as it turned out – to survive. However, Ampthill never looked in trouble and were camped on the Kettering line when Mr. Harrison's whistle sparked scenes of wild celebration from Ampthill's huge travelling support.

Skipper Dave Tomkins and his Ampthill side celebrate their first ever East Midlands Cup triumph in the final against Kettering

Ampthill: I. McGregor, A. Teague, R. Sheard, James Fletcher, G. Burger, P. McCarthy, L. Clark, R. Baber, D. Tompkins (capt.) P. Parker, G. Griffiths, I. Marshall, T. Gray, R. Beasley, P. Farthing,

replacements: G. Whitehall, Justin Fletcher, D. Welton, R. Campbell, Ian Burgess, A. Dadley

East Midlands Colts Cup in 1996

Ampthill Colts 15 pts. Wellingborough Colt 10 pts.

The Colts produced some notable performances and representative honours this season under the expert coaching of Denis Hardy and Dave Sprigg.

Ian Campbell and Will Sneath scored 27 and 23 tries respectively. Sean Jones, Ian Campbell, Fraser Newberry, Martin Scott, Terry Stokes and Dave Barry were all selected for Bedfordshire. Terry Stokes was in the East Midlands squad for the Colts Championship final at Twickenham.

On Sunday 28 April Ampthill beat Wellingborough 15-10 in a close-fought East Midlands Cup Final at Dillingham Park.

Ampthill: I. Campbell, W. Sneath, B. Venthem, J. Hurrel, A. Green, J. Offer, M. Troiano, A. Shindler, D. Barry, F. Newberry, A. Best, M. Cresswell, T. Stokes, S. Jones. M. Scott

Replacements: **J. Rolls, D. Dexter, P. Saunders, J. Lothian, D. Mechem**

Ampthill Colts celebrate their victory over Wellingborough in the East Midlands Cup Final

The Colts also were runners up in the East Midlands Colts seven a side competition, this season.

Bedfordshire County Challenge Shield (Silver Jubilee)

Bedfordshire County RFU was inaugurated at Silsoe College to give exposure to players from junior clubs who would not otherwise feature in an East Midlands XV. The County celebrated its Silver Jubilee with a game against Ampthill. This game was played at Dillingham Park before the Colts Final against Wellingborough. Ampthill 1st XV defeated a strong County XV by 36-10 to win the Bedfordshire County Challenge Shield.

Ampthill: Robert Campbell, Gavin Burger, Ian Burgess, Richard Sheard, Andy Teague, Phil McCarthy, Leigh Clark, Peter Boyd, Dave Tomkins (capt.), Phil Parker, Ian Marshall, Gavin Griffiths, Paul Farthing, Richard Beasley, Tom Gray replacements: Andy Dadley, Justin Fletcher, Graham Whitehall, Simon Spavins

Bedfordshire: Andy Moffatt (Queens), Andy Carne (L. Buzzard), Stewart Pestell (S. Park), Colin Sandford (Dunstablians), Chris Janes (S. Park) – capt., Alban Turney (L. Buzzard), Darren Stapleton (Queens), Jon Wray (L.

Buzzard), Jon Kately (Biggleswade), Richard Skar (L. Buzzard), Andy Williams (S. Park), Chris Fripp (L. Buzzard), Tim Clarke (Queens) **replacements:** Chris Smith (L. Buzzard), Matthew Southgate (Dunstablians), Andy Martin (S. Park)

Referee: **Peter Cook (East Midlands Society)**

1995-96	played	won	drawn	lost	pts. for	pts. against
1st XV	31	26	0	5	760	388
Exiles XV						
3rd XV						
4th XV						
5th XV						
Extras XV	24	8	1	15	521	435
Colts XV	30	19	1	10	737	452

Season 1996-97 – (Captain – Richard Sheard)
Officers

President	R. Dillingham
Chairman	B. Clark
Hon. Treasurer & Hon. Sec.	R. G. Churchill
Assist. Hon. Secretary	H. Cornforth
Fixture Secretary	G. Whitehall
Membership Secretary	D. Williams
Director of Rugby	T. Phillips
Committee	A. Teague, S. Templeman, I. Cooper, A. Clark, J. Wilkinson

Playing

1st XV Captain	R. Sheard
Exiles XV Captain	I. Burgess
3rd XV Captain	D. Park
4th XV Captain	I. Morgan
5th XV Captain	F. Dimmock
Extras XV	R. Duffin
Colts XV	T. Stokes (Capt.) Denis Hardy & Dave Sprigg (coaches)
Coach	B. Hughes – Head Coach, G. McIlroy

Bryn Hughes took over as head coach and had, at the time, unparalleled success. Bryn was a popular and thoughtful personality. He was unstinting in giving his time and impressive in his attention to detail.

Richard Sheard returned as 1st XV Captain, he headed up the most talented set of players the Club had ever produced and mostly, locally born. However, even Richard and new coach, Bryn Hughes, could not have anticipated the continued success that was to come this season. The Club were to become both Bedfordshire Cup Winners & East Midlands Champions, for the second year running.

Pilkington National Cup Competition

Widnes 30 pts. Ampthill 19 pts. – 14th September 1996

The Club was now in Midlands League Two and the 1st XV were to play in the Pilkington National Cup Competition, away to Widnes, on 14th September 1996. The mass of visiting supporters, ready for an upset, were silenced early on as Widnes went 12-0 up. Ampthill, however, were not fazed by this and after a couple of early misses from Wilkinson, Robert Campbell calmly slotted over two penalties to pull Ampthill back. Then a late score saw Widnes 17-6 at the break and well on top.

The second half saw Ampthill's best spell, but although Widnes were forced back, they conceded penalties rather than tries, Campbell pulling Amps. back to within 5 points. Indeed, only strong defence and the occasional missed pass kept Ampthill from taking the lead. In a vital spell Widnes upped a gear and only a superb tackle from John Wilkinson kept them out. The continued pressure was rewarded with two converted penalties, while with minutes remaining Widnes finally made the game safe with a converted try. Ampthill finally went over, James Fletcher crossing, while Campbell converted, but it was too late.

Ampthill: John Wilkinson, Andy Teague, Richard Sheard (capt.), James Fletcher, Robert Campbell, Phil McCarthy, Leigh Clark, Bob Baber, Dave Tomkins, Phil Parker, Gavin Griffiths, Justin Fletcher, Paul Farthing, Richard Beasley, Tom Gray

Replacements: Ian MacGregor, Simon Spavins, Derek Welton, Ian Campbell

Midlands League 2

Ampthill 1st XV began their league campaign in confident fashion winning seven of their first eight games thus: Bedford Athletic 24-13, Bedworth 16-11, Huntingdon 39-10, Keresley 51-27, Matlock 43-19, Paviours 16-10 and Bromsgrove 24-13. Thereafter, performances were inconsistent and disappointing. Though, there were good wins over Long Buckby 25-13 and Sutton Coldfield 36-6

Team	played	won	drew	lost	pts. for	pts. against	points
Banbury	17	13	2	2	511	231	28
Kenilworth	17	14	0	3	442	283	28
Old Laurentians	17	13	1	3	406	177	27
Kettering	17	13	1	3	457	234	27
Luctonians	17	12	2	3	426	168	26
Dudley	17	13	0	4	434	212	24
Bedford Athletic	17	11	1	5	362	206	23
Bromsgrove	17	10	0	7	271	293	20
Ampthill	**17**	**9**	**0**	**8**	**384**	**310**	**18**
Sutton Coldfield	17	7	1	9	344	413	15
Newport	17	6	1	10	261	353	13
Towcestrians	17	7	0	10	286	283	12
Paviors	17	4	2	11	286	441	10
Huntingdon	17	5	0	12	255	506	10
Keresley	17	4	0	13	218	352	6
Long Buckby	17	3	0	14	269	550	6
Matlock	17	3	0	14	257	555	6
Bedworth	17	0	1	14	185	450	1

To be fair, the 1st XV were the holders of the Bedfordshire and East Midlands Cups and were desperate to retain the silverware and maintain their ascendancy locally.

Bedfordshire Knockout Cup

Quarter-Final

Ampthill overcame a spirited Bedford Swift XV in the quarter final, though at half-time an upset seemed possible as the hosts led by only 8-6 at Dillingham Park. The second half was altogether different with the home pack on the rampage. MacGregor, Teague (3), Parke, Tomkins, Gray all scored in a seven try blitz – a 46-13 result which headed Ampthill onto a semi-final clash, at home, to none other than Stockwood Park.

Andy Teague commented, "We have been without a match for almost a month now and the entire side is desperate to get out there and get a game under their belts. We won't underestimate Stockwood Park on the day, but we are confident we can go to the final again." As champions, Ampthill were helped with automatic home games.

Semi-Final

Ampthill were too strong for Stockwood Park as they came back from behind at half-time to win 23-8. Two Ian MacGregor penalties to one from Huw Davies for the visitors gave an early 6-3 lead. Then a Leigh Clark kick rebounded into the in-goal area, Rob Campbell appeared to touch down first but Stockwood's Chris Johnson was awarded the try. Ampthill's Ian Marshall then scored after good work from the forwards with MacGregor converting. A third MacGregor penalty put the game out of reach for the visitors before a Tom Gray, late score confirmed Ampthill's place in the cup final.

Ampthill's Sixth Bedfordshire County Cup Final

Ampthill 13 pts. Bedford Athletic 12 pts., - 2nd February 1997

In a low-key final played at Dillingham Park on 2nd February, Ampthill retained their Bedfordshire Cup title.

However, Bedford Athletic had only themselves to blame as they did all the hard work in the first half but then failed to take advantage. With the slope and wind in their favour in the first half, Ampthill needed to build up a sizable lead, so the Athletic must have been delighted to turn around just 6-10 down.

Bedford Ath. did not make the most of the conditions and, failed to trouble Ampthill's line. They did take a 12-10 lead but were sunk by an Ian MacGregor penalty 15 minutes from time.

Overall, it was a disappointing match, with most of the play confined to midfield and the boot dominating. Athletic ruled the line-outs through Chris Wright, Ian Simpson and John Egan at the back. Otherwise the forward battle was pretty even.

Ampthill showed rather more invention and it was no surprise they scored the only try, in the first half. After MacGregor had missed two early penalties, they opened the scoring after a powerful rolling maul gave John Wilkinson the chance to hit the line at pace and crash over. MacGregor converted for 7-0.

The Athletic clawed their way back with two penalties by Steve Turner, before MacGregor stretched the lead with a successful kick at goal. Forays into Ampthill's half brought a drop-goal and penalty for Turner, but the hosts managed to keep them out until MacGregor kicked the crucial winning points.

Interestingly, the game was refereed by a visiting American, Ed Todd, who had also officiated at Goldington Road on the Friday before.

Ampthill Squad: **J. Wilkinson, A. Teague, R. Sheard (capt.), J. Fletcher, R. Campbell, I. MacGregor, L.Clark, M. Cahill, S. Spavins, D. Tompkins, P. Parker, C. McClean, G. Griffiths, I. Marshall, G. Whitehall, R. Beasley, P. Farthing, T. Gray, P. McCarthy, D. Welton, I. Campbell**

Bedford Athletic: **J. McKay, T. Cassidy, M. Norman (capt.), J. Chandler, S. Turner, C. Eldridge, D. Norman, N. Paterson, S. Flemming, I. Simpson, C. Wright, M. Swift, D. Goodwin, J. Egan, A. Donnelly, M. Buckle, C. Pollard, C. Molloy, S. Platt**

East Midlands Cup

Quarter-Final versus Long Buckby, 1st March 1997

Ampthill 34 pts. Long Buckby 7 pts.

Ampthill achieved the expected win over Long Buckby with a powerful performance. After the first 30 minutes of deadlock, there was never any doubt who would come out on top as the Ampthill rattled in 15 points in a devastating ten-minute spell. Paul Farthing scampered for the opener, while Rob Campbell fired over a penalty. Then James Fletcher charged his way over for a try before the break.

There was no let-up in the second half, Ampthill ran riot, with the ball kept in hand due to the strong wind. James Fletcher collected his second after a surging run from Andy Teague was stopped.

Then a thrilling backs move ended with Fletcher going over and the victory was completed by a Tom Gray score.

Semi-Final v. Wellingborough, April 1997

Ampthill, as reigning champions, travelled to Cut Throat Lane to take on Wellingborough in the semi-final. They were without some regular players, injured or unavailable. Andy Teague, Phil Parker, Ian MacGregor, Phil McCarthy, were all major doubts, although on the plus side Gavin Burger was to make his first start since Christmas. Ampthill were favourites to overcome Wellingborough who played in Midlands East 1, the league below.

Wellingborough 8 pts. Ampthill 15 pts.

In a tense semi-final contest, there was little room for error but the holders put on a supreme display to boss the contest throughout.

With the trip to Northants still in their system, Ampthill struggled to get a grip early on, despite the advantage of wind and pronounced slope. The deadlock was finally broken when the backs linked up to provide Richard Sheard with the opening score, which was converted by Rob Campbell.

Wellingborough upped a gear and a forward tussle ensued. But Ampthill held firm and struck a crucial blow just before the break when John Wilkinson linked with James Fletcher to score, although the conversion was missed. Ahead 12-0 at the break, Ampthill went onto the defensive, but Wellingborough fought their way back into the contest, first closing the gap with a penalty.

Further hard work was rewarded soon after, as Wellingborough went across for an unconverted try, and at 12-8, Ampthill's grip on the Cup looked shaky. But the visitors turned defence into attack and halted the Wellingborough charge by making inroads into home territory. A Rob Campbell penalty gave Ampthill a vital seven-point cushion and, to the joy of the travelling faithful, the visitors held firm to book the final berth against Old Northamptonians on May 4th.

Squad: **Phil McCarthy, Ian Marshall, Paul Farthing, S. Spavins, Phil Parker, Tom Gray, Gavin Griffiths, Graham Whitehall, Bryn Hughes, John Wilkinson, Andy Teague, Martin Cahill, James Fletcher, Richard Sheard, Dave Tomkins, Gavin Burger, Ian MacGregor, Leigh Clark**

East Midlands Cup Final – May 4th 1997 at Dillingham Park

Ampthill were to play Old Northamptonians who had finished second in Midlands East 1 – the league below- after a meteoric rise through the leagues. They had been promoted for the past two seasons, both as champions. Ampthill had had their opponents watched and knew exactly what to expect. The word was that ONs had a powerful front five and a strong defence. In spite of this, Ampthill were the hot favourites.

Ampthill 20 pts. Old Northamptonians 12 pts. 4th May 1997 A bumper crowd saw Ampthill retain the East Midlands Cup and earn themselves another crack at the Pilkington Cup. On a windy day at Dillingham Park, they made hard work of defending their trophy, especially after making a dream start. However, in the end a score-line of three tries to none tells its own story.

Within a minute Ampthill had made the first score. Playing down the slope but into the wind, Amps. put pressure on from the kick-off and forced an error. The ball was spun wide, James Fletcher made a crucial half-break and looped a pass out to Andy Teague for the winger to canter in. Any thoughts that ON's heads would drop and the floodgates would open were soon dispelled.

Some huge kicks from hand kept Ampthill pinned back and, apart from a couple of bursts, the home side never threatened a second try before half-time.

The line-out was a shambles, not helped by the elements, and the referee did not endear himself to the home faithful with some interesting decisions. He regularly penalised Ampthill, but ONs full-back John Deeks could not convert two kicks at goal.

In the first five minutes of the second half, Deeks kicked a penalty and fly-half John McConkey dropped a goal to put the visitors 6-5 up.

Ian MacGregor landed a penalty to restore the lead, only for Deeks to make it 9-8 with 25 minutes to go. That was the signal for Ampthill to move up a gear and the backs conjured a superb try. Ampthill had suggested all afternoon that, if they got some decent ball, they had the beating of their opposite numbers.

So, it proved, after 56 minutes MacGregor spotted a gap and shimmied through before passing to Richard Sheard to score.

Another Deeks' penalty cut the lead to 13-12 but Ampthill stretched away to two scores ahead with 15 minutes to go. The forwards made good ground, albeit slowly, before the backs took over. Sheard appeared on the blind and drew the defence before sending in replacement Lee Matthews for a try which MacGregor converted.

ONs threw everything into attack and were only denied a try under the posts by the intervention of Tom Gray, who plucked a loose ball from nowhere under his own bar and hung on long enough to win a penalty. Ampthill had to survive six minutes of injury time to reclaim their title.

Ampthill: John Wilkinson, Andy Teague, James Fletcher, Richard Sheard, Gavin Burger, Ian MacGregor, Martin Cahill, Phil Parker, Dave Tomkins, Simon Spavins, Ian Marshall, Gavin Griffiths, Paul Farthing, Justin Fletcher, Tom Gray, Lee Matthews, Phil McCarthy, Ian Campbell, Colin McClean, Keith Garwood, Derek Welton

Roy Duffin

This season Roy Duffin left the Club – moving to France. He was sadly missed, his contribution to the Club as a player and administrator was massive. Now sadly passed away, those who counted him as a friend can still sense his presence at a club he loved. He would have been so proud of what the Club has achieved and also his beloved Extras being managed by his son Liam.

Clubhouse Extension

The Clubhouse extension was ready for the new season, it was officially opened by Norman Brown on Saturday 26th October 1996.

It included an extended dining area, a ladies room, 4 more changing rooms a fitness room, physio room and reception area, tractor shed and two additional floodlight columns.

It was partly funded by National Lottery money to the tune of £121, 550, part of a legacy from the late George Jenkins and the balance by loan. The extension cost £177,000 and the main contractor was Mick Battams (Builders) Limited.

The 1st XV played Matlock, in the league on clubhouse extension day. The club was in a party mood and this was reflected in the score-line of 43-19 to the home team.

Richard Dillingham receiving National Lottery funding

	played	won	drew	lost	pts. for	Pts. lost
1996-97						
1st XV	34	27	0	7	905	495
Exiles XV						
3rd XV						
4th XV						
5th XV						
Extras XV						
Colts XV	24	13	1	10	483	299

Season 1997–98 – (Captain – Paul Farthing)

Management Committee

President	R. Dillingham MBE
Chairman	B. Clark
Treasurer	D. Temperley
Secretary	H. Cornforth
Assistant Secretary & Membership	T. Earp
Director of Rugby	T. Phillips
Sponsorship / Fundraising	S. Rogers
Grounds Maintenance	J. Wilkinson
Clubhouse Maintenance Mini & Youth Liaison	I. Cooper

Appointed Officers

League Registration	D. Williams
Fixtures & Referees	G. Whitehall
Medical	A. Bass
Publicity	A. Teague

Playing

1st XV Captain	P. Farthing
2nd XV Captain	A. Morgan
3rd XV Captain	D. Park
4th XV Captain	F. Dimmock
5th XV Captain	L. Duffin
Colts XV	D. Sprigg (Manager)
Coach	B. Hughes, G. McIlroy

At least three significant events happened this season. Firstly, the famous Exiles XV was no more – the more prosaic title of 2nd XV was to be used, though there would be two more variations in future years. Secondly, Richard Churchill retired as Hon. Treasurer and Hon. Secretary. Thirdly, a Management Committee was created with a sub-committee structure beneath.

Brian "Slim" Clark, in his tenth season as Chairman, struck an ominous tone in his welcome to the new season.

"Who would have believed it! East Midlands Champions for the second season …. Well done to all concerned. But we can't dwell on that for too long. As we face a new season several of the old faces have retired, and others have been offered lucrative contracts elsewhere. Whatever the reason for their going we wish them well and thank them for their efforts in the past. The future will be testing, but also very exciting. Under Paul Farthing's forthright northern leadership, we will go into the season with one of the youngest squads in our history. It is a tribute to our mini and youth section and all of the coaches that so many of our homegrown talent will now get its chance in the big time. It will be tough, but they won't lack for commitment and early training has shown a tremendous team spirit already growing. Please get behind them – they're our boys and we're proud of them!"

Paul Farthing was Club Captain for this season, a very popular no-nonsense leader – he led by example and from the front. Together with Tom Gray, Justin Fletcher and Richard Beasley he was one of the best wing-forwards to have represented the club.

Richard Churchill stood down as Treasurer (and Honorary Secretary) this season after 30 years in the post. He continued to carry out tasks around the Club and grounds which others would not tackle and for which he sought no recognition – though he was awarded the Clubman of the Year in 2014.

Pilkington Cup

Ampthill faced a difficult trip to Vale of Lune RUFC in Lancaster.

Vale of Lune 27 pts. Ampthill 25 pts. – 13h September 1997

Despite a late recovery, Ampthill crashed out of the senior cup against a well organised Vale of Lune XV. The home side were the better side for much of the encounter but a spirited fight-back from travelling Ampthill ensured that the closing moments were nail-biting.

Vale of Lune ran in two quick converted tries to thrust themselves into a 14-0 lead, but Rob Campbell reduced the arrears before the break with a well struck penalty kick, and an unconverted try from Justin Fletcher left the half-time score at 14-8.

A further penalty and a converted try from Lune after the restart put Ampthill further in arrears, but this only kicked the visitors into action. First, Mark Upex forced himself over the try line, and then Lee Matthews scored an excellent try to ensure the visitors were still in the game to the end, but victory eluded them.

Midlands League 2 East

Ampthill spent the league campaign trying to avoid relegation, which they just managed to do!

Bedford Athletic		away	postponed
Sutton Coldfield	36-16	home	won
Huntingdon	16-18	away	lost
Longton	19-34	home	lost
Moderns	21-31	away	lost
Paviours	13-12	home	won
Bromsgrove		away	*
Dudley	18-28	home	lost
Stafford	11-3	away	won
Kettering	29-33	home	lost
Leamington	29-3	away	won
Newport (Salop)	39-21	home	won
Luctonians	0-48	away	lost
Old Laurentians	19-22	home	lost
Sutton Coldfield	16-16	away	draw
Towcestrians	37-6	home	won

*2 points deducted from Ampthill for not honouring a fixture

Bedfordshire Cup

In the first round of the cup Ampthill beat Luton by 16-12, as might have been expected since their opponents were playing two leagues below. However, big-spending Luton had strengthened their side considerably in the two previous seasons, their ranks swelling with players from Bedford as well as Ampthill.

However, despite having plenty to prove, Luton suffered as Ampthill took a grip on the game early on, John Wilkinson getting the first points on the board as he slammed over a penalty inside the first five minutes. Luton missed the chance to level almost immediately and Wilkinson added to the lead with a massive penalty kick. However, all the good work was undone as Luton scored two penalties. Luton now had their tails up and ran the ball at every opportunity. Ironically, this was to prove their downfall as the game took a twist on 35 minutes, Luton losing possession allowing Rob Campbell to score beneath the posts. Wilkinson converted and kicked another penalty for 16-6, but Luton themselves converted a penalty to reduce the arrears to 7.

The second half proved to be a tense affair, and with Luton coming down the hill it was backs to the wall defending from the home side. A penalty did close the gap to 16-12 but crunching tackles from Ampthill and lack of composure from Luton saw the Amps. home.

However, Ampthill were to progress no further, losing to Dunstablians in the next round.

1997-98	played	won	drawn	lost	pts. for	pts. against
1st XV	32	18	1	13	798	539
2nd XV						
3rd XV						
4th XV						
5th XV	25	16	0	9	677	444
Colts XV						

Season 1998-1999 – (Captain – John Wilkinson)

Management Committee

President	R. Dillingham MBE
Chairman	M. Larby
Club Captain	John Wilkinson
Treasurer	S. Powell
Secretary	H. Wright
Director of Rugby	T. Phillips
Sponsorship / Fundraising	S. Rogers
Grounds/Clubhouse Maintenance	Jack Wilkinson
Mini & Youth Liaison	I. Cooper

Elected / Appointed Officers

League Registration	D. Williams
Fixtures & Referees	T. Phillips
Medical	A. Bass
Publicity – Assistant Secretary	R. Churchill
Membership	T. Earp

Playing

1st XV Captain	J. Wilkinson
2nd XV Captain	A. Morgan
3rd XV Captain	D. Park
4th XV Captain	L. Duffin
Colts XV	D. Sprigg (Manager), N. Macklin (coach)
Coach	B. Hughes, G. McIlroy

Mike Larby, a great servant of the Club, succeeded Brian Clark as Chairman, agreeing to serve for just one year. The Club ran no 5th XV this season.

League Results – Midlands 2 East

Derby	39-20	home	won
Stockwood Park	6-3	away	won
Huntingdon	17-3	home	won
Moderns	32-7	home	won
Lincoln	12-0	away	won
Bromsgrove	12-8	home	won
Newbold	7-16	away	lost
Stafford	29-16	home	won
Longton	6-21	away	lost
Kettering	8-27	away	lost
Leamington	37-12	home	won
Newport	13-12	away	won
Old Laurentians	21-10	away	won
Sutton Coldfield	42-14	home	won
Towcestrians	53-15	away	won
Luctonians	18-13	home	won

Midlands League 2 East

Captained by John Wilkinson, the 1st XV finished a creditable third in Midlands League Two, on points difference, behind Newbold-on-Avon.

#	Team	P	W	D	L	PF	PA	+/-	TB	LB	Pts	Adj
1	Longton	16	14	0	2	400	154	246	0	0	28	
2	Newbold on Avon	16	12	2	2	374	177	197	0	0	26	
3	Ampthill	16	13	0	3	352	197	155	0	0	26	
4	Old Laurentians	16	9	1	6	431	249	182	0	0	19	
5	Kettering	16	8	2	6	305	197	108	0	0	18	
6	Sutton Coldfield	16	8	2	6	318	269	49	0	0	18	
7	Newport (Salop)	16	8	0	8	298	304	-6	0	0	16	
8	Luctonians	16	8	0	8	298	310	-12	0	0	16	
9	Nottingham Moderns	16	8	0	8	253	317	-64	0	0	16	
10	Stockwood Park	16	7	1	8	303	287	16	0	0	15	
11	Derby	16	6	1	9	225	294	-69	0	0	13	
12	Huntingdon & District	16	6	1	9	242	315	-73	0	0	13	
13	Lincoln	16	6	0	10	224	310	-86	0	0	12	
14	Bromsgrove	16	5	1	10	262	229	33	0	0	11	
15	Stafford	16	6	1	9	240	321	-81	0	0	11	-2
16	Towcestrians	16	4	0	12	168	524	-356	0	0	8	
17	Leamington	16	2	0	14	164	403	-239	0	0	4	

The first league game saw Ampthill at home to Derby who had been relegated the previous season.

Ampthill 39pts. Derby 20 pts. – 12th September 1998

Ampthill played with renewed vigour to take the spoils against a good Derby side.

Skipper, John Wilkinson played a major role in events and he scored the first try within five minutes and converted it. Derby hit back with a try after ten minutes but Martin Cahill scored in the corner to make the score 12-5 after 20 minutes. A Wilkinson penalty and a Derby try and penalty made the half-time score 15-13.

The second half was all Ampthill with tries from Wilkinson again, Garwood, Burger and Campbell seeing them out of sight before Derby made it a little more respectable with a late converted try.

N.P.I. Cup

Ampthill enjoyed a good NPI Cup campaign, reaching the fourth round of this competition for "junior" clubs:

Round 1	Towcester	55-12	home
Round 2	Manor Park (Nuneaton)	36-5	away
Round 3	Mellish (Nottingham)	60-14	away
Round 4	Stow on the Wold	19-15	home

Ampthill 19pts. Stow on the Wold 15 pts. – 5th December 1998

Solid defence saw Ampthill squeeze through the fourth round of the NPI Cup at the expense of Stow on the Wold.

However, the home pack were in trouble for most of the game. Two Ian MacGregor penalties had Ampthill 6-3 in front by 15 minutes, and the first try arrived 5 minutes later when John Wilkinson joined the line from full-back and released wing Chris Saunders.

Stow responded with a try and conversion on 25 minutes. The visitors then took the lead early in the second-half with a catch and drive score.

Ampthill were only briefly in arrears, MacGregor missed from a penalty but, when the ball was cleared to the 22, the forwards rumbled on from a line-out and Andy Weeks touched down in the corner when the ball was spun down the line.

A further MacGregor penalty completed the scoring on the hour, and a try saving tackle from Saunders typified the Ampthill resistance.

Ampthill were knocked out in round 5 by Aylesbury. Aldwinians Rugby Club, from Audenshaw in Manchester were to go on to win the NPI Final at Twickenham beating Dudley Kingswinford 21-10.

1998-99	played	won	drawn	lost	pts. for	pts. against
1st XV	30	25	0	5	779	358
Exiles XV						
3rd XV						
4th XV						
Colts XV						

Season 1999-2000 – (Captain – Keith Garwood)

Management Committee

President	R. Dillingham MBE
Chairman	T. Phillips
Club Captain	K. Garwood
Treasurer	H. Cornforth
Secretary	H. Wright
Director of Rugby	M. Upex
Sponsorship / Membership	H. Cornforth
Mini & Youth Liaison	I. Cooper

Appointed Officers

League Registration	D. Williams
Fixtures & Referees	T. Phillips
Grounds Technical Advisor	R. Mills
Grounds Maintenance	John Wilkinson
Health & Safety Officer	T. Willison
Publicity	P. Sherry

Playing

1st XV Captain	K. Garwood
1st XV Vice-Captain	R. Campbell
2nd XV Captain	C. McClean
3rd XV Captain	D. Park
4th XV Captain	L. Duffin
Colts XV	D. Sprigg (Manager), N. Macklin (coach)
Coach	B. Hughes

Keith Garwood took over as 1st XV Captain and Mark Upex, the former Bedford player, became Director of Rugby. Keith joined from Stockwood Park and was a widely respected player and captain, he became a hooker but had played his early rugby in the three-quarters. Keith was an inspirational leader and a fine rugby player and a good clubman.

League Results

Derby	11-8	away	won
Stockwood Park	33-5	home	won
Huntingdon	33-19	away	won
Leighton Buzzard	24-9	home	won
Moderns	32-17	away	won
Lincoln	58-7	home	won
Bromsgrove	15-16	away	lost
Malvern	12-20	home	lost
Wolverhampton	5-5	away	draw
Kettering	9-28	home	lost
Wellingborough	12-16	away	lost
Newport (Salop)	3-21	home	lost
Luctonians	10-25	away	lost
Old Laurentians	3-30	home	lost
Sutton Coldfield	12-27	away	lost
Mansfield	30-11	home	won

Midlands League Two East

#	Team	P	W	D	L	PF	PA	+/-	TB	LB	Pts	Adj
1	Malvern	16	15	0	1	552	208	344	0	0	28	-2
2	Bromsgrove	16	12	0	4	407	229	178	0	0	24	
3	Luctonians	16	12	0	4	364	220	144	0	0	24	
4	Wellingborough	16	12	0	4	375	244	131	0	0	24	
5	Kettering	16	11	0	5	343	221	122	0	0	22	
6	Newport (Salop)	16	9	0	7	419	253	166	0	0	18	
7	Old Laurentians	16	9	0	7	426	286	140	0	0	18	
8	Ampthill	16	7	1	8	302	264	38	0	0	15	
9	Mansfield	16	7	0	9	288	262	26	0	0	14	
10	Sutton Coldfield	16	8	0	8	342	404	62	0	0	14	-2
11	Huntingdon & District	16	7	0	9	253	343	-90	0	0	14	
12	Lincoln	16	7	0	9	258	394	-136	0	0	14	
13	Nottingham Moderns	16	6	0	10	237	343	-106	0	0	12	
14	Derby	16	5	0	11	254	380	-126	0	0	10	
15	Leighton Buzzard	16	4	0	12	250	384	-134	0	0	8	
16	Stockwood Park	16	3	0	13	226	481	-255	0	0	6	
17	Wolverhampton	16	1	1	14	140	520	-380	0	0	3	

It was a curious league campaign, the first six games won, mostly quite comfortably, home, and away. Then a falling away in performance and results, with the coach left scratching his head!

Bedfordshire & East Midlands Cup Finals

However, in an exciting finale to the season Keith Garwood's team were runners-up in the Bedfordshire (10-20) & East Midlands Cups to Dunstablians who had an outstanding season. The Dunstable Club enjoyed a the near-perfect 1999/2000 season which delivered victory in all RFU competitions entered, along with League, County and East Midlands Cup success. This culminated in Dunstablians becoming National Intermediate Cup Champions at Twickenham. This meant that in the following season Ampthill would play Scunthorpe, at home, in the Tetley Bitter Cup.

1999-2000	played	won	drawn	lost	pts. for	pts. against
1st XV	28	17	1	10	586	423
Exiles XV						
3rd XV						
4th XV						
Colts XV						

10 Year Fixture Comparison (1st XV) 1990-2000

Sept.	1990/91 Syston Huntingdon Lutterworth * Shelford	Sept.	2000/01 Old Albanians Derby * GPT Coventry (NPI Cup)
Oct.	Long Buckby * Bedford Athletic * Aylestone St. James *	Oct.	Stockwood Park * Huntingdon * NPI Cup 2nd round Leighton Buzzard * Aylesbury
Nov.	Bletchley Belgrave * Northampton Trinity Biggleswade	Nov.	Moderns * Olney (NPI Cup 3rd round) Lincoln * Bromsgrove *
Dec.	Datchworth Barnet Royston Kettering Leighton Buzzard	Dec.	Luton (NPI Cup 4th round) Beds. Cup 1st round Malvern * Beds. Cup 2nd round
Jan.	Bedford Swifts Luton * Hitchin Milton Keynes	Jan.	Wolverhampton *(NPI Cup 5th round) Kettering * London Welsh Beds. Cup semi-finals Wellingborough * (NPI Cup 6th round)
Feb.	Brackley Coalville * Wigston Nuneaton 3rds.	Feb.	Old Verulamians Newport * Old Northamptonians Beds. Cup Final Luctonians (NPI Cup Quarter-finals)
Mar.	Harpenden Wellingborough * Wigston Stoneygate * Colworth	Mar.	Old Merchant Taylors Old Laurentians * Long Buckby (NPI Semi-Finals) Sutton Coldfield *
Apr.	Olney Northampton Old Scouts Stewarts & Lloyds Rushden	Apr. May	Mansfield * Towcestrians (NPI Cup) Aylesbury

*League matches E.M/Leics. League   *League matches Midlands League 2

Chapter 7 – 2000 to 2010 – The Road to Twickenham

Season 2000-01 50th Anniversary – (Captain - Keith Garwood)

Management Committee

President	R. Dillingham MBE
Chairman	H. Cornforth
Hon. Treasurer	C. Browning
Hon. Secretary	H. Wright
rector of Rugby	D. Hardy
Mini & Youth Representative	I. Cooper
1st XV Manager	P. Sherry
Ex Officio	B. Ewart, T. Phillips
Elected /Appointed Officers	
Referee Liaison	I. Owen
Publicity Officer	H. Cornforth
Membership Secretary	H. Wright
Grounds Maintenance	J. Wilkinson
Structural Maintenance	I. Cooper
Health & Safety Officer	T. Willison
Sponsorship & Advertising	B. Muncaster
Fixture Secretary	T. Earp
Registration Officer	D. Williams
Playing	
1st XV Captain	K. Garwood
1st XV Vice-Captain	R. Campbell
2nd XV Captain	I. Bell
3rd XV Captain	D. Park
4th XV Captain	L. Duffin
Vets XV Captain	A. Teague
Colts XV	D. Sprigg (Manager), N. Macklin (coach)
Coach	M. Davis

Harry Cornforth became Chairman, a post he would hold for two years, before taking on the role of Director of Rugby.

Bryn Hughes stood down after five very successful years as coach. Denis Hardy in his new role as Director of Rugby was charged with tracking down and appointing a new coach. He put out feelers nationally and internationally and eventually appointed Martin "Marty" Davis, a New Zealander, from Auckland. Marty had been a club coach for eight years and was awarded top coach by North Harbour Rugby Union in 1999. He had played for Christchurch and represented Royal New Zealand Air Force and the Combined Services.

In what seems now to be of great significance, the Club Membership Card contains no mention of a first team captain - Keith Garwood – only the manager, Pat Sherry.

Denis Hardy and Marty Davis "saw the need to change the whole approach to rugby in the senior club." The policy of 'No Train – No Play' would take some time to have an effect but with hindsight it was clearly the correct policy. Colin Cresswell, captain in the late 1960s, would have certainly approved!

Denis Hardy vividly remembers the effect Marty Davis had on the Club both in unit skills and individual player analysis and development. "In many ways he was ahead of his time and not everyone was ready for what he had to offer," said Denis. "Some, like skipper Keith Garwood, relished his professional and challenging approach. A few could not handle what he was offering and left the Club." Overall, there was an impressive increase in numbers of players coming along to training in Marty Davis' time. Denis Hardy (then DOR) recalls that Martin Hines an ex-Orrell and Northampton prop also offered his services to the Club, at this time, as a part-time coach.

The 1st XV narrowly lost their Tetley Bitter Cup match against Scunthorpe by 22 points to 24.

In the Bedfordshire Cup, Ampthill went out in the semi-final stage losing 3-72 to Dunstablians. Dunstablians retained their title by beating Bedford Athletic in the final by 74-5 – a record score for the final.

This season clubs competed home and away in the league for the first time.

League results

Dunstablians	20-29	home	lost	away	0-48	lost
Kettering	17-17	home	draw	away	8-21	lost
Leighton Buzzard	20-23	away	lost	home	23-21	won
Lincoln	23-20	home	won	away	10-25	lost
Luton	9-9	home	draw	away	10-30	lost
Mansfield	5-9	home	lost	away	22-26	lost
Huntingdon	8-20	away	lost	home	10-10	draw
Stockwood Park	13-6	home	won	away	10-10	draw
Syston	0-28	away	lost	home	37-22	won
Moderns	15-18	away	lost	home	28-12	won
Wellingborough	19-25	home	lost	away	3-58	lost

Ampthill points shown first

Midlands 2 East

#	Team	P	W	D	L	PF	PA	+/-	TB	LB	Pts	Adj
1	Dunstablians	22	22	0	0	950	195	755	0	0	42	-2
2	Wellingborough	22	18	0	4	575	323	252	0	0	36	
3	Luton	22	15	1	6	510	264	246	0	0	31	
4	Kettering	22	14	1	7	572	306	266	0	0	29	
5	Syston	22	13	0	9	451	451	0	0	0	26	
6	Mansfield	22	10	1	11	370	380	-10	0	0	21	
7	Huntingdon & District	22	9	2	11	296	406	-110	0	0	20	
8	Lincoln	22	9	0	13	308	453	-145	0	0	18	
9	Ampthill	22	5	4	13	310	487	-177	0	0	14	
10	Nottingham Moderns	22	6	0	16	323	554	-231	0	0	12	
11	Leighton Buzzard	22	5	0	17	266	675	-409	0	0	10	
12	Stockwood Park	22	1	1	20	171	608	-437	0	0	3	

Ampthill's away form was very poor this season, only one game on the road was not lost, the draw away at Stockwood Park. All five wins in the league were, therefore, home fixtures. Ampthill only just escaped the spectre of relegation by defeating Syston in the last game of the season.

Keith Garwood in his first season as captain did not enjoy a very successful campaign and, being the competitor that he was, he would have hated the 3-72 drubbing in the cup at the hands of Dunstablians who also beat Ampthill 48-0 at Bidwell Park. Keith did not have a settled team this season and Midlands 2 East was a very competitive league. However, morale remained high, not least because the players enjoyed Marty Davis' coaching and, as always, Denis Hardy's presence as Director of Rugby was a positive one.

Dunstablians dominated the league winning all their 22 matches, Stockwood Park were relegated. One striking feature of home and away league matches was the loss of traditional fixtures that had been maintained over many years, for example, Aylesbury, Old Verulamians, Biggleswade, Stamford and Olney.

2000-01	played	won	drawn	lost	pts. for	pts. against
1st XV	26	6	3	17	369	612
2nd XV	27	13	0	14	465	543
3rd XV	26	21	0	5	619	240
4th XV	26	19	0	7	676	268
Vets XV						
Colts XV	20	12	0	8	340	220

Season 2001-02 – (Captain Danny Phillips & Keith Garwood)

Management Committee

President	N. Brown
Chairman	H. Cornforth
Hon. Treasurer	R. Ewart
Hon. Secretary	H. Wright
Director of Rugby	D. Hardy
Mini & Youth Representative	John Wilkinson
1st XV Manager	P. Sherry
Sponsorship & Advertising	B. Muncaster
Ex Officio	H. Gray

Elected / Appointed Officers

Referee Liaison	I. Owen
Publicity Officer	R. Ewart
Membership Secretary	H. Wright
Grounds Maintenance	John Wilkinson
Structural Maintenance	I. Cooper

Playing

1st XV Captain	D. Phillips/K. Garwood
2nd XV Captain	P. New/S. Rogers
3rd XV Manager	C. Hopgood
4th XV Captain	L. Duffin
Colts XV	D. Sprigg (Manager), N. Macklin (coach)
Coach	M. Davis

League Results

Ilkeston	14-20	away	lost	home	40-15	won
Huntingdon	21-5	home	won	away	5-33	lost
Kettering	16-41	away	lost	home	16-24	lost
South Leicester	28-26	home	won	away	14-23	lost
Lincoln	32-15	away	won	home	75-14	won
Luton	23-0	home	won	away	17-25	lost
Mansfield	13-26	away	lost	home	16-14	won
Spalding	18-21	home	lost	away	18-21	lost
Syston	35-13	home	won	away	0-29	lost
Hinkley	12-28	away	lost	home	6-5	won
Wellingborough	17-11	away	won	home	21-14	won

Ampthill's point shown first

League: Midlands 2 East

#	Team	P	W	D	L	PF	PA	+/-	TB	LB	Pts
1	Hinckley	22	18	2	2	729	188	541	0	0	38
2	Spalding	22	15	2	5	603	326	277	0	0	32
3	South Leicester	22	15	1	6	603	333	270	0	0	31
4	Kettering	22	13	1	8	447	368	79	0	0	27
5	Mansfield	22	13	0	9	392	344	48	0	0	26
6	Ampthill	22	11	0	11	457	423	34	0	0	22
7	Syston	22	9	1	12	386	439	-53	0	0	19
8	Wellingborough	22	9	1	12	437	526	-89	0	0	19
9	Luton	22	7	3	12	398	432	-34	0	0	17
10	Ilkeston	22	7	0	15	287	685	-398	0	0	14
11	Huntingdon & District	22	6	1	15	368	530	-162	0	0	13
12	Lincoln	22	3	0	19	266	779	-513	0	0	6

In Midlands 2 East, the Ampthill 1st XV had a mixed season finishing in mid-table. They inflicted only the second defeat of the season on champions Hinckley. However, they did not gain many points on the road, beating only Lincoln 32-15 and Wellingborough 17-11. At home there were big wins over relegated Lincoln 75-14, Syston 35-13, Ilkeston 40-15 and Luton 23-0.

In "friendlies"; there were good victories against Stewarts & Lloyds 35-10 and Bishop Stortford 33-22. Sadly, the Club had no impact in the Bedfordshire Cup, Luton were champions defeating Stockwood Park 22-7 in the final.

Powergen Intermediate Cup

Ampthill had a reasonable run in this competition

round 1	Oadby Wyggestonians	45-3
round 2	Wellingborough	23-20
round 3	Stewart & Lloyds	35-10
round 4	Mansfield	12-31

2001-02	played	won	drawn	lost	pts. for	pts. against
1st XV	27	15	0	12	605	480
Exiles XV						
3rd XV						
4th XV						
Colts XV						

Season 2002-03 – (Captain - Danny Phillips)

Management Committee

President	N. Brown
Chairman	I. Cooper
Vice Chairman (Mini/Youth Chair)	C. Freeman
Hon. Treasurer	H. Cornforth
Hon. Secretary	C. Page
Director of Rugby	H. Cornforth
Facilities Manager	N. Woodward
Senior East Midlands Representative	H. Cornforth
Senior Representative	P. Sherry
Ex Officio	H. Gray

Elected / Appointed Officers

Child Protection	J. Sexton
Schools Liaison	A. Radley
Finance Sub-Committee	J. Cresswell, H. Wright, J. Wilkinson, N. Tinker, B. Muncaster, C. Freeman. Y. Russon, L. Barlow & V. Kaye

Playing

1st XV Captain	D. Phillips/K. Garwood
2nd XV Captain	P. New/S. Rogers
3rd XV Manager	C. Hopgood
Extras XV Manager	L. Duffin
Colts	D. Sprigg (Manager), N. Macklin (coach)
Coach	A. Hughes

Ian "Coops" Cooper, after distinguished service in the mini & youth section and the senior club, was elected Chairman. Cliff Page, website manager, began a long and significant period of service on the Club Committee.

Ampthill's kiwi coach, Marty Davis, left to coach Dijon, in eastern France. The new coach Alan Hughes had been the National Under 18's Coach. Denis Hardy having re-located to Dubai, Harry Cornforth took over as Director of Rugby and his tenure would witness further developments in playing standards and the overall management of the Club.

Apart from the improvement in playing standards that Harry Cornforth was about to engender with Mark Lavery, he also had a major effect on Club finances. He saw the need to increase income through sponsorship. For a number of years Barry Muncaster oversaw sponsorship income and proved to be particularly adept at involving local business in the scheme.

For the next four seasons the 3rd XV became the Bucks – the reason is lost in the mists of time! Of greater significance was the 4th XV becoming the Extras and being run by Liam Duffin. Seventeen seasons later Liam is still in charge – his father, Roy would have been proud!

League Results

Banbury	away	13-24	lost	home	35-0	won
Kettering	home	3-10	lost	away	16-17	lost
South Leicester	home	20-15	won	away	20-30	lost
Market Bosworth	home	31-5	won	away	12-14	lost
Luton	away	12-43	lost	home	10-15	lost
Mansfield	home	20-12	won	away	5-19	lost
Ilkeston	home	44-25	won	away	33-7	won
Northampton Old Scouts	away	40-3	won	home	64-7	won
Moderns	home	34-10	won	away	48-10	won
Syston	away	15-11	won	home	20-11	won
Wellingborough	home	75-9	won	away	54-24	won

Ampthill points shown first

1st XV League: Midlands 2 East

#	Team	P	W	D	L	PF	PA	+/-	TB	LB	Pts	Adj
1	Kettering	22	18	2	2	622	223	399	0	0	38	
2	Luton	22	18	1	3	712	301	411	0	0	37	
3	Mansfield	22	17	1	4	551	262	289	0	0	35	
4	South Leicester	22	15	2	5	734	305	429	0	0	32	
5	Ampthill	22	14	0	8	624	321	303	0	0	28	
6	Market Bosworth	22	14	0	8	542	361	181	0	0	26	-2
7	Banbury	22	7	0	15	409	594	-185	0	0	14	
8	Syston	22	7	0	15	433	451	-18	0	0	12	-2
9	Nottingham Moderns	22	6	0	16	334	712	-378	0	0	12	
10	Northampton Old Scouts	22	6	0	16	389	775	-386	0	0	12	
11	Wellingborough	22	5	0	17	298	741	-443	0	0	10	
12	Ilkeston	22	2	0	20	250	852	-602	0	0	2	-2

Although Ampthill's league position shows only a modest improvement, this disguises the increased capability of the 1st XV this season. Scoring 624 points, made Ampthill the second top scorers, behind Luton on 712. Conversely, the firsts conceded only 321 points, a great improvement on previous seasons. The team's away form improved too, notably in the victories at Syston, Ilkeston, Old Scouts, Moderns and Wellingborough.

After an indifferent start to their league season Ampthill had a run of five consecutive victories in October, including the following:

East Midlands Cup Semi-Final

Huntingdon 18 pts. Ampthill 25 pts.

Ampthill won through to the final of the East Midlands Cup with a fine win at Huntingdon. Games between Huntingdon and Ampthill are always tough encounters and this was no exception.

It was first blood to Huntingdon when they went over for a try which was converted, but Ampthill hit back within two minutes with a try from John Wilkinson. Ampthill then took the lead when Richard Hillier came up with his first try of the season at an opportune moment and David Garwood converted.

Huntingdon were back in front again before half-time though, thanks to a penalty and an unconverted try. The game was decided in the opening minutes of the second-half. Garwood kicked a penalty to level the scores at 15-15 and another one took Ampthill ahead. Phil Lane then crossed for a try and Garwood's conversion made it 25-15 with 20 minutes to go.

A Huntingdon penalty seven minutes later raised the home side's hopes, but Ampthill deservedly held out to reach the final.

East Midlands Cup Final – Saturday, 10th May 2003 at Peterborough

Peterborough 6pts. Ampthill 13pts.

I am indebted to Ian Hamilton, Hon. Secretary of Peterborough Rugby Club, for this match report from the Peterborough Telegraph of 12th May 2003. It was written by Bob French, the recently retired Sports Editor of the Telegraph, who played for Peterborough in the 1970s, when Ian Hamilton himself joined the club.

Borough are off target in final loss

"Borough went for it with all guns blazing, determined to make up for the disappointment of losing their promotion play-off a fortnight ago.

And, to their credit, they fired more than enough bullets to have won this fiercely-contested cup final. Only trouble was the bullets missed the target.

Visitors Ampthill were within their sights and came under siege for long spells. But Borough just couldn't hit where it hurt. Resolute defence certainly played a part but the main reason for Borough's lack of reward points was an acute bout of dropsy. Butter-fingered Borough just couldn't get those vital passes to stick and so much good work in the bruising, bone-crunching battle up front was undone by wayward finishing outside.

Ampthill were bigger, but that didn't stop Borough winning their fair share of set-piece possession - Darian Uys and Pete Kolakowski did particularly well at the lineouts – and in the loose Borough proved equally adept. Huge hits went in – everyone in the side managed at least a couple – and more often than not Borough turned possession over.

Yet the tries wouldn't come. Just when they needed it most, the crisp, quality passing which had served them so well throughout the season deserted them. Knock-on, forward passes – it was so disappointing. And it was especially disappointing for winger John Sismey and centre Pete Brudnell. Both are potential match winners but the ball never reached them all afternoon.

And for some reason the "crash ball", normally Brudnell's forte, seemed to go to the other centre Ben Chan, and although he tried his best, he lacked the bulk to penetrate. Super-heavyweights Nobby Coupland, James Hannam, Joel Burpitt and Michael Royal were better equipped for battering-ram raids, but even their thrusts were repelled.

Ampthill really did defend well, though. They were rock solid and if there were chinks in their armour, Borough failed to find them, although young Hannam did have try disallowed early on for – wait for it – a forward pass.

With a stiff wind behind them Borough dominated the first half territorially. But for all their huff and puff they led just 3-0 at the break, through a Chan penalty.

Soon Dave Garwood cancelled that out after the turn-around, a flood of Ampthill scores were anticipated. But Borough made them fight every inch of the way and they mustered only two touchdowns – one after 60 minutes by winder Wilkinson and another after 68 minutes by giant second-row Dilley – for a 13-3 lead.

Borough were beaten but refused to admit it. Despite losing key players like Burpitt, Coupland and Sismey through injury, they were still able to spend much of the remainder of the game camped on the Ampthill line. They got a penalty through Paul Booth but a try? No way. In fact, you couldn't see one of those if they'd stayed out on the park until dusk. It was one of those days.

It was a brave effort by Borough against a side from a league above but hard work on this occasion wasn't enough. Handling errors and injuries certainly didn't help their cause, but they did not possess a player with the flair to prise open that stubborn Ampthill defence.

It was a sad way to end the season but it's still been a good one. Runners-up in the league and runners-up in the cup is no mean achievement and if they can stick together, they could easily go one better in each competition."

Ampthill: S. Wilson, J. Wilkinson, D. Garwood, L. Matthews, S. Belcher, J. Offer, J. Lasbrey, J. Steele, K. Garwood, S. Ward, C. Dilley, N. Cafferty, S. Jarvis, P. Lane, D. Phillips (capt.) Replacements: P. Timewell, D. Park, D. Burns, R. Hillier, A. Hill, L. Roby, K.Simpson

Peterborough: D. Brundell, S. Sismey, P. Brudnell, P. Goodley, N. Thomas, G. McDougall, N. Coupland (capt.), P. Cook, M. Royal, P. Kolakowski, M. Hodges, J. Hannam, D. Uys, J. Burpitt Replacements: A. Ray, R. MacIntyre, J. Smythe, G. Rayner, P. Booth, R.Woolley, D.Stuffins

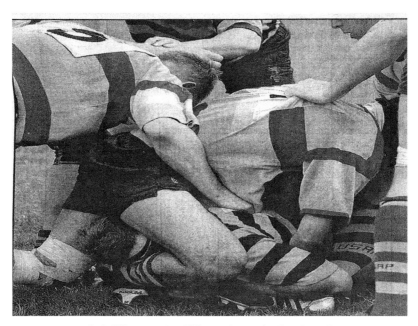

Craig Dilley scores Ampthill's second try against Peterborough

Intermediate Cup

After an inconsistent start in Midlands Two East, Ampthill needed to reproduce the kind of form that saw them cruise into the third round of the Intermediate Cup with a 34-5 win over Northampton Casuals.

After two missed penalties in the first ten minutes by David Garwood, he calmed Ampthill's nerves with a successful attempt. The first try of the day followed from a 30-metre jinking run from centre Lee Matthews. Northampton Casuals got their only points on the half-hour from an intercepted pass on their own five metre line.

But the Ampthill responded five minutes later with a score from full-back Phil Timewell. On the stroke of half-time James Offer went over for a try which again Garwood converted. And after the break constant forward pressure enabled captain Danny Phillips to crash over and extend the visitors dominance. A try from winger Stuart Belcher capped a comfortable win.

Ampthill 10 Luton 15 – Dillingham Park – February 15, 2003

James Offer launches an attack. Left to right Andy Hill, Simon Spavins, James Offer, John Lasbrey, Phil Lane

Market Bosworth 14 pts. Ampthill 12 pts. – 18th January 2003

After months of winning, Ampthill were beginning to remember what losing felt like with two successive defeats. But Ampthill came within inches of stealing victory as James Offer's last-gasp drop goal attempt floated just wide.

A Market Bosworth converted try within five minutes was countered by an Offer score on the stroke of half-time. The hosts pulled away with another seven points but John Lasbury dived over under the posts and David Garwood converted. Then came much Ampthill pressure and the near miss.

2002-03	played	won	drawn	lost	pts. for	pts. against
1st XV	26	18	0	8	680	338
Exiles XV						
3rd XV						
4th XV						
Colts XV						

Season 2003-04 – (Captain – Keith Garwood)

Management Committee

President	N. Brown
Chairman	I. Cooper
Vice Chairman (Mini/Youth Chair)	R. Ewart
Hon. Treasurer	H. Cornforth
Hon. Secretary & Website Manager	C. Page
Director of Rugby	H. Cornforth
Facilities Manager	I. Owen
General Committee Members:	P. Sherry & B. Muncaster
Elected / Appointed Officers	R. Browning, Nigel Macklin, Y. Russon, B. Muncaster, N. Tinker, K. Belcher, T. Willison, J. Cresswell, J. Cresswell, A. Radley, H. Wright, F. Sherry, P. Thompson, I. Owen & V. Kaye

Playing

1st XV Manager	P. Sherry
2nd XV Manager	S. Bell
Bucks XV Manager	C. Hopgood
Extras XV Manager	L. Duffin
Colts XV Manager	T. Howe
Coach	A. Hughes

The league season began brightly enough but six games were lost, home and away, either side of Christmas, leaving the 1st XV in midtable for the third season running. However, excellent wins were recorded against Nottingham Moderns 81-18, South Leicester 48-17, Dixonians 81-3 and Banbury 36-10 at home.

League Results

Newark	13-13	away	draw	home	24-22	won
Northampton Old Scouts	31-15	home	won	away	25-13	won
Loughborough Students	19-43	away	lost	home	24-17	won
Market Bosworth	17-40	home	lost	away	20-41	lost
Syston	27-17	away	won	home	3-24	lost
Huntingdon	27-5	away	won	home	18-23	lost
Moderns	81-18	home	won	away	27-25	won
Mansfield	17-38	away	lost	home	14-37	lost
Banbury	36-10	home	won	away	29-41	lost
South Leicester	27-18	away	won	home	48-17	won
Hinckley	27-32	home	lost	away	14-19	lost

Ampthill points shown first

1st XV League: Midlands 2 East

#	Team	P	W	D	L	PF	PA	+/-	TB	LB	Pts	Adj
1	Mansfield	22	19	0	3	772	287	485	0	0	**38**	
2	Hinckley	22	19	0	3	609	294	315	0	0	**38**	
3	Market Bosworth	22	18	0	4	684	343	341	0	0	**36**	
4	South Leicester	22	16	0	6	577	416	161	0	0	**32**	
5	Ampthill	22	11	1	10	568	528	40	0	0	**23**	
6	Newark	22	10	2	10	466	460	6	0	0	**22**	
7	Loughborough Students	22	10	0	12	583	461	122	0	0	**20**	
8	Syston	22	8	1	13	408	547	-139	0	0	**15**	-2
9	Huntingdon & District	22	7	0	15	330	718	-388	0	0	**14**	
10	Northampton Old Scouts	22	6	0	16	335	575	-240	0	0	**12**	
11	Banbury	22	4	1	17	373	616	-243	0	0	**9**	
12	Nottingham Moderns	22	1	1	20	302	762	-460	0	0	**3**	

2003-04	played	won	drawn	lost	pts. for	pts. against
1st XV	30	16	1	13	755	602
2nd XV						
Extras XV						
Colts XV						

Season 2004-05 – (Captain – Lee Matthews)

Management Committee

President	N. Brown
Chairman	I. Owen
Vice Chairman (Mini/Youth Chair)	R. Ewart
Club Captain	D. Burns
Hon. Treasurer	H. Cornforth
Hon. Secretary & Website Manager	C. Page
Facilities Manager	I. Owen
General Committee Members:	P. Sherry & B. Muncaster
Elected / Appointed Officers	R. Browning, K. Tonkin, B. Carey, B. Muncaster, H. Parrish, K. Belcher, C. Stallwood, V. Martin, Y. Russon, A. Radley, C. Browning, E. Muncaster, C. Welton, F. Sherry, P. Thompson, I. Owen, V. Kaye

Playing

1st XV Manager	P. Sherry
2nd XV Manager	S. Bell
Bucks XV Manager	D. Welton
Extras XV Manager	L. Duffin
Colts XV Manager	T. Howe
Coach	J. Wilkinson

The 1st XV had an indifferent season in the league finishing in 9th. position in Midlands 2 East.

League Results

Newark	22-5	home	won	away	24-31	lost	
Old Northamptonians	46-12	away	won	home	34-58	lost	
Loughborough Students	3-45	home	lost	away	9-50	lost	
Market Bosworth	27-45	away	lost	home	14-86	lost	
Syston	27-19	home	won	away	17-15	won	
Huntingdon	18-12	home	won	away	28-18	won	
Spalding	21-17	away	won	home	7-10	lost	
Peterborough	18-35	home	lost	away	15-31	lost	
Luton	9-37	away	lost	home	12-17	lost	
South Leicester	27-27	home	draw	away	19-33	lost	
Melton Mowbray	away	6-24	lost	home	39-8	won	

Ampthill points shown first

1st XV League: Midlands 2 East

#	Team	P	W	D	L	PF	PA	+/-	TB	LB	Pts	Adj
1	Luton	22	20	0	2	791	258	533	0	0	40	
2	Market Bosworth	22	20	0	2	675	269	406	0	0	40	
3	Peterborough	22	18	0	4	737	334	403	0	0	36	
4	Loughborough Students	22	12	2	8	563	385	178	0	0	26	
5	South Leicester	22	10	2	10	479	392	87	0	0	22	
6	Old Northamptonians	22	9	1	12	445	513	-68	0	0	19	
7	Spalding	22	8	2	12	325	438	-113	0	0	18	
8	Newark	22	9	0	13	355	554	-199	0	0	18	
9	Ampthill	22	8	1	13	442	644	-202	0	0	17	
10	Melton Mowbray	22	6	0	16	243	542	-299	0	0	12	
11	Syston	22	4	0	18	272	557	-285	0	0	8	
12	Huntingdon & District	22	4	0	18	289	730	-441	0	0	6	-2

Another disappointing season of inconsistent performances for Lee Matthews' team, relegation being just avoided. Old Northamptonians were beaten away but lost to at home by 34-58. Similarly, Spalding were beaten on the road, but succumbed to at home 7-10. There were crushing defeats by Loughborough Students and Market Bosworth, but champions Luton were beaten 12-7 in December – one of their only two losses that season.

In a throw-back to the 1950s, lack of players meant that some second XV games had to be cancelled.

Ampthill's Eighth Bedfordshire Cup Final

Bedford Athletic 27 pts. Ampthill 13 pts.

The club reached its eighth Bedfordshire Knockout Cup Final, losing to Bedford Athletic at Putnoe Woods.

Ampthill took an early 13-3 lead, but tries from Gareth Graham, Matt Aldwinckle, Andy Bennett and Rob Dunne saw Athletic home 27-13.

Ampthill: S. Wilson, M. Hemmingway, L. Matthews (capt.), J. Lasbrey, J. Offer, J. Steele, K. Garwood, S. Spavins, C. Dilley, N. Cafferty, S. Jones, P. Jones, P. Lane, A. Hill, R. Campbell, D. Bell

Bedford Athletic: P. Ryder, M. Aldwinckle, K. Palm, G. Graham, A. Bennett, R. Dunne, E. Axon, D. Conaway, N. Paterson, S. Watson, M. Hudson, A. Phillips, C. Barrett, A. Bond, B. Gander

replacements: S. Williams, C. Mitcherson, M. Ireland, J. Marsh, P. Elphick, C. Philips, D. Jenkins

National Under 17s Plate Title

Ampthill 33pts. North Walsham 20pts.– Sixways – 12 March 2005

Fly-half Dan Lavery helped Ampthill to a first-ever National U17s Plate Title, scoring 18 points in a 33-20 win over North Walsham at Worcester's Sixways Stadium.

Ampthill dominated possession from the start and Lavery went over after good work from Simon Jones and Richard Tonkin. Lavery added the conversion before North Walsham stormed into a 13-7 lead with a converted try and two penalties. Ampthill missed two kicks of their own, but Lavery made amends when he converted his second try. After the re-start they continued to take the initiative with Lavery in the thick of things. He burst through the midfield to set up Richard Barnard's try before adding the conversion. Barnard then grabbed his second try thanks to a clever break from prop Chris Perrett and a good offload from Matt Higgins.

Lavery missed the conversion but he had another shot at goal minutes later when Perrett barged his way over for Ampthill's fifth and final try, and even a consolation effort from North Walsham's Jake Tittering did not dampen their celebrations.

Ampthill: Graham Day, Max Thomas, Chris Perrett, Josh Williamson, Phil Hoy, John Cresswell, Joe Williams, Tom Ball, Tom Warfield, Daniel Lavery, Coll Davis, Simon Jones, Richard Tonkin, Richard Barnard, Matthew Kay. Reps.: Dan Woodward, Matt Burke, Craig Isaacs, Martin Chalkley, Adam Andrews, Matthew Higgins, Ben Ashton

A tremendous achievement, these were local young men, the product of mini and youth and many would progress to the first XV.

2004-05	played	won	drawn	lost	pts. for	pts. against
1st XV	22	8	1	13	442	644
2nd XV						
3rd XV						
4th XV						
Colts XV						

Season 2005-06 – (Captain -Simon Spavins)

Management Committee

President	D. Williams
Chairman	Pat Sherry
Vice Chairman (Mini/Youth Chair)	N. Macklin
Club Captain	D. Burns
Hon. Treasurer	P. Aatkar
Hon. Secretary & Website Manager	C. Page
Facilities Manager	L. Barlow
General Committee Members:	A. Radley & B. Muncaster
Elected / Appointed Officers	I. Browning, K. Tonkin, J. Thomas, B. Muncaster, H. Parrish, K. Belcher, C. Stallwood, V. Martin, G. Thomas, M. Pearce, S. Heley, D. Thomas, F. Sherry & I. Owen

Playing

1st XV Manager	I. Bremner
2nd XV Manager	S. Bell
Extras XV Manager	L. Duffin
Colts Manager	N. Ashton
Coach	D. Welton

In what now seems a natural progression Dave Williams succeeded Norman Brown as Club President and Pat Sherry became Chairman. Alex Radley, a future Chairman, joined the Management Committee.

The Club was reduced to running only three senior teams, undoubtedly Ampthill players had been lured away to local clubs who could afford to pay them.

League Results

Newark	5-20	away	lost	home	38-13	won
Old Northamptonians	5-17	home	lost	away	25-30	lost
Loughborough Students	3-83	away	lost	home	22-40	lost
Matlock	10-46	home	lost	away	28-13	won
Towcestrians	5-48	away	lost	home	20-27	lost
Derby	3- 86	away	lost	home	0--57	lost
Spalding	3-28	home	lost	away	24-36	lost
Peterborough	5-84	away	lost	home	3-57	lost
Mansfield	5-35	away	lost	home	20-46	lost
Paviors	10-7	home	won	away	0-25	lost
South Leicester	7-62	away	lost	home	7-20	lost

Ampthill's point shown first

1st XV League: Midlands 2 East

#	Team	P	W	D	L	PF	PA	+/-	TB	LB	Pts
1	South Leicester	22	20	1	1	627	233	394	0	0	41
2	Peterborough	22	19	1	2	889	263	626	0	0	39
3	Derby	22	17	0	5	782	268	514	0	0	34
4	Loughborough Students	22	16	0	6	759	294	465	0	0	32
5	Old Northamptonians	22	10	0	12	487	467	20	0	0	20
6	Matlock	22	9	1	12	417	441	-24	0	0	19
7	Mansfield	22	9	1	12	401	498	-97	0	0	19
8	Paviors	22	8	1	13	383	480	-97	0	0	17
9	Newark	22	7	1	14	281	828	-547	0	0	15
10	Towcestrians	22	6	0	16	360	614	-254	0	0	12
11	Spalding	22	5	0	17	277	645	-368	0	0	10
12	Ampthill	22	3	0	19	248	880	-632	0	0	6

The 1st XV lost its first ten league games and nineteen in total; rare victories were recorded away at Newark and Matlock and at home to Paviors. The Club was relegated to Midlands 3 East (South) and the future looked bleak.

Ian Bremner

Iain Bremner began his long reign as first team manager. He had been assisting Pat Sherry since 2003-04, so the continuity was invaluable to the team. At the end of his first season if you had told him he would still be going strong fourteen seasons later – and in the Championship – he would have given you one of his trade-mark long stares! However, the Club owes Iain a debt of gratitude, he is part of the team that has delivered, season on season.

Mark Lavery – the journey begins

I am indebted to Mark Lavery for his contribution to this history, he provided a fascinating, and very personal insight, into what was to occur to the Club over the next 13 seasons.

Mark Lavery had played for Orrell in the 1980s. Orrell were an ever-present in the English First Division until 1997. They were runners up to Bath in 1991–92, losing the title on the final day of the season following a defeat by London Wasps.

Mark re-located the family to mid-Bedfordshire from Lancashire in 1995. Graham Whitehall remembers him as a "very useful player". However, he really got involved when his son Daniel joined the Mini & Youth. Daniel played for two seasons in the side coached by Colin Burke and Laurie Barlow.

The premier competition for U/9 and U/11 was the East Midlands Mobbs Cup. Mark was asked to coach the U/10 in season 1997-98 . The following season as U/11, they won the Mobbs Cup-Final at Franklins Gardens with Daniel Lavery at fly-half.

In 2002-03, Mark Lavery's team toured South Africa, raising money for the tour with an event at Parkside Hall involving Jonathan Davies, Terry Holmes, and Peter Osgood. The squad flew into Cape Town and followed the Garden route, they were to win three games and lose one, including a game against a township team.

As we have seen in 2004-05, the team won the National U/17 Plate at Sixways Stadium, with Mark as coach. This was to be the end of Mark's coaching as he had now taken the group through the Mini & Youth system. However, Harry Cornforth, having watched the success of the U/17 team, asked Mark to look after the 1st XV for one weekend whilst Harry was away. The 1st XV were playing Spalding at the Memorial Field on 21st January 2006. Four 16-year-olds, and one 17-year-old, were in the team that played against Spalding and lost 24-36. Mark Lavery and Harry Cornforth worked manfully from January to April to keep Ampthill from relegation, but on 23 January they lost 0-57 to Derby having lost the away fixture in September by 86-3.

The Mini and Youth at Ampthill have produced a number of outstanding players including Josh Bassett at Wasps and Lewis Ludlow at Gloucester. Regrettably, the senior section had been in decline for the last two seasons and the Mini and Youth players were not aspiring to play first team rugby at Ampthill.

Mark Lavery – "The trigger was when we finally dropped to level seven from level six, where we'd been for twenty years. We just said, "Listen this isn't good enough, it's not good enough for the kids." In what became known as the Club's "night of the long knives" the old committee went out, a new one came in and plans were put in place to take the Club forward. The new committee included Colin Burke (Chairman), Mark Lavery, Bill Warfield and Warren Kay who had all been involved with the U/17 XV.

Most men would have walked away from what was a daunting task of rebuilding the squad. The better players had been lured away by financial inducement – they were young men making their way in the world – and it was a rapidly changing world. However, Ampthill now had a determined leader and Mark was to prove himself a resourceful, serial winner in the seasons to come.

Ninth Bedfordshire Cup Final

Simon Spavin's side actually enjoyed a good cup run, reaching the final but losing 25-36, to Dunstablians. Simon was a capable and popular 1st. XV captain and an excellent player.

As successful season resulted in promotion for the 2nd XV.

2005-06	played	won	drawn	lost	pts. for	pts. against
1st XV	22	3	0	19	248	880
2nd XV						
Extras XV						

Season 2006-07 – (Captain – Danny Phillips)

Management Committee

President	D. Williams
Chairman	C. Burke
Vice Chairman (Mini/Youth Chair)	J. Creswell
Club Captain	D. Burns
Hon. Treasurer	B. Warfield
Hon. Secretary	W. Kay
Director of Rugby	H. Cornforth
Facilities Manager	L. Barlow
General Committee Members:	A. Radley & B. Muncaster
Elected / Appointed Officers	H. Cornforth, K. Tonkin, J. Thomas, B. Muncaster, H. Parrish, K. Belcher, V. Martin, G. Thomas, M. Pearce, S. Heley, D. Thomas, J. Thomas, M. Stanbridge & V. Kaye

Playing

Head of Coaching & Playing Development	M. Lavery
1st XV Manager	I. Bremner
2nd XV Manager	S. Bell
Extras XV Manager	N. Ashton
Colts Manager	K. Tonkin
Coach	D. Marshall
Physiotherapist	M. Dwyer

Harry Cornforth returned as Director of Rugby and he was joined by Mark Lavery as Head of Coaching and Playing Development. Dave Marshall, the RFU CRC for Bedfordshire, was appointed as coach to the 1st & 2nd XVs. Mick Dwyer became resident physiotherapist. This would prove to be a winning combination.

1st XV League: Midlands 3 East (South)

#	Team	P	W	D	L	PF	PA	+/-	TB	LB	Pts	Adj
1	Ampthill	22	17	1	4	686	266	420	0	0	35	
2	Banbury	22	17	0	5	675	302	373	0	0	34	
3	Leighton Buzzard	22	16	1	5	511	217	294	0	0	33	
4	Wellingborough	22	15	3	4	584	390	194	0	0	33	
5	Leicester Forest	21	12	1	8	466	362	104	0	0	25	
6	Towcestrians	22	11	1	10	521	398	123	0	0	23	
7	Stewarts & Lloyds	22	10	1	11	343	395	-52	0	0	21	
8	Daventry	21	7	2	12	338	442	-104	0	0	16	
9	Huntingdon & District	22	6	1	15	292	489	-197	0	0	13	
10	Northampton Casuals	22	5	1	16	260	517	-257	0	0	11	
11	Northampton Mens Own	22	5	1	16	302	786	-484	0	0	11	
12	Bugbrooke	22	3	1	18	208	622	-414	0	0	5	2

Danny Phillips' (an outstanding player) 1st XV were the champions this season, the Cornforth-Lavery-Marshall combination proving to be a very potent source of rugby success, almost immediately. However, this does not tell the whole story and in fact Ampthill lost three of the first four league matches: 3-18 away to Leighton Buzzard, 18-41 away to Banbury and 0-6 away at Stewart & Lloyds. However, Ampthill were to taste defeat in the league on only one more occasion; a surprising loss to Daventry 12-16 at Stefen Hill.

The 1st XV would play in Midlands 2 East the following season,

League Results

Leighton Buzzard	13-18	away	lost	home	21-3	won
Banbury	18-41	away	lost	home	12-10	won
Stewart & Lloyds	0-6	away	lost	home	40-13	won
Leicester Forest	39-5	home	won	away	36-17	won
Northampton Casuals	42-20	away	won	home	19-10	won
Wellingborough	33-9	home	won	away	19-19	draw
Huntingdon	22-15	away	won	home	27-6	won
Daventry	12-16	away	lost	home	42-5	won
Bugbrooke	26-14	away	won	home	62-3	won
Towcestrians	23-11	away	won	home	55-5	won
Northampton Men's Own	66-14	home	won	away	59-6	won

Ampthill points shown first

The 1st XV enjoyed a good run in the EDF Cup competition beating Old Halesonians 16-8, Brackley 37-5 and Sutton Coldfield – before losing to Leicester Forest, away, by 25-29.

2006-07	played	won	drawn	lost	pts. for	pts. against
1st XV	22	17	1	4	686	266
2nd XV						
Extras XV						

Season 2007-08 – (Captain - Phil Lane)

Management Committee

President	D. Williams
Chairman	C. Burke
Vice Chairman (Mini/Youth Chair)	J. Creswell
Hon. Treasurer	B. Warfield
Hon. Secretary	W. Kay
Director of Rugby	H. Cornforth
Facilities Manager	H. Parrish
General Committee Members:	A. Radley, B. Muncaster
Elected / Appointed Officers	C. Page, J. Thomas, B. Muncaster, J. Woodward, K. Belcher, C. Stallwood, V. Martin, S. Morgan, D. Thomas, L. Elston, M. Stanbridge, J. Cresswell

Playing

1st XV Manager	I. Bremner
2nd XV Manager	A. Walker
Extras XV Manager	L. Duffin
Colts Manager	J. Cresswell
Coach	A. Brown
Physiotherapist	M. Dwyer

Coach, Dave Marshall left the Club to become head coach of the East Midlands elite player academy. The Club was fortunate to secure the services of Alan Brown, former RFU East Midlands RDO, to coach the 1st & 2nd XVs. Alan joined the Club from Bedford Blues after successfully leading their Colts side to win the National Colts Cup. Phil Lane became 1st XV captain, a post he was to hold for six seasons – an astonishing feat in modern rugby times and a tremendous commitment. In Ampthill's history, only Norman Brown has captained the 1st XV for longer – 9 seasons – from 1951 – 1960.

1st XV League: Midlands 2 East

After gaining promotion to Midlands 2 East, a number of new players were signed. Most notably Phil Lane returned from Luton after helping them get into the national leagues. J.J. Raven also arrived from Bedford University and brought along Sam Bates, Matt Loon and Zav Swinbourne. The Club also reversed the trend of losing their best players to local semi-pro teams, indeed players began to arrive in numbers to Dillingham Park.

This was a season of consolidation, the 1st XV finished in mid-table (7th) in the very competitive Midlands 2 East, winning 10 games and losing twelve. Seven of these losses were by less than a score and three by a single point. Mark Lavery, however, knew there was a still great deal of work to be done.

League Results

Derby	17-6	home	won	away	18-10	won
Hinckley	20-34	home	lost	away	9-28	lost
Paviors	10-35	away	lost	home	17-20	lost
Newark	24-30	home	lost	away	17-18	lost
Old Northamptonians	19-13	away	won	home	54-20	won
Syston	11-12	home	lost	away	3-8	lost
Matlock	21-22	away	lost	home	12-11	won
Banbury	24-11	home	won	away	18-14	won
Kettering	13-41	away	lost	home	12-20	lost
Melton Mowbray	20-6	home	won	away	25-22	won
Market Bosworth	15-19	away	lost	home	25-19	won

Ampthill points shown first

Phil Lane's 1st XV lost all six games against the top three clubs but scored a notable 18-17 away win at fourth-placed Newark.

Midlands 2 East

#	Team	P	W	D	L	PF	PA	+/-	TB	LB	Pts
1	Kettering	22	18	1	3	688	260	428	0	0	37
2	Hinckley	22	16	2	4	444	236	208	0	0	34
3	Syston	22	16	2	4	400	264	136	0	0	34
4	Newark	22	16	0	6	574	381	193	0	0	32
5	Paviors	22	13	0	9	442	382	60	0	0	26
6	Matlock	22	12	1	9	406	401	5	0	0	25
7	Ampthill	22	10	0	12	404	429	-25	0	0	20
8	Market Bosworth	22	9	2	11	338	368	-30	0	0	20
9	Derby	22	9	1	12	372	434	-62	0	0	19
10	Old Northamptonians	22	4	0	18	377	541	-164	0	0	8
11	Banbury	22	3	0	19	215	618	-403	0	0	6
12	Melton Mowbray	22	1	1	20	274	620	-346	0	0	3

Ampthill 1st XV 2007-08

back row: **Mark Lavery, Phil Donbavand, Gareth Farbon, Danny Phillips, Phil Lane, Nick Lewis, (Iain Bremner's head) Simon Rose, Lee Matthews, Simon Spavins, Greg Mathers, Giles Witheat, Alan Brown, Harry Cornforth**
front-row: **Kieran Davies, Adam Shaw, John Lasbrey, Bruce Thomas, Rex Hedges, James Swinbourne, Ed Swannick, J.J. Raven**

The 1st XV also enjoyed an extended run in the EDF Energy Cup reaching the last sixteen - losing away to Chester, the eventual winners. Bromsgrove 80-12, Walsall 33-19, Loughborough Students 5-3 were beaten on the way.

The 2nd XV played in the Bombardier Merit Table 1 with the likes of Peterborough, Luton, Dunstable, and Kettering all clubs on a par, or a league above, at first team level. It was a much-changed squad through long-term injuries or promotion to the 1st XV. However, the 2nd XV survived the league, taking points off all the teams, except Kettering.

The Extras enjoyed a very successful season winning their East Midlands Merit Table League Division 4. Only one league game was lost, away to Peterborough and that by just one point. Arch- rival, Luton were beaten home and away.

2007-08	played	won	drawn	lost	pts. for	pts. against
1st XV	27	13	0	14	521	477
2nd XV						
Extras XV						
Colts XV						

Season 2008-09 – (Captain - Phil Lane)

Management Committee

President	D. Williams
Chairman	C. Burke
Vice Chairman (Mini/Youth Chair)	J. Creswell
1st XV Captain	P. Lane
Hon. Treasurer	B. Warfield
Hon. Secretary	W. Kay
Director of Rugby	M. Lavery
Facilities Manager	H. Parrish
Legal Representative	A. Radley
General Committee Members:	P. Farthing, B. Muncaster, J. Thomas, D. Hoy, P. Carter, P. Sherry
Elected / Appointed Officers	C. Page, J. Thomas, B. Muncaster, J. Woodward, K. Belcher,
	C. Stallwood, V. Martin, S. Morgan, E. Muncaster,
	D. Thomas, L. Elston, M. Stanbridge, S. Watson J. Cresswell
	S. Watson, M. Stanbridge

Playing

1st XV Manager	I. Bremner
2nd XV Manager	N. Stephenson
Extras XV Manager	L. Duffin
Colts Manager	J. Cresswell
Vets Manager	n/a
Coach	S. Evans (Forwards Coach) & A. Brown (Backs Coach)
Physiotherapist	M. Dwyer

1st XV League: Midlands 2 East

Harry Cornforth stood down as Director of Rugby to devote more time to his family. Mark Lavery took over the reins and appointed Stuart Evans, the former Wales, Swansea, Neath, Great Britain, and St. Helens prop, as Forwards' Coach. Mark had played for Orrell against Neath and formed a firm friendship with Stuart Evans

Director of Rugby Mark Lavery, coaches Alan Brown, Stuart Evans and physio Mick Dwyer oversaw an outstanding series of results securing a Midlands 2 East Championship and East Midlands Cup double for the 1st XV.

The second-place finish for the 2nd XV and third-place finish for the Extras in their respective merit tables was testimony to the increasing strength in depth across the Club. Nick Stephenson took over as 2nd XV's (1881s) Team Manager – an important role which he has successfully fulfilled to this date.

In his first season as captain, Phil Lane led the 1st XV to promotion, as champions of Midlands 2 East. Only two games were lost; an early 30-24 reverse at Dunstablians and a surprise home defeat in the last game of the season against Scunthorpe - Ampthill having won the fixture at Clifton Lane. During the campaign Leighton Buzzard were overwhelmed by 67-14 and Newark 64 -7, both at Dillingham Park. The division was won with the highest points scored in Midlands 2 over the last 10 years – 809.

Midlands 2 East

#	Team	P	W	D	L	PF	PA	+/-	TB	LB	Pts	Adj
1	Ampthill	22	20	0	2	809	321	488	0	0	40	
2	Scunthorpe	22	17	0	5	636	329	307	0	0	34	
3	Paviors	22	16	0	6	532	368	164	0	0	32	
4	Syston	22	15	0	7	554	277	277	0	0	30	
5	Dunstablians	22	14	1	7	594	432	162	0	0	29	
6	Newark	22	13	1	8	534	349	185	0	0	27	0
7	Mansfield	22	9	0	13	398	503	-105	0	0	18	
8	Leighton Buzzard	22	7	1	14	350	715	-365	0	0	15	
9	Matlock	22	6	0	16	370	422	-52	0	0	12	
10	Derby	22	5	1	16	267	563	-296	0	0	11	
11	Market Bosworth	22	5	0	17	323	542	-219	0	0	10	
12	Wellingborough	22	3	0	19	348	894	-546	0	0	6	

League Results

Derby	29-10	away	won	home	39-12	won
Dunstablians	24-30	away	lost	home	38-25	won
Paviors	53-10	home	won	away	41-10	won
Wellingborough	54-19	home	won	away	52-13	won
Syston	37-15	away	won	home	20-16	won
Matlock	44-7	home	won	away	13-8	won
Leighton Buzzard	29-13	away	won	home	67-14	won
Mansfield	47-8	home	won	away	34-11	won
Scunthorpe	29-13	away	won	home	18-19	lost
Market Bosworth	35-29	home	won	away	35-26	won
Newark	7-6	away	won	home	64-7	won

Ampthill points shown first

East Midlands Cup Final - March 21st 2009 - at Goldington Road

Ampthill 10 pts. Peterborough 9 pts.

A stirring second half comeback saw Ampthill edge out Peterborough 10-9 in the final of the East Midlands Senior Cup at Goldington Road and close in on the most successful season in the Club's history.

Ampthill, top of Midlands Two East, defeated a side currently sitting fifth in Midlands One with a superb Kieran Davies penalty in the seventh minute of injury time.

On a breezy, but glorious spring afternoon, at the home of Bedford Blues, the final made up in endeavour and commitment for what it lacked in flair and execution. Despite Ampthill's dominance in the tight, the two packs generally cancelled each other out. But Peterborough offered a step up in physicality and went 6-0 in front by half-time thanks to two penalty goals from forced errors.

Playing down the famous slope in the second half, Ampthill conceded another early penalty before one of the few backs moves from either side presented left wing Adam Shaw with a clear scoring chance on 50 minutes.

The defender made a desperate last-ditch tackle which was judged outside the law by the referee who, after consulting with his ideally placed assistant, awarded a penalty try, converted from under the posts by fly-half Davies. Ampthill dominated territory for the remaining half an hour but uncompromising defence saw them unable to trouble the scoreboard.

Twice they crossed the whitewash, but both times were correctly disallowed with the ball held up.

Then Ampthill missed with a drop goal attempt before, with time up on the clock, Peterborough conceded a penalty, five metres from touch on their left side and bang on the ten-metre line.

Despite having a torrid time with the boot earlier, Davies confidently placed the ball and stroked an excellent kick which hung in the air before just clearing the bar.

There was time for Peterborough to mount one last response and, ignoring the drop goal option, the favourites chose to run the ball. But four defenders finally bundled the carrier into touch by the left corner flag enabling Ampthill to clear off the park for a famous triumph.

2nd XV - The Bombardier League

#	Team	P	W	D	L	PF	PA	+/-	TB	LB	Pts
1	Peterborough 2nd XV	17	15	0	2	650	142	508	0	0	62
2	Ampthill 1881 XV	16	13	0	3	438	185	253	0	0	55
3	Luton 2nd XV	18	12	0	6	600	244	356	0	0	54
4	Kettering 2nd XV	16	11	0	5	388	348	40	0	0	49
5	Old Northamptonians 2nd XV	16	8	0	8	314	373	-59	0	0	40
6	Leighton Buzzard 2nd XV	18	7	0	11	227	312	-85	0	0	39
7	Wellingborough A	16	7	0	9	307	384	-77	0	0	37
8	Towcestrians 2nd XV	16	6	0	10	194	388	-194	0	0	34
9	Northampton Old Scouts 2nd XV	17	3	0	14	299	593	-294	0	0	26
10	Bedford Athletic 2nd XV	18	2	0	16	62	510	-448	0	0	24

It would be season 2013-14 before the 2nd XV (or the Exiles as old-timers remember them) became the 1881s – named after the year when Messrs. Tanqueray etc famously formed the Club at the King's Head Inn, in Woburn Street.

The 2nd XV, as named in the club handbook had a successful league campaign finishing second to a dominant Peterborough team. On 7 March 2009, Ampthill beat Peterborough 35-14 at home but lost the away fixture at Fengate by 14-17. The only other reverses were a 0-20 loss to Leighton Buzzard at home and a defeat by 6-27 to Luton away.

Other Senior Teams Leagues

Jets (3rd XV) – Division 2
played   won   drawn   lost   pts. for   pts. against   points
21   11   0   10   423   358   60
The Jets finished in sixth place in a league of 14 teams

Extras (4th XV) – Eagle IPA League

played   won   drawn   lost   pts. for   pts. against   points
17   9   0   8   337   249   44
The Extras finished in third place in a league of ten teams.

2008-09	played	won	drawn	lost	pts. for	pts. against
1st XV	24*	22	0	2	809	321
2nd XV	16	13	0	3	438	185
Extras XV	17	9	0	8	337	249
Vets XV						
Colts XV						

excludes pre-season friendlies*

During the close season Mark Lavery was instrumental in securing the services of former Wales coach and latterly head coach at Worcester Warriors, Clive Griffiths, to oversee defence and skills. Simon Emms, former Wales, and Northampton Saints prop added the role of forwards coach to his playing duties. For 2009-10, Stuart Evans became Head Coach and Alan Brown would concentrate on attack. It was also announced that the Club would field a 4th XV again who would share fixtures with the Vets in an East Midlands Merit Table.

Colin Burke

The Club Chairman, Colin Burke, made the following announcement in March 2009:

"The 2008-09 season has been one of unprecedented achievement and progress due entirely to the efforts of many club member volunteers, coaches, parents and players of all ages.

On the playing side the senior, youth and mini squads have brought more silverware to Dillingham Park than ever before. Across the Club player development has reached a new zenith with more players pulling on representative shirts while more and more of our youth system are receiving CB, RFU elite player and GP academy recognition.

The on-field success has been matched by improvements to the clubhouse, the award of the RFU "Seal of Approval" and confirmation by East Midlands and the RFU of Ampthill's preferred status for financial support for infrastructure development.

Olney Field

Off the field we have negotiated an agreement with local land-owner David Olney, whose sons have been through our mini & youth system, to acquire the field immediately adjacent to Dillingham Park and are currently preparing a Whole Club Development Plan in conjunction with the RFU which is the last hurdle before funding commitments from Sport England, the Rugby Football Foundation and other partners can be confirmed for the project to transform the new land into pitches and training areas.

To raise funds to purchase the freehold for the two new pitches every age group from under 6 all the way through to the senior sides were required "to raise at least £750 per season over the next few years to achieve this."

FOAR - Friends of Ampthill Rugby

The Friends of Ampthill Rugby is a new fund-raising concept from the committee whose proceeds will be held in a separate, ring-fenced, bank account to be used for the acquisition and development of the infrastructure and facilities at Dillingham Park. We are asking the members and supporters to commit to a regular monthly payment of at least £10 for a period of 3 years (£120/yr., £360 in total, you may of course make a single payment) and hope that we will find at least 100 parties prepared to commit who will raise a total of £360,000 between them by the end of the third year. We are confident that, should we be able to raise this amount, it will seed up to £300,000 further funding from external partners enabling us to transform our facilities.

In return every individual or company who becomes a FOAR will have their name recorded on a plaque in the clubhouse and a monolith to be located in the new field after development."

POAR – Partners of Ampthill Rugby

The Partners of Ampthill Rugby is a scheme specifically for businesses and based on the POAR principles. Your company commits to a regular payment of at least £50 per month or £600 per year for a minimum period. This will give you a pitch-side advertising board for free, your business name on a plaque in the clubhouse and be on the monolith that is being located in the new field development to serve as a permanent reminder of your company's commitment and involvement with the club for future generations

RFU Seal of Approval

Off the field, the Club achieved RFU "Seal of Approval" status after a great deal of work from many volunteers led by vice chair Jonny Cresswell.

Jonny Cresswell (Vice-Chairman & Chair of Mini & Youth) receiving the RFU Seal of Approval from East Midlands President, Derek Watkins

Season 2009-10 – (Captain – Phil Lane)

Management Committee

President	D. Williams
Chairman	C. Burke
Vice Chairman (Chair of Youth Rugby)	J. Cresswell
1st XV Captain	D. Phillips
Hon. Treasurer	B. Warfield
Hon. Secretary	W. Kay
Director of Rugby	M. Lavery
Facilities Manager	H. Parrish
Legal Representative	A. Radley
Chair of Mini Rugby	B. McTavish
General Committee members:	B. Muncaster, J. Thomas, D. Hoy, C. Ashby, P. Carter
Elected / Appointed Officers	C. Page, J. Thomas, B. Muncaster, J. Woodward, K. Belcher, C. Stallwood, V. Martin, S. Morgan, D. Thomas, L. Elston, M. Stanbridge, S. Watson J. Cresswell, C. Ashby & L. Barlow & E. Muncaster

Playing

1st XV Manager	I. Bremner
2nd XV Manager	N. Stephenson
Extras XV Manager	L. Duffin
4th XV/Vets Manager	D. Wheeler
Colts Manager	N. Woodward
Coach	S. Evans, A. Brown, C. Griffiths
Physiotherapist	M. Dwyer

National League 3 Midlands (level 5)

This season new players included, Simon Emms, Andy Rees, Matt Burke, Dan Lavery and Tom Warfield.

Ampthill topped National Division 3 Midlands, having been crowned winners after round 23, following a 41-7 victory over Hereford at Wyeside on April 3rd 2010, as results elsewhere also went their way.

The champions earned yet another first-half bonus point with four tries before the interval despite the game being played in terrible weather conditions, with standing water on some parts of the pitch.

Scrum-half Thomas Warfield was the first of Ampthill's six try scorers to cross the whitewash.

Prop Andrew Reece, centre Jonathan Raven and flanker Matthew Burke all went over before the interval, while Hereford hit back through the Fijian Rabuka and Gary Preece converted the home sides effort to make the half-time score 29-7.

Tries from winger Ben Brierley and second-row Gareth Ellis sealed the victory in the second-half while Kieron Davies added four conversions and a penalty for a personal haul of 11 points.

Phil Lanes' 1st XV topped the league, 11 points clear of second placed Luctonians and scored over 1,000 points for the season. The only real disappointment was the loss at home 0-53 to Luctonians on the last game of the season, May 1st 2010, with promotion already gained. However, the greatest game in the Club's history to date, the clash with mighty Jersey, was to take place at Twickenham on Saturday May 8th.

Bedford Athletic had a wretched season, losing all 26 games, including 10-71 to Ampthill at Putnoe Woods and 6-64 at Dillingham Park.

National League 3 Midlands

#	Team	P	W	D	L	PF	PA	+/-	TB	LB	Pts	Adj
1	Ampthill	26	22	0	4	1012	377	635	19	3	100	-10
2	Luctonians	26	18	1	7	743	349	394	11	4	89	
3	Hinckley	26	18	1	7	649	427	222	10	4	88	
4	Luton	26	17	1	8	898	501	397	15	2	87	
5	Bromsgrove	26	16	2	8	611	581	30	10	2	80	
6	Longton	26	14	0	12	498	443	55	7	7	70	
7	Peterborough	26	12	2	12	572	561	11	10	5	67	
8	Hereford	26	13	2	11	550	558	-8	7	2	65	
9	Kenilworth	26	11	0	15	505	726	-221	6	4	54	
10	Newport (Salop)	26	10	1	15	535	552	-17	6	6	54	
11	South Leicester	26	10	1	15	483	553	-70	8	4	54	
12	Malvern	26	8	2	16	423	604	-181	5	5	46	
13	Kettering	26	6	1	19	437	627	-190	5	5	36	
14	Bedford Athletic	26	0	0	26	283	1340	-1057	2	4	1	-5

League Results – 1st XV

South Leicester	20-6	home	won	away	51-13	won
Bedford Athletic	71-10	home	won	away	64-6	won
Bromsgrove	26-28	away	lost	home	37-14	won
Hereford	50-8	home	won	away	41-7	won
Hinckley	24-19	away	won	home	52-13	won
Kenilworth	42-19	home	won	away	40-17	won
Kettering	26-8	away	won	home	56-14	won
Longton	66-3	home	won	away	15-21	lost
Luctonians	27-10	away	won	home	0-53	lost
Malvern	26-19	home	won	away	53-0	won
Newport (Salop)	14-16	away	lost	home	38-13	won
Peterborough	29-6	home	won	away	35-28	won
Luton	30-7	away	won	home	79-19	won

Ampthill points shown first

On 30th January 2010 Ampthill postponed the match against Kettering without a referee being present, but denied it was it was to gain "premeditated advantage." The following news appeared in the national press:

Champions Ampthill Rapped on Disrepute Charge

National Three Midlands club Ampthill have been summoned to appear before a Rugby Football Union disciplinary panel next Tuesday on a charge of allegedly bringing the game into disrepute. Ampthill have been charged with an offence of conduct prejudicial to the interests of Union/or the game contrary to Rule 5.12 of the RFU. It is alleged that an officer of the Club deliberately attempted to mislead an RFU Competitions Appeal Panel by fabricating false evidence.

The Club has also been charged with a breach of Game Regulation 16.3 that they allegedly failed to field their strongest team in their league match against Luctonians on May 1st. Ampthill will appear before an RFU disciplinary panel at the Coventry M6 Holiday Inn Hotel on May 18th at 6.30pm.

The panel comprised of chairman Antony Davies, John Brennan and Mike Curling recommended that Hinckley should be promoted to take Ampthill's place in National Two North the following season. Ampthill had ten points deducted, which still made them champions, although promotion was denied them.

Mark Lavery remembers feeling that the Club was not really ready to compete at National 2 level, so this, long-term, may be seen as a blessing in disguise.

Ampthill would level transfer to National 3 London & SE the following season, where they would finish fourth. Hinckley would finish in 15th place in National Two North, one place above relegated Newbury Blues.

Other Senior Teams Leagues

Jets (3rd XV) – Waggledance League

played	won	drawn	lost	pts. for	pts. against	points
14	11	0	3	512	96	47

The Jets finished as runners-up, 18 points behind Bedford Swifts 2nd XV.

Extras (4th XV) – Eagle IPA League

played	won	drawn	lost	pts. for	pts. against	points
16	9	0	7	338	427	43

The Extras finished fourth, out of ten teams.

National Three Champions Cup Final at Twickenham

Ampthill 12pts. Jersey 21 pts.

Ampthill's Director of Rugby Mark Lavery said his team can be proud that they gave Jersey the "fright of their lives" despite being edged out in the in the Champions Cup Final at Twickenham.

The showpiece proved one step too far for the National Three Midlands title winners as they came up against an all-conquering Jersey side whose victory gave them an historic treble, after being crowned League and Siam Cup Champions.

"We've given a good account of ourselves and certainly flown the flag for Bedfordshire," said Lavery. "In the end it was probably the difference between an amateur and a professional team. They have got ten full time players in their team and some from South Africa, Australia, New Zealand and the South Pacific, whereas we've got a head coach who travels from Wales.

We've had 11 weeks without a break and I think that showed in the end, but I am extremely proud of the effort from the entire squad. I wouldn't say it was a disappointment. If anything, we've overachieved and given a very good side the fright of their lives. I think we can be proud of that. We didn't come to lose but we were the underdogs. I think it would have been disappointing if we'd played poorly but our forwards played extremely well against a formidable pack and Jersey seemed to score all their points from our mistakes."

Mark Lavery is certain that the club's first trip to the national rugby stadium combined with their triumphant league season, romping to the title despite a ten-point reduction, will push the club on to greater heights next season.

"Winning the National Three title has put us on the map and got people calling us," he said. "When we went into that league it was a step up, so next year will be another challenge, but I think we will equip ourselves well."

A strong Jersey ran in a try within five minutes, but Ampthill levelled on 20 minutes with the best score of the game, moving the ball through the entire length of the field for Ben Brierley to cross over to the right of the posts.

A penalty saw Jersey leave Ampthill 8-5 down at the break, though they felt they should have had a penalty try five minutes before that for one of the many Jersey infringements at the scrum that went unpunished throughout the game.

The Reds scored again straight from the restart with an unconverted try and another penalty midway through the half, doubled Jersey's first half tally, before a sin-binning offered Ampthill the chance to attack a chink in the Jersey armour. But a concerted ten-minute period of Ampthill pressure saw phase after phase repelled close to the try line, while scrums were spun and collapsed by the Reds without being penalised.

Then from deep in their territory on 70 minutes Jersey scored an intercepted try. A never say die Ampthill were finally awarded a penalty try five minutes from time and Kieron Davies converted though it was too late for a comeback.

Proud Ampthill captain Phil Lane admitted it was "just a game too far. All the boys have put in an awesome performance today. They have been great all year and, to top it of with a Twickenham final you can't ask for anymore. We were in the game at half-time and then in the second half we camped on their line, put pressure on them and, had we scored again early, it could have been a different game. But we conceded another try and it was game over."

As we have seen Ampthill under Mark Lavery and Harry Cornforth had recruited extensively to strengthen the side. There were, though, locally-born players in the squad that faced Jersey.

Shane Allen, Phil Lane, John Lasbrey, Nicholas Lewis, and Thomas Warfield were all Bedfordshire born.

Nick Lewis (pictured above – third player from the right) is worthy of mention. Born in Maulden, Nick had forced his way into the 1st XV having started his Ampthill career with Liam Duffin's Extras, but when the "cavalry" arrived he maintained his place in the first team. The second-rower had made his debut on the 2000 tour to Doncaster.

The Mob at Twickenham

Rebecca Lane with Freddy

A proud Phil Lane leads the Ampthill team from the field

Ampthill squad: **Shane Allen, Keni Barrett, Benjamin Brierly, Matthew Burke, Kieron Davies, Philip Donbavand, Gareth Ellis, Simon Emms, Thomas Jankowski, Phil Lane, John Lasbrey, Daniel Lavery, Nicholas Lewis, Matthew Loon, Ryan Price, Jonathan Raven, Andrew Rees, Samuel Richbell, Adam Shaw, Ryan Spence, James Swinbourne, Thomas Warfield, Oliver Wills.**

Management: **Stuart Evans, Simon Emms, Alan Brown, Clive Griffiths, Iain Bremner, Michael Dwyer, Rhiannon Parry & Farouk Boudissa.**

2nd XV - Bombardier League

For reasons best forgotten the 2nd XV was called the All Stars this season – but this was probably justified, as like the 1st XV they finished as champions of the Bombardier League six points clear of Luton.

#	Team	P	W	D	L	PF	PA	+/-	TB	LB	Pts
1	Ampthill 1881 XV	19	16	0	3	606	217	389	0	0	67
2	Luton 2nd XV	19	14	0	5	466	302	164	0	0	61
3	Kettering 2nd XV	19	12	0	7	552	233	319	0	0	55
4	Peterborough 2nd XV	18	11	0	7	516	304	212	0	0	51
5	Old Northamptonians 2nd XV	19	8	0	11	492	424	68	0	0	43
6	Dunstablians 2nd XV	18	8	0	10	284	363	-79	0	0	42
7	Leighton Buzzard 2nd XV	18	7	1	10	279	505	-226	0	0	40
8	Wellingborough A	18	7	0	11	299	395	-96	0	0	39
9	Northampton Old Scouts 2nd XV	15	7	0	8	351	419	-68	0	0	36
10	Milton Keynes 2nd XV	18	5	0	13	212	628	-416	0	0	33
11	Towcestrians 2nd XV	17	3	1	13	258	525	-267	0	0	27

The 1881s won the Bombardier League by six points, this being the highest league for non-1st XV's in the East Midlands. Runners up Luton were beaten 39-5, Dunstablians 50-15 & 53-0 and Old Northamptonians 41-12.

2009-10	played	won	drawn	lost	pts. for	pts. against
1st XV	29	24	0	5	1100	430
2nd XV	19	16	0	3	606	217
4th XV/Vets						
Extras XV	16	9	0	7	388	427
Colts XV						

Iain Bremner (1st XV Manager) & Mick Dwyer (Lead Therapist)

10 Year Fixture Comparison (1st XV) 2000-2010

	2000/01		2010/11
Aug.	Banbury		
	Olney		
Sept.	Dunstablians*	Sept.	South Leicester*
	Scunthorpe (Tetley Cup)		Bedford Athletic*
	Huntingdon & District*		Bromsgrove*
	Kettering*		Hereford*
	Leighton Buzzard*		
Oct.	Lincoln*	Oct.	Hinckley*
	Luton*		Kenilworth*
	Mansfield*		Kettering*
			Longton*
			Luctonians
Nov.	Kettering*	Nov.	Malvern*
	Nottingham Moderns*		Newport (Salop)*
	Syston*		Peterborough*
Dec.	Wellingborough*	Dec.	Bedford Athletic*
	Leighton Buzzard (Beds. Cup)		Bromsgrove*
	Stockwood Park*		
Jan.	Nottingham Moderns*	Jan.	Hereford*
	Mansfield*		Hinckley*
	Dunstablians (Beds. Cup)		Kenilworth*
	Luton*		
	Lincoln*		
Feb.	Leighton Buzzard*	Feb.	Longton*
	Dunstablians (Beds. Cup)		
	Kettering*		
Mar.	Huntingdon & District*	Mar.	Malvern*
	Dunstablians*		Newport (Salop)*
	Kettering*		Peterborough*
	Wellingborough*		Luton*
Apr.	Syston*	Apr.	South Leicester*
			Morley
			Luctonians
			Jersey (Champions Cup Final)

*League matches Midlands League Two East   *League matches National 3 Midlands

Chapter 8 (2010–2019) – The Race to the Championship!

Season 2010-11 (Captain – Phil Lane)

Management Committee

President	D. Williams
Chairman	C. Burke
Vice Chairman	J. Cresswell
Hon. Treasurer	B. Warfield
Hon. Secretary	I. Titman
Director of Rugby	M. Lavery
Chair of Mini Rugby	B. McTavish
General Committee members:	B. Muncaster, J. Thomas, D. Hoy, C. Ashby, P. Carter, J. Bishop, R. Blumire
Elected / Appointed Officers	C. Page, J. Thomas, B. Muncaster, J. Woodward, K. Belcher, C. Stallwood, V. Martin, S. Morgan, W. Kaye, D. Thomas, L. Elston, M. Stanbridge, S. Watson J. Cresswell, C. Ashby & E. Muncaster

Playing

1st XV Manager	I. Bremner
2nd XV Manager	N. Stephenson
Extras XV Manager	L. Duffin
4th XV Manager	S. Jones
Vets XV Manager	D. Wheeler
Colts XV Manager	N. Woodward
Coach	S. Evans (Head Coach), A. Brown, C. Griffiths

New players appearing for Ampthill this season included; Stuart Riding (Barking), Tom Jankowski (Bedford), Paul Davies (Neath), Lee Ankar (Luton), Danny Pointon (Northampton Saints and England U18s), Andy Rees (Neath), Daniel Lavery (Ampthill, England U/16), Ryan Price (- Cardiff), Karl Braband (Rugby Lions), Benjamin Forbes (prop), Stuart Riding (Rushden) and Paul Davies (Neath). For the first time in the history of the Club, former Welsh international and British Lion Darren Morris travelled from Wales with Stuart Evans.

Entrance Charges for 1st XV Home Games

This season Colin Burke, Club Chairman, wrote to all members concerning the levying of entrance charges for National 3 home games:

"Running a successful team at this high level is very expensive and requires all sorts of additional expenses and club commitments – and this doesn't include paying **any** players. An entrance charge to watch all the other teams in this league is levied to ALL spectators for exactly the same reasons. Our Ampthill 1st XV team is successful; we were Champions of National League Three last season and went all the way to Twickenham to play in the Cup Final. We expect another great season this year!"

The charges would be:

All ages from 17 and below	Free
All Members	£3 on production of yellow membership Card
All Non-Members	£5
Life Members	Donations at your discretion

1st XV League Results

Barnes	22-44	home	lost	away	12-43	lost
Bracknell	32-18	away	won	home	30-10	won
Tring	50-7	home	won	away	14-13	won
Gravesend	53-24	away	won	home	29-21	won
Bishop Stortford	38-25	home	won	away	39-19	won
Diss	41-17	away	won	home	64-7	won
Hertford	26-29	away	lost	home	12-17	lost
Dorking	57-13	home	won	away	17-31	lost
Havant	40-14	home	won	away	20-32	lost
Staines	20-20	away	draw	home	28-14	won
North Walsham	40-5	home	won	away	42-7	won
Basingstoke	25-21	away	won	home	41-5	won
CS Stags 1863	26-38	away	lost	home	30-24	won

Ampthill points shown first

This was a very competitive league and Ampthill's campaign was commendable – a 4th place behind Barnes, Hertford and Dorking. With these three teams, Ampthill finished well clear of the rest of the league. In October, Ampthill beat Dorking 57-13 at home, the Surrey-based club would finish third. Narrow losses were achieved against second-placed Hertford, but champions Barnes beat Ampthill comfortably home and away.

1st XV National 3 London & South-East

#	Team	P	W	D	L	PF	PA	+/-	TB	LB	Pts
1	Barnes	26	24	0	2	1006	471	535	23	1	120
2	Hertford	26	24	0	2	1067	353	714	21	1	118
3	Dorking	26	19	0	7	902	563	339	18	2	96
4	Ampthill	26	18	1	7	848	518	330	16	2	92
5	Bracknell	26	14	0	12	660	611	49	10	5	71
6	Gravesend	26	13	0	13	690	601	89	10	6	68
7	CS Stags 1863	26	12	0	14	701	781	-80	13	5	66
8	Bishop's Stortford	26	13	0	13	621	715	-94	7	1	60
9	Staines	26	10	2	14	576	517	59	7	6	57
10	Tring	26	11	0	15	584	668	-84	8	4	56
11	Havant	26	8	0	18	546	848	-302	10	6	48
12	Basingstoke	26	7	0	19	466	822	-356	2	7	37
13	North Walsham	26	5	1	20	353	861	-508	5	4	31
14	Diss	26	2	0	24	329	1020	-691	2	5	15

It became apparent, very quickly, that the National 3 London and South-East Division was significantly stronger than National 3 Midlands League with a number of southern hemisphere players playing for the various clubs in and around the capital.

1881 XV - Bombardier League

#	Team	P	W	D	L	PF	PA	+/-	TB	LB	Pts
1	Luton 2nd XV	17	14	0	3	484	202	282	0	0	59
2	Kettering 2nd XV	18	13	1	4	423	245	178	0	0	58
3	Old Northamptonians 2nd XV	17	12	0	5	682	198	484	0	0	53
4	Peterborough 2nd XV	18	10	0	8	434	276	158	0	0	47
5	Ampthill 1881 XV	16	11	0	5	374	240	134	0	0	46
6	Leighton Buzzard 2nd XV	18	9	1	8	414	332	82	0	0	45
7	Dunstablians 2nd XV	18	5	0	13	229	662	-433	0	0	31
8	Wellingborough A	17	3	3	11	299	498	-199	0	0	29
9	Bedford Athletic 2nd XV	18	3	1	14	228	658	-430	0	0	24
10	Northampton Old Scouts 2nd XV	15	3	0	12	139	395	-256	0	0	18

The 2nd XV won a creditable 11 matches in the Bombardier League and finished a respectable fifth.

Other Senior Teams Leagues

Jets (3rd XV) – Waggledance League

played	won	drawn	lost	pts. for	pts. against	points
18	15	0	3	753	118	63

The Jets finished as champions on points difference over Kempston 2nd XV, scoring 753 points.

Extras (4th XV) – Eagle IPA League

played	won	drawn	lost	pts. for	pts. against	points
17	10	0	7	359	245	47

The Extras finished in fifth position in a league of ten.

	played	won	drawn	lost	pts. for	pts. against
2010-11						
1st XV	27	19	1	7	827	456
2nd XV	16	11	0	5	375	240
Jets XV	16	8	0	8	339	284
Extras XV	8	3	1	4	196	214
5th XV	13	6	0	7	330	322
Vets XV						
Colts XV						

The Creation of Two New Pitches

Author's note: - The following article was written by Martin Wythe, Ampthill Rugby Club's Head Groundsman. It appeared in the Pitchcare Magazine issue 55, on 18th July 2014. I include it here, with only minor amendments, with Martin's permission.

The Ampthill Job – two new pitches and major renovations

Martin Wythe with Wallace

Situated smack bang in the middle of an imaginary triangle formed by Bedford, Milton Keynes and Hitchin, Ampthill Rugby Club has seen rapid development over the past ten years, propelling the club from the local leagues to the fist team being runners-up in National 2 South. The club has seen success not only in the first team; the Development side (1881s) and the Extras winning their respective leagues. Established in 1881, the club has over a thousand senior members in addition to 520 junior members aged 6-17. Ampthill RUFC is proud to hold onto community values, offering a standard of rugby for everyone, with five senior teams and a ladies team. The current President, Dave Williams, has been a member for fifty years and held the post of president for the past nine years.

Poor Soil: Having taken core samples, it was clear that the soil profile was very layered where enthusiastic volunteers had put varying layers of "topsoil" over some well-draining sand. My initial suggestion was to dig up the pitches – as one can imagine – this met with some rather sceptical reactions and I was asked to work on a less radical approach!

The Two Original Pitches 2005 – 2011

As their groundsman, and a contractor in my own right, the club asked me to look at their two pitches and produce a programme of works to improve, what were, poor playing surfaces.

Pitch Flooding: The first task was to stop water pouring from the adjacent road, across the car park and down the 1st team pitch. This involved the installation of 100mm drain and a 3m deep soakaway along the edge of the car park, which solved the initial ingress of water.

Until this year, I have worked on aeration, fertilising, and topdressing. From week to week, I use a Sisis DP 36 Slitter, but also hire in a contractor to verti-drain annually: once during renovations and again in October or November.

I have soil analysis carried out annually and fertiliser selection is made according to the report. As and when club finances allowed, we would top-dress with sand (60 tonnes per pitch) in order to improve levels and drainage. These two pitches are located adjacent to the clubhouse. One is floodlit and used for training six days a week, so it takes quite a battering, and the other is used most weekends.

New Pitch Development 2011 – Present

In 2011, with the help of the RFU and many supporters, Ampthill Rugby Club began the construction of two brand new pitches set back behind the clubhouse on Olney Field.

Perched on the side of the Greensand Ridge, the new pitches are set amongst ancient woodland and adjacent to a Site of Special Scientific Interest and Ampthill Great Park – Capability Brown circa 1771.

All works carried out in this project had to be as sympathetic as possible to the surrounding landscape and wildlife. Close liaison with the Wildlife Trust and various other agencies ensured that these obligations were met and we are in the process of developing a sympathetic management plan for the areas surrounding the pitches; this is likely to include sheep grazing to encourage flora and fauna.

Dig It Up!

Full excavation of the existing landscape was necessary to achieve a level playing surface. This was a mammoth task and took around eight weeks to complete. Works began in early May 2011 and, as we had no facility for water, we were very much at the mercy of the rain gods!!

The RFU's Jim Hacker designed the pitches and the RFU's preferred contractor was John Greasley Ltd. The new pitches were terraced out of the Greensand Ridge using huge 3600 excavators, bulldozers, and dumpers. Laser levelling ensured a precise construction and TerraCottem was used to improve water retention and increase Cation Exchange Capacity (CEC).

After consultation with the club, Jim Hacker decided to start with a combination of perennial rye grass and smooth stalk meadow grass mix, as this would be a hard wearing and drought resistant combination. We now use a 100% rye grass mix for quick establishment.

Having had the soil analysis back this spring, there is a high phosphate content, which appears to be the nature of the sand, plus a manganese deficiency. I applied a 12:0:6+2 Mn to help remedy these problems. Early in June, I sprayed with seaweed (Maxicrop Triple) to improve root growth and increase microbial activity.

In March 2013, following completion of the pitches, Keith Kent, the RFU Twickenham Head Groundsman, was on a national road trip visiting junior league grounds and we were lucky enough that he paid us a visit. He gave me a rather concerned look upon being told we had not installed a drainage system of any kind. Concern soon turned to relief when I informed him that we had been blessed with thirty feet of pure sand under the new pitches!

The first game played on the new pitches was in March 2013 (our last game of the 2012/13 season). This season has been the first full seasons use, having had the wettest winter in living memory; the pitches could not have performed better. They were never "heavy" and have suffered little wear, which is a testament to the fantastic drainage.

As the pitches are quite remote from the clubhouse, it is quite amusing to see the reaction of visiting supporters when they get to the top of the hill and look down on the vast natural amphitheatre.

The Committee Relents

This spring, having two new pitches to fall back on, the committee felt they were in a position to allow me to deep cultivate and re-level the original pitches next to the clubhouse. We initially looked to employ the services of a sportsground contractor to laser level these pitches. After receiving quotations for the proposed works, the club decided that, having made a huge financial commitment to the new pitches, this would be a step too far. I proposed to carry the work out "in-house" and was set the task of bringing together costings and a programme of works.

To overcome the layering, root breaks and consequent capillary lock I proposed using a local agricultural contractor to initially rotavate to a depth of 300mm and then power harrow overall three times. The aim was to produce a consistent soil profile. Using a 6m harrow, we reduced undulations and produced fine tilth. This enabled me to use my John Deere 855 and bed grader to create smooth running levels. This was never a perfect solution but was cost effective,

Carrying out this cultivation has had the added benefit of removing a growing annual meadow grass problem. The seed was then drilled using my ancient Gandy seeder. As we have an unusual soil analysis showing a large amount of phosphates, we are again using a 12:0:6+2% Mn as a pre-seeder. I will also apply seaweed to improve root growth and drought tolerance, in mid to late June.

Keith Kent has written up a short report on the club grounds, including this observation: "There is a plan to plough up this pitch, if the club can get a grant. It does undulate and runaway in the corners and I know that, in Martin, they have a guy who will be able to do a proper job for the club."

The seed is in, and now our fingers are crossed for a damp start to the summer. In conclusion, it has been an interesting journey over the past decade, developing the pitches and working with a forward-looking and ambitious committee who are committed to maintaining and improving the grounds to meet the aspirations of all our playing members.

Season 2011-12 - (Captain Phil Lane)

Management Committee

President	D. Williams
Chairman	C. Burke
1st XV Captain	P. Lane
Hon. Treasurer	B. Warfield
Hon. Secretary	I. Titman
Director of Rugby	M. Lavery
Chair of Mini Rugby	B. McTavish
General Committee members:	B. Muncaster, P. Carter, J. Bishop, K. Belcher
Elected /Appointed Officers	C. Page, J. Thomas, B. Muncaster, J. Woodward,
	K. Belcher, C. Stallwood, V. Martin, S. Morgan, W. Kaye,
	D. Thomas, L. Elston, M. Stanbridge, S. Watson J.
	Cresswell, C. Ashby & E. Muncaster

Playing

1st XV Manager	I. Bremner
2nd XV Manager	N. Stephenson
Extras XV Manager	L. Duffin
4th XV Manager	S. Jones
Vets Manager	D. Wheeler
Colts Manager	N. Woodward
Coach	S. Evans, A. Brown, C. Griffiths

New players for this season included Kyle Palmer (South African winger), Joe Sproston (prop – North Wales Region RGC), Ross Davies (prop - Neath), Gavin Williams (scrum-half – Warrington Wolves), Craig Ross (winger - Caldy), Richard Emms brother of Simon Emms (hooker - Ospreys), Chris Anderson (fly-half – Neath), Liam Munro (flanker – Rugby Lions) and Ben Saville (hooker – Gloucester).

Stuart Evans knew Paul Turner, who had stepped down as Head Coach of Newport Gwent Dragons, and invited him to act as a part-time backs coach. Paul would also work with Wasps as skills coach.

Grand Opening of New Pitches

In April 2012, a spokesman for the Club told the local press: "The £260,000 project which was grant and loan-aided by the Rugby Football Union via their Sport England funding, the Rugby Football Foundation and Central Bedfordshire Council, would not have been possible without the generosity of Sally and David Olney. As well as those many individuals and organisations who together make up the Friends and Partners of Ampthill Rugby."

On Sunday 15th April 2012, the new pitches were officially opened by Sally Bacon, Mayor of Ampthill, and rugby legend Jason Robinson. Sally Bacon had this to say, "It is an honour to open the new rugby pitches for Ampthill & District Community Rugby Club. The club is a great asset to Ampthill and the surrounding area and has always strived to encourage the youth of Ampthill to achieve their rugby potential with great success. I am pleased to welcome our friends from Nissan-Lez-Ensérune and surrounding area, and hope that they have an enjoyable visit. "Bonne chance!"

The day included rugby activity between Nissan and Ampthill under 14s and a social during the evening. Twinning with Nissan had begun two years previously. In 2011, the Ampthill under 13 rugby team travelled to Nissan for their end of season tour where they received a very warm welcome and a weekend of fun both on and off the pitch.

Writing in the programme of the day Dave Williams, Club President, had this to say:

"These pitches will be enjoyed by the Mini and Youth players of Ampthill Rugby Club for many years into the future. This is a Rugby Club with strong roots in the local community and has been established for many years.

To find the start of Mini and Youth at the club we have to go back to 1971 when Colin Tanner, the local Cub/Scout leader, asked me to teach his cubs to play rugby, in order that they could obtain the Sportsman's badge. They had to do two sports and everyone played soccer. This I agreed to do, so I coached them for six weeks on Saturday mornings and set a little exam at the end."

Opening of new pitches: Jason Robinson and Bruce McTavish (Mini & Youth) – Sunday 15th April 2012

1st XV League: National League 3 London & South-East

#	Team	P	W	D	L	PF	PA	+/-	TB	LB	Pts	Adj
1	Canterbury	26	24	0	2	1108	422	686	22	0	118	
2	Tonbridge Juddians	26	20	1	5	997	431	566	20	1	103	
3	Ampthill	26	19	1	6	957	473	484	20	5	103	
4	Bishop's Stortford	26	21	0	5	900	498	402	15	1	100	
5	Dorking	26	18	0	8	855	490	365	15	4	91	
6	CS Stags 1863	26	13	0	13	660	628	32	11	3	66	
7	Tring	26	13	0	13	669	673	-4	10	4	66	
8	Staines	26	11	0	15	518	679	-161	6	5	55	
9	London Irish Wild Geese	26	11	1	14	579	681	-102	5	4	50	-5
10	Westcliff	26	9	1	16	611	796	-185	7	4	49	
11	Gravesend	26	8	1	17	547	783	-236	7	5	46	
12	Bracknell	26	6	0	20	526	739	-213	7	4	35	
13	Luton	26	4	0	22	351	891	-540	3	1	20	
14	Havant	26	2	1	23	328	1422	-1094	3	2	15	

Ampthill finished third with the same points as second placed Tonbridge who had lost one game less.

League Results

Tonbridge Juddians	22-32	home	lost	away	8-8	draw
Tring	21-22	away	lost	home	33-6	won
Bracknell	56-16	home	won	away	60-24	won
London Irish Wild Geese	20-21	away	lost	home	52-12	won
Westcliff	44-40	home	won	away	39-15	won
Gravesend	37-10	away	won	home	35-26	won
Dorking	30-23	home	won	away	21-17	won
Havant	70-13	away	won	home	66-0	won
Staines	49-3	home	won	away	36-10	won
Canterbury	24-31	home	lost	away	33-24	won
Luton	33-18	away	won	home	32-3	won
CS Stags 1863	35-23	home	won	away	52-17	won
Bishop's Stortford	22-28	away	lost	home	27-31	lost

Ampthill points shown first

This was a season of what might have been for Ampthill. They started the season slowly, three of the first four games were lost, albeit narrowly. Ampthill beat Canterbury at Merton Lane, one of only two losses that season for the champions. Home and away defeats at Bishop's Stortford did not help the cause The second game of the season saw a narrow loss to Tring at Cow Lane, whilst in the reverse fixture the visitors were trounced 33-6. Still, there remained a feeling that Ampthill were gathering strength to push for promotion!

Mark Lavery remembers thinking that Ampthill had probably played more new clubs in the past two seasons than in the previous twenty seasons, because of the various leagues the Club found itself in.

East Midlands Cup Campaign

How they got there ……

Quarter Finals			Semi-Finals		Final
Towcestrians	0		Kettering	23o	
v.					
Ampthill	85		v.		Ampthill
Wellingborough	27				
v.			Ampthill	36	
Peterborough	12				v.
			Wellingborough	17	
Luton	25				
v.			v.		Luton
Bedford Athletic	3				
			Luton	37	
Kettering	31				
v.					
Old Northamptonians	11				

Wells Bombardier East Midlands Cup Final – Wednesday 4th April 2012

Ampthill 45 pts. Luton 32 pts.

A ding-dong battle at Goldington Road saw rampant Ampthill triumph against a spirited Luton side.

An 11 try fest saw National League 3 London & South East promotion hopefuls A's do just enough to see off the already relegated Luton. Chris Anderson for Ampthill and Jake Harris for Luton exchanged early penalties before Amps scored the first try on nine minutes when, after Jamie Crawford's initial break, Craig Ross scored in the corner. Luton hit straight back, Tesh Edwards touching down on 15 minutes with Harris adding the extras. An Anderson penalty on 31 minutes nudged Ampthill ahead before they scored their second try moments later when a lovely move through the middle and miss pass saw hooker Ben Saville cross in the corner, Anderson's conversion drifted wide, but he landed a penalty to put Ampthill 21-10 up at the interval.

After half-time, a great break by Gavin Williams eventually saw Phil Lane cross the whitewash with Anderson on target. Luton's response was immediate as Mahendran's probing ended in a try for Jack Elston – then Luton's Jake Hobbs touched down.

Spells of pressure saw Stuart Riding score for Amps, while Harris went in at the corner on the hour. More pressure from Ampthill saw Paul Davies go over for a fifth try.

Dogged Luton gained an injury-time consolation as Wayne Hemson burrowed over. But Ampthill had the last say as fleet-footed replacement Lee Anker raced in out-wide.

Ampthill: Dan Lavery, Peter Brierley, Paul Davies, Wayne Kelly, Craig Ross, Chris Anderson, Gavin Williams, Joe Sproston, Ben Saville, Tristan Wati, Nick Lewis, Karl Braband, Phil Lane (capt.), Jamie Crawford, replacements: James Wright, Bryce Titman, Terry Cooper, Liam Munro, Peter Vickers, Jonathan Raven, Lee Anker

Luton: Alex Sutherland, Rik Hobbs, Jake Hobbs, Utah Taylor, Teshurn Edwards, Jake Harris, Thomas Mahendran, Marc Tindall, David Irvine, Dan Blinkhorn, Karl Rodell, Jack Elston, Adam Harris, Mike Western, Matt Yang, replacements: Bob Barba, Ryan Shepard, Laurence Alden, Philip Guildersleve, Jonathan Wright, Josh Button, Chris Meehan, Wayne Hemson

Action from the East Midlands Cup Final

1881 XV - Bombardier League

#	Team	P	W	D	L	PF	PA	+/-	TB	LB	Pts
1	Ampthill 1881 XV	10	9	0	1	336	151	185	0	0	37
2	Luton 2nd XV	10	5	1	4	117	92	25	0	0	24
3	Kettering 2nd XV	7	4	0	3	127	202	75	0	0	19
4	Peterborough 2nd XV	7	3	1	3	185	155	30	0	0	17
5	Old Northamptonians 2nd XV	8	2	1	5	171	190	-19	0	0	14
6	Leighton Buzzard 2nd XV	8	0	1	7	95	241	-146	0	0	8

Bombardier League Results

Kettering 2nd	29-30	away	lost	home	85-5	won
Leighton Buzzard 2nd	50-12	home	won	away	AWO	won
Old Northamptonians 2nd	51-41	home	won	away	32-29	won
Peterborough 2nd	39-22	home	won	away	50-12	won
Luton	HWO	home	won	away	AWO	won

Ampthill points shown first

The 2nd XV were worthy winners of the Bombardier League finishing 7 points clear of runners-ups and old-rivals Luton. The only loss was away to Kettering 30-29. Nick Stephenson could be justly proud of his team's achievement.

Other Senior League Results

Ampthill Jets (3rd XV) – Red Stripe League

P	W	D	L	PF	PA	Pts.
16	16	0	0	690	70	64

Jets finished as champions 9 points clear of Stewart & Lloyds 2nds. (conceding just 70 points an average of 4.4 points per game)

Extras (4th XV) – Directors League

P	W	D	L	PF	PA	Pts.
11	4	1	6	226	232	34

Extras finished runners in fourth place in a league of eight.

| 2011-12 | played | won | drawn | lost | pts. for | pts. against |

1st XV	29	22	1	6	1132	528
2nd XV*	10	9	0	1	336	151
Extras XV*	11	4	1	6	226	236
5th XV*	13	6	0	7	330	322
Vets XV						
Colts XV						

*League results only

Colin Burke

At the end of the season Colin Burke stood down as chairman after six years of great personal achievement and progress for the club, including the opening of Olney Field. It is possible now to see these years under Colin's leadership as providing the impetus to what was to come by the end of the decade. Colin would continue to serve with distinction as a Committee member.

Season 2012-13 - (Captain - Phil Lane)

Management Committee

President	D. Williams
Chairman	M. Lavery
Hon. Treasurer	B. Warfield
Hon. Secretary	I. Titman
Director of Rugby	M. Lavery
Chair of Youth Rugby	C. Stallwood
General Committee members:	B. Muncaster, D. Wheeler, J. Bishop, K. Belcher, C. Burke, I. Cooper, D. Phillips
Elected /Appointed Officers	C. Rempel, Liz Barlow, K. Belcher, P. Allen, D. Hoy, N. Ashton, B. McTavish, C. Stallwood, M. Stanbridge, C. Ashby, I. Titman, C. Page, J. Bishop, S. Morgan, J. Thomas, E. Muncaster, N. Eastwood & C. Jones

Playing

1st XV Manager	I. Bremner
Development XV Manager	N. Stephenson
Extras XV Manager	L. Duffin
4th XV Manager	S. Jones
Vets Manager	D. Wheeler
Colts Manager	P. New
Coach	P. Turner Head Coach, A. Brown (Development Squad)

Stuart Evans stepped down after four seasons, having won two league titles in that time, in what Mark Lavery described as "an incredible record." Paul Turner came on board as coach as Ampthill's first team squad was becoming semi-professional.

New players included Viliami Ma'asi (hooker - London Welsh, Tonga), Sam Walsh (prop – Bedford Blues), Dean Adamson and Elliot Clements-Hill (Bedford Academy), Tony Begovitc (Shelford), Mark Popham, brother of Alex Popham (flanker – Cross Keys) and Lee Bray (second-row – Cardiff).

For season 2012-13, the second XV, was called the Development XV.

1st XV League Results

South Leicester	20-3	away	won	84-7	home	won	
Broadstreet	74-7	away	won	59-15	home	won	
Hinckley	36-26	home	won	21-6	away	won	
Bournville	35-33	away	won	75-19	home	won	
Derby	80-6	home	won	59-5	away	won	
Mansfield	20-20	away	draw	76-3	home	won	
Nuneaton	18-15	home	won	45-21	away	won	
Longton	51-17	away	won	70-8	home	won	
Sandbach	43-14	away	won	43-13	home	won	
Sutton Coldfield	10-13	away	lost	34-0	home	won	
Syston	32-0	home	won	49-27	away	won	
Scunthorpe	52-17	home	won	43-14	away	won	
Newport (Salop)	84-3	home	won	33-3	away	won	

Ampthill points shown first

1st XV League: National League 3 Midlands (transferred from National 3 London & SE)

National 3 Midlands

#	Team	P	W	D	L	PF	PA	+/-	TB	LB	Pts
1	Ampthill	26	24	1	1	1246	315	931	21	1	120
2	Sutton Coldfield	26	23	1	2	862	267	595	17	1	112
3	South Leicester	26	19	0	7	804	576	228	14	3	93
4	Nuneaton	26	16	1	9	761	515	246	12	5	83
5	Newport (Salop)	26	14	0	12	607	630	-23	10	5	71
6	Hinckley	26	13	2	11	672	547	125	10	5	71
7	Sandbach	26	13	0	13	655	504	151	8	5	65
8	Broadstreet	26	12	1	13	711	708	3	11	2	63
9	Longton	26	12	0	14	590	718	-128	8	7	63
10	Bournville	26	11	0	15	683	759	-76	13	5	62
11	Scunthorpe	26	11	0	15	622	801	-179	10	1	55
12	Syston	26	8	1	17	494	727	-233	12	4	50
13	Mansfield	26	1	1	24	267	1052	-785	3	3	12
14	Derby	26	1	0	25	329	1184	-855	3	2	9

This season was a two-horse race between Ampthill and Sutton Coldfield. On Saturday 24 November 2012, Ampthill played Sutton Coldfield, at the Roger Smoldon Ground. In what Mark Lavery remembers as being an uncompromising game, Vili Ma'asi received a battering and was unable to see out of one eye and was moved to the back row. The home side won the game by 13-10, Ampthill's only defeat of the season. Vili Ma'asi, the most professional of players and hugely respected by his team-mates, stored away these experinces for what would prove to be a pivotal match, the return fixture of the season at Dillingham Park.

Ampthill 76pts. Mansfield 3pts. – February 9th 2013

In October, Ampthill were given a real fright when held to a 20-20 draw by Mansfield. Mansfield were also the only side whose pack had given Ampthill's forwards a hard time in the scrummage, but that earlier aberration was well and truly avenged on the day.

However, Mansfield's front row again proved troublesome for the whole game, while Ampthill's recent intensity appeared to be absent at first.

Loose-head, James Wright touched down a catch-and-drive on four minutes and repeated the dose in almost identical fashion three minutes later. Centre Paul Davies finished off a backs' move on 13 minutes, before the visitors, having missed an earlier attempt, converted a penalty midway through the half.

Winger Dean Adamson, scored the first of his hat-trick of tries when he beat the last man wide on the right in the 23rd minute. Blindside flanker Lee Bray touched down the first of a brace on 33 minutes, before full-back Elliot Clements-Hill chipped the cover, won the foot race, and hacked on to touch down and round off a move that had started inside the home 22.

Leading 36-3 at the break – the second half continued in the same vein with Adamson adding two more tries on 47 and 80 minutes. Number eight Phil Lane capitalised on scrum turnover in front of the visitors' posts on 56 minutes, centre Jonathen Raven touched down on 67 minutes before Bray added his second, two minutes from time.

Clements-Hill converted seven of the 11 tries as Amps ran out easy winners. With seven games left Ampthill remained in pole position, three points ahead of Sutton Coldfield who had a game in hand but who still had to visit Dillingham Park later in the season.

Tom Warfield bursts past his Mansfield opposite number

The Showdown with Sutton Coldfield

This occurred on 6 April 2013 and Viliami Ma'asi, virtually single-handedly, demolished the Sutton Coldfield pack in an inspired performance. The opposition were beaten 34-0, a result which ended their ambitions for the title. Ampthill won the title, 8 points clear of runners-up Sutton Coldfield and were promoted to National 2 South.

Ampthill 84pts. South Leicester 7pts. – 20th April 2013

Dean Adamson grabbed five tries as Ampthill crushed third-placed South Leicester to take the National 3 Midlands title in style. The hosts, who needed only a bonus point from the game to be sure of top spot, ran in a dozen tries. Adamson got the first of his five in the opening minute and the job was effectively done when Nick Lewis went over after 38 minutes following a second Adamson try and one for the leading points scorer in the national leagues, Elliott Clements-Hill.

Matt Lord pounced on a rare slip to get the visitors on the board, but it was all Ampthill from that point on. Adamson completed a hat-trick before the break and then Mark Popham, brother of Welsh second-row Alex, ending a nine minute try-less drought. He was followed over by Adamson, Sam Walsh, Adamson again, and Kyle Palm twice. In injury time tight-head prop Joe Sproston charged down a kick to go in under the posts and then converted himself adding to a Paul Davies penalty and five conversions and a further three for Clements-Hill.

Ampthill were worthy champions, losing just that one game away at Sutton Coldfield, who finished second and drawing one game 20-20 with Mansfield at Eakring Road. Scoring 1,246 points (100 tries for the three-quarters) there were some dominant performances this season from the 1st XV.

On the road, Broadstreet were beaten 7-74 and Derby 5-59 whilst at Dillingham Park, Derby were despatched 80-6, Newport 84-3, South Leicester 84-7, Mansfield 76-3 and South Leicester 84-7.

Paul Turner

Paul Turner was born in Newbridge, and still holds the Newbridge Rugby Club points scoring record of 405 points from season 1983-84. Paul remains the only three-quarter capped from that club.

His playing career included spells at Newbridge, Newport, Pontypool, Bedford, and Sale, dazzling with his skills and tactical genius, accumulating hundreds of points along the way, kicking goals with both feet, for good measure. He won three caps for Wales, all of them in 1989, sharing in the 12-9 victory over England at a rain-soaked National Stadium which denied the old enemy the Five Nations' title. It should be remembered that in the same era Jonathan Davies, Mark Ring, Bleddyn Bowen, Tony Clement and Neil Jenkins won international caps for Wales at outside-half.

Paul also played three times for the Barbarians. Turner represented the Crawshays at the Hong Kong Sevens in 1985 & 1987 and the Penguins in 1988.

Paul Turner takes on the English defence in Wales' 1989 victory over the old enemy

Paul Turner left Newport RFC and became player/coach at Sale FC in 1992, leaving in 1996 to join Bedford RFC as player/Head Coach. He took both clubs into the English Premiership during his tenure. In 1998/99 he joined Saracens as backs coach and then spent 2 seasons at Rugby Lions as player/coach, winning promotion to Division 1.

In 2001, he left Rugby Lions to work under Philippe Saint-André at Gloucester, winning the inaugural Premiership Grand Final. He then moved on to Harlequins as backs coach from 2002-05. In 2005 he was appointed Head Coach for the Newport Gwent Dragons. Paul was Magners' League Coach of the Year for the 2010 season but stepped down from the Dragons in February 2011.

The Dragon's loss was Ampthill's gain, since Paul joined the Club and assisted Stuart Evans for the rest of the season. He also spent a year at Wasps as skills coach before accepting the Head Coach role at Ampthill Rugby Club; the rest is history.

Paul Turner has formed a potent partnership with Mark Lavery, Director of Rugby – their achievements are vastly appreciated by the members of Ampthill Rugby Club, of which, there are currently more than 1100.

League Success

All four senior sides would gain promotion from their leagues this season:

1st XV	National 3 Midlands,
Development XV	League Division 3 North
Jets	Courage Best League
Extras	Directors League

East Midlands Cup Campaign

How they got there ……

Quarter Finals			Semi-Finals		Final
Peterborough		W/O			
v.			Kettering		
Luton					
			v.		**Ampthill**
Bedford Athletic		11			
v.			**Ampthill**	W/O	
Ampthill		23			v.
			Peterborough Lions	15	
Bugbrroke					
v.			v.		Luton
Kettering					
		W/O			
			Luton	28	
Peterborough Lions		65			
v.					
Old Northamptonians		30			

Wells Bombardier East Midlands Cup Final – Wednesday 8th May 2013

Ampthill 17pts. Luton ,13 pts.

At Goldington Road, Luton belied their lower league status with a tenacious performance and even led 13-7 with 10 minutes to go, only for National League Three Midlands champions Ampthill to show their class in the closing minutes to score two tries and snatch victory.

A fleet-footed burst from deep by Jonathen Raven took Ampthill upfield early on and, after some patient build-up play, Lee Anker found a gap to cross on seven minutes and Paul Davies converted.

Ampthill started to concede too many penalties as Steve Ellis took full advantage to slot home a simple penalty for Luton on 13 minutes. Luton should have had their first try midway through the half when Ampthill struggled to stop a buccaneering run by Ellis and, as the ball was spread wide, Dave Brennan was just bundled into touch. Ellis sent a drop goal attempt just wide for Luton, while a Tesh Edwards run from deep put the Luton side in trouble just before the whistle, but Ampthill were adjudged to be held-up over the line.

Both teams continued to fight manfully and it was Luton who wrestled the lead on 58 minutes when Ampthill failed to deal with a Tom Mahendren's giant clearance kick and, although Edwards was unable to gather, Mahendren was on hand to collect and dart over. However, full-back Will Affleck's kick lacked legs.

It was another steepling kick that led to Luton's second try on 68 minutes when Kyle Palmer fumbled and Ryan Staff was on hand to pick up the scraps and break before finding replacement Aiden Kenny on the outside to score, although Affleck's difficult conversion fell short. However, Ampthill hit straight back as substitute Clements-Hill's quicksilver break opened up Luton's defence and Lee Bray was on hand to power over, although Davies shanked his conversion.

With just one point in it, that set up a grandstand finish and Ampthill claimed victory with four minutes to go when Sproson's juggernaut run from close in proved impossible to stop.

Lee Anker scoring on 7 minutes, with referee Max Barnard in close attendance

Ampthill: Gavin Williams, Lee Anker, Paul Davies, Jonathan Raven, Dean Adamson, Dan Lavery, Tom Warfield, James Wright, Vili Ma'asi, Joe Sproston, Nick Lewis, Karl Braband, Lee Bray, Tom Begovic, Phil Lane (capt.) replacements: Josh Smith, George Warner, Haydn Edwins, Jake Foster, Elliott Clements-Hill, Felix Stretton, Jake McCloud

Luton: Will Affleck, Chris Davies, Dave Brennan, Steve Ellis, Tesh Edwards, Tom Wilmore, Tom Mahendren, Sam Pacey, Dave Irvine, Daniel Blinkhorn, Chris Depper, Pat Nelly, Jack Elston, Adam Harriss, Michael Western, replacements: Ryan Duffy, Marc Tindall, Ben Murphy, Ryan Staff, Ben Kay, Matt Yang, Aiden Kenny, Ross Geraghty.

This was Ampthill's fourth East Midlands title and it gave the Club a league and Cup double that was a fitting tribute to a truly outstanding effort for all concerned with the senior squad.

Development XV (1881 XV) - League Division 3 North

#	Team	P	W	D	L	PF	PA	+/-	TB	LB	Pts	Adj
1	Ampthill 1881 XV	8	6	0	2	184	168	16	4	0	30	0
2	Westcliff II	6	4	0	2	194	128	66	3	0	20	-1
3	Richmond Normans (4th XV)	5	4	0	1	185	158	27	3	0	20	0
4	Amersham & Chiltern II	4	1	0	3	67	118	-51	1	1	9	0
5	Hampstead 2nd XV	4	0	0	4	94	122	-28	2	2	8	0
6	Ealing Men's 1sts	0	0	0	0	0	0	0			0	0
7	Staines II	3	0	0	3	0	30	-30	0	0	0	-3

The 1881s were clear champions this season, ten points clear of runners-up Westcliff. Impressive wins were achieved on the road including, 18-20 against Hampstead, 0-10 at Staines and 5-38 over Amersham & Chiltern at Ash Grove. Nick Stevenson's 1881s were promoted to League Division 2 North for the following season

Other Senior Teams Leagues

Jets (3rd XV) – Courage Best League

played	won	drawn	lost	pts. for	pts. against	points
15	15	0	0	696	133	60

Like the 1st XV and 1881s, the Jets finished champions of the Courage Best League, a clear 18 points ahead of Stewarts & Lloyds in second place. All fifteen matches were won. Jonny Cresswell's team enjoyed an outstanding season including wins against Northampton Heathens 105-12, 93-5 against Wellingborough, 60-20 over Leighton Buzzard and 64-12 versus Sharnbrook.

Extras (4th XV) – Directors League

played	won	drawn	lost	pts. for	pts. against	points
12	8	1	3	399	233	37

The Extras were second out of eight teams, 5 points behind champions - Huntingdon

Phil Lane

This would turn out to be Phil Lane's sixth and final season as captain, though he would continue to play. Phil was a formidable player and undoubtedly one of Ampthill's finest forwards. Phil's contribution to the success of Ampthill Rugby Club cannot be over-stated, when he retired as a player, Mark Lavery insisted on still registering him to play. Phil came out of retirement for 2019-20 and more than held his own in the strongest 1881 squad that the Club has ever put into the field. It should also be remembered that Phil came through the Club's Mini & Youth system. In Chapter 9, page 311, you will see that Phil Lane was voted into the Ampthill Team of the Decade 2010-2020.

2012-13	played	won	drawn	lost	pts. for	pts. against
1st XV	29	27	1	1	1286	339
Development. XV*	8	6	0	2	184	168
Jets XV*	15	15	0	0	696	133
Extras XV*	12	8	1	3	399	166
5th XV*	13	6	0	7	330	322
Vets XV						
Colts XV						

*League results only

Season 2013-14 - (Captain Viliami Ma'asi)

Management Committee

President	D. Williams
Chairman	M. Lavery
Hon. Treasurer	B. Warfield
Hon. Secretary	I. Titman
Director of Rugby	M. Lavery
Chair of Youth Rugby	C. Stallwood
General Committee members:	P. Sherry, D. Wheeler, J. Bishop, K. Belcher, C. Burke, I. Cooper, D. Phillips
Elected /Appointed Officers	C. Rempel, Liz Barlow, K. Belcher, P. Allen, D. Hoy, N. Ashton, B. McTavish, C. Stallwood, M. Stanbridge, C. Ashby, I. Titman, C. Page, J. Bishop, S. Morgan, J. Thomas, E. Muncaster, N. Eastwood & C. Jones

Playing

1st XV Manager	I. Bremner
1881 XV Manager	N. Stephenson
Extras XV Manager	L. Duffin
4th XV Manager	D. Burns
Vets Manager	D. Wheeler
Colts Manager	P. New
Coach	P. Turner Head Coach, A. Brown (1881s)

This was Ampthill's first step into the big leagues after winning National 3 Midlands, the A's would ply their trade in National 2 South. Pretty much every team in this competition was semi-professional and once more they would be playing teams never faced before.

The drive to become a semi-professional 1st team squad really gained momentum this season. New players included "the legend that is Maama Molitika", (back-rower - Rugby San Donà) , Kevin Barrett (scrum-half - Saracens), Alex Bloisi, Darrel Dyer, Joe Bercis, Matt Collins (all Bedford Academy), Steff Myberg (Chiltern) Tom Aviss (scrum-half – Pontypool), Jonny Morgan (winger – Bedford Academy).

The skipper Viliami Ma'asi "changed everything" according to Mark Lavery. Through his professional approach, his controlled fury and modest demeanour, he inspired those around him. Sadly, Vili was to break his leg in the first ten minutes of the opening league match against London Irish Wild Geese at Sunbury. "It was like we'd been shot", said Mark Lavery of his captain. Vili would play in only six games that season.

A typical match day pack would be a front-row of Walsh, Ma'asi & Sproston, locks from Braband, Lane or Bray, back row of Burke, Popham and Molitika with Bercis on the bench – a formidable unit.

The campaign became a three-way contest between Hartpury College, Bishop's Stortford, and Ampthill. Hartpury were to beat Ampthill home and away and were worthy winners of National 2 South. Ampthill also found Clifton a tough nut to crack.

At the end of September, Ampthill travelled to Cambridge, having won two games, and drawn the third against Bishop's Stortford. Cambridge had just come down from National 1 and must have regarded the result as a formality. As Ampthill took the field, the Cambridge announcer said, "And the team to beat Ampthill today is …." Buoyed by a big pack of forwards and disciplined fury Ampthill prevailed by 25 points to 15.

With more victories, confidence grew, and Ampthill were climbing up the table, but Hartpury kept on winning. In mid-December, Hartpury were the visitors and it was decided to play them on Pitch 2, near the clubhouse, to restrict space to their rapid three-quarters. After 20 minutes Ampthill were leading 24-3 when they were awarded a penalty near Hartpury's try line. Coaches and spectators expected a rumble through the forwards, but Josh Sharp attempted a grubber kick which was scooped up by the Hartpury winger who dashed 60 metres to score. Ampthill never recovered and were beaten 41-24.

In April, the return fixture was described by Mark Lavery as a "titanic battle that could have gone either way", but the result was 30 – 39 to Hartpury.

1st XV League Results

London Irish Wild Geese	37-10	away	won	40-24	home	won
Bishop's Stortford	28-28	away	draw	41-22	home	won
Clifton	20-37	home	lost	12-36	away	lost
Cambridge	25-15	away	won	40-10	home	won
Launceston	56-11	home	won	38-23	away	won
Southend Saxons	21-30	away	lost	17-14	home	won
Chinnor	21-11	home	won	35-31	away	won
Taunton Titans	22-26	away	lost	40-12	home	won
Bournmouth	36-0	home	won	61-23	away	won
Exmouth	42-20	away	won	43-10	home	won
Dings Crusaders	78-10	home	won	34-19	away	won
Shelford	31-20	away	won	36-10	home	won
Redruth	38-17	home	won	36-41	away	lost
Canterbury	30-33	away	lost	41-8	home	won
Hartpury University	24-41	home	lost	30-39	away	lost

Ampthill points shown first

This was a step up in class from previous league campaigns and Ampthill were clearly competitive, finishing runners-up behind Hartpury whose own progress through the leagues had been impressive.

Apart from the two losses to Hartpury, Ampthill also lost home and away to Clifton. Other losses followed lengthy trips to Taunton, Canterbury, Redruth. These are not easy places to gain victories and these clubs have sporting traditions that predate Ampthill's precocious ambitions.

The subsequent narrow loss in the play-offs to Darlington Mowden Park was a blow, Ampthill had come so close. Paul Turner told the Rugby Paper: "We were 10 seconds away from promotion and it would have thrown a small junior club like Ampthill into fixtures we could never have dreamed of two years ago. To have played against the likes of Richmond and Rosslyn Park would have been unbelievable, but we've put that disappointment behind us now and we're planning to have another good season and make a big push to go up. We've lost some boys to Championship sides who we might otherwise have kept so we've got to rebuild a bit, but we've signed some good players and Paino Hehea has a great pedigree."

Elliot Clements-Hill was the top points scorer in the league with 366 points. Dean Adamson was top try scorer in National 2 with 24 tries. Ampthill scored 151 tries to champions Hartpury's 142, and conceded 77 tries to Hartpury's 85 tries.

Considering the standard of the opposition the season was considered a "spectacular success."

SSE National League 2 South

#	Team	P	W	D	L	PF	PA	+/-	TB	LB	Pts
1	Hartpury University	30	23	0	7	1019	666	353	22	3	117
2	Ampthill	30	21	1	8	1053	631	422	20	3	109
3	Bishop's Stortford	30	18	2	10	841	687	154	19	7	102
4	Canterbury	30	19	0	11	781	715	66	18	6	100
5	Clifton	30	18	0	12	739	702	37	11	3	86
6	Taunton Titans	30	17	1	12	785	718	67	10	6	86
7	Cambridge	30	16	0	14	749	668	81	14	7	85
8	Southend Saxons	30	15	0	15	735	740	-5	12	8	80
9	Redruth	30	13	1	16	641	759	-118	13	5	72
10	Shelford	30	13	2	15	646	664	-18	6	7	69
11	Dings Crusaders	30	12	0	18	679	745	-66	10	10	68
12	Launceston	30	15	0	15	605	730	125	4	2	66
13	Chinnor	30	12	0	18	676	775	-99	8	9	65
14	London Irish Wild Geese	30	11	0	19	754	808	54	11	8	63
15	Bournemouth	30	8	1	21	670	996	-326	10	5	49
16	Exmouth	30	5	0	25	591	960	-369	7	7	34

Play-off for promotion versus Darlington Mowden Park, DMP won 30-28

#	Team	P	W	D	L	PF	PA	+/-	TB	LB	Pts
1	Ampthill	0	0	0	-2	-56	-62	6	0	0	0
2	Darlington Mowden Park	-2	0	0	0	-62	-56	-6	0	0	0

Top scorers, Elliot Clements-Hill (Plymouth Albion) and Dean Adamson (Bedford) were leaving, but former Blues centre Brendan Burke arrived as player-coach plus full-back Karim Lynch, as well as Paino Hehea. Indeed, all the signs were that Ampthill Rugby Club was gaining momentum and improving season on season. Yet again, due to re-structuring, the Club was transferred to National 2 North for next season.

1881s XV – Bombardier League

#	Team	P	W	D	L	PF	PA	+/-	TB	LB	Pts	Adj
1	Ampthill 1881 XV	17	16	0	1	727	91	636	0	0	65	
2	Towcestrians 2nd XV	17	12	0	5	708	245	463	0	0	53	
3	Luton 2nd XV	18	11	0	7	345	307	38	0	0	50	
4	Cambridge Wanderers	13	10	0	3	213	109	104	0	0	42	
5	Kettering 2nd XV	14	8	0	6	274	389	-115	0	0	37	
6	Bedford Athletic 2nd XV	18	7	0	11	275	492	-217	0	0	36	
7	Old Northamptonians 2nd XV	14	5	0	9	214	427	-213	0	0	28	
8	Peterborough 2nd XV	14	5	0	9	240	456	-216	0	0	28	
9	Leighton Buzzard 2nd XV	11	1	0	10	58	309	-251	0	0	11	
10	Peterborough Lions 2nd XV	16	1	0	15	66	295	-229	0	0	9	

The newly named 1881 XV finished comfortable champions 12 points clear of Towcestrians. Only one game was lost against Cambridge Wanderers 5-15. Notable wins included; 91-0 v. Old Northamptonians 2nds, 79-0 v. Peterborough 2nds, 68-0 v. Kettering 2nds. And 50-7 v. Luton 2nds.

They also won the Zoo Sports Division 2 North and would be playing in Zoo League 1 next season.

Other Senior Teams Leagues

Jets (3rd XV) – Courage Best League

played	won	drawn	lost	pts. for	pts. against	points
15	15	0	0	696	133	60

Undefeated, the Jets were champions for the third successive year.

Extras (4th XV) – Eagle IPA League

played	won	drawn	lost	pts. for	pts. against	points
16	14	0	2	342	172	58

The Extras were second on points difference to champions Wellingborough A and earned their fifth promotion in five years. They would be playing in the Herts. & Middlesex Merit Table next season.

5th XV – Youngs London Stout League

played	won	drawn	lost	pts. for	pts. against	points
14	6	0	8	232	310	32

The 5th XV were third in a league of eight.

Playing Record

2013-14	played	won	drawn	lost	pts. for	pts. against
1st XV	30	21	1	8	631	422
1881s XV	18	8	0	10	389	509
Jets XV	15	15	0	0	696	133
Extras XV	20	12	0	8	420	412
5Th XV	14	6	0	8	232	310
Vets XV						
Colts XV						

Season 2014-15 - (Captain - Viliami Ma'asi)

Management Committee

President	P. Sherry
Chairman	M. Lavery
Hon. Treasurer	B. Warfield
Hon. Secretary	I. Titman
Director of Rugby	M. Lavery
General Committee members:	C. Burke, J. Bishop, K. Belcher, D. Phillips, I. Cooper, D. Wheeler, P. Carter, A. Spavins
Elected /Appointed Officers	C. Rempel, K. Belcher, J. Reid, P. Davies, D. Hoy, B. MacTavish, C. Stallwood, L. Threader, M. Stanbridge, H. Christy, C. Page, J. Bishop, R. Marshall, P. Carter, V. Martin, J. Abbott & C. Jones
Playing	
1st XV Manager	I. Bremner
1881 XV Manager	N. Stephenson
Extras XV Manager	L. Duffin
4th XV Manager	D. Burns
5th XV Manager	R. Mardle
Vets Manager	D. Wheeler
Colts Manager	I. Barclay
Coach	P. Turner Head Coach, A. Brown (1881s)

New players included Paino Hehea (second-row – Calvisano & Tonga), Brendan Burke (centre - Bedford Blues), Karim Lynch (full-back – Bournemouth), Kieran Duffin (scrum-half – Bedford), Gareth Clarke (winger – Rugby Lions), Lewis Brunger (prop – Southend) and Will Goodge (Ampthill Mini & Youth.)

Pre-Season

"After the disappointment of missing out narrowly in the National 2 play-offs against Darlington Mowden Park, we arranged to play DMP again at Dillingham Park on 23rd August which resulted in a narrow loss 28pts. to 31pts. We also played Henley Hawks again at Dillingham Park on 30th August and won well at 40pts. to 24pts. This gave us some confidence going into the new season." (Mark Lavery).

August 23rd 2014 Ampthill 28 pts. Darlington Mowden Park 31 Pts.

August 30th 2014 Ampthill 40 pts. Henley Hawks 24 pts.

The transfer to National 2 North meant yet another campaign against little known opponents. The league developed into a two-horse race between Ampthill and Hull Ionians

Three away losses this season cost Ampthill the outright title. The 19-30 defeat at 11th place Leicester Lions was unexpected and the narrow defeat at Chester was disappointing. The 6-7 loss to champions Hull Ioanians at Brantingham Park was not unexpected, but the decisions to ignore kickable penalties in such a tight game baffled some Ampthill followers.

Mark Lavery has described Ampthill as having a "brilliant offence that year." Joe Tarrant with 310 points was top scorer in the league. Joe Bercis was top try-scorer in National 2 North with 31 tries. Joe Tarrant scored 18 tries as did Darrel Dyer. Ampthill scored 171 tries to Ionians 141 and conceded 54 tries to Ionians 52.

Maama Molitika was to have shoulder reconstruction this season and played only 20 of the 30 games, one can only speculate at how this affected the outcome of Ampthill's campaign, since he was a such a magnificent rugby player.

Overall, though, it was a very satisfactory season, the victory in the play-offs made it the greatest day in the Club's history to date.

1st XV League Results

Stockport	48-0	home	won	59-17	away	won
Leicester Lions	66-7	home	won	19-30	away	lost
Sedgley Park	32-20	away	won	27-8	home	won
Birmingham & Solihull	33-17	home	won	31-14	away	won
Preston Grasshoppers	57-9	away	won	22-17	home	won
Hull Ionians	25-15	home	won	6-7	away	lost
Chester	13-15	away	lost	28-23	home	won
Harrogate	53-7	home	won	26-9	away	won
Luctonians	29-7	away	won	45-29	home	won
Stourbridge	44-12	home	won	37-12	away	won
Huddersfield	17-17	away	draw	48-7	home	won
Caldy	18-13	home	won	36-29	away	won
Hull	67-3	away	won	45-14	home	won
Otley	41-10	home	won	53-12	away	won
Broadstreet	52-33	away	won	36-26	home	won

Ampthill points shown first

National League 2 North

#	Team	P	W	D	L	PF	PA	+/-	TB	LB	Pts
1	Hull Ionians	30	27	0	3	976	409	567	25	1	134
2	Ampthill	30	26	1	3	1113	439	674	23	2	131
3	Sedgley Park	30	18	1	11	883	666	217	16	4	94
4	Harrogate	30	17	3	10	720	653	67	11	4	89
5	Chester	30	16	1	13	706	595	111	12	6	84
6	Caldy	30	16	1	13	696	720	-24	11	7	84
7	Broadstreet	30	17	0	13	773	687	86	11	4	83
8	Otley	30	13	1	16	676	682	-6	13	8	75
9	Huddersfield	30	14	2	14	585	658	-73	7	4	71
10	Stourbridge	30	12	1	17	740	803	-63	12	7	69
11	Leicester Lions	30	13	0	17	612	804	-192	10	2	64
12	Preston Grasshoppers	30	11	0	19	621	664	-43	10	10	64
13	Luctonians	30	11	1	18	599	766	-167	10	5	61
14	Birmingham & Solihull	30	9	2	19	724	809	-85	8	10	58
15	Hull	30	10	1	19	543	836	-293	9	3	54
16	Stockport	30	2	1	27	445	1221	-776	4	5	19

One abiding memory of this season to Lancastrian, Mark Lavery, was the match against Preston Grasshoppers, at Lightfoot Green Lane, in October 2014. This famous old club, home to Wade Dooley and Steve Bainbridge, resulted in a great 57-9 victory for Ampthill. "It was a massive game for us," said Mark, "Grasshoppers said Ampthill were the best side they had ever seen." From such an eminent club, this was praise indeed!

National 2 North – top points & try scorers 2014-15

leading points scorers			leading try scorers		
Joe Tarrant - Ampthill		310	**Joe Bercis - Ampthill**		31
Adam Canning - Birmingham		297	Harry Hudson - Otley		22
Lewis Allen - Preston Grasshoppers		273	Sam Wilson – Hull Ionians		19
Steve Depledge - Otley		234	Andrew Riley – Sedgley Park		18
Will Goodwin - Chester		186	**Joe Tarrant - Ampthill**		**18**
Ben Palmer - Broadstreet		176	**Darrel Dyer - Ampthill**		**18**
Isaac Green – Hull Ionians		175	Rob Young Leicester Lions		15

Promotion Playoff – Saturday 2nd May 2015

Ampthill 19pts. Bishop's Stortford 10pts.

Ampthill secured promotion to National One as they beat an impressive Bishop's Stortford side 19-10 at Dillingham Park. A record crowd of 1,213 was in attendance to witness Ampthill make history and secure third tier rugby for next season making them one of the 40th highest ranked rugby clubs in England.

Tries from Matthew Burke, Viliami Ma'asi and Joseph Sproston, all in the first half, came either side of scores for the well-supported visitors by George Cullen and Jimmy Rea.

The hosts were, however, under the cosh straight from kick-off as some good hands from Stortford allowed the visitors to gain some threatening territory coupled with quick ball. A number of five-metre lines-out followed and Ampthill lock Karl Braband was brandished an early yellow for continuing to penalise as the rolling mauls were being set-up. It was no surprise that the visitors went for another attempt at a maul, however, the defence stood firm as Stortford sensibly decided to ship the ball into the hands of the backs. A number of phases followed before an overlap on the right allowed full-back Cullen to dot down in the corner and it was the ideal start for the Hertfordshire side.

After Braband returned from the bin in the 17th minute, the home side began to get their hands on the ball as fly-half Joe Tarrant started to spot gaps in Stortford's defence. This meant that the territory moved into Stortford's half and a number of phases followed with Ampthill just metres out. Blindside flanker Burke was on hand to trundle his way over after some good leg power, Tarrant converted, and to the delight of the home fans Ampthill were 7-5 ahead after the first quarter.

Referee, Marcus Caton, gave very few decisions in favour of the home side in the opening exchanges, but a penalty in the 28th minute allowed Paul Turner's side to have an attacking line-out of their own. What followed was very impressive, as the shove rumbled its way to the line for what was a trademark score for Ampthill this season, from a catch and drive line-out. Hooker Ma'asi was credited with the try, but there was no doubt it was an effort made and created by the whole forward pack.

Just six minutes later, another attacking maul followed and the visitors pack were able to learn from their earlier mistakes and quash the rolling maul. However, the defence didn't hold out for much longer as front row forward Sproston burrowed his way over from a ruck, and Ampthill led 19-5 going into the half-time interval.

The start of the second half period showed neither side overly dominating, until on the hour when Bishop's Stortford began to stretch the home defence. A deliberate knock-on in the 57th minute by winger Gareth Clarke meant Ampthill were down to 14 for the second time. However, unlike earlier in the match, the visitors were unable to utilise their extra man and convert that into points on the scoreboard, as a superb effort from the home defence kept them out.

Then on the hour mark, an incident that proved to be the one that decided the match. Referee Caton looked to have awarded the visitors a try after Hugh Mitchell peeled off a five metre line-out, but after consultation with his touch-judge, the man with the whistle reversed his decision after believing he lost control of the ball over the line.

With that decision going against the National Two South side, the result always looked out of their reach in the closing moments as their momentum was quashed, despite consistently getting their hands on the ball. The visitors began to dominate at scrum time though, and after winning one against the head, they flung the ball to the left wing where Rea was able to dot down inside the left touchline.

The conversion was missed and with Stortford needing two more scores in the final five minutes, there only looked like there would be only one winner. That side was Ampthill and to the delight of those in attendance, the team in amber and maroon secured the 19-10 victory and a place in National One for next season.

Ampthill: Joseph Sproston, Viliami Ma'asi, James Wright, Paino Hehea, Karl Braband, Matthew Burke, Joseph Bercis, Maama Molitika, Gavin Williams, Joseph Tarrant, Gareth Clarke, William Goodge, Brendan Burke, Darrel Dyer, Karim Lynch **Replacements:** Lewis Brunger, Alexander Bloisi, Lee Bray, Kevin Barratt, Lee Anker

Paino Hehea leads the driving maul towards Stortford's line

The faithful celebrate Ampthill's victory

Try time: Viliami Ma'asi forces his way over the try-line

1881s XV – Zoo League Division 1

#	Team	P	W	D	L	PF	PA	+/-	TB	LB	Pts	Adj
1	Richmond Vikings (2nd XV)	18	17	0	1	849	303	546	16	0	85	
2	Esher Cardinals (2nd XV)	18	13	0	5	542	304	238	10	0	67	
3	Cinderford United (2nd XV)	17	13	0	4	420	285	135	6	0	62	
4	Jersey Athletic	17	11	0	6	454	344	110	10	0	60	
5	Blackheath Heathens (2nd XV)	19	11	0	8	491	418	73	7	0	59	
6	Ampthill 1881 XV	18	8	0	10	389	509	-120	8	0	49	-1
7	Barnes 2nd XV	19	6	2	11	464	470	-6	8	0	47	
8	London Scottish 2nd XV	20	7	0	13	365	622	-257	4	0	44	-1
9	Old Albanians 2nd XV	20	6	0	14	358	749	-391	7	0	43	-2
10	Henley II	18	5	1	12	460	475	-15	9	0	43	
11	Worthing Raiders A (2nd XV)	18	4	1	13	311	537	-226	4	0	34	-1
12	Ealing Trailfinders 2nd XV	0	0	0	0	0	0			0	0	

Other Senior Teams Leagues

Jets (3rd XV) – Herts. & Middlesex Merit Table 1

played	won	drawn	lost	pts. for	pts. against	points
20	16	1	3	883	244	69

Jets were champions, 10 points clear of Peterborough 2nd XV. The Jets had won their last 5 league campaigns losing only 3 games in the process. They were also cup winners.

Extras (4th XV) – Bombardier League

played	won	drawn	lost	pts. for	pts. against	points
20	12	0	8	420	412	56

This season the Extras finished in third place in a league of eleven, in the top Merit Table in East Midlands.

5th XV - Youngs London Stout League

played	won	drawn	lost	pts. for	pts. against	points
14	6	0	8	232	310	32

In their first season in the leagues, the 5th XV achieved a creditable third-place in a league of eight teams

2014-15	played	won	drawn	lost	pts. for	pts. against
1st XV	30	26	1	3	1113	439
1881s XV	18	8	0	10	389	509
Extras XV	20	16	1	3	838	244
4th XV	20	12	0	8	420	412
5th XV	14	6	0	8	232	310
Vets XV						
Colts XV						

Rugby Paper National 2 Dream Team – May 17th 2015

Hull Ionians and Ampthill would be playing their rugby in National One next season and when the Rugby Paper selected its "Dream Team" it analysed what made both teams tick and all signs pointed to forward dominance. Seven Ionians or Ampthill players were selected to pack down in the scrum for the team of the season, including front-row veterans Vili Ma'asi and Steve Johnson who proved age is just a number.

Team: 15. Carolan Ryan (Stourbridge), 14. Andy Riley (Sedgley Park), 13. Lewis Manikin (Harrogate), 12. Joe Barker (Hull Ionians), 11. Harry Hudson (Otley), 10. Adam Canning (Birmingham & Solihull), 9. Stephen Depledge (Otley), 1. **Joe Sproston** (Ampthill), 2. **Vili Ma'asi** (Ampthill), 3. Steve Johnson (Hull Ionians), 4. Joe Makin (Hull Ionians), 5. **Paino Hehea** (Ampthill), 6. Nigel Mukarati (Stourbridge), 7. **Joe Bercis** (Ampthill), 8. **Maama Molitika** (Ampthill)

This is how the Rugby Paper assessed the Ampthill players in its Dream Team:

Joe Sproston

Ampthill's pack was a dominant beast throughout the campaign and the impressive Sproston more than played his part. The 23-year-old has been a virtual ever present for Ampthill since joining in 2010 and has developed into an all-rounder in the front-row – grabbing 13 tries this season. With quick hands for a prop, he is much more than a powerful scrummager.

Vili Ma'asi

Not many players in this league can boast to have played in a World Cup but in Ma'asi Ampthill have a captain who has gone around the globe and back. Despite approaching 40, the Tongan hooker leads by example, including scoring a try in their promotion play-off victory over Bishop's Stortford.

Paino Hehea

Chris Goddard of Birmingham was also a popular choice with our correspondents for a second-row berth in this team, but Makin is joined by another of Ampthill's Tongan veterans. The former Racing Metro lock formed the backbone of a powerful engine room and a driving maul that got the better of most teams.

Joe Bercis

Caldy's Nyle Davidson and Laurence Cohen of Hull Ionians thrived at openside this season but no-one comes close to Bercis. The Ampthill man has developed into the complete No.7, regularly topping both the tackle count and turnovers, while his eye for the line is unrivalled. With 31 tries in 29 games the former Ireland youth international touched down over ten more times than anyone else this year and will join Moseley in the summer. (A great favourite at Dillingham Park, Joe was to return to the fold after his season with Moseley.)

Ampthill's Joe Bercis

Tongahill – The priceless contribution of the Pacific Islanders

Viliami Ma'asi

In 2011, Viliami Ma'asi was the first of the Tongan internationals to join Ampthill.

Vili played for Tonga 36 times including participation in the 2003 World Cup, his career included playing 195 games in the English National Leagues, for Yorkshire Carnegie, Cornish Pirates, London Welsh and five seasons for Ampthill. He represented, East Midlands at Twickenham for their first ever County Championship trophy in 2016.

He was an integral part of the Club for more than five years leading the 2012/13 National 3 Midlands Championship side and making a substantial and important contribution to our National 2 campaign that ultimately led to promotion to National 1 via the 2014/15 season-ending promotion playoff against Bishop's Stortford at Dillingham Park.

Vili and his family moved to Marston Moretaine in the summer of 2012 and his children Suva, Sonny and Rikess have all played for our Mini & Youth throughout the time that the family have been in the area. Vili was often at the club on a Sunday offering both skilled coaching (with his boots on) and encouragement from the side-lines.

Viliami Ma'asi, 2006 vintage

DOR Mark Lavery said, "When Vili arrived he had an immediate impact on all aspects of the senior Club bringing a new level of professionalism and application to the senior set-up. I sometimes liken it to the impact Eric Cantona had at Manchester United, so profound was Vili's impact on everybody with whom he worked".

Maama Molitika

Maama, 45 (1.96m, 108kg), in a rugby career spanning 21 seasons that started at Bridgend Ravens in 1999 and included short spells in Japan with IBM Big Blue and Italy with Rugby San Dona. However, the majority of his career has been in the UK. He made his name in Wales with Bridgend, helping them to their first Welsh Premiership title in 2003 and finished the season as joint top try scorer. Following the regionalisation of Welsh Rugby in 2003/04, Maama joined the Celtic Warriors for their only season of existence and played for them in both the Celtic League and Heineken Cup.

When the Warriors were dissolved, Maama played a season at Harlequins in the Premiership and then spent a year in Japan. He returned to Wales and joined Cardiff Blues in 2007 where he went on to made 112 appearances over 7 seasons, winning the Anglo-Welsh Cup in 2009 and the Amlin European Challenge Cup against Toulon in 2010 – the first Welsh side to win a European trophy! Maama also played in the Heineken Cup semi-final in 2008 at the

Millennium Stadium that was decided on penalties (finishing 6-7 to Leicester) after an extra-time stalemate. To date the only rugby match game to be decided in this way.

Maama was capped by Tonga 18 times and played in the 2007 World Cup against England at Parc de Princes and represented the Pacific Islanders 3 times in 2006. Maama joined Ampthill in 2013, going on to make 160 1st XV appearances over the past 7 seasons and was a key member of the squad's winning promotion to firstly National One and then the Greene King IPA Championship. Having helped the Mob to a 5th place finish in their first season in Level 2, Maama has decided against "one more year!"

Maama had this to say about his decision, "I would just like to say a big thank you to Mark Lavery and Paul Turner for giving me the opportunity to be part of Ampthill Rugby and to carry on my career. I've been at Ampthill for 7 seasons, and seen the club move from National 2 status to Championship and I will continue to track its performance and follow and support the club every step of the way.

Maama Molitika - pre-Championship season at Twickenham

My professional rugby career has spanned over 21 years and I am lucky to have experienced all the things I have, from playing for my country at international level to being selected for the Barbarians, through to playing for each and every club I have. I am now moving onto the next chapter which will hopefully include me staying within the game and allowing me to coach others using my experience and knowledge."

Head Coach, Paul Turner comments "Thanks Maama for your huge contribution to Ampthill Rugby. You will remain as one of the key figures in our great climb up the leagues into the Championship. Both your on-field performances and your off-field manner have been outstanding. All the very best in your retirement from the game."

Paino Hehea

After the disappointment of the loss in injury time to Darlington Mowden Park, Mark Lavery moved to strengthen his squad for the campaign in National 2 North. Paino Hehea joined in the close-season having played for Racing Metro, Lyon in France and Calvisano, in Italy. He represented Tonga in the Rugby World Cup in 2007 & 2011 and in the Pacific Nations Cup in 2006, 2008 and 2011.

The 6' 6", 18 stone lock joined Ampthill in 2014 and made 83 appearances in National 1 and National 2, scoring 14 tries. Injury forces Paino's retirement in April 2018 – he was sorely missed.

Paino in action against France in the 2011 World Cup – Tonga won 19-14

Aleki Lutui

Aleki played 38 times for Tonga & 7 games for the Pacific Islanders. He made 9 appearances in three World Cups. He previously played for Chiefs in the international Super 14 competition, as well as the Bay of Plenty in the Air New Zealand Cup. He was also the top try scorer for the Bay of Plenty in the 2002 National Provincial Championship. The 5' 11", 17 stone Lutui, also played for Worcester, Edinburgh, and Gloucester before joining Ampthill for the 2015-16 season.

Aleki is a prolific try scorer for Ampthill and a wrecking-ball around the pitch. On Friday October 9th, 2015, Aleki played against the All-Blacks in the World Cup at St. James' Park, his next game was the following day for Ampthill against Blackheath!

Aleki made his debut for Tonga in March 1999 against Georgia. He played for Tonga in their 2001 Pacific Rim campaign and later in the year toured Scotland and Wales. On June 5, 2004 he captained Tonga for the first time in a match against Fiji. In June 2005 he captained Tonga in four matches; two against both Fiji and Samoa.

Aleki went on tour with the Pacific Islanders rugby union team in 2004 for a series of Tests against a number of southern rugby nations. He was included in the Pacific Nations tour to Europe in late 2006 and also played in the game against England at Twickenham in 2008.

Lutui joined Worcester in September 2006, on a two-year deal. The Tongan international was a former police officer before he took up rugby.

He became an important player for Worcester at Sixways with his all-action displays and eye for the try line. After a spell with Edinburgh, he joined Gloucester.

Lutui, was named in the Tonga squad for the 2007 Rugby World Cup in France, the 2011 Rugby World Cup in New Zealand and the 2015 Rugby World Cup in England.

Soane Tonga'uhia

Tongan born, but New Zealand educated, Soane played for Auckland before moving to Bedford Blues in 2005-06. He was capped 15 times for Tonga. Tonga'uhia moved to Northampton Saints at the start of the 2006/07 season and became something of a crowd favourite at Franklin's Gardens with the nickname 'Tiny' – an ironic take on his size (6' 3" & 20 1/2 stone).

He developed into the most formidable prop of his generation. Soane Tonga'uhia left the Saints at the end of the season 2012-13 to join the Top 14 Paris club Racing Metro. Soane left Racing Metro to join Top 14 rivals Oyonnax from the 2014-15 season.

In June 2016, Tonga'uhia returned to England to join new Aviva Premiership side Bristol Rugby. In 2018 Tonga'uhia took up a player/coach role at Ampthill RUFC.

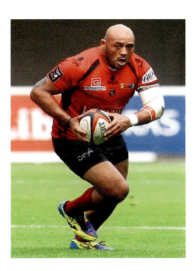

It is impossible to overstate the contribution that these amazing athletes have made to the success of Ampthill Rugby Club. They are warriors, as fearsome on the pitch as they are charming and modest off it. Many opponents have made the mistake of assuming, because of age, they will run out of steam in the second half, but they are eighty minutes warriors.

Paul Turner – on the Tongans:

"I'd seen Vili Ma'asi years before, I always had agents telling me we've got to sign this Tongan hooker for the Dragons, but at the time he was too old to bring into the Welsh system, given I had two or three young Welsh hookers. We used to play him in pre-season when he was at Cornish Pirates and he was some player.

Anyway, we signed him – I think he was about 38 when he joined – and he is the sole reason for what is happening now. He was the glue that made it happen, he'd been released by London Welsh but he was great for us for three years – when Vili Ma'asi didn't play we were a completely different side. It's good for England that he's got three sons around the scene now who have or will play for England at age level."

Just before Vili left to take up the coaching role at Peterborough Lions, he ensured there was a successor, Maama Molitika. "They were good mates at Calvisano, but I knew Maama from my time at Quins, and he was at Blues too, he was some player as well. Paino Hehea, who I'd tried to sign for the Dragons, came along – he'd been at Racing. All of them were at the end of their careers, sort of 36-38."

Next came Lutui. "I tried to get him at the Dragons about ten years earlier. We wanted a hooker and I remember watching the first game of the Lions tour in 2005, the one where we had one hell of a battle against Bay of Plenty. I saw this hooker for Bay of Plenty and thought, Christ I wouldn't mind signing him, he's bloody good. But he couldn't get a work permit – two years later he signed for Worcester." Ever the patient man, a decade or so later Paul got his hooker. "They've all been good for us. The way Lutui joined us was remarkable. He'd played the second half against the All-Blacks in a rugby world cup game at Newcastle on a Friday night and then, the next morning he drove down to us, arrived just before half-time and played the second half against Blackheath. Amazing. It was a really physical game too. Completing the set, prop Soane Tonga'uhia joined as player-coach from Bristol."

Paul Turner

Leon Fukofuka

Ampthill's "youngest Tongan", Leon is the son of former Auckland and Tonga Prop, Kalau Fukofuka. Leon was born and raised in West Auckland, New Zealand. After graduating from high school, he began playing for Marist in Auckland's Premier club rugby competition and also turned out for Auckland's sevens team. He was first named in Auckland's senior squad for the 2014 ITM Cup and made a total of 7 appearances in the competition.

He was a member of the New Zealand Under-20 side which finished 3rd at the 2014 IRB Junior World Championship. Leon played for both Waikato Chiefs and Canterbury Crusaders. He has been capped 7 times for Tonga including the World Cup in Japan.

A 6' 1", 15 stone scrum-half, Leon joined Ampthill for season 2019-20. Fukofuka causes massive problems for match-day commentators!

Leon Fukofuka in action against Newcastle Falcons – February 2nd 2020 at Kingston Park

Season 2015-16 - (Captain - Viliami Ma'asa)

Management Committee

President	P. Sherry
Chairman	M. Lavery
Hon. Treasurer	B. Warfield
Hon. Secretary	I. Titman
Director of Rugby	M. Lavery
Chair of Mini/Youth	K. Garwood
General Committee members:	J. Bishop, D. Phillips, A. Spavins, C. Burke, K. Belcher, I. Cooper, A. Clarke
Elected /Appointed Officers	C. Rempel, Liz Barlow, K. Belcher, P. Allen, D. Hoy, N. Ashton, B. McTavish, C. Stallwood, M. Stanbridge, C. Ashby, I. Titman, C. Page, J. Bishop, S. Morgan, J. Thomas, E. Muncaster, N. Eastwood & C. Jones

Playing

1st.XV Manager	I. Bremner
1881 XV Manager	N. Stephenson
Jets XV	J. Cresswell
Extras XV	L. Duffin
5th XV	R. Mardle
Vets Manager	D. Wheeler
Coach	P. Turner Head Coach, A. Brown (1881s)

Pre-Season

"After winning the National 2 play-off against Bishops Stortford and as part of our preparation to go into National 1 for the first time in the Club's history, we arranged two highly prestigious friendlies travelling away to play Stade Rouen, the club of former England captain and scrum-half Richard Hill. Stade Rouen is in Normandy and Richard Hill's brief is to get Rouen into the equivalent of the English Championship Pro D2. After a torturous journey which included a 6 hour wait at Folkestone for the Channel Tunnel to re-open, we arrived in Rouen at 2am on the morning of game day! Rouen had the biggest forward pack that Ampthill's Head Coach Paul Turner had ever seen and I can safely say it was the first time in recent history that we would run into a side that completely demolished Ampthill. Whilst the final score was respectable at 35-19, it didn't really tell the full story. Ampthill were down 35-5 with 6 minutes to go and managed to score two consolation tries when Rouen bought on a number of squad players.

The second pre-season friendly took place on Saturday August 29th when Ampthill hosted Pontypool from the Principality Championship. For those from older generations, they will remember the mighty Pontypool front row who played for the British Lions, - Falconer, Windsor, and Price. Pontypool were now playing in the Principality Championship in Wales which meant they were in the equivalent to National 1 in Wales. The main Pontypool sponsor flew up to the Club in his helicopter and was a little shocked when Ampthill ran out easy winners by 50pts to 10. Whilst the score line was not as Pontypool expected, it was still a huge prestigious occasion for Ampthill to host a club with such history and tradition." (Mark Lavery).

August 10th 3-way Bedford Blues / Old Albanians / Ampthill
August 23rd Rouen 35 pts. Ampthill 19 pts.
August 29th Ampthill 50 pts. Pontypool 10pts.

Recruitment was massive for this season including Aleki Lutui (hooker - Gloucester), Ben Gulliver (lock - Bedford Blues), Syd Blackmore (flanker/hooker - Bath Academy), Jack Culverhouse (prop – Bedford Blues), Will Massie (fly-half – Nottingham), Kennet O'Neil (flanker – Saracens Academy), Elliot Reeder (centre – Saracens Academy).

For the first time dual-registered players made a massive impact. Ralph Adams-Hale, Max Wilkins, Billy Walker, Brian Tuilagi (Saracens), Will Evans (Leicester Tigers), James Fish, Tom Nuttley (Northampton Saints) all appeared for the Club. Will Goodge, through sheer effort, came through the 2nd XV to play in the centre.

Those of us who are regular away supporters are, by now, used to being asked where Ampthill is situated. The first game of the season in National 1 was a visit to Esher in Surrey. Mark Lavery tells the story of being greeted by a "posh" official who said, "Excuse me old chap where exactly is Ampthill? - I've never heard of you!"

The first three games of the season, against Esher, Blaydon and Cinderford were won – all with bonus points and, "We were beginning to cause a ripple," said Mark. However, losses to Blackheath home and away, and on the road to Rosslyn Park, Darlington Mowden Park, Hartpury College, Plymouth Albion, and Coventry left Ampthill in 4th position in National 1.

Five points were deducted through playing an ineligible player, Jack Culverhouse from Bedford, whose dual registration had expired. This would have placed Ampthill equal 3rd with Blackheath on points, though Blackheath had won one more game.

National League 1

#	Team	P	W	D	L	PF	PA	+/-	TB	LB	Pts	Adj
1	Richmond	30	23	2	5	854	534	320	16	4	116	
2	Hartpury University	30	21	0	9	966	558	408	15	5	104	
3	Blackheath	30	21	2	7	794	488	306	9	6	103	
4	Ampthill	30	20	2	8	746	620	126	14	5	98	-5
5	Rosslyn Park	30	20	0	10	745	578	167	12	3	95	
6	Darlington Mowden Park	30	19	0	11	766	640	126	11	4	91	
7	Esher	30	17	0	13	801	603	198	14	6	88	
8	Plymouth Albion	30	22	0	8	733	647	86	11	3	72	-30
9	Coventry	30	13	2	15	710	653	57	9	6	71	
10	Fylde	30	11	1	18	736	804	-68	11	10	67	
11	Blaydon	30	10	0	20	565	772	-207	10	7	57	
12	Hull Ionians	30	9	0	21	645	872	-227	10	11	57	
13	Loughborough Students	30	9	0	21	680	774	-94	10	9	55	
14	Wharfedale	30	6	1	23	592	869	-277	10	7	43	
15	Cinderford	30	7	1	22	545	969	-424	7	4	41	
16	Henley	30	6	1	23	478	975	-497	5	3	29	-5

1st XV League Results in National 1

Opponent	Score	Venue	Result	Score	Venue	Result
Esher	27-16	away	won	20-13	home	won
Blaydon	41-12	home	won	19-12	away	won
Cinderford	27-25	away	won	47-14	home	won
Henley	14-14	home	draw	38-16	away	won
Darlington Mowden Park	32-20	home	won	29-45	away	lost
Blackheath	10-15	home	lost	15-21	away	lost
Rosslyn Park	10-17	away	lost	21-5	home	won
Wharfdale	29-12	away	won	35-29	home	won
Loughborough Students	21-19	home	won	21-19	away	won
Hartpury University	10-37	away	lost	24-18	home	won
Richmond	10-46	home	lost	19-19	away	draw
Plymouth Albion	13-18	away	lost	52-13	home	won
Hull Ionians	22-21	home	won	36-34	away	won
Coventry	31-25	home	won	19-25	away	lost
Fylde	29-19	away	won	25-21	home	won

Ampthill points shown first

Richmond were worthy winners of National 1 this season, they were a highly-organised team and were well-served at half-back. Ampthill were well-beaten at home by the champions 10-46, but later in March gave the leaders a scare with a well-earned 19-19 draw at the Athletic Ground.

Other notable triumphs included a 31-25 home win over Coventry, a 24-18 defeat of Hartpury and a rare 52-13 demolition of Plymouth Albion. Blackheath, of course beat Ampthill home and away, otherwise the results were as might be expected.

1881s XV – Herts. & Middlesex Merit Table 1

#	Team	P	W	D	L	PF	PA	+/-	TB	LB	Pts
1	Richmond Vikings (2nd XV)	20	19	0	1	993	260	733	17	0	93
2	Blackheath Heathens (2nd XV)	20	15	0	5	677	350	327	12	2	79
3	Esher Cardinals (2nd XV)	20	14	0	6	689	399	290	13	0	74
4	Jersey Athletic	20	13	0	7	490	421	69	11	0	70
5	Barnes 2nd XV	20	13	0	7	639	430	209	9	0	67
6	Ampthill 1881 XV	20	11	0	9	491	479	12	10	3	66
7	Cinderford United (2nd XV)	20	7	0	13	432	537	-105	4	6	50
8	Henley II	20	7	0	13	272	536	-264	5	1	45
9	Old Elthamians 2nd XV	20	6	0	14	291	590	-299	3	2	41
10	Worthing Raiders A (2nd XV)	20	3	0	17	286	656	-370	4	3	31
11	London Scottish Highlanders (Amateurs 1st XV)	20	2	0	18	245	847	-602	3	3	30

Other Senior Teams Leagues

Jets (3rd XV) – Merit Table 1

played	won	drawn	lost	pts. for	pts. against	points
18	15	0	3	697	203	84

Jets were again champions, finishing 2 points clear of Belsize Park 2nd XV

Extras (4th XV) – Bombardier League

played	won	drawn	lost	pts. for	pts. against	points
13	11	0	2	243	126	46

The Extras finished second in a league of eight, 2 points behind champions Towcestrians 2nd XV.

5th XV Youngs London Stout League

played	won	drawn	lost	pts. for	pts. against	points
16	12	2	2	316	151	54

In only their second season in leagues, the 5th XV were champions, 6 points clear of Leighton Buzzard 3rd XV. There were notable wins against: Men's Own 80-12, Leighton Buzzard 46-7 and Olney 48-0.

2015-16	played	won	drawn	lost	pts. for	pts. against
1st XV	30	20	2	8	746	620
1881s XV	20	11	0	9	491	479
Jets XV	18	15	0	3	697	203
Extras XV	13	11	0	2	243	126
5th XV	16	12	2	2	232	165
Vets XV						

Season 2016-17 - (Captain - Viliami Ma'asa)

Management Committee

President	P. Sherry
Chairman	M. Lavery
Hon. Treasurer	B. Warfield
Hon. Secretary	I. Titman
Director of Rugby	M. Lavery
Chair of Mini/Youth	K. Garwood
General Committee members:	A. Clark, D. Phillips, A. Spavins, C. Burke, K. Belcher, I. Cooper
Elected / Appointed Officers	C. Rempel, Liz Barlow, K. Belcher, P. Allen, D. Hoy, N. Ashton, B. McTavish, C. Stallwood, M. Stanbridge, C. Ashby, I. Titman, C. Page, J. Bishop, S. Morgan, J. Thomas, E. Muncaster, N. Eastwood & C. Jones

Playing

1st XV Manager	I. Bremner
1881 XV Manager	N. Stephenson
Jets XV Manager	J. Cresswell
Extras XV Manager	L. Duffin
5th XV Manager	R. Mardle
Vets XV Manager	D. Wheeler
Coach	P. Turner Head Coach, A. Brown (1881s)

Pre-Season

"As part of our preparations for our second season in National 1 we once more arrange two prestigious friendlies against Jersey and Bridgend and a third with South Leicester. The 1st team and 1881's travelled to Championship side Jersey to renew acquaintances after we had played them at Twickenham in the Champions Final a number of seasons ago. Jersey ran out 35-22 winners but unlike the previous season against Stade Rouen, the Maroon and Gold were a very different prospect and the game could have gone either way.

The second pre-season game was against another legendary Welsh side, Bridgend Ravens. The game played at Dillingham Park was again pretty one-sided and ended up with an Ampthill win of 43pts to 15.

The next "friendly" was notable for a strong performance from South Leicester, but Ampthill ended up winning 24-7. Another reason this fixture was notable is because this is the first time that Nick Isiekwe and Ben Earl wore the Maroon and Gold. Both players are commented on later in this article.

So, pre-season preparation had been good and the team went into the 2016-2017 with a lot of confidence." (Mark Lavery).

August 13th. 2016 Jersey Reds 35 pts. Ampthill 15 pts.

August 20th. 2016 Ampthill 43 pts. Bridgend Ravens 15 pts.

August 25th 2016 South Leicester 7 pts. Ampthill 24 pts.

New players this season included Steph Jones, (fly-half - Bedford Blues), Sam Baker (winger – Cinderford), Sam Hanks (centre - Cinderford), and Brett Sturgess (prop - Exeter Chiefs), Loti Molitika cousin of Maama (flanker – Cinderford), Peter Wakeman (winger – North-East), Josh Walker (lock – Bury St. Edmunds), Rob Bell (flanker – Henley).

The season was notable because of two factors. The first was Hartpury's perfect season; 30 wins from 30 games, finishing 22 points above runners-up Plymouth Albion. This had never been achieved before or since.

The second factor was the quality and impact of Ampthill's dual registered players. Flanker, Ben Earl from Saracens played 7 times for Ampthill before being capped for England. Nick Isiekwe, also Saracens, played 7 times for Ampthill before being selected for England's tour to Argentina. In April 2017 Eddie Jones named him in the team to play the Pumas in Buenos Aires. Mark Lavery and Paul Turner described Earl and Isiekwe as being "two absolute superstars to work with, humble and hyper-professional."

Alex Mitchell, the Northampton Saints scrum-half, played 13 games for Ampthill, this season before going on to represent England Under 20s at the World Cup in Georgia. He is considered a future successor to Ben Youngs in the national team.

Reece Marshall played 10 games, Matt Beasley 9 games, James Fish 9 games, Will Allman 9 games, Tony Trinder 2 games – all from Northampton Saints. Ralph Adams-Hales ex-Ampthill now at Saracens, played twice.

The geographical position of Ampthill is of major importance, giving access to Saracens, Northampton, Leicester, and Wasps rugby clubs. Paul Turner and Mark Lavery had developed excellent working relationships with these premiership clubs, as the Club entered its third season in National 1. As Mark Lavery observed, "To have finished third in National 1 in our second season, " was a massive achievement when you consider the teams around little old Ampthill!"

National League 1

#	Team	P	W	D	L	PF	PA	+/-	TB	LB	Pts
1	Hartpury University	30	30	0	0	1455	532	923	28	0	148
2	Plymouth Albion	30	24	0	6	879	523	356	17	5	118
3	Ampthill	30	22	0	8	844	584	260	17	3	108
4	Coventry	30	20	1	9	974	733	241	17	2	101
5	Birmingham Moseley	30	20	0	10	854	682	172	15	3	98
6	Rosslyn Park	30	16	1	13	867	682	185	13	7	86
7	Blackheath	30	14	1	15	692	724	-32	13	4	75
8	Esher	30	13	0	17	828	854	-26	16	6	74
9	Old Albanians	30	13	0	17	749	926	-177	14	5	71
10	Darlington Mowden Park	30	13	1	16	695	791	-96	10	5	69
11	Loughborough Students	30	10	1	19	905	966	-61	16	8	66
12	Fylde	30	10	0	20	691	1050	-359	15	4	59
13	Hull Ionians	30	10	1	19	679	944	-265	9	7	58
14	Cambridge	30	8	1	21	779	994	-215	18	6	58
15	Blaydon	30	8	2	20	642	1010	-368	10	6	52
16	Macclesfield	30	4	1	25	579	1117	-538	8	5	31

Hartpury were promoted, on route they amassed almost 1500 points. Ampthill finished a very pleasing third, ten points off runners-up spot. Perhaps as important was the step up in performance as exemplified by wins against Blackheath, Coventry and doubles over Moseley, Rosslyn Park, Cambridge, and Loughborough Students. Their nemesis Darlington Mowden Park did the double over Ampthill as did, of course, the runaway champions Hartpury University.

1st XV League Results

Rosslyn Park	24-15	home	won	27-21	away	won
Old Albanians	18-17	away	won	43-19	home	won
Darlington Mowden Park	20-39	home	lost	12-14	away	lost
Loughborough Students	37-29	away	won	25-3	home	won
Birmingham Moseley	26-8	home	won	35-18	away	won
Macclesfield	28-12	away	won	36-10	home	won
Blackheath	17-31	home	lost	24-17	away	won
Hartpury University	14-49	away	lost	25-51	home	lost
Esher	29-24	home	won	46-15	away	won
Fylde	11-13	away	lost	43-24	home	won
Coventry	22-8	home	won	19-29	away	lost
Hull Ionians	49-13	away	won	31-11	home	won
Blaydon	50-14	home	won	40-17	away	won
Plymouth Albion	24-22	home	won	14-19	away	lost

Cambridge   20-10   away   won   35-12   home   won

Ampthill points shown first

1881s XV – Zoo Sports Division 1

#	Team	P	W	D	L	PF	PA	+/-	TB	LB	Pts
1	Richmond Vikings (2nd XV)	21	21	0	0	1036	162	874	18	0	102
2	Bishop's Stortford Blues	24	18	0	6	748	410	338	15	1	94
3	Ampthill 1881 XV	24	17	0	7	679	516	163	14	1	89
4	Jersey Athletic	23	16	0	7	642	451	191	12	0	83
5	Barnes 2nd XV	24	14	0	10	710	528	182	12	5	83
6	Blackheath Heathens (2nd XV)	24	13	1	10	622	533	89	12	3	77
7	Old Elthamians 2nd XV	24	13	0	11	637	591	46	11	2	76
8	Bury St Edmunds Wolfhounds 2nd XV	23	10	1	12	496	625	-129	8	2	63
9	Henley Wanderers II	23	7	1	15	485	697	-212	9	2	55
10	Cinderford United (2nd XV)	22	8	0	14	407	529	-122	6	3	52
11	Worthing Raiders A (2nd XV)	24	5	0	19	302	856	-554	6	2	43
12	London Scottish 2nd XV	22	3	1	18	332	860	-528	6	3	39
13	Esher Cardinals (2nd XV)	24	4	0	20	346	684	-338	5	3	36

The 1881s improved their league position, recording a pleasing 17 victories, but Richmond Vikings ran away with the title winning all 21 matches this season.

However, creditable Ampthill results include, 40-14 against London Scottish, 57-7 over Old Elthamians, 37-20 defeat of Blackheath Heathens and the 38-33 win over Esher Cardinals.

Other Senior Teams Leagues

Jets (3rd XV) – Merit Table 1

played	won	drawn	lost	pts. for	pts. against	points
15	13	0	2	605	203	71

Jets were runners-up in the league to Tring 2nd XV, six points in arrears.

Extras (4th XV) – Bombardier League

played	won	drawn	lost	pts. for	pts. against	points
6	3	0	3	123	207	15

The Extras finished second of six teams.

Extras (4th XV) – Bombardier/Eagle 2017 League

played	won	drawn	lost	pts. for	pts. against	points
9	5	1	3	209	174	25

The Extras finished third of six teams.

5th XV – Youngs Bitter

played	won	drawn	lost	pts. for	pts. against	points
16	8	0	8	355	446	40

The 5th XV were third in a league of ten teams.

2016-17	played	won	drawn	lost	pts. for	pts. against
1st XV	30	22	0	8	844	584
1881s XV	24	17	0	7	679	516
Jets XV	15	10	0	5	441	307
Extras XV	15	8	0	8	332	381
5th XV	16	8	0	3	355	446
Vets XV						

Season 2017-18 - (Captain - Billy Johnson)

Management Committee

President	P. Sherry
Chairman	I. Titman
Hon. Treasurer	B. Warfield
Hon. Secretary	A. Clark
Director of Rugby	M. Lavery
Chair of Mini/Youth	J. Wiggett
General Committee members:	D. Phillips, A. Spavins, C. Burke & K. Belcher
Elected / Appointed Officers	A. Spavins, B. Brown, P. Davies, K. Belcher, D. Phillips, C. Stallwood, J. Wiggett, M. Stanbridge, L. Threader, H. Christey, C. Page, W. Kay, F. Dimmock, C. Burke, L. Palmer, J. Abbott, N. Sugrue K. Miller & B. McTavish
Playing	
1st XV Manager	I. Bremner
1881 XV Manager	N. Stephenson
Jets XV Manager	J. Cresswell
Extras XV Manager	L. Duffin
5th XV Manager	R. Mardle
Vets Manager	D. Wheeler
Coach	P. Turner Head Coach, A. Brown (1881s)

Pre-Season

"Ampthill's only pre-season game was against Championship side Nottingham at Lady Bay and was the first time in a number of years that it felt that Ampthill were playing the role of boys in a game of men against boys! Nottingham won 64-14 and frankly Ampthill were lucky to get 14. The difference in calibre between the two sides was enormous and a sobering experience for the squad and the management." (Mark Lavery)

Nottingham 64 pts. Ampthill 14 pts. - August 26th, 2017

New players this season included Billy Johnson (Old Albanians) equally at home at lock or blindside and he made an excellent captain. James Pritchard, the Australian born Canadian international (62 caps) joined Ampthill from Coventry after a stellar career at Bedford Blues and having played in 4 World Cups. James made a major impact at the Club and was immensely popular with the players and fans. Also joining the Club were - Karl Garside (tight-head prop - Old Albanians), Stef Leibenburg (scrum-half – Cambridge), Lawrence Rayner (fly-half – Nottingham), Carl Burgess (second-row – Old Northamptonians).

Coventry were worthy champions this season, finishing nine points clear of Darlington Mowden Park. The Club drew four games they might have won against; Old Albanians (a), Moseley (a), Esher (a) and Loughborough Students (h), this could have made things much tighter at the top.

In April Ampthill inflicted a rare 22-10 defeat on the champions at Dillingham Park. Ampthill were as convincing that day, as Coventry were disappointing. Still, it was Coventry's season. As it was, Ampthill finished in fourth place, the first time in Mark Lavery's tenure that the Club did not improve on the previous season, which was cause for regret. The great Viliami Ma'asi retired at the end of this season because of a neck injury, he moved to Peterborough Lions as Head Coach, he was an enormous loss.

Richard Churchill – (1937-2017)

Richard Churchill passed-away peacefully, on Monday August 14th at Willen Hospice, Milton Keynes. Richard was a pillar of Ampthill rugby for much of the club's history, as a player for the 1st XV for a decade, Honorary Treasurer for thirty years, volunteer (Clubman of the Year in 2014) and supporter, where he continued to attend home games after recovering from a stroke.

Whilst at Bedford Modern School, Richard played one game for the club in 1951, and then joined Bedford for four seasons where he appeared the first team. He re-joined Ampthill in 1956 and played outside half for the 1st XV for ten years. Afterwards he played for the Exiles but became fixture secretary for nine years before taking on the onerous task of Club Treasurer in 1968.

When he took over this task the only source of income was match fees (3/6 per game), four Jumble Sales, one Dinner Dance and one Summer Fete – no sponsorship was allowed. It is known by a few that from time to time Richard contributed sums from his own pocket to keep the club afloat.

During his tenure of office, we acquired a second pitch, our first club house and our present clubhouse. We expanded from two teams to six teams and we established the mini and youth section.

When Richard retired from the post of Treasurer, he continued to support the Club by painting the club fences and many other jobs that few would undertake, including every Monday he would travel from Milton Keynes and collect rubbish from around the pitches. People with such dedication to the Club are very rare. The Club has been privileged to have had such a member as Richard Churchill.

The author is proud to have been a friend of Richard Churchill – a true gentleman and a very fine man.

Richard Churchill

National League 1

#	Team	P	W	D	L	PF	PA	+/-	TB	LB	Pts
1	Coventry	30	27	0	3	1213	495	718	26	0	134
2	Darlington Mowden Park	30	23	1	6	838	637	201	19	2	115
3	Plymouth Albion	30	20	2	8	844	549	295	18	6	108
4	Ampthill	30	19	4	7	797	540	257	17	5	106
5	Blackheath	30	17	2	11	764	636	128	13	3	88
6	Old Elthamians	30	15	1	14	714	709	5	14	5	81
7	Bishop's Stortford	30	15	1	14	750	713	37	8	8	78
8	Birmingham Moseley	30	14	2	14	680	770	-90	12	6	78
9	Esher	30	11	2	17	774	827	-53	18	8	74
10	Cambridge	30	14	0	16	613	600	13	8	8	72
11	Caldy	30	12	0	18	726	743	-17	12	8	68
12	Rosslyn Park	30	10	2	18	766	863	-97	15	7	66
13	Loughborough Students	30	10	3	17	756	894	-138	10	6	62
14	Hull Ionians	30	10	1	19	685	941	-256	14	3	59
15	Old Albanians	30	9	1	20	620	941	-321	11	5	54
16	Fylde	30	3	0	27	405	1087	-682	4	4	20

1st XV League Results

Birmingham Moseley	21-21	away	draw	36-5	home	won
Old Albanians	28-24	home	won	35-35	away	draw
Blackheath	15-16	away	lost	21-14	home	won
Esher	45-5	home	won	29-29	away	draw
Bishop's Stortford	41-22	away	won	22-12	home	won
Loughborough Students	36-14	away	won	17-17	home	draw
Cambridge	7-8	home	lost	8-20	away	lost
Caldy	39-22	away	won	30-14	home	won
Old Elthamians	33-7	home	won	18-6	away	won
Plymouth Albion	9-16	away	lost	33-28	home	won
Rosslyn Park	29-23	home	won	31-21	away	won
Darlington Mowden Park	15-21	away	lost	15-17	home	lost
Coventry	14-63	away	lost	22-10	home	won
Hull Ionians	45-17	home	won	42-16	away	won
Fylde	35-12	home	won	26-5	away	won

Ampthill points shown first

1881s XV – Zoo Sports Division 1

#	Team	P	W	D	L	PF	PA	+/-	TB	LB	Pts
1	Richmond Vikings (2nd XV)	24	21	0	3	809	287	522	19	2	108
2	Ampthill 1881 XV	24	20	0	4	747	362	385	14	2	100
3	Old Elthamians 2nd XV	24	17	0	7	672	522	150	15	2	91
4	Richmond Saxons (3rd XV)	22	15	1	6	703	482	221	14	2	84
5	Jersey Athletic	24	12	0	12	605	633	-28	11	4	75
6	Barnes 2nd XV	23	12	0	11	580	648	-68	8	3	70
7	Cambridge Wanderers	23	9	0	14	579	599	-20	12	5	66
8	Coventry 2nd XV	23	10	1	12	473	453	20	8	3	60
9	Esher Cardinals (2nd XV)	24	9	0	15	461	686	-225	7	1	56
10	Cinderford United (2nd XV)	23	7	1	15	480	659	-179	6	4	54
11	Chinnor II	24	5	0	19	433	727	-294	8	6	49
12	London Scottish 2nd XV	24	8	1	15	338	546	-208	6	0	48
13	Bishop's Stortford Blues	24	5	2	17	412	688	-276	5	4	47
14	Blackheath Heathens (2nd XV)	0	0	0	0	0	0	0	0	0	0

The 1881 league campaign saw them finished as runners up to Richmond Vikings by eight points and well-clear of Old Elthamians from Bromley.

During the season they inflicted a 30-24 defeat on the champions and also beat Richmond Saxons 40-28 & 44-12. Jersey Athletic were despatched 38-19 & 23-22; Esher Cardinals 53-12 & 53-14. Coventry were beaten 26-14 at the Butts Park Arena.

Other Senior Teams Leagues

Jets (3rd XV) – Merit Table 1

played	won	drawn	lost	pts. for	pts. against	points
16	13	1	2	571	305	75

Jets were champions 6 points clear of runners-up, Bishop's Stortford Chindits.

Extras (4th XV) – Bombardier League

played	won	drawn	lost	pts. for	pts. against	points
6	4	0	2	113	103	18

The Extras finished in second place, 11 points behind champions Bedford Athletic 2nd XV.

Extras (4th XV) – Merit Table 1

played	won	drawn	lost	pts. for	pts. against	points
18	17	1	0	840	133	89

The Extras finished unbeaten as champions, 2 points clear of Bedford Athletic 2nd XV, whom they beat 32-10 at home and drew with 17-17 at Putnoe Woods.

5th XV – Youngs Bitter

played	won	drawn	lost	pts. for	pts. against	points
9	4	0	5	173	188	21

The 5th XV finished in third position in a league of six teams.

2017-18	played	won	drawn	lost	pts. for	pts. against
1st XV	30	19	4	7	797	540
1881s XV	24	20	0	4	747	362
Jets XV	16	13	1	2	571	305
Extras XV	24	21	1	2	953	236
5th XV	9	4	0	5	173	188
Vets XV						
Colts XV						

Season 2018-19 - (Captain - Billy Johnson)

Management Committee

President	P. Sherry
Chairman	A. Radley
Hon. Treasurer	B. Warfield
Hon. Secretary	A. Clark
Director of Rugby	M. Lavery
Fixture Secretary	I. Titman
Chair of Mini/Youth	J. Wiggett
General Committee members:	D. Phillips, A. Spavins, C. Burke, K. Belcher
Elected / Appointed Officers	P. Allen, D. New, M. Wythe, D. Thomas, D. Phillips, J. Wiggett, M. Stanbridge, H. Christey, D. Sibilia, M. Plant, W. Kay, C. Hampshaw, C. Burke, B. McTavish, K. Miller

Playing

1st.XV Manager	I. Bremner
1881 XV Manager	N. Stephenson
Jets XV Manager	J. Cresswell
Extras XV Manager	L. Duffin
5th XV Manager	R. Mardle
Vets Manager	D. Wheeler
Academy XV Manager	T. Gray
Coach	P. Turner Head Coach, A. Brown (1881s)

Pre-Season

"Just one pre-season fixture was organised. Ampthill would host Ebbw Vale on Saturday 18th August at the home of Bedford Blues, Goldington Road, due to the pitches at Ampthill being unplayable. The A's came out of a close contest by winning 20pts to 15. Ampthill scored 4 tries and missed all conversions and the steelmen, unusually for a pre-season friendly, kicked 5 penalties."

Goldington Road – Boxing Day 2018

"We were also invited to play our first game against Bedford Blues in a friendly on Boxing Day on Goldington Road. An epic match which Ampthill came out with a 31-28 win in front of a capacity crowd. This certainly gave the members, supporters and players of Ampthill pause for thought that they be on the edge of realising their dream and the possibility of playing Championship rugby in the future." (Mark Lavery).

This season, the first four senior teams won their leagues and the 5th XV were only deprived of the championship through a rule change.

Paul Turner and Mark Lavery had a clear internal goal for season 2018-19 - to win National 1. New players included the stellar signing of loose-head prop Soane Tonga'uhia from Bristol. Also arriving were - Will Allman (flanker – Northampton Saints), Oliver Waliker (hooker – Old Albanians), Mickey Waters (full-back/fly-half – Leeds Carnegie), George De-Coti (Loughborough University), Spencer Sutherland (winger – Esher), Will Foster (Loughborough Students), Euan McKirdy and Ciaran Whyte came from the Scottish borders. Henry Williams a line-out specialist from the Dragons came on loan, but eventually signed forms. Sam Hudson joined from Loughborough Students and proved to be an influential No.8.

This was a simply titanic season in which the top four teams; Ampthill, Old Elthamians, Rosslyn Park and Blackheath were competing hammer and tongs for the title. The top positions were changing week by week and anxious supporters after a game would sip their pints and wait for Club statistician, Cliff Page to text the results of matches.

Few observers of Ampthill's early fixtures could have imagined they were watching the future champions. After a 43-34, unconvincing win over Loughborough Students, Ampthill lost the next two games.

In particular, the 33-38 loss at Chinnor and 6-13 reverse at home to Cambridge gave no clues to the success to come. In fact, Ampthill were abject in these games. The Club had recruited a significant group of new players and hindsight suggests they were taking some time to gel, but of the first thirteen games, five were lost and one drawn.

Rosslyn Park were the form side at the season's start. On 13th October, Ampthill lost to Caldy at Paton Field by 19-18, they selected too many inexperienced dual-registered players against a street-wise team and failed to use the elements in the second half. Old Elthamians were thrashing Loughborough Students 48-24 away, on the same day.

The ding-dong changes in fortunes continued when, on 20th October Ampthill beat Cinderford 54-20 at Dillingham Park and Old Elthamians drew 22-22 with Chinnor.

In November Ampthill beat Rotherham Titans 22-18 at home, Old Elthamians beat Plymouth Albion away and Rosslyn Park could only manage a draw at Chinnor. Old Elthamians' form was "bubbling-up".

On 17th November, Ampthill visited high-spending Old Elthamians at College Meadow. The match was played on a pitch covered in water and in incessant rain and freezing temperatures. Unsurprisingly, flanker Joe Bercis, had to be substituted before he perished from hypothermia. With minutes remaining Ampthill scored a try to tie the match at 13-13, with James Pritchard's conversion in front of the posts to win the match, a seeming formality. Pritchard, wrongly, thought he needed to convert the try to achieve a draw and he missed the kick he would normally have managed blind-folded. Bear in mind that James is Bedford Blues all-time points scorer with 2,833 points and Championship all-time points scorer with 2673 points and also Canada's all-time points scorer with 606 points!

In early December, Ampthill were beaten 6-10 by Rosslyn Park at The Rock. It was not the strongest of Ampthill sides and they only got going in the final quarter. In truth, Rosslyn Park were the most difficult side Ampthill met that season and Ampthill were more soundly beaten than the score suggested. The return match at Dillingham Park was a thriller.

In mid-December, Ampthill, showing good form, beat Sale 25-17 at Heywood Road. Old Elthamians beat Bishop Stortford 17-3 at College Meadow and Rosslyn Park beat Caldy 26-10 at the Rock.

Before Christmas, Ampthill overcame a spirited Chinnor side by 38-27 at Dillingham Park. Rosslyn Park beat Bishop's Stortford 27-25 at Silver Leys, and Old Elthamians were narrowly beaten at home by Blackheath 11-12.

Going into the new year Old Elthamians were National 1 leaders, Rosslyn Park second and Ampthill lay in third place.

The game at Esher, in the new year, typified Ampthill's inconsistency. In what John Inverdale, Esher's Deputy President, described as "the most bizarre game I have ever seen", Ampthill contrived to lose to the home side 49-48, in a game they had dominated, by gifting interception tries to the opposition. The game ended in a farcical fashion when scrum-half Gavin Williams, mistakenly thinking his side were leading, kicked the ball out of play in injury time. He was inconsolable afterwards but, in truth, the defeat could not be laid at his door.

However, on the same day Old Elthamians were beaten by Darlington Mowden Park, at the Northern Echo Arena, by 26-41 and Rosslyn Park beat Rotherham 46-24 at the Rock to stay in contention.

In late January, Ampthill beat Blackheath 31-26 at Eltham, in what Mark Lavery has described as a "war zone", this result effectively ended the Londoners' bid for the title. Old Elthamians beat Moseley 14-10 at Billesley Common and Rosslyn Park were beaten 31-32 by Darlington Mowden Park at The Rock.

The title was now a two-horse race between Old Elthamians and Ampthill.

In early March, Ampthill beat Rotherham 36-24 at Clifton Lane. Old Elthamians beat Plymouth Albion 40-29 at Brickfields and Rosslyn Park beat Chinnor, who had fallen away in 2019, by 38-31.

On 9th March, Old Elthamians came to Dillingham Park in what seemed certain to be the title clincher. On the day Ampthill physically dominated the visitors and the three-quarters ran rings around their opponents, in a convincing 36-6 victory.

At the end of March Ampthill faced Rosslyn Park at Dillingham Park in front of 1,000 spectators. For 40 minutes Park dominated and Ampthill were 20-0 behind. In the second half the Ampthill forwards got stuck in and Park became rattled and lost their discipline, conceding 3 yellow cards. A try by flanker Syd Blackmore after a break by fly-half Sharp, was followed by a penalty-try. An excellent third try by Josh Sharp on 78 minutes took the score to 21-20 in Ampthill's favour.

Most teams would have thrown in the towel, but Rosslyn Park fought back strongly and won a penalty pretty much in front of the posts and only 20 metres out. With Ampthill supporters expecting the worst, the kick was astonishingly missed. This result maintained the gap between Ampthill and Old Elthamians.

The last twelve games of the season were won, nine with bonus points. On the 13th April Ampthill comprehensively demolished Sale 57-12 at Dillingham Park ,which meant going into the final game they needed just one point for the title.

On 27 April, Ampthill travelled to Loughborough students for the final game of the season, with Old Elthamians hoping for a miracle.

The National 1 Decider

Loughborough 20 pts. Ampthill 52 pts.

Ampthill Director of Rugby Mark Lavery revelled in a "truly historic day" as his side sealed the National 1 title and will play in the Championship after an eight-try demolition of Loughborough students.

Ampthill came into the game needing just a solitary point to rubber-stamp the title and had that by half-time after running in four tries in 40 minutes.

They kicked on after the break to finish top of the pile by five points from Old Elthamians – while defeat relegates Loughborough to National 2 – and Lavery admits next year will be very different.

"It's a truly historic day," he said. "To have the division won by half-time was perfect, this meant we could play a bit more rugby in the second half. Loughborough came back at us really well, moved the ball around and tested the defence. The bottom line is we are going to enjoy the night, it's been a momentous year, and our lives just became a little more complicated!"

Ampthill dominated the early stages with a combination of effective phases and breakdowns, culminating in Maama Molitika crossing on three minutes. Despite Loughborough struggling to contend with the Ampthill scrum, they narrowed the deficit following a spell of pressure resulting from a lineout deep in the Ampthill 22, as Max Hill dotted down.

It didn't take the away side long to extend their lead with an additional two tries from Matthew Collins and Aleki Lutui, after several strong mauls. The students weren't easily deterred and continued to put bodies on the line but Ampthill clinched the title by securing the four try bonus point with the final play of the half, as Joe Bercis touched down.

Sam Hudson capitalised on a gap in Loughborough's defence two minutes after the break, widening the score to 33-5. But Loughborough got a second try as Hill took the ball and, with the help from his fellow forwards, scrambled over the line before Will Allman got Ampthill's sixth score.

The students followed up with two quick tries – hooker Jamie Harding scoring after some forceful carrying in the 62nd minute and Austin Beckett elegantly outmanoeuvring his opposite man to dot down on 65 minutes.

In the last ten minutes the champions extended their lead though, as Sam Baker scored from a 70th. minute scrum and crossed again in the final minute for try number eight.

Skipper Billy Johnson receiving National 1 Trophy in front of his jubilant team mates.

National League 1

#	Team	P	W	D	L	PF	PA	+/-	TB	LB	Pts
1	Ampthill	30	23	1	6	970	583	387	21	5	120
2	Old Elthamians	30	23	2	5	845	562	283	17	2	115
3	Rosslyn Park	30	21	1	8	873	699	174	16	4	106
4	Blackheath	30	20	1	9	794	601	193	17	6	105
5	Plymouth Albion	30	16	0	14	701	690	11	13	6	83
6	Rotherham Titans	30	16	0	14	717	705	12	13	5	82
7	Darlington Mowden Park	30	13	1	16	739	790	-51	16	7	77
8	Cinderford	30	13	1	16	624	710	-86	11	7	72
9	Bishop's Stortford	30	13	0	17	758	627	131	12	8	72
10	Chinnor	30	11	2	17	735	862	-127	15	9	72
11	Sale FC	30	12	1	17	732	873	-141	12	6	68
12	Birmingham Moseley	30	11	1	18	768	857	-89	13	9	68
13	Cambridge	30	12	1	17	574	617	-43	5	9	64
14	Caldy	30	11	0	19	579	771	-192	9	9	62
15	Esher	30	11	0	19	627	803	-176	9	8	61
16	Loughborough Students	30	8	0	22	821	1107	-286	19	6	57

1st XV League results

Loughborough Students	43-34	home	won	52-20	away	won
Chinnor	33-38	away	lost	38-27	home	won
Esher	35-20	home	won	48-49	away	lost
Plymouth Albion	5-17	away	lost	48-15	home	won
Blackheath	33-22	home	won	31-26	away	won
Cambridge	6-13	home	lost	22-11	away	won
Caldy	18-19	away	lost	59-7	home	won
Cinderford	54-10	home	won	26-20	away	won
Bishop's Stortford	29-10	away	won	34-24	home	won
Rotherham Titans	22-8	home	won	36-24	away	won
Old Elthamians	13-13	away	draw	36-6	home	won
Darlington Mowden Park	40-29	home	won	33-26	away	won
Rosslyn Park	6-10	away	lost	21-20	home	won
Birmingham Moseley	25-17	home	won	40-26	away	won
Sale	27-10	away	won	57-12	home	won

Ampthill points shown first

Iain Bremner, team manager since 2005, with club captain Billy Johnson and the National One trophy.

Ampthill: Pritchard (Waters 25), Foster, Morris, Hanks, Baker, Sharp, Barrett, (Williams 59), Tonga'uhia, Lutui (Blackmore 40), Collins (Garside 52), Burgess, Johnson, Hudson, Bercis, Molitika (Allman 40)

James Pritchard

James (Skippy) Pritchard confirmed he would hang up his boots at the end of the season and return to Australia.

James began playing Rugby Union for Randwick in 1999 after playing Rugby League in his youth. In 2000 Randwick won the Citibank/MasterCard Cup and he was named player of the year. Skippy joined Bedford Blues in 2001and left in 2004, only to return in 2006 and stay until 2016 where he became a firm favourite. In between he played for Plymouth Albion, Perpignan, and Northampton Saints. He remains the leading points scorer in the Championship (2,673) and is Bedford's highest ever point scorer with 2,833.

After short spells with Coventry and Old Albanians he joined Ampthill in 2017, since when he has made 47 appearances scoring 7 tries and 332 points. Over the past two seasons he has made a significant contribution to Ampthill's on-field success both through his performances and his coaching. Internationally, he represented Canada in four Rugby World Cups (2003, 2007, 2011, 2015) where he made 10 appearances and has 62 caps for Canada in total, scoring more than 600 points.

1881s XV – Zoo Sports Division 1

#	Team	P	W	D	L	PF	PA	+/-	TB	LB	Pts
1	Ampthill 1881 XV	24	20	1	3	725	438	287	14	2	101
2	Richmond Vikings (2nd XV)	24	19	1	4	895	359	536	15	2	99
3	Cambridge Wanderers	24	16	0	8	755	395	360	15	4	89
4	Bishop's Stortford Blues	24	15	0	9	632	563	69	14	3	86
5	Old Elthamians 2nd XV	24	13	2	9	615	510	105	11	5	79
6	Jersey Athletic	24	12	0	12	584	665	-81	13	2	74
7	Richmond Saxons (3rd XV)	24	12	0	12	567	514	53	9	1	67
8	Rams II	24	10	0	14	503	653	-150	9	1	62
9	Cinderford United (2nd XV)	24	9	1	14	449	582	-133	9	3	62
10	Barnes 2nd XV	24	9	1	14	506	598	-92	7	1	58
11	Wimbledon 2nd XV	24	8	0	16	421	664	-243	6	3	57
12	Esher Cardinals (2nd XV)	23	5	0	18	385	722	-337	8	1	41
13	Chinnor II	23	4	0	19	254	628	-374	6	2	31

Although the 1881s were pushed hard by Richmond Vikings, they emerged as worthy winners. Convincing victories included: Richmond Vikings 20-19, Bishop's Stortford 52-34, Rams 2nds. 59-28, Wimbledon 2nds. 61-0, Esher Cardinals 38-22.

Nick Stephenson, Michael Lavery, Sean Fitzpatrick & Alan Brown – Zoo League Presentation

The Zoo League trophy was presented by Sean Fitzpatrick at the Rugby Room, East India Club, St. James Square, London on Thursday, 30th May 2019.

Other Senior Teams Leagues

Jets (3rd XV) – Merit Table 1

played	won	drawn	lost	pts. for	pts. against	points
18	18	0	0	826	103	90

The undefeated Jets were champions, 12 points ahead of Fullerians 2nd XV.

Extras (4th XV) – Bombardier League

played	won	drawn	lost	pts. for	pts. against	points
4	1	0	3	105	159	13

The Extras were sixth out of seven teams.

Extras (4th XV) – Merit Table 2

played	won	drawn	lost	pts. for	pts. against	points
14	7	0	7	575	240	79

The Extras were champions, 3 points ahead of Letchworth 2nd XV.

5th XV - Banana Bread Beer Merit Table

played	won	drawn	lost	pts. for	pts. against	points
12	10	0	2	302	104	34

The 5th XV finished second in their league of eight teams.

This season all the Club's senior teams won their league except Richard Mardle's 5th XV, who finished runners up to Sharnbrook & Colworth.

5th XV Denied Championship

The 5th XV team was more that somewhat aggrieved when the rules concerning scratched fixtures was changed. In previous seasons a scratched game meant the award of a 20-0 win to the team who had honoured the fixture. This rule was changed to an award a result of an average season's victory. This effectively denied Ampthill 5th XV the championship. To rub salt in the wound Richard Mardle's team had beaten the winners Sharnbrook & Colworth 29-7 at Dillingham Park and 27-14 at Channels End Road.

2018-19	played	won	drawn	lost	pts. for	pts. against
1st XV	30	23	1	6	970	583
1881s XV	24	20	1	3	725	438
Jets XV	18	18	0	0	826	103
Extras XV	21	15	0	5	680	399
5th XV	10	8	0	2	302	104
Vets XV						
Academy XV						

Ian Titman, Mayor of Ampthill, & Lady Mayoress Maggie

Honorary Secretary (ex-Chairman & Fixture Secretary) was elected mayor of Ampthill for 2019-20 on 15th May. Ian joined the Club in 1987 and played in the front-row for the 1st XV.

Ampthill Ladies 1st XV

back row: **Bethan Scarr, Sisi Bomolo, Bex Lane, Nikki Milward*, Gemini Forster*, Sophie Ward*, Gemma Bear*, Sian Mills, Chloe Pearce** front row: **Nichole Neate*, Erica Larkins*, Megan Parry, Sammie Godleman, Gloria Mills, Jules Gale, Annie Tomblin, Charlotte Saunders.** *playing first ever game.

On 8th September 2019, the Ampthill Ladies travelled to Biggleswade on a momentous day for women's rugby for the club. Five years of development of the girl's teams and hard work by the coaches meant that Ampthill for the first time in its 138-year history fielded a women's team.

Author's note – I am grateful to Ian Scarr, coach of the Ladies squad for the following:

The Girls U13 and U15's were reformed in 2014-15 by Dave Dunstan and Ian Scarr after Ian's daughter Bethan, frustrated with not getting any game play with Alameda School, asked Dad to form an U15 side at Ampthill and she brought all her schoolmates to play. The first season was an introduction with some friendlies against the newly formed Bedford Junior Blues U15 girls coached by Gloria Mills. This meeting of coaches and daughters (Sian Mills and Bethan Scarr) soon became the driving force behind Ampthill's success over the coming years. With a merger of the two sides in 2016-17 for U18's and Gloria being the first Ladies 1st XV captain in Ampthill history in the 2019-20 season. Bedford Blues have now formed a ladies side for 2020-21 season and the rivalry will continue in men's and women's senior rugby.

Local Press - August 2019 - Chairman Alex Radley expects a battle for A's

Ampthill have completed a remarkable rise to reach the Championship for the first time in the club's history but chairman Alex Radley is under no illusions that the real work starts now.

Last season saw the Dillingham Park club secure their fifth promotion in 12 years to reach the Championship, scoring almost 1,000 points in their National One title win.

Now in the second tier of English rugby with the likes of Newcastle Falcons and Bedford Blues, Radley is cautious when predicting how the season will pan out given the strengths of the respective sides they will face.

"We had an exceptional season last year but we have no illusions about the task in front of us this year," said Radley at the Championship launch event at Twickenham earlier this month. He added, "Seeing the professionalism of the other squads, we hope we will be able to compete and do our best."

With that in mind, the summer has seen a raft of changes to the squad with experience brought into the side in the form of ex-Harlequins hooker Dave Ward as player/coach and scrum-half Darrel Veenendaal from Nottingham. Fly-half Louis Grimoldby and lock Shay Kerry have also joined head coach Paul Turner's side as they look to add extra quality to the core group that earned promotion.

Radley added, "We've got a couple of good additions with Daryl Veenendaal and Dave Ward coming in who are leading training this year. We are still trying to build our squad. We've still got some opportunities for more people to come in and we've kept the core from last year. We have a very strong group of boys who took us up to the Championship and they've been here for a while and we believe they can perform at this level."

Although there is caution, an overriding sense of excitement exists among a squad that cannot wait to get going at such a high level. Long-serving forward Maama Molitika said, "We're so glad to be here, it's been a long journey for Ampthill. It's my seventh season and we've come a long way. Just to be here in this environment is a massive achievement for the club. To play against Newcastle Falcons for all the boys at the club will just be a great experience for us to play against one of the most historic clubs in the league. It's so exciting not just for myself but for Ampthill RFC and the whole team. I can't wait to get out there and make sure I'm ready to go."

Alex Radley – Chairman of Ampthill & District Rugby Club

Running a Championship Club

Author's note - I am grateful for the input of many Club members for this section, but particularly Karen Radley, whose care and attention to detail was greatly appreciated.

It is doubtful if anyone truly understood how different being in the Championship would prove to be for the running of the Club. Virtually everything changed or became more complicated or enlarged.

Director of Rugby, Mark Lavery and Club Chairman Alex Radley attended regular Championship Club meetings at Twickenham. As preparations for the next season got underway it became known that the Club must meet thirty-seven criteria and that these would be inspected by the Championship officials. Any failure to meet any of the criteria would mean a fine of between £750 and £1,000 fine per breach – potentially a £37,000 bill and a possible ejection from the league. Chairman of Bedford Blues and the Championship, Geoff Irvine, was generous with his time and expertise. His advice was crucial to the Club's preparation for the Championship.

At that time, the Club was run mainly by volunteers. Only the Head Coach, bar staff, medical, kitchen staff and cleaning staff were paid. The players were semi-professional and most had part or full-time employment outside rugby. In National 1, the players trained on two evenings per week. For the Championship season, training was increased to three evenings per week. However, there was a great deal of underlying concern about how the Club could compete with the likes of Newcastle Falcons, Ealing Trailfinders, Coventry, Jersey, Nottingham, London Scottish, Cornish Pirates and Bedford. These clubs were professionally run, had outstanding stadiums and full-time players and coaching staff. Their infrastructure was well practised and sophisticated. They were also much better supported home and away than was little Ampthill. This in itself would put pressure on the Club's infrastructure.

Ampthill Rugby Club would continue to be run by volunteers – but there would need to be more of them and they would need to work smarter and respond quickly to the lessons learned with each home game. Mistakes would be made and it was vital that the Club reacted immediately and rectified them. Internal communications, generally problematic at most rugby clubs would need to improve and regular feed-back meetings for a newly arranged Championship Group were scheduled.

Match-day Volunteers & Employed Staff

Over-page, Alan Dymock of Rugby World meets Ampthill's, Paul New, in his match day kit! Paul works tirelessly to ensure everything pitch-side is ready for kick-off and also signage for spectators. Paul has played in all the senior sides from 1st XV to Vets and also assists with the coaching of the Ladies XV. Paul is an ex-fireman, like Tony Willison, Paul Dobson, Richard Beasley, and Pat Sherry. Paul also coached the national fire-brigade XV. On matchdays Paul and Dominic New (Site Agent) assist Head Groundsman, Martin Wythe with all arrangements pitch-side.

Cleanliness of Site

On a Friday, before home games, ex-player Paul Titchener ensures the cleanliness of the four pitches, the car park, and surrounding areas. From time to time, this will include Woburn Road and its laybys next to the Club entrance.

Event Managers

Ian Scarr (Management Committee and Head Coach of the Ladies XV) and Kev Miller (Commercial & Marketing Manager) alternate as Event Managers for home Championship games. They lead the pre-match briefing, co-ordinate the volunteer teams and ensure efficient deployment of personnel to their various functions. During games they act as additional stewards, as and where required. For the Championship season the Event Managers ensure that tickets are booked, and match-day programmes printed. They also ensure volunteers have identity lanyards to access refreshments and match-day entry.

Paul New (photographer- Sam Riley, courtesy of Rugby World)

Match-Day Hospitality

The team includes Alex Radley, Club Chairman, and other members of the Management Committee who look after official hospitality. Away officials are wined and dined before home games and in the bar afterwards by Club officials.

Front of House

Tony Willison and Mike Plant look after front of house duties for home match-days. This involves contacting opposition clubs to learn of travel arrangements e.g. arrival times of vehicles with kit and paraphernalia, team, and supporters coaches. Also, any parking requirements for named travelling officials. David Thomas, Fixture Secretary, confirms details of match-day fixtures. These details are passed to Team Managers and Vic Kaye, by front of house.

On the morning of match days, Ian Bremner will direct which changing rooms are to be used. The 1st XV generally use Changing rooms 4 & 6, the opposition are allocated rooms 1-3. Team names & logos are placed on changing room doors. The foyer notice board is also chalked-up in the traditional manner. On Championship home games, Ampthill team managers are contacted to ensure that no away team cars are left on site, by front of house.

Mary Stanbridge, referee liaison, supplies the names of officials and this list is posted on Changing Room 5 by Mike Plant and officials' names are checked as they arrive. There are four officials plus a referee's assessor and also a coach. During the week after a game, the referee and his assessor communicate and come to an "agreement" over the performance of the referee. This data is processed and builds-up over time and is available world-wide to those entitled to access.

Pre-match "goody-bags" for the RFU match officials are prepared by Club Steward, Bex Lane, these are named and put into the referees' room which also contains each official's name and RFU logo. Matchday programmes are placed in home and away changing rooms and for all RFU officials.

Players, officials, and spectators are greeted and given information about bars, toilets and how to access tickets and pitches (the famous walk through the woods).

Changing rooms are locked when teams exit and are opened at half-time, if required, and after games.

Post-match drinks are taken to referees (coffee) and to fourth officials Cliff Page and Ian Titman (beer).

Fourth Officials

Cliff Page and Ian Titman act as fourth officials submitting match-day data to the RFU GMS software system. This includes ensuring all players are registered and eligible to play. They also collect data during the game: including timings of scores, substitutions, yellow and red cards and liaising with their equivalent opposition staff and with refereeing officials. After the game they are ensconced for about an hour feeding this data into a laptop computer into the RFU GMS system and transmitting to RFU Headquarters. Each match is filmed and this too is sent to Twickenham. Interestingly, these films are made available to all clubs and Paul Turner and his coaching team will give feedback to the first team squad after each game and also review the footage of the opponents for the next game.

Car Parking

Vic Kaye is the car park attendant working to an agreed parking plan for match-day staff, opposition officials, players and RFU officials. Spectator parking is not permitted on site due to limited space. Those travelling to the match by car are asked to park at the nearby Alameda Sports Hall or Queensmen F.C. where stewards are on duty. At approximately 7.30am on matchdays Vic cones off the laybys next to the Club entrance. If more than two coaches are due, these will be sent to "overspill" parking at The Firs Lower School in Station Road, where stewards are on duty.

Car parking stewards are Richard Benson, Stuart Palmer, Jules Gale, Charlotte Saunders, Sarah Marchant, Bill Dunham, Christina Dunham, Mark McKinley, Rachel Worthington. These volunteers are deployed according to the needs of particular games.

Health & Safety

Pat Sherry, Club President and Ground Safety Officer, is on duty from at least two hours before kick-off. He liaises closely with first-aiders, other medical personnel, and stewards. He is also involved with the safety of spectators and those using the Media Tower. The latter is regularly checked for safety by external professionals. If the Queensmen Car Park is in use on match-day, Pat will open the adjacent ground.

Spectator First Aid

A minimum of two First Aiders oversee the wellbeing of the crowd at each match. Richard Roberts, Emma Muncaster, Grace McGreevy, and Angharad Spavins – all volunteer qualified first-aiders – share match-day first aid duties. Andrew Allison, a paramedic, is on standby each week in case the crowd size exceeds 2000 when a Crowd Director, or Event Practitioner, is a mandatory requirement.

Security

Because of the increased size of Championship crowds and because of the need for a Ticket Office it was necessary to employ qualified, professional security staff. They are deployed near the ticket office and clubhouse before the game and at the clubhouse after the game. Spectators may only use the marquee after the game. The Clubhouse is restricted to players, RFU and Club Officials for one hour after games, with spectators being directed to the marquee by the security staff.

The Club Steward

Bex Lane, Club Steward, is first to arrive on match-day mornings. In addition to the clubhouse bar, she runs bars in the marquee in front of the club and a bar up on pitch 3 – the Championship pitch. Her extensive staff run these bars before, during and after games. Bex also prepares pre-match refreshments for the referee and match officials.

Kitchen

Tracey Holywell is in charge of the kitchen and its staff. Refreshments are available before and after the game for spectators and lunches provided for hospitality purposes. The players are served hot food after games. Tracey and her staff have a well-deserved reputation for high standards of catering and quality of service.

Ticket Office

Lyn Palmer, Ann Plant, Tracey Gray, and Anna Hornibrook are volunteer ticket office staff for ticket and programme sales. Lyn Palmer counts the takings and ensures these are banked. Tickets can be pre-booked on-line, via the Club's web-site.

Club Website

Kev Miller is responsible for the Club web-site and social media. The biggest change for the Championship was the provision for pre-booking match-day tickets. This was to prove to be popular and successful.

Medical and Therapy Provision

Author's note: I am grateful for the medical and therapy teams input to this section.

The move into Championship rugby meant the Club was required to comply with RFU Minimum Standards Criteria for the safety and welfare of players and spectators. This was to prove no mean feat and the leap from National 1 to the Championship, in respect of the level of medical and therapy provision, was enormous. Meetings with the senior management team at the RFU post qualification/pre-season demonstrated a lack of confidence on their part that the Club would get to where it needed to be.

For many years, the Club had relied on the services of Mick Dwyer, an Irishman living in England, to provide injury management, strength, conditioning, and rehabilitation for the senior squad. In 2006 Mick had been a final year Sports Therapy Student at the then University of Luton when he was invited to interview for the position of Club 'physio' through a local connection and friend of the Club, Tim Stanbridge. Mick met with Mark Lavery, the then Chairman Harry Cornforth, and first team manager Iain Bremner. This meeting was to be the catalyst of a thirteen-year journey to the Championship and all the hard work that was to follow.

Mick's role evolved to that of Lead Therapist where his responsibilities involved stock ordering and cleaning as well as his clinical role with the players. Fast forward to 2019 and suddenly the Club was also required to have a lead doctor, match day doctors, physiotherapists, and a Clinical Governance Lead for what was now being referred to as its 'elite' playing squad.

The first position to be recruited was the Clinical Governance Lead. Karen Radley, the Chairman's wife, was a former registered nurse and sister in intensive care. She had just retired as Head of Clinical Risk and Governance in the NHS. The Club appointed Karen to the role of Clinical Governance Lead with a degree of optimism that her NHS skills would be transferrable to the rugby setting. Due to her close ties with the Club, Karen agreed to work pro bono.

The Club were extremely lucky to have a number of medical and therapy professionals who were willing to be involved. Dr Richard Collins had worked in the NHS for 20 years, including 11 years as a local Bedford GP and 8 years in musculoskeletal medicine. Additionally, Richard was a member of the Faculty of Sport and Exercise Medicine and had worked with the English Institute of Sport providing medical care to British Olympic and Paralympic athletes. He was also a match day doctor for Northampton Saints Rugby Club. Richard was appointed as Lead Doctor which meant he was ultimately responsible for the clinical care of all players on both matchdays and non-matchdays.

To support Richard, the Club was extremely fortunate to secure the help of 3 further medical practitioners to provide clinical care to players on match days.

The first was Dr. Will Allingham, a former mini and youth player at Ampthill who was working as a Registrar in Emergency Medicine at University Hospital Coventry and who had experience of Sports Medicine through his work with Coventry Blaze Ice Hockey Team. Will was to prove a great asset to the medical set up, covering most Championship games, both home and away.

GP trainees, Dr. Aoife Kelly and Dr. Tom Axon further strengthened the medical team. Both with an interest in Sports Medicine and working with the University of Cambridge Rugby Union Football team, they were keen to gain additional game day trauma care and player welfare experience. The responsibilities of the newly formed medical team were extensive, with duties involving player welfare, concussion surveillance, anti-doping, and therapeutic use exemptions alongside the 'usual' care of game related injuries and their diagnosis and treatment. The team also possessed qualifications and skills for musculoskeletal ultrasound and joint injections, advanced trauma life support and transfer of critically ill patients. The Club felt extremely fortunate to have found a medical team with such an excellent breadth to their skills and knowledge.

To supplement the medical team the Club bolstered its therapy team with the recruitment of Kelly Ryder, Simon Jones, and Nick Allen, three extremely skilled and competent physiotherapists with a wealth of experience in a variety of sports including Rugby Union.

James MacLagan, a graduate of the Strength and Conditioning programme at the University of Bedfordshire, completed the team as the Club's Strength and Conditioning Coach.

With all the medical personnel in post the Clinical Governance Lead began working through the RFU criteria to ensure the Club would be Championship ready for the start of the season. A season which would see the Club undergo its first ever audit for fulfilling the RFU minimum standards.

The facilities at the Club were to prove the biggest challenge to achieving compliance. The lack of a pitch-side medical room for players meant many down at Twickenham doubted that the Club would actually get where it needed to be in order to participate in the second tier of English rugby. Planning permission was sought for a temporary pitch-side medical facility and subsequently a portacabin was purchased. The building duly arrived on the back of a low-loader but, frustratingly, the overhanging trees at the A507 entrance and soft ground along the roadway to pitch 3 prevented the 25-ton lorry load from getting through. The portacabin was taken back to the Club carpark where it sat for a week while the Committee scratched their heads about how to get it into the correct position.

There were no main utilities to Olney Fields so the team had to think creatively about how to get water and electricity to the medical centre on game days along with managing the disposal of effluent. It was established that the hose used for watering the pitches was likely contaminated with fertiliser so therefore was deemed unsuitable. Instead a water pump, run from a Land Rover battery, was attached to a clean water tank each week to create a fresh water supply. Wastewater was filtered into an IBC and electricity was provided by generator. Security grills were fitted to the medical centre by Barwest Fabrication Ltd.

Two days before the first game we were as ready as we were going to be. The medical centre and the pitch were looking great. Policies and protocols were all written and approved by the Committee. All players had undergone the necessary pre-screening and baseline SCAT5 test, a standardised tool used to aid in the evaluation of players suspected of having sustained a concussion during a game or training session and we had taken delivery of all the required equipment, including lifesaving and trauma equipment, emergency drugs and medical gases.

A typical matchday for the medical team involved arrival at the club two hours before kick-off to commence kit checks and touch base with the therapy and strength and conditioning teams. Following this there would be an opportunity to see any players requiring assessment pre-game or a medical team opinion. As no equipment was left in the pitch-side medical centre for security reasons all the kit needed to be carried from the clubhouse 'over the hill' to the pitch-side medical centre where it was set up ready for the game. As the kit consisted of a 7-foot spinal board, a pitch-side trauma bag and gas cylinders it always provided a good warm up!

At pitch-side the medical team have access to oxygen and entonox, spinal immobilisation and splinting, a defibrillator and associated drugs, and the medical centre contains all the equipment for blood and head injuries. The medical centre also provides a space for the pitch-side RFU Head Injury Assessment (HIA) protocols new to Ampthill in the 2019/20 Championship season.

After the final whistle, the therapy team continue to play a key role in assessing and treating any injuries picked up during the game. More serious injuries may require referral for further investigation or consultant review. The team also arrange ice baths and post-match massages where required.

The role of the medical and therapy teams extends far beyond match day though. A large proportion of work goes on behind the scenes and spans across a 7-day week. With almost 30 games scheduled in the playing season, a typical week requires the medical and therapy teams to be accessible 24/7 to ensure players remain in optimum condition.

The day after a game involves a triage session with the squad to update on any injury information and check on player wellbeing, including hydration, nutrition, and sleep. There are three training sessions throughout the week where members of the therapy team are always on site to carry out injury assessments, soft tissue therapies and monitored rehabilitation. A further key role of the therapy team is to complete a fitness test with players returning from injury, to confirm their readiness to play.

A pitch-side paramedic crewed ambulance was mandatory for all Championship games. The ambulance and crew were primarily assigned to the players but could be utilised to provide emergency care for members of the crowd if needed. If the ambulance needed to leave the ground for any reason during a game, the game would not be allowed to continue until a replacement ambulance was on site. The biggest challenge for the crews was mastering the slope up to the medical centre, roadway matting being needed during the wetter winter months.

The first season for Ampthill in the Championship saw its players suffer a few head injuries, a broken jaw, a broken thumb, a ruptured bicep, a ruptured hamstring, and some torn ligaments, all perhaps to be expected at this level of elite sport. In all, albeit cut short because of coronavirus, the 2019/20 season was considered a great success with frequent praise from visiting sides regarding the pitch-side facilities, professionalism, and protocols in place by the new kids on the block!

Crowd Cover & First-Aid

Emma Muncaster oversees the well-being of the crowd. First-Aiders include Richard Roberts, Grace McGreevy, Angharad Spavins, and Andrew Allison. The crowd paramedic is Anna Bright.

Team Managers

Iain Bremner (1st XV), Nick Stephenson (1881s), Jonny Cresswell (Jets), Liam Duffin (Extras, Richard Mardle (5ths.), Dave Wheeler (Vets), Tom Gray, Steve Everitt, Alaine Clark (Academy).

The Club Shop

The Club Shop is run by Andy and Christine Hampshaw. The shop normally opens on 1st XV match days and Sunday mornings either in the Clubhouse or the Hague Bar, in the Marquee. The opening Hours: Match Days 1.5hrs before kick-off, Sundays 1000-1200. The shop supplies playing kit & accessories for All Mini, Youth and Senior Squads, including supporters sweater, hoodies, scarves, umbrellas etc.

Post-Training Meals

The players really appreciate the provision of hot meals after training. During the season these were cooked by Martin Wythe, Paul New and Bex Lane.

Mini & Youth

An enthusiastic group of youngsters act as ball-boys/girls, maintain the manual score-board and wave the players through a welcoming tunnel of flags.

Close-Season Preparation

A large Marquee was hired, sited in front of the clubhouse to cater for the anticipated increase in support. A secure bar and beer cooler were installed, and seating and tables. The additional bars were painted in Club colours.

 The Ticket Office and Club Shop would also operate from the marquee which was called The Hague Bar. The Ticket Office staff deserve particular praise for the way this tricky operation was managed, both on-line and on match-days.

A medical room was created near the changing rooms in addition to the major Medical Centre by pitch 3. A shop store was created in the Club foyer.

New ground entrances were constructed on pitch 3 for spectators and, separately for players, support staff and medics.

Around pitch 3, a spectator barrier was installed as specified for the Championship and the dug-outs were re-sited to the west side of the pitch. These dug-outs were weather-proofed and painted in Club colours.

An extra catering marquee was installed in addition to the existing facilities.

An irrigation system was installed from the Club through the woods to pitch 3. Provision was made to hire a generator for all home games to supply the Championship pitch with power and lighting for the first time.

Numerous spectator safety barriers were installed on the east and south sides of pitch 3.

A huge Media Tower was hired and installed. The roadway from the by-pass entrance to the pitch-side was cleared and made accessible for ambulances, tractors, kit-vehicles etc.

Extra toilet facilities were hired for pitch 3 and by the marquee in front of the clubhouse.

2019-20 Club Management Committee

Pat Sherry, Alex Radley, Ian Titman, Bill Warfield, Mark Lavery, James Wiggett, Angharad Spavins, Colin Burke, Ian Scarr and Alaine Clark

The Marquee installed for the Championship season – Dillingham Park

Dominic New (Site Agent) – supervises preparation of media tower, dug-outs, and medical centre footings

Ann Plant inspects Bex's new Pitch-side Bar

Phil Lane, Martin Wythe and Vic Kaye erecting the pitch-side fencing

Medical Centre arrives – Karen Radley's Pride & Joy

Media Tower under construction

Things taking shape – Pitch 3

The famous walk through the woods - Jarryd Sage (photographer- Sam Riley, courtesy of Rugby World)

Chapter 9 – The Championship & Covid-19

Season 2019-20 – (Captain – Louis Grimoldby)

On January 27th 2020, it was seventy years since the Club was reformed in The Wingfield Club in 1950. The 1st XV celebrated by beating Doncaster Knights by 30 points to 26.

Management Committee

President	P. Sherry
Chairman	A. Radley
Hon. Treasurer	B. Warfield
Hon. Secretary	I. Titman
Director of Rugby	M. Lavery
Chair of Youth Rugby	J. Wiggett
Club Safeguarding	A. Spavins
General Committee members:	C. Burke, I. Scarr, & A. Clarke
Elected / Appointed Officers	P. Allen, D. New, M. Wythe, D. Thomas, D. Phillips, M. Stanbridge, H. Christey, D. Sibilia, M. Plant, W. Kay, C. Hampshaw, B. McTavish, K. Miller

Playing

1st XV Manager	I. Bremner
1881 XV Manager	N. Stephenson
Jets XV	J. Cresswell
Extras XV Manager	L. Duffin
5th XV	R. Mardle
Vets Manager	D. Wheeler
Academy XV	T. Gray
Coach	P. Turner Head Coach, M. Botha, A. Brown (1881s)

Mouritz Botha – joins Coaching Team

Ampthill pulled off a coup by appointing former England and Saracens lock Mouritz Botha as assistant coach. Botha, who coached Germany during their bid to reach the World Cup last year, recently assisted Georgia in their pre-tournament preparations and was keen to gain hands-on league experience as he built an increasingly impressive coaching CV. Botha, capped ten times by England, said, "Germany was a great experience but I wanted something closer to home and Ampthill were interested." Botha, 37, spent five hugely successful seasons at Saracens and also enjoyed stints at Bedford, Newcastle, and Super Rugby giants, Sharks.

He said: "Guys like Alex Sanderson and Paul Gustard were big mentors for me at Saracens and a lot of what I do as a coach is based on stuff I took from there. Being at the Sharks and Newcastle after that meant I've seen how things are done by a lot of different people and I'll add my own flavour to it. I love the ambition here and it's a club in a unique stage of transformation having come through the leagues in the last few years. It's a brilliant story and I'll be here for the season assisting with defence, lineout and having an input elsewhere."

Ex-Harlequins hooker Dave Ward joined Ampthill as player-coach over the summer and his arrival would underpin the Club's bid to become established in Level 2.

Dave Ward – player coach

1st XV League Results

Nottingham	20-44	home	lost		away	cancelled
Yorkshire Carnegie	53-12	home	won	52-10	away	won
London Scottish	6-6	away	draw	13-5	home	won
Hartpury University	19-13	home	won	16-5	away	won
Cornish Pirates	11-40	away	lost	13-30	home	lost
Jersey Reds	38-47	home	lost		away	cancelled
Bedford Blues	23-10	away	won		home	cancelled
Coventry	19-17	home	won		away	cancelled
Ealing Trailfinders	26-77	away	lost		home	cancelled
Doncaster Knight	30-26	home	won		away	cancelled
Newcastle Falcons	29-47	away	lost		home	cancelled

The Championship – positions when the was league suspended after March 14th 2020, by the RFU

#	Team	P	W	D	L	PF	PA	+∆	TB	LB	Pts
1	Newcastle Falcons	15	15	0	0	486	151	335	11	0	71
2	Ealing Trailfinders	14	11	1	2	491	253	238	7	0	53
3	Cornish Pirates	15	11	0	4	377	234	143	6	2	52
4	Coventry	15	8	1	6	399	318	81	6	1	44
5	Ampthill	15	8	1	6	368	399	-31	6	0	40
6	Nottingham	14	6	0	8	308	254	54	4	4	32
7	Jersey Reds	14	6	0	8	320	350	-30	5	3	32
8	Bedford Blues	15	6	0	9	253	325	-72	3	4	31
9	Doncaster Knights	15	6	0	9	268	351	-83	3	1	28
10	London Scottish	14	4	1	9	299	314	-15	4	5	27
11	Hartpury University	14	4	0	10	225	317	-92	3	5	24
12	Yorkshire Carnegie	14	0	0	14	192	720	-528	2	0	2

Cup Competition – Pool 1 Results

Ampthill	17	Coventry	47	
Ealing Trailfinders	43	Ampthill	5	
Bedford Blues	12	Ampthill	25	
Coventry	64	Ampthill	26	
Ampthill	17	Bedford Blues	14	

It seemed clear, from the squads selected for the cup games, that the Club was concentrating on league survival. Only against local rivals, Bedford Blues was the strongest squad selected and the results then spoke for themselves. For travelling away supporters, the beatings at Ealing and Coventry were hard to take, particularly when the bench replacements made the games competitive in the final quarter. However, no one seriously doubted the wisdom of the strategy as valuable players were protected for the league campaign.

Author's note - The following match reports are reproduced with the kind permission of David Emery, Editor in Chief of The Rugby Paper.

Bedford 12pts. Ampthill 25pts. – Saturday, October 5th 2019 - Championship Cup

Ampthill took the spoils in the "Battle of Bedfordshire" with winger Kwaku Aseidu, a constant thorn in the Blues' side. Head coach, Paul Turner said. "It's a massive day – to win the first competitive game against Bedford Blues in the club's history."

In what was a scrappy, error strewn first ten minutes Ampthill opened the scoring after sustained pressure saw Aseidu dive in at the corner. Ampthill's Karim Lynch was sent to the sin bin on 18 minutes after a dangerous aerial challenge but despite a period of pressure, it was only towards the end of Lynch's 10 minutes off the field that Bedford capitalised, with Dan Temm going over in the corner to restore parity at the half hour mark.

Bedford could not penetrate further, conceding regular penalties in dangerous positions, and Louis Grimoldby restored Ampthill's lead with a penalty. It was a first half more notable for its mistakes and ill-discipline than its quality, as both teams squandered good openings with handling errors and poor set piece play.

Bedford made a more composed start to the second half with a quickly taken penalty opening up the Ampthill defence, but a knock-on in the corner left them empty-handed. A good break from scrum-half Kevin Barrett, followed by a precise cross-field kick from Grimoldby led to Jarryd Sage diving over to give Ampthill a 15-5 lead. With 15 minutes remaining, Ampthill extended their lead with assured handling and composed attacking play, ending with a second try for Aseidu.

Jarred by the 20-5 score-line in front of a bumper crowd at Goldington Road, (who saw the Blues don pink in aid of Macmillan Cancer on Ladies Day) Blue's persistence was rewarded with a scrappy try with five minutes remaining when Huw Worthington bundled over the try-line. Ed Coulson kicked the conversion to reduce the deficit to 20-12, however, it was Ampthill who had the last laugh.

Karim Lynch touched down in the corner to secure a famous victory for the visitors which earned them their first points in the Championship Cup, at the half-way stage of the pools.

Ampthill: Lynch, Aseidu, Bardoli, Sage, Baker, Grimoldby (Sharp 69), Barrett (Veenendaal 78), Christie, Ward (Blackmore 62), Lutui (Collins 62), Williams (Johnson 55), Kerry, Hudson, Bercis, Molitika (Langley 55).

Attendance – 3,287

Ampthill 17pts Bedford 14 pts. – Saturday, December 14th 2019 - Championship Cup

Ampthill head coach Paul Turner hailed his benchmen as a dramatic late Billy Johnson try clinched victory over near rivals Bedford. Turner was not so happy with his side's indiscipline after conceding 17 penalties, but he said, "No-one would have believed ten years ago that Ampthill would be hosting Bedford in a competitive game at Dillingham Park. Our line-out was poor and our discipline worse, but this result defines our attitude. Our defence in the second half gave us a chance and our bench won the game in the last five minutes."

Blues dominated the early exchanges up front and No.9 James Lennon crossed for the first try after five minutes, Will Hooley converting. Ampthill responded, exerting their own pressure within the visitors 22 and scrum-half Barrett broke blind from a scrum deep inside Bedford's half and sent wing Spencer Sutherland, making his season debut after recovering from injury, over in the corner. Ampthill lock Kerry and Bedford No.8 Daniel Temm saw yellow cards for technical offences and Sutherland followed them minutes later when he was pinged for not releasing.

In between the sin-binnings, Blues winger Ryan Hutler was tackled just short of the line and with 13 now playing 14, Bedford forced a series of phases inside Amps. red zone which led to the referee awarding a penalty try on 36 minutes, after he lost patience with the hosts once too often.

Ampthill managed to get three points back before the half-time whistle, with a Grimoldby penalty, following a ruck offence pulling them back to within four points at 14-10.

For the second week in a row Ampthill's line-out was not functioning and ill-discipline was costing them territory. Bedford had several opportunities to take advantage of line-outs inside the home 22, but an improved mauling defence from Ampthill and wrong option-taking by Bedford saw those chances go begging. Another breakdown infringement gave Hooley the chance to extend the lead but his kick turned almost 90 degrees in the wind after it left the tee.

Ampthill's replacements sparked a revival with scrum-half Fukofuka breaking down the blindside leading to a series of phases and lock Billy Johnson fought his way across the line in the 78th minute for the win. Bedford director of rugby Mike Rayer said, "We got what we deserved. We needed to get a couple of scores in front but we failed to take our opportunities."

Ampthill: Lynch, Sutherland (Foster 55), Sage, Hanks (Bardoli), Baker, Grimoldby, Barret (Fukofuka 64), Schroder (Tonga'uhia 60), Ward (Blackmore 50), Lutui (Pupuma 50), Burgess (Johnson 53), Kerry, Arthur, Bercis, Molitika (Hudson 53) Attendance – 2,151

Championship – The First Season

Mark Lavery and Paul Turner had recruited heavily in the close season for this first campaign in the Championship. New players included Darryl Veenendaal, Dave Ward, Facundo Dominguez, Jac Arthur, Jarryd Sage, Louis Grimoldby, Robert Langley, Serafin Bordoli, Shay Kerry, Leon Fukofuka, Luvuyo Pupuma and Tomi Lewis. Additionally, there were a raft of dual-registered players principally from Saracens, Northampton, and Wasps. These included, Ben Christie, Tommy Matthews, Sam Costelow, Jon Kpoku, Reuben Bird-Tulloch, Josh Gillespie, Conner Anderson, Olly Morris, and Michael Van Vuuren. A decision was made not to play any pre-season "friendlies" – therefore, it was reasonable to assume that the new squad would take a while to find its feet.

However, the main difference in recruitment from previous seasons was the quality of the new players. After a shaky start against Nottingham, it was noticeable how much quicker the players gelled than in previous campaigns.

Ampthill 20pts. Nottingham 44pts. – Saturday, 12 October 2019

Ampthill were given a tough introduction to the Championship by a physical and clinical Nottingham side. Trailing just 17-13, with a minute to half-time, Ampthill conceded a try and then two more in the second half, after being reduced to 14, as Nottingham dominated territory and possession. Ampthill's director of rugby Mark Lavery said, "For 39 minutes of the first half we were okay, the gifted try just before half-time was a blow but it was the second half, where we played in all the wrong areas and showed very poor discipline, that was most disappointing. We played for more than 45 minutes with 14 men against an efficient, well-drilled championship side and we got what we deserved."

The opening exchanges were even despite Ampthill losing full-back Lynch to a yellow card after just eight minutes for foul play. Both sides slotted penalty goals before Nottingham grabbed the first try. A penalty against Ampthill for a breakdown offence was kicked inside the 22 and the lineout catch was driven over with hooker Luke Cole credited with the score.

Fly-half Thomas Mathews added the conversion before lock Llewelyn Jones crashed over from close range for Nottingham's second try, a repeat of the first try. Mathews added the conversion.

Ampthill's replacement centre Sam Hanks hit back immediately after intercepting a loose pass just inside the Nottingham half and scampering 45m to score wide on the left. Grimoldby converted from the touchline and Ampthill were back in the game at 17-13. Grimoldby added a penalty to narrow the gap, but lock Shay Kerry was then sin-binned for a technical foul and Nottingham blindside James Connolly powered over to punish them.

Ampthill lost their way in the second half, as Mathews punished ill-discipline, before wing Ben Foley collected a grubber to score Nottingham's fourth try wide on the left with Ampthill's. flanker in the bin for hands in the ruck. Lock Jon Kpoku crashed over for a close range try on 63 minutes as Amps. showed their fighting qualities, but Kerry was shown a second yellow, followed by a red on 71 minutes, for more team infringements.

Ampthill conceded a fifth try on 79 minutes as impressive Nottingham centre Harry Strong found a way though to cap a professional display from the Green and Whites.

Ampthill: Lynch, Asiedu, Bardoli, Sage, Baker, Grimoldby, Veenendaal, Tonga'uiha (Collins 63), Ward (Blackmore 52), Lutui (Christie 52), Williams (Kpoku 46), Kerry, Johnson (Dominguez 64), Bercis, Molitika (Williams 61) Attendance – 762

Ampthill 53pts. Yorkshire Carnegie 22pts. – Saturday, 19th October 2019

Ampthill skipper Dave Ward hailed a terrific all-round display as the newcomers hit shell-shocked Carnegie for eight.

The visitors showed signs of promise during an opening half-hour in which Tom Varndell shone and Dan Lancaster – son of Stuart – grabbed a try. However, over eighty minutes Yorkshire had no answer - as Ampthill went through the gears to finish with a half-century of points. Ward said, "We wanted five points and to deny Yorkshire four tries, so job done. We're not getting ahead of ourselves but we've got to enjoy these moments."

A hectic opening saw Joe Ford and Louis Grimaldby exchange penalties before Ampthill went close to the first try when Soane Tonga'uiha was held up. Ampthill joy was not long delayed as Jon Kpoku smashed over from Kevin Barrett's pop pass after good work from Karim Lynch, Tonga'uiha and Ward.

Yorkshire replied with a quick-fire try double. Lancaster was first to score after Varndell's dash before Varndell telegraphed Barrett's mid-field pass to race home from 45m. Carnegie butchered the restart, enabling the alert Sam Baker to scorch clear for a try that Grimoldby converted to restore Ampthill's lead. Baker was soon involved again when, following an excellent turn-over from Joe Bercis, the wing forced his way through Lancaster and Tim Bitrim at the corner.

Ampthill began to dominate and bagged their bonus-point try when Tonga'uiha , Kpoku, Aleki Lutui and Shay Kerry softened up the defence with punishing runs before Lutui surged on to Barrett's offload to crash over.

Ampthill led 27-15 at the break, but it was Carnegie, with replacement flanker Bustin, making an immediate impact, who struck first after the restart when Varndell's chip ahead enabled James Elliott to run under the sticks. Yorkshire promptly committed hara-kiri, however, as Ben Sowery overthrew a lineout and Ward pounced for Ampthill's fifth try. Sowery's second overthrow ruined a good Carnegie position and despite making changes they were unable to create any pressure.

Ampthill's tackling became crisper as the finishing line hoved into view, with Kerry, Will Allman and human dynamo Bercis forcing turnovers in the lead up to a game-clinching try on 70 minutes after Josh Gillespie's forceful run. Rapid recycling saw Allman go close before the impressive Kpoku roared onto Barrett's pass for his second five-pointer. Yorkshire rallied through Ryan Shaw's jinking run, but Ampthill rounded things off when Matt Collins forced his way over before Baker raced clear to send in Gillespie for try eight.

Yorkshire boss Martyn Wood said, "Our back division's looking sharp and when we got the ball, we were good. But individual errors cost us, along with a high penalty count, and we didn't hold the ball long enough to build pressure."

Ampthill: **Lynch, Gillespie, Sage, Hanks (Bird-Tuloch 52), Baker, Grimoldby (Walters 52), Barrett (Veenendaal 74), Tonga'uiha (Christie 66), Ward (Blackmore 56), Lutui (Collins 66), Kpoku, Kerry, Johnson (Allman 60), Bercis, Dominguez (Molitika 56)**

Attendance 640

London Scottish 6pts. Ampthill 6pts. – Saturday, 26th October 2019

This was a mature, morale boosting, performance and Ampthill were the happier of the two sides with the result.

Defending stoutly in the wind and rain, Ampthill's defence continually thwarted the attacking ambitions of an error prone Scottish side. The conditions meant this was never going to be a spectacle, but Ampthill would reflect that they were ahead until the 77th minute when Dan Barnes' successful pressure kick squared the game for the Exiles.

This, after replacement Sam Costelow's penalty, was controversially adjudged to have flown wide of the uprights which would have given Ampthill a six-point lead. Ampthill head coach, Paul Turner said, "We had a game plan and I thought we grew up today. We didn't make as many errors as in the first two league games. It's a shame that Sam's kick at goal wasn't given as, for me, it went over. However, London Scottish are a very good side and I am very proud of the way we performed as a team. We're growing slowly."

Scottish started the stronger of the sides and although Josh Burton's grubber fired them into a good position, a messy maul and misfiring lineout saw them fail to capitalise. Good link play between the Scottish back-row kept the Amps. defence honest, but poor ball retention led to turnover and Ampthill cleared their lines.

Having absorbed the early pressure Ampthill half-backs, Kevin Barrett and Louis Grimoldby were quick to plant the ball behind the defence when given the opportunity. Grimoldby, twice punished the Exiles for holding-on, to open a 6-0 lead.

Scottish rebounded towards the end of the half and, with Mark Bright, Matt Eliet and Lewis Wynne carrying well. Harry Sheppard reduced the deficit after slotting over a penalty in front of the posts.

Scottish rung the changes in the second-half and, given an injection of pace by the lively Bobby Beatie, should have added to their tally during a ten-minute spell of pressure close to the line, but unyielding Ampthill defence kept them out from both five-metre scrum and a line-out drive close to the line with Shay Kerry to the fore.

With fresh impetus from some precision kicking by half-back replacements, Darryl Veenendaal and Costelow, Ampthill pinned Scottish back and could have sealed a famous victory but Costelow's strike was agonisingly wide. It was even more agonising when the Exiles late charge earned another kickable penalty and Barnes ensured that it was honours even.

Exiles captain Lewis Wynne commented, "Our lineout didn't function and our set piece and discipline wasn't all it should have been. We gave away too many penalties and Ampthill had a good kicking game which put us under a bit of pressure."

Ampthill: **Lynch, Gillespie, Sage (Anderson 71), Bird-Tullock, Baker, Grimoldby (Costelow 57), Barrett (Veenendaal 57), Tonga'uiha (Christie 71), Ward, Lutui (Collins 71), Kpoku (Johnson 54), Kerry, Allman, Bercis (Blackmore 69), Hudson.**

Attendance – 788

Ampthill's Matt Collins getting to grips with Falcon's Sinoti Sinoti (Image: Chris Lishman, Newcastle Falcons)

Ampthill 19pts. Hartpury University 13pts. – Saturday, 2nd November 2019

Ampthill held out for their second win of the league campaign in a tight game where defences dominated. Head coach Paul Turner observed, "Despite a nerve-wracking last few minutes, this was a good win against old rivals. Our half-backs showed good control in the first half but might have made our lives easier if they'd have used their kicking game more in the second. If before the season you had offered me two wins and a draw from our first four league fixtures, I'd have bitten your hand off. It's been a good start but we still have work to do."

The opening exchanges were even with both sides incurring the wrath of the referee resulting in an exchange of penalty goals. Hartpury fly-half Joshua Bragman grabbing the first, before opposite number Samuel Costelow levelled after both sides were penalised for breakdown offences. Ampthill took the lead on twenty minutes with another Costelow penalty.

The forward battle was intense, but Ampthill gradually established control at the set piece with former Tongan Test props Soane Tonga'uiha and Aleki Lutui prominent.

However, Hartpury took the lead on 25 minutes when Ampthill were penalised in midfield and Hartpury kicked deep to set up an attacking lineout which set up Akapusi Qera for a driving maul try. Bragman converted from wide out. The hosts responded with a period of pressure and Costelow knocked over his third penalty for 10-9.

Tough defence from Hartpury repelled a series of Ampthill drives but Veenendaal eventually made the breakthrough with a grubber for centre Reuben Bird-Tullock to touch down. Costelow converted to put Ampthill ahead 16-10 at half-time.

Defences were on top in the second-half, with only another penalty exchange adding to the scoreboard. With Ampthill down to 14 men after a yellow card to lock Shay Kerry, Hartpury threw everything at them but they could not find a way through the solid home wall.

Ampthill: **Lynch, Gillespie, Anderson, Bird-Tulloch, Baker, Costelow (Grimoldby 78), Veenendaal, Tonga'uiha (Christie 76), Ward, Lutui (Collins 76), Kpoku (Johnson), Kerry, Allman, Bercis (Blackmore 53), Hudson (Molitika 70).**

Attendance – 701

Cornish Pirates 40pts. Ampthill 11pts – Sunday, 10th November 2019

Ampthill travelled to Mennaye Field, Penzance to face Cornish Pirates in the first ever game between the two clubs, to find the well-drilled and efficient host in an uncompromising mood as their warm welcome turned into a dominant performance.

Ampthill started well, taking the game to the hosts from the off, winning a penalty on 4 minutes which was well-struck by fly-half Samuel Costelow, to take the lead. The home side responded immediately forcing the visitors to concede a penalty, but their fly-half"s kick drifted wide. The remainder of the first quarter was well contested and evenly matched but the Pirates gradually gained the upper hand securing possession and territory. On 23 minutes, a lost Ampthill line-out deep in their own half led to the host's full-back Cant crossing the whitewash, fly-half Rojas Alvaraz adding the conversion giving the Pirates a 7-3 lead they were never to lose.

In the 27th minute a visitor's clearing kick from Costelow was charged down, several phases later Pirates' winger Wedlake squeezed over out wide, Alvarez missing the touchline conversion. On 34 minutes, home centre Patterson touched down from a maul, having benefitted from some generous defending, Alvarez adding the extras to put the hosts firmly in control. Ampthill struck back with a 40th minute penalty goal, to leave the score 19-6 at the whistle.

From an Ampthill perspective, the second-half started badly with the Pirates attacking down the left-wing, Wedlake benefitting from a couple of missed tackles resulting in his second try and the hosts had a bonus point try converted by Rojas Alvarez.

Following a number of substitutions in the 60th minute, saw the return of Dave Ward to his former club. After a line-out catch and drive Dave Ward forced his way over the line, the conversion was missed leaving the score at 26-11.

Almost immediately a turnover saw Ampthill pressing hard deep in the hosts half, but a knock-on gave the ball back to the Pirates and the visitors rarely threatened again.

Chasing the game, Ampthill conceded two more tries, the first on 72 minutes by Pirates', right wing O'Meara and the second, at the death by flanker Matavesi, both converted by Alvarez.

Head coach Paul Turner commented, "At certain points we showed that we can compete at this level, but we played too much rugby in the wrong areas and failed to take a couple of opportunities that could have made the game more interesting. We will have to learn our lessons quickly and it doesn't get any easier next week when we welcome Jersey Reds to Dillingham Park."

Ampthill: **Lynch (Grimoldby 59), Aseidu, Anderson, Hanks (Walters 23), Baker, Costelow, Veenendaal (Barrett 31), Christie (Tonga'uiha 52), Blackmore (Ward 51), Collins (Lutui 51), Kerry, Johnson, Bercis, Dominguez (Molitika 59), Hudson**

Replacements: **Ward, Tonga'uiha, Lutui, Williams, Molitika, Barrett, Grimoldby, Waters.**

Ampthill 38pts. Jersey Reds 47pts. – Saturday, 16th November 2019

Defence appeared optional for both sides as the crowd were treated to a 12 try festival. Ampthill began brilliantly, with fly-half Samuel Costelow charging down a clearance kick from his opposite number Greg Dyer, then hacking on for open side Joe Bercis to dive on the ball under the posts for a first minutes try converted by Costelow.

The next 20 minutes were dominated by the visitors ruthlessly capitalising on Ampthill errors to score three tries, through open side Joshua Bainbridge, hooker Antonio Harris and a penalty try. All came from penalties kicked into the home 22, followed by line-out catch and drives. The last one also resulted in a yellow card for Dave Ward.

As often happens going a man down was the catalyst for the home team to raise their game. First Costelow missed a 48m penalty in the 28th minute before converting another on 31 minutes. Then, after a period of concerted pressure, lock forward Jon Kpoku finished from 5 metres out on 37 minutes, Costelow adding the extras. The half-time whistle came with Ampthill leading 19-17.

The second half began with a bang as another penalty, line-out catch and drive brought the bonus point try for the visitor's Harris. Dyer's conversion bisecting the posts.

Almost immediately, with Ampthill on the attack, the home spectators let out a roar as a high tackle on Costelow was ignored by the officials, but the resulting interception, a 60m scamper by Jerseys right-wing Morgan and conversion by Dyer adding to the crowds' discontent.

Trailing by 17 points, Ampthill once again responded well, Bercis scoring his second try before the hosts try of the season was created by the home backs with quick passing, a chip by Obatoyinbo recovered by wing Sam Baker and great support from Louis Grimoldby which saw him under the posts. At 31-33 the game was again in the balance, but another penalty try in the 65th minute gave breathing space to the visitors.

In the 67th minute a turnover in the Jersey 22 saw them break out of defence for a length-of-the-field try for Homer.

Ampthill scored another fine try as Costelow ghosted through. Ampthill head coach said, "I was proud of how hard we fought; however, this was a harsh lesson. Give penalties away against this standard of opposition and we will be punished."

Ampthill: Steward (Lynch 79), Gillespie, Obatoyinbo, Grimoldby, Baker, Costelow, Barrett (Fukofuka 57), Tonga'uiha (Christie 55), Ward (Lutui 55), Collins (Pupuma 46), Kpoku, Kerry (Williams 55), Blackmore (Molitika 38), Bercis (Ward 70), Hudson.

Attendance 790

Bedford Blues 10pts. Ampthill 23pts. – Thursday, 26th December 2019

Ampthill upped the ante in the second half to earn the bragging rights over local rivals Bedford. Trailing 10-3 at half-time, Paul Turner's side put in a dominant second 40-minute display, winning the half 20-3 to rack up a third win of the season over Mike Rayer's Blues.

Head coach Turner said, "I am proud of the passion and improved accuracy shown in the second half which proved decisive. We just did enough against a good Bedford side and I'm very pleased for the group who responded to the pressure we placed on them during our preparation."

It was now eight games since the Blues had notched up a win, they had been beaten 11 times this season in the league and cup. The decision to move the fixture to the day after Christmas to ensure a bumper crowd was astute in terms of people through the gate, but it was a sell-out crowd that also witnessed a Blues team wilt away in the second period.

Ampthill did a job. Steered by the impressive Grimoldby, they were good for their win, but they did not have to play well. They defended resolutely, finishing off a couple of well worked tries but Bedford outfoxed themselves on more than one occasion. Such is the story at Goldington Road this year.

Bedford led at half-time. New signing Alafoti Fao'siliva bundled his way through a crowd from close range to give the home fans something to hope for. Indeed, the ascendancy at set piece, both scrum and lineout, was pleasing for those in Blue, sipping at their interval pints.

But the game quickly turned in the second half with Ampthill playing the game in the right areas and Blue's indiscipline costing them any chance of overcoming a growing deficit. Syd Blackmore stole in on the back of an impressive rolling maul for the Ampthill's first, and then Sam Baker was found out on the left wing by a lofty pass from Grimoldby exploiting an overlap.

The Blues fluttered late on with a surge against 14 men after the Mob's lock forward Shay Kerry was shown a yellow for bringing down a maul. But even then, the ball found the floor too often and the Blues trudged from the field having fumbled a losing bonus point.

"We've just got to cut out the silly penalties and stop getting involved in things that we shouldn't be," said a beleaguered Will Hooley. "We put ourselves under a lot of pressure, but this is fixable stuff. We've got to stick together, as we are the only ones that can get this right."

Ampthill: Lynch, Sutherland, Sage (Foster 31), Bardoli, Baker (Hanks 64), Grimoldby, Fukofuka (Veenendaal 61), Tonga'uiha (Pupuma 55), Blackmore (Ward 55), Lutui (Collins 64), Johnson (Burgess 61), Kerry, Arthur (Dominguez 64), Bercis, Hudson.

Attendance – 5,000

Kevin Barrett helped the A's to a win in the rain at Hartpury under the Friday Night Lights!
(Image: Lauren Couchman, LNCImages)

Ampthill 19pts. Coventry 17pts. – Saturday, 11th January 2020

A last kick of the game penalty by Louis Grimoldby secured victory for Ampthill. Coventry had dominated early on and took a fifth minute lead when wing Ratu Bulumakau finished by the corner flag.

Ampthill came back into the game through their forwards, winning a penalty at a breakdown. Grimoldby popped the ball between the posts.

Defences then held firm until wing Max Trimble intercepted a Grimoldby pass on the 10m line to scamper untouched under the posts, Tony Fenner adding the extras. Ampthill hooker Syd Blackmore capitalised on a period of pressure on 39 minutes, with Grimoldby bringing the score to 10-12 at half-time.

Ampthill came out firing in the second-half, gradually turning the screw and winning two back to back penalties. Grimoldby hit both through the uprights for Ampthill to take the lead. The second penalty was the result of fine skills from full-back Karim Lynch who fielded a difficult kick-off before returning the ball behind the visitors' defence where the kick chase cornered the isolated defender and won the penalty.

Coventry raised their game forcing Ampthill to defend. Referee Dean Richards repeatedly penalised the home side until flanker Facundo Dominguez was yellow carded on 66 minutes. Just two minutes later Serafin Bartoli deliberately handled the ball in front of the posts and joined his Argentinian colleague in the bin. With the hosts deep in their 22 the home side's cover eventually ran out leaving prop James Gibbons to touch down. Replacement fly-half Rory Jenkins kick crucially slid past the posts leaving the visitors in the lead 16-17.

The next few minutes were key as Ampthill, playing with 13 playing 15, held out until restored to a full complement with two minutes remaining. A knock-on saw an Amps. scrum outside the visitors' 22. The roar from the Ampthill support resounded as the referee awarded a penalty for the hosts.

Cool as a cucumber, Grimoldby stepped up to secure the win with the last kick of the game.

Coventry coach Roland Winter said, "We didn't take advantage of the wind in the first half." Ampthill director of rugby Mark Lavery said, "The interception try was a blow but we fought back and deserved to win."

Ampthill: **Lynch, Sutherland (Gillespie 73), Sage (Hanks 76), Bardoli, Baker, Grimoldby, Barrett, Tonga'uiha (Pupuma 50), Blackmore (Ward 50), Lutui (Collins 62), Johnson (Kpoku 50), Kerry, Arthur (Dominguez 58), Bercis, Hudson.**

Attendance – 1,016

Ealing Trailfinders 77 pts. Ampthill 26 pts. – Saturday, 18th January 2020.

Ealing Trailfinders made it back-to-back wins with a big victory over Ampthill thanks largely to their dominant driving maul. The West Londoners scored 11 tries in total as the attack fired in impressive fashion, although a late rally from the visitors ensured they left with a gutsy try bonus point.

Ealing forwards coach Glen Townson said, "That intensity is what we strive to get. We were disappointed to concede four tries but to score 77 points is a great effort and we'll look to build towards London Scottish next weekend."

Backing up last week's win at Nottingham, Trailfinders got off to the perfect start when Jordan Els opened the scoring after just four minutes. The South African broke away from a powerful driving maul to dot down. The lead doubled with eight minutes on the clock in identical fashion, with another maul allowing Dave McKern to score. Tommy Bell then gathered Elijah Niko's audacious offload for try number three, as the Green and Whites started to pull away.

Ampthill got onto the scoreboard at the end of the first quarter as Henri Williams went over from close range, but that would be as good as it got for the visitors, who saw three tries conceded in the remainder of the first half. Alun Walker scored two tries in ten minutes from rolling mauls to extend the lead to 35-7, just after Jac Arthur was sent to the sin bin for Ampthill after killing the ball on the line. Pat Howard then powered over from two metres out to give his side a 42-7 advantage at the break.

The second half started in similar fashion to the first, with Reon Joseph scoring the try of the match to put the result beyond doubt. Steven Shingler's cross field kick was judged to perfection and Joseph gathered it before racing 40 metres to the delight of the home crowd. Howard was sent to the sin bin for the Trailfinders as a brilliant counter-attack from Ampthill saw them go the length of the field, and with men outside the ruck, Howard failed to roll away giving the referee no option.

Tommy Bell brought up the half century for Ealing as he was the beneficiary of Jody Reid's inside pass to score under the posts for his second of the match.

Ampthill crossed for their second try, shortly after as Sam Baker pounced on a counter-attack as the game headed into the final quarter. Craig Hampson had a clear run to the line with an overlap on the wing before Ampthill registered a deserved bonus point as Rob Langley and Sam Hanks both score from close range.

There was still time for Lewis Jones and Matt Cornish to add more gloss to the score-line, confirming a huge victory for the hosts.

Ampthill: **Lynch (Bordoli 61), Sutherland, Sage, Hanks, Baker, Grimoldby, Veenendaal (Fukofuka 31), Tonga'uiha (Christie 56), Ward (Lutui 65), Pupuma (Collins 71), Johnson (Langley 49), Williams, Arthur, Bercis (Dominguez 49), Hudson.**

Attendance – 680

Ampthill 30pts. Doncaster Knights 26pts. – Saturday, 25th January 2020.

Ampthill held firm in the face of a fierce second half fightback to take the spoils over former coach Clive Griffiths' charges, in their first ever match against Doncaster.

Cruising at 30-14 with just over five minutes to go, late tries from Jack Roberts and Kyle Evans ensured a nervy finale at Olney Field with Ampthill's ill-discipline almost costing them dear. Ampthill Director of Rugby, Mark Lavery said, "We played well for large parts but when leading 30-14 in the second half we failed to put the game away and allowed them back in – this wasn't good enough. Now we focus on our away trip to Newcastle, an experience no one associated with Ampthill could have imagined a few years ago!"

Flanker, Joe Bercis touched down after five minutes for the first try following huge pressure on the visitors' defence. Wing Sam Baker caught in stride a fine cross kick from fly-half Louis Grimoldby to race over for the second in the left corner. Grimoldby missed both conversions but landed two penalties to extend the lead to 16-0 after Doncaster twice cynically infringed with the hosts on the attack in front of the posts.

A bad leg break suffered by Doncaster No.8 Ollie Stedman stopped the game for a few minutes and when it resumed the Knights seemed galvanised. Ampthill appeared to have lost focus and Doncaster scored either side of the half-time. Ben Hunter touched down from a driving maul and Tyson Lewis finished off a backs' move immediately after the interval.

Ampthill hit back with two more converted tries; Jared Sage's midfield break was followed by Bercis second from close range on 61 minutes.

But leading 30-14 with 20 minutes remaining, Ampthill allowed the visitors off the hook after a yellow card to centre Sam Hanks for going in at the side, and Knight's replacement wing Jack Roberts touched down. Just three minutes later, while again under the cosh, home No.8 Sam Hudson was sent to join Hanks in the bin for sacking a maul. Despite the best efforts of the remaining 13 Ampthill players the Knights ran in another try on 78 minutes through centre Kyle Evans, but Ampthill held firm for the final knockings after Roberts came back on to help clinch their fifth victory of the season.

Doncaster coach Clive Griffiths said, "Ampthill thoroughly deserved their win. Our squad was warned what to expect but we did not follow the game plan in the first-half, choosing to play rather than concentrating on territory. We had chances to win but failed to take them. A sad day for Doncaster, but a great day for Ampthill.

Ampthill: Lynch, Sutherland (Foster 64), Sage (Hanks 59), Bardoli, Bakr, Grimoldby, Barrett (Fukofuka 62), Tonga'uiha (Pupuma 49), Ward (Blackmore 51), Collins (Lutui 49), Johnson, Kerry (Langley 48), Arthur (Allman 62), Bercis, Hudson.

Attendance – 980

Newcastle Falcons 47pts. Ampthill 29pts. – Sunday, 2nd February 2020

On what can only be described as a truly historic day, Ampthill travelled to Kingston Park, home of Premiership and Heineken Cup participants Newcastle Falcons. This was a huge honour and for a club of Ampthill's size it does not get any bigger or better than that!

The Newcastle welcome could only be described as incredible and very humbling for all our members, supporters, and committee members. If one had said twelve years ago that Ampthill would be playing Newcastle Falcons in a competitive fixture, most of the town would have laughed at you.

Ampthill eventually got themselves off the mark on 36 minutes when full-back Tomi Lewis scored after collecting an inside pass from left wing Will Foster, Louis Grimoldby converting

After a one-sided and dominant start, the hosts had a 33-7 lead at half time and lesser teams would have folded. Ampthill closed the half with 13 players after Leon Fukofuka was yellow carded for a high tackle and Dave Ward was also carded for an infringement at a 5m line-out.

Playing a Premiership side is hard enough with a full team never mind when outnumbered, Ampthill conceded 19 points when down to 13.

The visitor's management had their hands full trying to restore some confidence back into the team at the break, but Falcons scored two more tries to lead 45-7 after 48 minutes. With the home team enjoying a dominant lead, the Maroon and Gold had a huge challenge on their hands and what could be a season-defining half an hour was to start.

The bench entered the fray with Tongan international hooker Aleki Lutui taking a leading role as he carried hard and gave a rallying point for the forward pack. Replacement pops Ben Christie and Luvuyo Pupuma made good yards, while Rob Langley had his best game for the visitors.

Kevin Barrett had come on at scrum-half with Leon Fukofuka moving to inside centre. Sam Hudson came on at number eight but lasted twelve minutes before going off injured and was replaced by returning flanker Will Allman. Serafin Bardoli replaced Jarryd Sage at centre. Henri Williams replaced Jack Arthur.

Newcastle didn't score again, while lock Billy Johnson bagged a hat-trick, and with wing Spencer Sutherland scoring another try, the final score was 45-29. The Falcons had conceded on average 10 points a game going into the fixture, Ampthill scored five tries against the number one rated defence in the competition.

Head coach Paul Turner said, "It was a huge day for our club to come to Kingston Park and I think the occasion got the better of us early on, while Newcastle were exceptional and put us to the sword in the first half. It was important we got the bench on early in the second half and changed the game dynamic getting us back in the game. I thought Aleki led the charge well and the bench got us on the front foot earning us a well-deserved bonus point.

We have now completed the first half of our Championship fixtures and at the halfway point we are in a deserved sixth place and beginning to understand the competition. I think this playing and coaching group can give a lot more and we can look at the second half of the season with some confidence whilst understanding there is a lot to work on and improvements to come."

Director of Rugby, Mark Lavery commented, "Very proud of the second half fightback and in lots of ways it sums up this playing group when facing a Premiership side and against real adversity they showed great resolve to get the try bonus point. A year ago, Toulon came to Kingston Park and won and whilst we couldn't quite pull off a win, we are pleased to come away with a point."

Tomi Lewis making his debut against Falcons and scoring a 33 - minute try (Image Chris Lishman)

Ampthill: Lewis Tomi, Spencer Southerland, Sage Jarryd, Sam Hanks, Will Foster, Louis Grimoldby, Leon Fokofuka, Soane Tonga'uiha, Dave Ward, Matt Collins, Rob Langley, Billy Johnson, Jac Arthur, Will Allman, Mama Molitika – replacements: Aleki Lutui, Ben Christie, Luvuyo Pupuma, Henri Williams, Kevin Barrett, Serafin Bordoli, Sam Baker

In January, Welsh U20s and Sevens International, Tomi Lewis joined Ampthill on loan from Scarlets for the remainder of the season. He had come through the Scarlets development programme and represented Wales U20s at the World Cup in 2019 and Wales in the IRB Sevens scoring 16 tries! He made 2 appearances this season for the Scarlets in the Guinness PRO14.

Ampthill 13pts. London Scottish 5pts. – Saturday, 15th February 2020

A last-minute try, against the run of play, by replacement wing Josh Gillespie made the game safe for Ampthill, as Scottish looked to get within range to strike for the winner.

Trailing 6-5, Scottish were on a rare visit into the Ampthill half when the ball went loose and Louis Grimoldby hacked clear. He chased his own kick and hacked into the in-goal area for Gillespie to win the foot race and touch down. Grimoldby converted from a wide angle with the last kick of the game.

Ampthill head coach Paul Turner said, "It was a game for the purists, conditions were awful and credit must go to all the players in both squads. Our defence was key in the first half and we executed professionally enough in the second to take the points."

Playing against the howling gale in the first half, Ampthill's defence restricted the visitors to a single try. With kicking from hand against the wind very difficult, both sides tried to play their way out of their own half, managing several double-figure sets of phases, but finding it hard to achieve significant territorial gains.

Scottish took the lead on eleven minutes with a try by flanker Luke Frost. After multiple red zone phases, he drove over from close range, but William Magee's conversion hit the post. Despite several occasions with similar possession deep in Scottish territory Ampthill were unable to score a point in the first half.

Grimoldby notched a penalty at the start of the second half to get Ampthill on the board and it was Scottish's turn to show committed defence, denying Ampthill for the next twenty minutes despite almost continuous pressure in their own half. Ampthill prop Aleki Lutui received a yellow card just before the hour mark for a dangerous tackle and Ampthill were forced to replace winger Will Foster to keep the front row competitive.

Despite being a man down, Grimoldby added a second penalty on 66 minutes to take the lead for the first time 6-5. Thereafter, Grimoldby kept Scottish in their own half with judicious placement of kicks behind their line forcing them to carry against the wind. As the Exiles tried to find a way through the Ampthill defence the ball spilled loose resulting in Gillespie's last-minute score.

London Scottish coach Steve Scott said, "The toughest time to lose a game is in the last couple of minutes and we've now had that happen three games in a row. Conditions were horrendous even playing with the wind."

Ampthill: Lewis, Sutherland, Sage (Gillespie 66), Matthews, Foster (Collins 58), Grimoldby, Barrett (Fukofuka 71), Pupuma (Christie 17), Ward (Van Vuuren 58), Lutui (Morris 66), Kpoku, Kerry (Arthur 40), Johnson, Bercis (Blackmore 66), Hudson.

Attendance – 467

The next fixture against Yorkshire Carnegie at the Emerald Headingley Stadium was postponed from Sunday 9th February because of poor weather.

Yorkshire Carnegie 10pts. Ampthill 52pts. – Sunday, 23rd February 2020

It was another tough afternoon for Yorkshire Carnegie as they suffered an eight-try defeat at The Emerald Headingley Stadium.

Despite conceding over 50 points once again Phil Davies director of rugby, spoke highly of the first half performance. "I know it sounds ridiculous but our defensive set up was pretty good, despite what the score-line says. We had to do too much of it against a physical team. It's important now that we keep our heads up and work on how we control the ball, build pressure and score points."

In blustery conditions, Ampthill took the lead after six minutes; Will Foster collecting a knock on from the home side to race away and touch down in the corner. Dan Lancaster cut the deficit to two points with a penalty goal but left the field with a leg injury after only 25 minutes.

Ampthill soon restored their lead as hooker Michael Van Vuuren crashed over off a flat pass by Leon Fukofuka on the 28-minute mark. A knock-on from the kick-off set up Carnegie to score their only try of the game; Humphrey going down the short side from a scrum to put youngster Harry Robinson in the corner. As the half drew to a close, the referee awarded a penalty try on the siren for collapsing a scrum to give the visitors a 19-10 lead going into the changing rooms. Unlike the evenly contested first period, the second half was dominated by Ampthill who secured a bonus point with five more tries.

Second row, Jon Kpoku crashed over to give the visitors a 16-point lead before flanker Syd Blackmore took advantage of Humphrey's sin-binning to make a strong drive from an Ampthill line out and get the ball over the whitewash with three defenders on him. Sam Baker sealed the points for the visitors with a seven-minute double. The winger first broke clean through the Carnegie defence to touch down under the posts on the hour mark, before then strolling into the corner untouched, thanks to quick passing and offloads from Paul Turner's side. Sam Wainwright secured the half-century from a dominant maul to make the full-time score 52-10.

Ampthill's head coach was happy to have taken the bonus point that lifts his side to fifth in the table. "It was difficult conditions today," he said. "The guys really dug in and we are happy with the bonus point. To be where we are in the league is great, but we've got some difficult games coming up."

Ampthill: Lewis (Anderson 62), Foster, Morris (Matthews 62), Bird-Tulloch, Baker, Grimoldby, Fukofuka (Barrett 54), Christie (Tonga'uiha 62), Van Vuuren (Ward 57), Collins (Wainwright 54), Kpoku (Williams 57), Kerry, Johnson, Blackmore, Hudson (Arthur 40).

Attendance – 840

Hartpury University 5pts. Ampthill 16pts. – Friday, 28th February 2020

Ampthill were good value for this victory on a dismal Gloucestershire evening. Neither side produced much on a saturated pitch, but the visitors were smart enough to take the chances that came their way. And in Louis Grimoldby, Ampthill had a reliable source of points.

Hartpury did have some moments of pressure, particularly in the second half, but lacked the composure to capitalise and their indiscipline was a constant encouragement to the visitors.

The surface at the Alpas Arena is generally good, but the sheer volume of rainfall meant the match started with standing water in areas. Although the pitch did not cut up badly, a greasy ball ensured that entertainment was at a premium.

The only score of the opening period came courtesy of a Grimoldby penalty after 18 minutes. Hartpury were penalised for coming in from the side and the fly-half struck well from 30 metres. Apart from that, the teams were unable to create any kind of sustained pressure, with territorial kicking being the order of the day. Hartpury finished the half with 14 men, after prop Ashley Challenger was singled out for an accumulation of smaller offences.

Things got marginally better after the break, although the pattern of the game remained largely the same. Hartpury were pressing for a try but an Ampthill break-out led to a penalty for blocking and Grimoldby did the rest. He extended the lead to 9-0 a few minutes later after Hartpury played the jumper at the lineout.

The hosts then had their best spell of the game, finally building some pressure in the visitors' 22. However, they lacked both the nous and accuracy to finish the job, as a series of promising positions were wasted. Eventually they did get some reward. With Ampthill down to 14 after a yellow card to Ben Christie for team infringements, the ball squirted out of a ruck and was floated wide for Jacob Morris to score in the corner. Hartpury could not build on that and the last rites were delivered with two minutes remaining.

Grimaldby launched a perfectly weighted crosskick which tortured the home defence and replacement wing, Sam Baker, was there to score. Grimoldby's touchline conversion capped a strong individual display.

"We were very disappointed with that performance," said Hartpury coach John Barnes. "It was always going to be a difficult night but we were particularly naïve against a solid Ampthill side,"

Ampthill: Lewis, Sutherland (Baker 70), Bird-Tulloch, Matthews, Gillespie, Grimoldby, Barrett (Fukofuka 65), Christie (Anderson 70), Ward (Van Vuuren 59), Collins, Kpoku (Williams 52), Kerry, Arthur (Molitika 50), Bercis, Blackmore.

Attendance – 578

Ampthill 13pts. Cornish Pirates 30pts. – Saturday, 14th March

Cornish Pirates produced a dominant second-half display to claim the bonus point win. Director of Rugby Chris Stirling said, "The result went our way but in truth, with third playing fourth, this was probably our best five points of the season so far."

Playing into the wind Ampthill began well, gaining territory with a combination of phase play through the forwards before full-back Tomi Lewis produced an elusive run, stepping through multiple tackles to touch down near the posts. Louis Grimoldby added the extras. Ampthill thought they had a second try minutes later through left - wing Sam Baker but referee Simon Harding ruled the ball had not been grounded.

Having taken play back for a penalty, Grimoldby made no mistake to extend the lead to 10-0.

Pirates began to exert some control through their forwards while Will Cargill took advantage of the wind to keep the hosts pinned deep in their own half. The pressure told with the home side twice penalised in front of the posts allowing Cargill to convert penalties for 10-6. Grimoldby extended the lead with another penalty of his own but it was scant reward for some fine attacking play.

A missed tackle then gave the visitors the chance to apply pressure inside Ampthill's 22, where centre Rory Parata squeezed over from close range to narrow the gap to 13-11. From there it was all Pirates, outscoring Ampthill 19-0 with tries from wing Robin Wedlake-Millecam and a double by hooker Sam Frost, with Cargill adding two conversions.

Ampthill were denied another try after a late charge down was judged to have gone Pirates' way. Ampthill's head coach Paul Turner said, "The 13-11 lead at half-time didn't do us justice. This has happened once or twice this season, we've kicked off, given a ball away and conceded a soft try and the momentum."

Ampthill: Lewis, Sutherland, Bird-Tulloch, Sage (Matthews 58), Baker (Anderson 51), Grimoldby, Barrett (Fukofuka 58), Tonga'uiha (Christie 65), Van Vuuren (Ward 49), Collins, Johnson (Williams 62), Kerry, Arthur (Molitika 49), Bercis, Blackmore.

Attendance 1,208

Covid-19, RFU Announced Championship Final League Positions

On Thursday 2nd April 2020, the RFU announced the final leagues positions for the abandoned Championship season 2019-20. The RFU decided to spilt the games played into home and away, averaging the number of points earned in each case and applying that to the remaining fixtures. This confirmed that Newcastle Falcons – currently top of the table by 18 points from second-placed Ealing Trailfinders– as champions and promoted back to the Premiership. The latter could yet resume, but Saracens have been confirmed in the relegation position already as punishment for their breaches of the salary cap.

FINAL LEAGUE STANDINGS 2019/20

Club	Points
1. Newcastle Falcons (P)	104.50
2. Ealing Trailfinders	83.42
3. Cornish Pirates	75.43
4. Coventry	65.80
5. Ampthill	**58.34**
6. Nottingham	50.88
7. Jersey Reds	49.04
8. Bedford Blues	46.36
9. London Scottish	42.43
10. Doncaster Knights	36.84*
11. Hartpury University	35.29
12. Yorkshire Carnegie (R)	2.75

*Doncaster Knights were deducted 5 points on 31/03/20 for the use of an unregistered agent contrary to Regulation 8.

Yorkshire Carnegie were relegated with a points difference of 528, an average losing margin of 37 points per game. Director of rugby Phil Davies announced that the club would revert back to its former name of Leeds. It is expected that Leeds will leave the Emerald Headingley Stadium.

Club Statement – 3rd April 2020

Following the RFU announcement this morning regarding final league positions for the Professional and Community game in England, we are proud to confirm that Ampthill & District Community Rugby Club has finished 5th in the Greene King IPA Championship at our first attempt!

We would like to extend our congratulations to Newcastle Falcon's on securing both the title and promotion back to the Gallagher Premiership and our thanks to the rest of the league for making us so welcome this season. We also extend our best wishes to Yorkshire Carnegie whom we feel sure will come back bigger and stronger in the future.

We should also take this opportunity to thank our corporate partners, Grange Jaguar Land Rover, British Car Auctions, Wheeler Electrical, O'Neills Sportswear, Powell Systems, Comfort Homecare, Global Wealth Management Solutions and FirstAid4Sport, plus our 1100 members without whose support we would not have achieved this result.

Mark Lavery, Director of Rugby at Ampthill Rugby, "It's a really unusual set of circumstances and our first thoughts are to all our members, supporters and those stakeholders affected by COVID-19. The important thing is to make sure we all stay home and stay safe. I think the coaching team led by Paul Turner has done an excellent job in securing fifth place at our first attempt in the Greene King IPA Championship. I know the circumstances are highly unusual, but to consider a club of our size finishing the season as the seventeenth highest ranked rugby club in England will certainly be a note

Top Scorers in the Championship – 2019-20

Leading points scorers			Leading try scorers	
Louis Grimoldby - Ampthill	112		Adam Radwan – Newcastle Falcons	10
Roy Jennings – Coventry	112		George McGuigan – Newcastle Falcons	10
Sam Oliver – Doncaster Knights	112		Callum Patterson – Cornish Pirates	9
Javier Alvarez – Cornish Pirates	108		Jack Spittle - Nottingham	9
Craig Willis – Ealing Trailfinders	82		Antonio Harris – Jersey Reds	8
Josh Bragman - Hartpury	77		Ryan Hutler – Bedford Blues	8
Steven Shingler – Ealing Trailfinders	70		David Williams - Nottingham	8
Shane O'Leary - Nottingham	65		Reon Joseph – Ealing Trailfinders	7
Brendan Cope – Jersey Reds	60		Luke Frost – London Scottish	7

When the RFU cancelled all non-Premiership rugby in March 2020, Ampthill 1881s were nicely placed in third place with return fixtures remaining against clubs they had already convincingly beaten. These would include Rams – beaten 57-6, Bishop's Stortford – beaten 22-7 and Cinderford United 33-16. Whilst it seems unlikely that the 1881s would have overtaken the two teams above, they should certainly expect to retain third spot this season.

1881s – Zoo Sports League - Division 1

#	Team	P	W	D	L	PF	PA	+/-	TB	LB	Pts
1	Richmond Vikings (2nd XV)	21	20	1	0	847	247	600	16	0	98
2	Old Elthamians 2nd XV	20	16	0	4	542	286	256	7	1	75
3	Ampthill 1881 XV	17	13	2	2	638	255	383	12	0	70
4	Rosslyn Park 2nd XV	21	12	1	8	579	368	211	8	1	63
5	Cinderford United (2nd XV)	19	9	3	7	386	407	-21	6	0	53
6	Wimbledon 2nd XV	19	7	3	9	428	480	-52	7	2	52
7	Jersey Athletic	18	7	0	11	373	423	-50	4	4	47
8	Richmond Saxons (3rd XV)	18	7	0	11	354	464	-110	5	2	46
9	Rams II	17	6	0	11	372	510	-138	8	3	46
10	Esher Cardinals (2nd XV)	16	7	1	8	339	446	-107	6	0	42
11	Bishop's Stortford Blues	19	5	0	14	375	516	-141	5	4	42
12	Canterbury 2XV Pilgrims	19	4	1	14	367	672	-305	5	2	37
13	Cambridge Wanderers	19	5	0	14	320	555	-235	7	1	36
14	Barnes 2nd XV	15	5	0	10	269	560	-291	5	0	35

Other Senior Teams Leagues

Jets (3rd XV) – Merit Table 2

played	won	drawn	lost	pts. for	pts. against	points
21	11	0	10	423	358	60

When the season ended prematurely, the Jets lay sixth in the league of fourteen teams.

Extras (4th XV) – Bombardier League

played	won	drawn	lost	pts. for	pts. against	points
8	3	1	4	196	214	18

When the season was fore-shortened in March, the Extras were in fourth place in a 7-team league

Extras (4th XV) – Merit Table 1

played	won	drawn	lost	pts. for	pts. against	points
14	7	0	7	239	262	56

When the season was ended in March the Extras lay fourth of 8 teams.

5th XV- Banana Bread Beer Merit Table

played	won	drawn	lost	pts. for	pts. against	points
13	6	0	7	330	322	31

The 5th XV were lying fourth of nine teams when the competition was stopped because of Covid-19

2019-20	played	won	drawn	lost	pts. for	pts. against
1st XV	15	8	1	6	368	399
1881s	17	13	2	2	638	255
Jets XV	21	11	0	10	423	358
Extras XV	22	10	1	11	435	476
5th XV	13	6	0	7	330	322
Vets XV	19	12	1	6	627	279
Academy XV	2	1	0	1	86	33

RFU Cuts Championship Funding

At 8am, on Tuesday 11th February 2020, Championship clubs each received an email detailing the cuts to funding and calling them to what was said to have been a highly charged meeting at Twickenham. Bill Sweeny, the RFU Chief Executive and Conor O'Shea, the Director of Performance, explained they would be reducing funding from £530,000 to £288,000 per club as part of a new 12-month deal starting in July. It would be reviewed again in six months.

The RFU insisted that the cut followed a review of spending called "Project Union" and that the Championship had failed to deliver on five key strategic targets after a significant hike in funding over the past four years from the profits of hosting the 2015 World Cup.

The press release from English rugby's governing body stated that "the RFU will continue to provide financial support" to the Championship next season, but that central funding will be reduced from £480,000 to £288,000 for 2020-21.

Premiership Rugby confirmed that it would also be reducing its funding to the Championship by half from £1.7 million to £850,000.

RFU chief executive Bill Sweeney said the reason for the 40% cut was the failure of the clubs to meet specific targets set in 2015. The five areas:

1. Make steps towards becoming a financially viable league, given the average annual club loss is £260,000.
2. Develop a league where more clubs have an ambition of winning promotion.
3. Increase the number of English-qualified players.
4. Develop future England coaches and referees.
5. Develop a community programme to grow the game in the club's region.

Sweeney insisted that the RFU was "not using this as a means to seal (the Premiership) off in any way", and that promotion and relegation remained in place for clubs with deep enough pockets to bridge the £6 million spending gap with the Premiership clubs and meet minimum-standards criteria.

"We don't think this is an amount of money which defines whether or not you can still go for that," Sweeney said. "But clearly there will be speculation that this is a direction (ring-fencing) in terms of the way the game is going."

The move sparked a furious reaction from clubs, who, indeed, accused the RFU of ring-fencing and claimed it would force them to become semi-professional and effectively close off the path to the top-flight. The clubs said they would honour existing contracts, but that there would be significant cuts to playing budgets.

"This is ring-fencing in all but name", Geoff Irvine, the Chairman of the Championship clubs, said. "The significant reduction has come as a shock to the clubs. The value of the Championship has not been recognised or rewarded by the RFU, when you consider how many of the England squad started their careers in the Championship."

Alistair Bow, chairman of Nottingham, accused the RFU of "handing professional rugby on a plate to Premiership Rugby and CVC, its private-equity investor. The implications of what they are going to do are going to be devastating to English rugby as a whole," Bow said. "Bill Sweeney could well go down as the man who ruined English rugby. They have sold their soul to Premiership Rugby and CVC."

Dicky Evans, the Cornish Pirates owner, whose club are building a new stadium, said receiving the letter from the RFU was "like being sacked by text message". "It stinks," he said "We are too far down the road with the stadium to pull out now. They are giving up on rugby in the second tier."

The RFU, however, insisted that there was already a gulf in standards between the tiers evidenced by the fact that that in the past five years the relegated Premiership sides were promoted the following season.

Sweeney said that the increase in funding to almost £6 million per season over the past four had not resulted in any of the five strategic targets being met, including becoming a financially viable second tier – the clubs are losing £260,000 per year on average – and developing English qualified players for the Premiership and England.

He said that while the Championship would remain important for player development, it was no longer "the primary route for discovering and developing Premiership and England players", following an analysis of the number who are breaking into the national squads from the second tier.

Sweeney admitted that the implications of the return to pre-2015 funding would force clubs towards a "semi-pro model". "We have looked at their financial situation and we don't think it will put any clubs out of business," he said.

"We think they will have to adjust their management philosophy and go more towards a semi-pro model, as opposed to a fully professional model."

The RFU will save about £3million next season from the cuts and could invest in new pathways, with a review expected of the Premiership A league, Premiership Cup and Shield and University "Super Rugby". Premiership Rugby said it would also be investing in areas such as its Under-18 league.

Open Letter from the Executive of the Championship to Bill Sweeney

In this open letter Geoff Irvine makes a number of points including:

1. A baseline funding of £1 million per club was necessary to fund full-time professional rugby
2. As the end of the four-year agreement period approached for Championship funding the RFU had failed to engage with Championship Clubs
3. The 50% cut in funding was announced with no warning or negotiation
4. No Championship club had any knowledge of the 5 strategic targets quoted by RFU
5. The Twickenham East Stand Project has an overspend of tens of millions of pounds
6. The reduction in funding a few months prior to season 2020/21 is a " a disaster for our finances"
7. CCC asked for a moratorium for 2 years to allow more considered debate

Graham Cattermole, former RFU Chairman, added his criticism to the slashing cuts to Championship funding. Cattermole argued that putting the Championship clubs in jeopardy without thinking through the funding plan has made the RFU look inept. He is certain that even though RFU chief executive, Bill Sweeney on Friday 21st February, revised the cuts from £220,000 a club to £135,000 (from this season's £530,000), it is a clear sign the RFU remains under fiscal pressure. Cattermole said, "Sweeney did not think this whole issue through sufficiently in order to formulate a realistic proposal to the clubs. This exercise has been messy in its concept and delivery but, more importantly, indicates a lack of professionalism and poor management by the RFU executive."

"As soon as I saw the announcement of the Championship cut-backs, I had no doubt it is cost-cutting because the financial situation is not rosy. Yes, the RFU made a profit of £3 million to the end of 2019, but when you consider the cost base at Twickenham that is a poor return, especially when you take into account the loan debt that has to be repaid."

"If the RFU saw this funding as an important issue, why was there not an annual review showing the clubs where appropriate action could and should be taken? The whole thing is a smoke-screen to ring-fence the Premiership clubs and curtail promotion-relegation without the RFU having to pass a formal vote. It will have been done by sleight of hand."

Cattermole asserts that the RFU Council has supported the transfer of power to the Management Board to such a degree that it can now be challenged only at an SGM or AGM. "There is no accountability at the moment, and no checks and balances, because half the RFU board is, in essence self-perpetuating."

Ampthill Captain Louis Grimaldby in The Rugby Paper – 23rd February 2020

"England ought to replicate the French system," says Ampthill Captain, Louis Grimoldby

Ampthill fly-half Louis Grimoldby urges English rugby to mirror the French system of having two professional leagues under one commercial umbrella.

Deemed surplus to requirements by Harlequins in 2015, Grimoldby opted to make a fresh start in France where he starred for Massy (Paris suburbs) in levels two and three, gaining an appreciation of how an integrated professional structure should look.

The Ligue Nationale de Rugby (LNR) administer both the Top 14 and ProD2 and Grimoldby would like that replicated in England. Vicious RFU cutbacks have thrown the future of England's Championship into doubt and Grimoldby, 25, told the Rugby Paper, "I'm not sure what the RFU are looking for but if you want two thriving leagues, it makes complete sense to have them under one governing body.

It's worrying to think English rugby just wants one professional league. In French rugby there are teams in Federale One, their third-tier division, who are now full-time professional. Massy had just been relegated from ProD2 when I went there, but we got back up and I had two enjoyable years in their second division playing in front of some sell-out crowds. After we got promoted, we played against teams like Perpignon, Biarritz and Oyonnax, often in front of 8,000, so I've experienced both second divisions and the difference is vast.

How can we be so far away from that here with the talent coming through the Championship? It is a shame that you might have just one full-time professional league here. The second tier will effectively be amateur – with no incentives that will happen."

Grimoldby is concerned that the standard in Tier Two will diminish significantly if teams are forced to go part-time. He added, "If you look at the standard of the Premiership's A League it seems to be a lot of 17- or 18-year olds bolstered by National One players who can't get a game at the weekend. If you water down the existing Championship I don't see where the development's coming from. Look at the number of dual-registered boys we're bringing through at Ampthill. We've got Josh Gillespie, Tommy Matthews (both Northampton), Jon Kpoku (Saracens), Oli Morris (Worcester) and Ben Christie (Wasps) who are being exposed to the Championship, getting good game time, and will be far better equipped for the Premiership because of it.

If all the clubs in the Championship go part-time the standard isn't going to be the same." Grimoldby believes twinning the Premiership and Championship would be win-win. "ProD2 in France commands big crowds and what LNR have done is move all their Tier Two games to Thursday or Friday nights. They've got a good TV deal and every game is available via Eurosport so the league gets tremendous exposure and benefits financially. The potential for the Championship here is really good, but the RFU have gone about things differently and you fear what might happen."

Reproduced with the kind permission of David Emery, Editor in Chief of The Rugby Paper.

Role of Championship in producing top-flight players

Many clubs took issue with much of the information contained in the email announcing cuts, it contained references to funding for the British and Irish Cup, which was disbanded two years ago, as well as downplaying the role of the Championship has played in developing England players. As Dicky Evans, the Cornish Pirates owner, put it bluntly, "To say we are not producing players is total b……..s.". The England squad that faced Scotland on 8th February 2020, contained 12 players who cut their teeth in the Championship.

In February, The Rugby Paper produced a club by club breakdown of how the Championship has produced Premiership, Pro14 and England players.

Nb Current team in brackets and Dual registered*

Ampthill

Karl Garside (Northampton Saints), Ben Earl* (Saracens), Nick Isiekwe* (Saracens), Ralph Adams-Hale* (Saracens), Samson Ma'asi* (Northampton Saints), Jon Kpoku* (Saracens), Oli Morris* (Worcester Warriors)

Bedford Blues

Michael Le Bourgeois (Wasps), Mark Atkinson (Gloucester), Dan Cole* (Leicester Tigers), Josh Bassett (Wasps), Will Chudley (Bath), Ben Ransom* (Saracens now Blackheath), Duncan Taylor*, Will Fraser*, Mako Vunipola*, Maro Itoje*, Owen Farrell*, George Kruis*, Jackson Wray*, Nick Tompkins*, James Short* (all Saracens), Aaron Morris (Saracens now Harlequins), Luke Baldwin (Saracens now Dragons – loan)

Cornish Pirates

Christian Judge (Bath), Alex Day (Saracens), Jamal Ford-Robinson (Gloucester), Sam Simmonds* (Exeter Chiefs), Jack Nowell* (Exeter Chiefs), Dave Ward (Harlequins now Ampthill), Ollie Devoto (Bath now Exeter Chiefs), Chris Cook (Bath)

Coventry

Biyi Alo (Wasps), Lewis Ludlam* (Northampton Saints), Beno Obano* (Bath), James Stokes (London Irish)

Doncaster Knights

Willgriff John (Sale Sharks), Will Hurrell (Bristol), Tomas Francis (Exeter Chiefs), Piers Francis (Northampton Saints), Michael Heaney (Worcester Warriors), Glen Young (Harlequins), Jack Yeandle (Exeter Chiefs), Jack Roberts (Leicester)

Ealing Trailfinders

Piers O'Connor (Bristol), Luke Daniels (Bristol)

Hartpury University

Sed Negri (Gloucester now Benetton), Jake Polledri (Gloucester), Ruaridh McConnochie (Bath), Lewis Ludlow* (Gloucester), Callum Braley* (Gloucester), Ellis Genge* (Bristol now Leicester), Ryan Mills* (Worcester Warriors), Henry Trinder* (Gloucester), Elliot Stooke* (Gloucester now Bath), Charlie Sharples* (Gloucester), Tom Savage* (Gloucester now Suntory Sungollath), Dan Robinson* (Gloucester now Wasps)

Jersey Reds

Brett Herron (Harlequins), Scott van Breda (Worcester Warriors), Jake Woolmore (Bristol), Tom Pincus (Bristol), Jake Armstrong (Bristol), Matt Rogerson (London Irish), Simon Kerrod (Harlequins), Gary Graham (Newcastle Falcons), Nick Haining (Bristol), Richard Barrington (Saracens), Guy Thompson (Leicester Tigers), Tom Howe (Worcester Warriors), Sam Lockwood (Newcastle Falcons), Tommy Bell (Leicester Tigers now Ealing Trailfinders), Elvis Taione (Exeter Chiefs), Jerry Sexton (Southern Kings), Keran Hardy (Scarlets), Sean McCarthy (Leinster)

London Scottish

Theo Vukasinovic (Wasps), Richard Palframan (Worcester Warriors), Elliot Daly* (Saracens), George Merrick* (Harlequins now Clermont Auvergne), Sam Twomey* (Harlequins now London Irish), Harry Sloan* (Harlequins now Ealing Trailfinders), Sam Stuart* (Harlequins now Newcastle Falcons), James Chisholm* (Harlequins)

Nottingham

Harry Williams (Exeter Chiefs), Toby Freeman (Harlequins), Calum Green (Leicester Tigers), Dan Cole* (Leicester Tigers), Ed Slater (Gloucester), Will Stuart (Bath), George Furbank* (Northampton Saints), Alfie Barbeary* (Wasps)

Yorkshire Carnegie

Sam Wolstenholme (Wasps), Paul Hill (Northampton), Alex Lozowski (Saracens), Lewis Boyce (Harlequins now Bath), Craig Hampson (Wasps), Dom Barrow (Newcastle Falcons now free agent), Ryan Burrows (Newcastle Falcons), Callum Green (Newcastle Falcons), Jack Walker (Bath), Max Green (Bath), Max Wright (Bath), Ollie Fox (Bath), Steve McColl (Gloucester), Tom Denton (Leinster), Ben Harris (Newcastle Falcons), Joel Hodgson (Newcastle Falcons), Jonah Holmes (Leicester Tigers), Alex Davies (Bath)

Alistair Bow, chairman of Nottingham Rugby Club, and the most trenchant critic of the RFU had this to say on why the Championship is invaluable for producing English qualified players:

"Virtually every club in the Premiership has England internationals who have been nurtured in the Championship and its value has been proven time and again. Championship clubs bring young EQP players through – and like Nottingham acknowledge that they can, and do , move on. Without adequate funding the Premiership will lose that proven model.

You need a second pro league for players to get the necessary development. We all have to learn a trade, and the Championship – and the National Leagues – have proved their worth in developing leading players, coaches, referees, administrators, and conditioning staff.

Premiership clubs put their trust in Championship clubs to bring along their promising players and coaches and we do the same with our loan deals to National One clubs. It is an absolutely proven model."

Reproduced with the kind permission of David Emery Editor in Chief of The Rugby Paper.

Other prominent ex-Ampthill players

Josh Bassett played youth team rugby for **Ampthill** where he helped the under-17s win the National Bowl with a try in the final—the team lost only one game all season.

He played for **Bedford Blues** in the RFU Championship. After being promoted from the academy in 2010, Bassett soon became a regular starter. He was linked with a host of Premiership teams after becoming a prolific try scorer for the Blues. On 3 April 2013, it was announced that Bassett had signed for **Wasps** for the 2013/14 season.

Lewis Ludlow attended Ampthill schools and came through the mini-youth system at the club. His father Paul, and grand-father Tony, were prominent playing members of the Club. Lewis represented England U/18 on their tour to South Africa and after Hartpury College he signed for Gloucester in 2015 and has had a stellar career in the back-row. Lewis is welsh-qualified through grandparents.

Dean Adamson came through the Club's mini & youth and was a member of the U/9 team who reached the Prudential Cup Final at Twickenham in 2002. A prolific points scorer (22 tries in National 2 for Ampthill), he signed for Bedford in 2014. By the end of 2017-18 he had amassed 60 tries from 85 appearances and was named in the Championship dream team.

The Saracens are coming!

Multiple salary-cap breaches meant that Saracens were relegated from the Premiership and would make the walk through the woods to Ampthill's Olney Field – a ground with no floodlights and no stand. The irony of Ampthill's strong links to Saracens via dual-registered players such as Ben Earl, Nick Isiekwe, Ralph Alex-Hales and Jon Kpoku and the coaching of Mouritz Botha was not lost on the Ampthill faithful.

The majority of Saracens stars conformed their loyalty to the club by signing new contracts and it seemed that Eddie Jones would be allowed to select Saracens players for England despite their playing in the Championship.

Heartland Championship Proposals

In July 2020, during the Covid-19 lockdown, it was disclosed that revolutionary plans for a new Championship league were being discussed with the compilation of a 76-page document by Edward Griffiths, the former Saracens CEO. From 2021/22, Griffiths proposed a new 16-team "Heartland" Championship split into North and South conferences, with top four in each moving forward to contest the title with play-offs and a grand-final. The bottom four in each conference would fight to avoid relegation to National 1.

Minimum ground standards aimed at encouraging new fans and ensuring that clubs aspiring to join the Heartland Championship are properly equipped are to be introduced. Flood lighting and adequate seating and covered accommodation would become mandatory. This proposal would place huge pressure on Ampthill's plans to relocate to a new stadium, half a mile from Dillingham Park (see below).

A collective commercial and bargaining agreement which would see Heartland Championship sides pool resources to attract new broadcasting and sponsorship deals. This would obviously help to off-set the drastic cut-backs in RFU funding to Championship clubs. A Heartland Championship XV would play second-tier nations such as Tonga, Samoa, and Georgia.

Significantly the plan from the ex-Saracens CEO contained the proposal that promotion to the premiership should be based on "agreed criteria" rather than a first past the post format. Griffiths also proposes a four-year moratorium on promotion and relegation. It is noticeable how Griffiths' proposals are careful not to propose an official ring fence to the Premiership, but in many peoples' eyes his plan, especially the four-year moratorium, is a step towards just that.

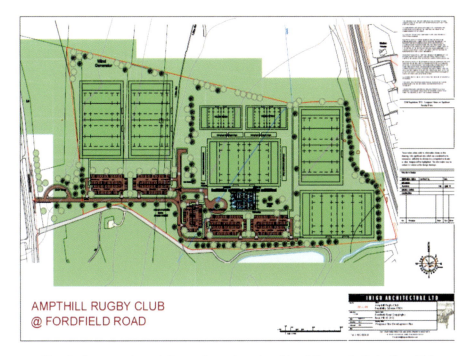

Plans for the proposed new stadium on the western edge of Ampthill opposite Center Parcs (sic)

Green King IPA Dream Team of the Season

All positions were decided by a public vote on Twitter – Joe Bercis convincingly took the 7 shirt with 45% of over 3200 votes against some strong competition!

Mark's Lavery's - Summary of the Journey to date:

2006-07 Midlands 3 East (South) – won the division with David Marshall as coach
2007-08 Midlands East – finished 7th with Alan Brown as coach
2008-09 Midlands 2 East – won the division with Stuart Evans as Head Coach
2009-10 National 3 Midlands – won the division with Stuart Evans as Head Coach but denied promotion for not following correct match postponement protocol – transferred to National 3 London & South-East (see page 196).
2010-11 National 2 London & South-East – finished 4th with Stuart Evans as Head Coach
2011-12 National 2 London & South-East – finished 3rd with Stuart Evans as Head Coach
2012-13 transferred back to National 3 Midlands – won division with Paul Turner as Head Coach
2013-14 National 2 South - finished 2nd to Hartpury and lost play-off at Darlington Mowden Park in extra time with Paul Turner as Head Coach
2014-15 National 2 North – finished 2nd to Hull Ionians but won the play-off at home to Bishop's Stortford with Paul Turner as Head Coach
2015-16 National 1 – finished 4th with Paul Turner as Head Coach
2016-17 National 1- finished 3rd with Paul Turner as Head Coach
2017-18 National 1 – finished 4th (the reader will note that this is the only season when the Club did not improve its league position in Mark Lavery's tenure as Director of Rugby) with Paul Turner as Head Coach
2018-19 National 1 champions with Paul Turner as Head Coach
2019-20 Green King IOA Championship – finished 5th with Paul Turner as Head Coach

Mark Lavery & Joe Bercis celebrate (photo by Daniele Colucciello – with kind permission of The Rugby Journal)

Our first season in the Championship created a lot of media interest and both the mainstream and rugby press became even more regular visitors to Dillingham Park.

In April 2020 the club featured in The Rugby Journal and Daniele Colucciello's breath taking image "The Calm before the Storm" was subsequently voted as "Rugby Photo of the Year".

Team of the Decade 2010- 2020

In May 2020, 10,000 votes on Twitter produced this "just for fun" Ampthill "Team of the Decade".

10 Year Fixture Comparison (1st XV) 2010-2020

	2010/11		2019/20
Sept.	Barnes Bracknell Tring Gravesend	Sept.	Coventry (Championship Cup) Ealing Trailfinders (Championship Cup)
Oct.	Bishop's Stortford Diss North Walsham Hertford Dorking	Oct.	Bedford Blues (Championship Cup) Nottingham Yorkshire Carnegie London Scottish
Nov.	Havant Staines Civil Service	Nov.	Hartpury University Cornish Pirates Jersey Reds Coventry (Championship Cup)
Dec.	Basingstoke Bracknell Tring	Dec.	Ealing Trailfinders (Championship Cup) Bedford Blues (Championship Cup) Bedford Blues
Jan.	Gravesend Bishop Stortford Diss North Walsham	Jan.	Coventry Ealing Trailfinders Doncaster
Feb.	Hertford Basingstoke Dorking Tring	Feb.	Newcastle Falcons Yorkshire Carnegie London Scottish Hartpury University
Mar.	Havant Staines Civil Service	Mar.	Cornish Pirates Jersey Reds Bedford Blues Coventry
Apr.	Basingstoke Barnes	Apr.	Ealing Trailfinders Doncaster Newcastle Nottingham

League matches - National 3 London & SE   League matches - The Championship

Chapter 10 – The Mini & Youth – The Jewel in the Crown – 1971-2020

The first 10 years

Ampthill Rugby Club, until comparatively recently, has been best known for the quality of its Mini & Youth section. It has been influential in the spread of youngsters' rugby throughout East Midlands and beyond. The person originally responsible for this is Dave Williams, these are his words in 2012:

"To find the start of Mini and Youth at the club we have to go back to 1971 when Colin Tanner, the local Cub/Scout leader, asked me to teach his cubs to play rugby, in order that they could obtain the Sportsman's Badge. They had to do two sports and everyone played soccer. This I agreed to do, so I coached them for six weeks on a Saturday morning and set a little exam at the end. It was so successful that a club member suggested that I should continue with the course during the next season, and so I did every other Saturday morning. I chose Saturday because at that time the Harpur Trust schools were open on Saturday mornings and they provided much better coaches than I, and I wanted to get the children that went to the local schools involved. The game of mini rugby had not been invented at this stage, but when two years later it was, we were ready for it, and Ampthill became the club to emulate. We now have a mini/youth section with 455 players and parental support that other clubs can only dream of."

When the Lions returned from their successful crusade to New Zealand in 1970-71, they brought back tales of how rugby was promoted in schools and clubs. The Lions' tour engendered a resurgence in interest in rugby - a revolution was about to begin. In the early 1970s Dave Williams recalls being called to a meeting at Rushden RUFC hosted by Ron Jacobs who had been tasked with developing mini-rugby in the East Midlands by the RFU.

Jacobs played a club record 470 games for Northampton over a 17-year period and appeared 29 times for England - captaining them for his final two games in 1964. After retiring from playing, Jacobs remained involved in rugby and became president of the Rugby Football Union in 1983 and was tour manager during the controversial 1984 England rugby union tour of South Africa.

The RFU recognised that the East Midlands region was ahead of its time in developing rugby for youngsters. Mini-rugby was inspired by a grass-roots up approach, particularly in the East Midlands but also in the valleys of South Wales, where the majority of the players for the Lions and their coach Carwyn James resided.

Ron Jacobs asked Dave about how he had introduced the shortened form of the game to youngsters at Ampthill. Dave explained that he had taught the boys to play sevens rugby as that was the only abbreviated form of the game he knew.

Thus, there were set and loose scrums, lines-out, set positions, tackling and even the occasional kick. It should be remembered that hailing from the Rhondda Valley Dave was a very accomplished player and a natural communicator.

Within a period of five years the game had become established in England and Wales and a publication "Mini Rugby – the real thing" was jointly issued by Don Rutherford (RFU Technical Administrator) and Ray Williams (Coaching Organiser, Welsh Rugby Union). This set out to "the basic philosophy behind the introduction of Mini-Rugby, how it should be played and administered." Both Unions wished to emphasise that it was a game for nine players, played in accord with rules advocated in the booklet.

Fortunately, Ampthill had a head start in the East Midlands – although at first there were no opponents to play against! However, by 1972, other local clubs, notably St. Neots, Dunstablians and Leighton Buzzard started mini teams. At this time, it was Dave Williams who continued to teach the boys rugby, moving from sevens to the nine-man mini-rugby format. Bill Edwards was Chairman of Mini-Rugby from 1973-79 and Bert Robinson was Secretary of the section.

In 1973, Alameda Middle School opened and two rugby players were appointed to the staff, PE teacher Will Hunt and science teacher Dave Parker, and they were joined by the author in 1977. These teachers were highly influential in the development of boys' rugby and a high proportion of Alameda pupils had fathers who had played rugby or were playing rugby at Ampthill or other local clubs.

Club fixtures were arranged and Ampthill was soon known for high quality teams and being "the team to beat." By the 1975-76 season, some fifty boys were playing at Ampthill and the club was able to field sides in three age groups. In that year they went to the St. Neots Festival and played 13 games overall, winning 9, losing 3 and drawing 1. From this time onwards, the Mini Section expanded at an amazing rate, thanks to the efforts of many volunteer members and parents.

At the Club's AGM in 1974, the Chairman Dave Williams, had this to say about mini-rugby, "To introduce players to the game is of course one of the primary objects of a junior club, and perhaps while on this subject I should define the objects of our Saturday morning training sessions for the 7 to 13 year olds. The object is simply to introduce young lads to the game at an early stage, it is not our intention to produce a squad of heavily coached rugby robots.

This season the Club is 25 years old, and while it may seem appropriate to review the history of the Club, I think it is more relevant to remind members what a large organisation we have become. The Club membership at this time is as follows:

Playing Members	98
Non-Playing Members	25
Vice Presidents/Life Members	78
Mini-Rugby Players	**61**
	262

The following year Dave Williams reported that there were now 62 boys in the mini youth section and the results of mini games were reported at the AGM for the first time

Mini-Rugby	p	w	d	l	pf	pa
Under 9	1	1	0	0	24	4
Under 10	1	0	0	1	0	4
Under 11	4	4	0	0	40	4
Under 12	3	0	0	3	10	56
Under 13	6	1	0	5	36	106

It was noted that the under 11 side had won all four games and gave away only one try. The other sides were, in some cases, unfortunate in that the opposing clubs have a different view on age limits. Dave Williams commented, "Sufficient to say that we have over sixty very young men very interested in our game."

The Club Fixture card for 1979-80 listed the sections fixtures for the first time:

AMPTHILL & DISTRICT – MINI RUGBY SECTION

Ground: Woburn Road

Organiser: Bill Edwards

Training: Sunday mornings at 10am. Commencing 7th October 1979

FIXTURES

Date	Opponent	H/A
28 Oct.	Dunstable	H
11 Nov.	Stockwood Park	A
25 Nov.	Leighton Buzzard	H
16 Dec	Bedford	H
20 Jan	Biggleswade	A
3 Feb.	Milton Keynes	H
24 Feb.	Stockwood Park	H
23 Mar.	South Beds. Festival	A
30 Mar.	St. Neots	A
20 Apr.	St. Neots Festival	A

It should be noted that Bill Edwards was a former 1st XV captain who had two sons at Alameda Middle School – both accomplished players. The Ampthill Rugby Club Mini-Youth and Alameda Middle School axis would bring through many players to the senior game. Woodland Middle School in Flitwick was also influential in introducing the game to 9 – 13-year-olds.

1980s

The rapid development of the section can be seen by the 1980-81 fixture list:

Youth

Date	Opponent	Ages	H/A
Oct 12	Dunstablians	U16 U14	H
Nov 9	Stockwood Park	U16 U14	A
Nov 23	Leighton Buzzard	U16 U14	A
Dec 7	Biggleswade	U15 U14	H
Jan 4	Milton Keynes	U16 U15 U14	H
Jan 11	St. Neots	U16 U14	A
Jan 25	Stockwood Park	U16 U14	H
Feb 8	Biggleswade	U15 U14	A
Feb 22	Dunstable	U16 U14	A
Mch 8	St. Neots	U16	H
Mch 22	Leighton Buzzard	U16 U14	H
Apr 5	Milton Keynes 7's		

Mini Rugby

SEPTEMBER: Training

Date	Opponent	H/A
Oct 5	St. Neots	A
Oct 19	Biggleswade/Letchworth	A
Nov 9	Stockwood Park	H
Nov 23	Leighton Buzzard	H
Dec 7	Bedford/Cambs	A
Jan 11	St. Neots	H
Jan 25	Stockwood Park	A
Feb 15	Dunstable	A
Mch 8	Biggleswade	H
Mch 22	Leighton Buzzard	A
Mch 29	Stockwood Park Festival	A
Apr 5	Dunstable	H
Apr 26	St. Neots Festival	A

By 1982-83 the Club was able to run a side in every age group from U7s to U17s and it was also the year when the Mini section became a financial success and able to support itself without funding from the senior sector of the Club.

By the 1984-85 season, the expansion of the section can be seen by the need for increased organisation:

1984-85 Mini/Youth Organisation:

Chairman	Roger Phillips
Hon. Secretary	Dave Baston
Hon. Treasurer	Mike Marsden
Social Secretary	Bob Campbell
Kit	Mike Johnson
Fixtures	Norman Brown
Youth Organiser	Larry Grant

New Clubhouse

The opening of the Dillingham Park Clubhouse by Budge Rogers, OBE – Sunday 5 April 1981.

Ampthill 1st XV versus Public School Wanderers

back row: P. Johnson, S. Moore, P. McGuckian, E. Hyde, M. Hobley, B. Kidner, N. Fox, C. Leeke (ref.) M. Truman, S. Watson, P. Argent, M. Nolan, B. Clark, G. Bailey, B. Clayton, K. Betts, S. Barker, I. Owen middle-row: R. Cheesman, T. Buttimoore, J. Raphael, M. Malic, R. Wilkinson, R. James, D. Rogers, D. Dillingham, B. O'Dell, S. Peacey (capt.), P.Day, J. Hindmarch, P. Cadigan, B. Hart front row: G. Wilson, P. Rossborough, I. Peck, G. Griffiths, A. Owen, D. Parker, P. Ogilvie, M. Plant.

Mini-rugby boys: **Liam Duffin, Adrian Downing, Russell Hart, Mark Bishop, Stewart Pegg, Michael Tanner, Justin Fletcher, John Wilkinson, Nigel Vicary, Steven Marsden, Richard Holmes, Graham Baston.**

Mini-Rugby Boys

Six of the 12 mini-rugby playing boys pictured above were to go on to play senior rugby for Ampthill. Liam Duffin, Michael Tanner, Justin Fletcher, John Wilkinson and Steve Marden were all to play in senior teams for the Club and beyond.

Liam Duffin: played for Ampthill senior teams and now is the Manager of the Extras
Michael Tanner: Ampthill, Bedfordshire, England Students, England U/21, Richmond, Royal Navy, Combined Services
Justin Fletcher: Ampthill, Bedford Colts, Midlands Colts, England Colts trials, Bedfordshire
John Wilkinson: Ampthill, Bedfordshire, East Midlands, Bedford
Steve Marsden: Ampthill senior teams

2000 – Ampthill Mini & Youth Taking Rugby to the Community

In Denis Hardy's time as Director of Rugby & Ian Cooper's time as Chairman of Mini & Youth circa 2000-2002 the "Taking Rugby to the Community" was published .

It sought to emphasise the Club's commitment to developing rugby in Mid-Bedfordshire and explaining how to make contact and join the Mini & Youth Section of the Ampthill & District Rugby Club.

Anyone can Play!

Ampthill & District Community R.U.F.C. is a thriving club situated in Mid Bedfordshire. We cater for all ages, both Boys and Girls. The differing levels of age and ability are categorised into four groups. Mini, Midi, Youth and Senior sections, along Rugby Football Union's Continuum guidelines. It is our Policy to check our coaches' backgrounds to assess their suitability to work with children.

Mini Section aged 6-11

We register junior players, from School year 2, into our under 7's Team. They enter competitions and play matches against other clubs in the East Midlands area. Our R.F.U. qualified coaches encourage, team work & self-discipline. Girls and Boys play in mixed teams until the Youth Section.

Midi Section aged 12

Now 12 a side, the intermediary game, an intense year, with players hopefully perfecting, all the skills required for the full 15 a side game. Along side a full calendar of matches and competitions.

Youth Section aged 13-17

Welcome to the full 15 a side game of Rugby Union. We have seven teams in this section. That's one at each age level plus a girls under 16 squad. Whether a new member to the club or someone who has come up through the Mini section all are welcome. If your talents shine maybe you will be selected to represent your county.

AMPTHILL RUFC UNDER 9 SQUAD 2000-2001

Membership Details

The annual subscription for the 2001-2002 season for Mini, Midi and Youth sections is £25 for the first child in each family and £5 for all additional children (to a maximum of £30 per family. This subscription includes Social (non-voting) membership for parents or guardians nominated upon the membership form.
For further details call
John Wilkinson 01525 840795

School Support Scheme

We have a team of R.F.U. qualified coaches who work with the teachers in Middle and Upper schools in the area, providing specialist coaching. We also visit Lower schools to "introduce Rugby" to the younger members of our community. During the last school year we have helped, Alameda, Parkfields and Woodlands Middle Schools, Harlington and Redbourne Upper Schools, and a number of Lower Schools.
For further details call
Lester Bull 01525 874287

Senior Section

Currently competing in Midlands Division 2 East (Level 6), The senior section has 4 full teams, in addition to an under 19 and under 21 side. In recent years the First XV has competed in the Tetley Bitter Cup, Won the East Midland Cup 1995/96, 1996/97. Bedfordshire County Cup. 1992/93, 1995/96, 1996/97. Training is held on Tuesday and Thursday nights under the guidance of Chief Coach Marty Davis, formerly of New Zealand Club, Takapuna. Players from all levels are invited to come along and participate.
For details call Denis Hardy
01234 751517 or 07747 618313

Major Achievements

Under 6s

An amazing first season of rugby has been had by all in the U6 Team. The children have been brilliantly behaved, but above all have displayed true sportsman qualities such as determination and perseverance. The winter months can be hard on the younger players!

We have been fortunate to have a fantastic team of coaches. I would like to thank Heather Sharrock, Russ Pitts, Anita Jarrett, Tony Barkell, Matt Ford, Steve Covington, Eric Murray, Stephen Nolan, Paul Dean, Ben Roger-Brown, Wayne Creamer and Alistair Middleton for their commitment and dedication throughout the season. We held a joint training session with Bedford Blues – the first away session for the children. It was a great day and wonderful to see so many families enjoying rugby.

We also had a successful year in terms of fundraising, raising over £1000. This money has purchased training equipment such as agility ladders and poles. In addition, in recognition of the players' weekly commitment, at such a young age, we rewarded them with their first rugby social, at Kidsworld Bedford. It was brilliant to see the children engaging socially off the pitch and gave the parents a chance to have coffee in the warmth for a change!

Robin Lamb – Head Coach - 2015/16 season

Under 6 Squad- season 2015/16

Under 7s

Rugby Lions & Peterborough Festival winners 2007/08, tour to Great Yarmouth, Bedfordshire Cup Winners 2008/09, 2015/16

Another fantastic season had by all in the U7s. Some great rugby and lots of fun. We welcomed some new players this year, they have settled in well with the old stagers, and the group is growing together.

I am pleased to report that we remain unbeaten this season. We have had some enjoyable fixtures against the likes of Olney, Bedford, Buckingham and Biggleswade. The ice-cold wind at Luton was less so, but we just about survived!! Well done to the players for maintaining a consistently high standard of play and improving over the season. We ventured on our first Ampthill mini rugby tour to Great Yarmouth in April – what an event that is!! Plenty of team bonding… Many thanks to James Wiggett for organising that on top pf his duties as Mini & Youth Chairman and his day job! The U7s have loved supporting the first team (and other senior sides) throughout this unbelievably successful season for the Club, merrily waving flags and cheering the teams on vociferously.

Head Coach – Gareth Farbon – season 2018/19

Under 7 Squad – season 2018/19

Under 8s

Bedfordshire Cup Champions 2008/09, 2011/12, 2012/13, 2013/14, 2015, 2016, Bedford Festival winners 2015/16, 2018/19

With speed, grace, and precision the Ampthill U8 squad wreaked havoc across Bedfordshire leaving a train of tags behind them.

It was a bumpy start to the season with players' salaries under negotiation, yet again. Grey clouds drew in closer, the wind whistled as it whipped bare legs and temperatures plummeted. Conditions were tough. "Tony the Tiger Millward" had no choice but to buckle up and do what he had sworn no man should ever have to do again – he gave out the weekly sweeties.

With the sugar filled team back in play, such determination continued onto the pitch, as they returned to their home ground, time and time again unbeaten. Of course, I reminded the parents that it is not about winning , it is about destroying the opposition, because we are the mighty Ampthill! "Hoooraaah!"

The players' dedication is second to none, and as a team of coaches we focussed their development around their strategic play. The team's understanding of defence has transformed into a solid wall of Maroon, Black and Gold. Coaches from other teams even went so far as to comment on this, and that of the teams' ability to pass on and then move, then look to off-load, before getting tagged. Such skills were put to the test at the Bedfordshire Festival. Despite low numbers, the team had never been so hungry for victory. The rival Bedford Blues could not match the speed, aggression and tactical play of the mighty Under 8's.

Head Coach, Robin Lamb & Team Manager Tony Millward – season 2018/19

Under 8s Squad - Bedfordshire Festival winners 2018/19

Under 9s

Mobbs Memorial Champions 2012/13, Bedfordshire Cup winners 2011/12, 2012/13, 2013/14

Under 9s in Prudential Cup Final at Twickenham – Sunday 26th May 2002

The pride of the mini and youth section the Clubs Under 9s were the first team in the Club's history to reach a Twickenham Final. The team qualified for the final by winning their group over two days of competition, at Nottingham, in early April. There were six teams in each of two groups, the first two places in each group playing off in a semi-final against the two highest placed in the opposing group.

Under 9s Coaches

    Clive Stallwood   Gareth Davies   Mike Adamson   Paul Hickey

Coach Gareth Davies gives the half-time team talk at Twickenham

| Dean Adamson | Callum Beasley | Steven Hickey | Josh Graham | Edward Stallwood | Morgan Phillips |
| William Wade | Joe Tidd | George Diffey | George Olney | Will Davis | |

Remainder of Under 9s Squad

Adrian Branscombe	Frankie Gill	Peter Jackson	Edward Janes	Oliver Jones
Aiden McKinstery	Joshua Peacock	James Smith	Rory Taylor	Joshua Ward
Max Warner				

Ironically, the final result on the day was a draw, with neither side scoring.

Under 10s

Under 10s Mobbs Memorial Champions 1985/86, 1986/87, 1988/89, 1998/99, 2000/01, 2002/03, 2007/08, 2011/12, 2012/13, 2013/14, County Cup winners, 2004-05, 2005/2006, 2006/07, 2007/08, 2014/2015, Prima Shield winners at Welford Road 2015/16

Under 10s - 2014/15 Bedfordshire Cup winners and Mobbs Memorial runners up

The under 10 squad had a fairly successful season. We started the season well with some good displays of rugby at the Peterborough tournament with our development squad winning their section of the tournament.

We learnt a lot from this and took the lessons into games with other clubs and really started impressing the coaches and parents.

In the Mobbs tournament we played some excellent rugby all round but unfortunately, we came second without losing a game and only came second due to try countback.

Further friendlies against some good teams saw the squad improving as the season went on and this culminated in us retaining the Bedfordshire Cup.

This was a keenly contested tournament with our first group game against Bedford ending in a draw and we ended up meeting the old foe in the final and this finished with us winning 1-0 in one of the most atrocious games of U10 rugby that the coaches had witnessed.

To end the season, we took two teams on tour that not only played some good rugby but cemented some old friendships and started some new ones. In the words of our esteemed departing Mini chairman "Rugby was the winner." On that note the Under 10s would like to thank Bruce McTavish for all his hard work and hope that he enjoys the rest.

Under 10 Team Manager – season 2014/15 – Simon Gibbs

Under 11s

Mobbs Memorial Champions 2003/04, 2008/09 2012/13, 2013/14, Bedfordshire County Champions, 2004/05, 2005,06, 2006/07, 2007/08, 2008/09, 2013/14, Sea-point Festival (Dublin) winners 2008/09, Land Rover Cup winners 2008/09, Guinness Premiership Finals Day 2008/09

With our third season of tackling, our players have continued to learn and develop their skills with enthusiasm this year. The players have continued to cope with the next change to the rules since September and tested our skills with numerous "friendlies" that have been organised. The boys and girls have been praised by a number of visiting coaches. The majority of our matches showed us in favourable light to Ampthill!

We attended he Cambridge Mini Festival as well as the Peterborough Festival and had some good matches at both. We also welcomed a number of new players who have settled in well and are now an integral part of the U11 team.

We took 27 players again on tour to Great Yarmouth this year and had two successful tri-angulars on both days which resulted in some great rugby being played even with the strange weather on the Sunday at Norwich! Opposing coaches remarked how strong and well-drilled our players were. All of our coaches were proud to be associated with these teams.

We bid a fond farewell to our girls, some of whom have been with us since U6s, who are moving across to the Girls squads – we will miss them and we all wish Evie, Isla, Harriet, Lola and Eleanor all the best of luck!

Head Coach – Stu Palmer & Team Manager Lyn Palmer

Under 11s season 2018/19

Under 12s

Under 12s Mobbs Memorial Champions 1994/95, 1999/00, 2002/03, 2003/04, 2012/13, 2013/14, 2014/15, Bedfordshire Cup winners, 2012/13, 2013/14, 2014/15

The U12s continued with their philosophy of playing two mixed ability teams and to their credit each team won more games that they lost. Mobbs (East Midlands Cup) qualifiers were played in November at Luton. The Ampthill U/12 team swept all teams aside to set up a Cup Final with old "frenemies" Old Northamptonians to be played at Goldington Road, Bedford in the following April. As cup holders for the last two years the U12s were looking forward to ending their mini careers with one last hurray! On the Sunday of the Mobbs qualifiers the Ampthill "B" team played against their counterparts at Old Scouts and Bedford in the annual triangular fixture where they came out as winners successfully ending years of being second best to these clubs!

Beds Cup was played in March and again Ampthill U12, established themselves as the best team in Bedfordshire beating Bedford in the final. During the Easter holidays the annual Mini Rugby Tour hit the Norfolk coast more specifically the Haven Holiday Park in Great Yarmouth. A "friendly" game against Wymondham saw the boys get their revenge, and then at the Holt Festival on the Sunday the team finished as Plate winners. A fantastic achievement after the late nights, karaoke and tour fun and games that all who went took part in.

The final game of the season, the Mobbs Cup Final was played at Goldington Road, home of the Bedford Blues. The large travelling Ampthill support witnessed a fantastic team performance resulting in an emphatic 7 tries to 2 victory against rivals Old Northamptonians. Once again, the Ampthill U12s are East Midlands champions and a fitting end to the boys' mini career that has consistently seen them exceed expectations and quite legitimately be known as the best U12 squad in the county and the region.

Under 12s Team Manager – season 2014/15 – James Wiggett

Under 12s Bedfordshire & East Midlands Champions – season 2014/15

Under 13s

Under 13s East Midlands Champions 2007/08, 2015/16 Bedfordshire Cup Champions, 2015/16, 2017/18, tour to Rouen 2015/16

As always, an eagerly anticipated start to the season, saw the boys fully embrace the transition from mini to youth rugby with full size pitches, 15 players and entry into the Herts. & Middlesex League (HML), as well as both the Bedfordshire and East Midlands Cups that they were more used to from the seasons playing mini rugby.

When planning the new season, the anticipation of playing on a full size pitch gave the coaches a little concern as they contemplated the overall fitness of the squad and as a result the boys were encouraged for the first time to try to stay in reasonable condition over the summer with a little bit of help provided hill runs in the park!! Registration Sunday in September, saw the summer recruitment strategies pay off, as the U13s had a squad big enough to run two sides throughout the whole season with the playing philosophy being two mixed ability teams for league and friendly games and in a cup game an "A" team would be selected. The season started in whirlwind fashion and the U13s were quickly facing friendly, league and cup matches week after week. This was pretty much the way it went for the season allowing all of the squad plenty of game time. The season saw games against some traditional opposition but also games against new clubs, Teddington, Market Harborough, and Maldon to name a few!! Many miles covered by travelling parents and their commitment was just as impressive as the boys!

The season finished with boys being crowned both Bedfordshire Cup and East Midlands Cup champions beating Leighton Buzzard and Northampton Old Scouts respectively in the final of each tournament. This proved yet again that not only are Ampthill the best U13 team in the county but also the East Midlands region. In particular, the East Midlands cup run was very impressive, as the draw for each round was not particularly kind to the boys pitching them against many of the stronger teams in the competition. This only proved to spur the boys on to produce some great rugby and also meant that no other club in the competition could question their "Champion" status.

Under 13 Team Manager – season 2015/16 – Head Coach – Hugh Christie & Ian White - Manager

Under 13s Bedfordshire & East Midlands Champions – season 2015/16

Under 14s

Under 14s East Midland Champions 1995/96, 2001/02, 2002/03, 2003/04, 2011/12, 2016/17 Bedfordshire Champions 2008/09, Herts & Middx. League Champions 2015/16

At the start of the season, our coaching team took the decision to enter the East Midlands League for our development squad. Our aim was to get as much rugby into the boys as we could for the season and make sure that game time was a priority. In the end it was an inspired decision as, not only did we get the rugby we desired, but we also saw new talent join the club and transition to the "A" squad through the season. In summary, the EML Challenger League saw us beat all-comers – playing 5, winning 5 and with a points difference of 166.

Our cup competition run also brought success, eventually. A semi-final exit from the Beds. Cup to Bedford was the boys' first defeat of the season. Rather than going away and mulling over the defeat, the squad to their credit took this as a sign that they wanted to improve. The introduction of our new rugby psychologist helped the boys understand that they had the skills, desire, and determination to beat Bedford and that all they needed to do was believe in themselves, and so they did!

Wins over Wellingborough and Long Buckby meant that we faced Bedford again away in the EM Semi-Final. A truly memorable game, not just for the end result but also for the way in which both teams played the game. The result, a 19-17 win to Ampthill, was met with huge roars from the large following crowd and grins over the playing and coaching squads faces which lasted for the remainder of the weekend. In the final, we came up against an excellent and very strong Kettering side, who came away with the win, but not without a valiant second half effort by the squad which they will take into next season.

Craig Ashby & Damon Blakey – Head Coaches – season 2014-15

Under 14 – season 2014/15 – winners of EM Challenger League, Easy Midlands Cup runners-up

Under 15s

Under 15s Bedfordshire Cup winners 2007/08, 2012/13, 2017/18, East Midlands Cup-winners 2003/04, 2006/07, 2007/08, 2008/09, 2009/10, 2010/11, 2011/12, 2012/13, Herts & Middx. League winners, 2010/11, 2011/12, 2012/13, 2013/14, National Champions Cup Winners 2012/13, East Midlands League winners 2014/15.

After many years of struggling against similar teams, the Under 15 took a huge leap forward this year. It was a year that saw them not only develop as individuals, but as a team that could challenge the best.

This is the first season we have been able to start with a squad large enough to almost play an "A" and "B" team. With this number of players, the competition for places proved invaluable, as players had to fight for their positions.

We played in two leagues, East Midlands, and Herts & Middlesex. We ran out easy winners of the latter and only lost the East Midlands by the smallest margin. Promotion next season in the Herts & Middlesex will provide a far more challenging prospect for the squad.

We also had an excellent cup run, with us losing out to Bedford in an amazing final under floodlights at the Bedford Swifts' ground.

Players from the squad have been selected to represent the Bedfordshire County team, the developing players' programme, and Welsh exiles. At the time of writing we have just found out that three of our players have also been selected for the East Midlands under 16 trials – we hope they succeed.

All in all, this has been a very rewarding and successful year from this age group, but there is more to come and next season we will really see this team challenge for all available trophies.

U15 Team Manager – Gary Taylor – season 2013-14

Under 15 - 2013/14 Herts & Middlesex League winners

Under 16s

Under 16s East Midlands 7s winners 1995/96, 2008/09, East Midlands Championship winners 2011/12, 2012/13, 2013/14, 2014/15, 2015/16, 2016/17, 2018/19 Bedfordshire Cup winners 2014/15, 2015/16, 2017/18, 2018/19

The U16s had yet another fantastic season. The 2018/19 season started in the first week of August with some pre-season fitness and fun. This ensured that the lads were at least a little prepared for the start of games in early September. The squad fulfilled East Midlands League, Bedfordshire Cup and East Midlands cup fixtures and friendlies this season with all players playing a part.

The boys convincingly won the Bedfordshire Cup 76-3 versus Biggleswade, on a dusty and hard pitch with some great off-loads and fantastic running rugby.

The traditional end of season show-down in the East Midlands Cup Final versus Northampton Old Scouts was the boys' final competitive game of the season. The game was played at Towcester and with an exceptional defensive display they were once again crowned champions of the region winning 36-14. This marked an exceptional achievement of being unbeaten in this competition for the last 7 years.

The boys will now move on and make the step up to the Academy under a new coaching team led by Tom Gray where new challenges await. However, the U16 coaches are sure they will have the skills, mentality, and ability to do very well and wish them all well in the next chapter of their rugby, hopefully staying in the game for many years to come.

Head Coach – Hugh Christey – season 2018/19

Under 16 squad – season 2018/19 – Bedfordshire & East Midland Champions

Under 17s

Under 17s National 17s representatives of East Midlands, Henry Staff plays for England against France and Scotland 2007/08, National Bowl winners 2009/10, 9 players selected for East Midlands in 2008/09, East Midlands Cup winners 2014/15, Herts & Middx. League winners 2015/16, Bedfordshire County Cup winners 2016/17

Lavery's tries give Ampthill National trophy – March 12th, 2005

Fly-half Dan Lavery helped Ampthill to a first-ever National U17s Plate title scoring 18 points in a 33-20 win over North Walsham at Worcester Sixways Stadium . Ampthill dominated possession from the start and Lavery went over after good work from Simon Jones and Richard Tonkin. Lavery added the conversion before North Walsham stormed into a 13-7 lead with a converted try and two penalties.

Ampthill missed two kicks of their own but Lavery made amends when he converted his second try. After the restart they continued to take the initiative with Lavery in the thick of things. He burst through the midfield to set up Richard Bernard's try before adding the conversion. Barnard then grabbed his second try thanks to a clever break from prop Chris Perrett and a good off-load from Matt Higgins.

Lavery missed the conversion but he had another shot at goal minutes later when Perrett barged his way over for Ampthill's fifth try, and even a consolation effort from North Walsham's Jake Tittering did not dampen their celebrations.

Ampthill: Graham Day, Max Thomas, Chris Perrett, Josh Williamson, Phil Hoy, John Cresswell, Joe Williams, Tom Ball, Tom Warfield, Daniel Lavery, Colin Davis, Simon Jones, Richard Tonkin, Richard Barnard, Matthew Kay.

Replacements: Dan Woodward, Matt Burke, Craig Isaacs, Martin Chalkley, Adam Andrews, Matthew Higgins, Ben Ashton

A tremendous achievement, these were local young men, the product of mini and youth and many would progress to the first XV.

Under 18s

Under 18s Herts & Middx. League winners 2014/15, Bedfordshire County Champions 2011/12, 2015/16, 2017/18, East Midlands League Champions 2011/12

For the first time in many years the Club fielded an Under 18 team. Despite some doom-laden prophesies about its sustainability, not only did the squad complete a full season, but also came back from a half-time deficit of 7-22 taking the Herts & Middlesex League title in the process. The squad's final record was played 12, won 8, lost 4 amassing 344 points for and 276 against.

On the weekends without a match, players took the opportunity to play for the 4ths., Extras, Vets and even the 2nd XV. Thanks go to the coaches and players of all those teams for giving them the chance to taste senior rugby and to inculcate them in the dark arts of rugby rituals. The "double gin, double brandy" inflicted by the U18s players on their Head Coach during the final presentation evening seemed to be a particular favourite.

A final end of season Tens tournament, at St. Neots, saw Ampthill field a mixed U17/U18 team. Despite not having played together before, and doing it "just for fun", the team reached the final of the competition, just losing to a Bedford team that had played and trained as an U17/U18 team throughout the season.

Two of our players – Josh White and Jerome Hallett made the East Midlands Colts team. Thanks go to the captain Conor Willetts and vice-captain Billy Ward for their work throughout the season and to the parents who have helped behind the scenes over the years. The age group has now travelled the road from Under 6s to Under 18s, with this year being the end of their Mini and Youth journey. The last event of the season was the Presentation Evening, with each player receiving a medal engraved with their name and a motto which is uniquely theirs "Ex Amicitia Victoria." Roughly translated "Through Friendship Victory".

The following season 2015/16, the Under 18s would become Bedfordshire County Champions

U18 Team Manager – Ian Barclay – season 2014-15

Colts

East Midlands Colts Cup winners 1995/96, Bedfordshire Colts Cup Winners 2002/03

1992/93 - Ampthill Colts – Rugby World's "Youth Team of the Month"

In its first full season the Colt's record was a remarkable:

played	won	drew	lost	pts. for	pts. against
22	20	0	2	709	194

The Colts lost only 2 games, both to Stockwood Park: 5 – 14 in the Bedfordshire Cup Final and 5 – 24, in the final of the East Midlands Cup. In December 1992, the Rugby World publication made Ampthill Colts "Youth Team of the Month". Robert Campbell, Simon Spavins, Paul Smedley, Jonathan Bugg, Mark Cheeseman, Mark Green, Johnny Sprigg and Steve Gyau-Awuah played for Bedfordshire Colts against the Army.

In the East Midlands Cup, the Colts beat Men's Own 51-0, Old Scouts 22-21, Wellingborough 86-0, Kettering 25-8, before losing to Stockwood Park in the final.

East Midlands Colts Cup Final

An injury-hit Ampthill Colts side lost 24-5 to Luton's Stockwood Park in the East Midlands Cup Final, at Dillingham Park. But they could look back on a fine campaign, with just two defeats in 22 games this season – ironically both to Stockwood. The visitors led 7-0 at half-time and added another try soon after, before Ampthill's hopes were raised by a try from Robert Campbell. But Stockwood added two more tries and a conversion to secure their victory.

Ampthill Colts won the East Midlands Cup in 1996

The Colts produced some notable performances and representative honours this season under the expert coaching of Denis Hardy and Dave Sprigg.

Ian Campbell and Will Sneath scored 27 and 23 tries, respectively. Sean Jones, Ian Campbell, Fraser Newberry, Martin Scott, Terry Stokes, and Dave Barry were all selected for Bedfordshire. Terry Stokes was in the East Midlands squad for the Colts Championship final at Twickenham.

On Sunday 28 April Ampthill beat Wellingborough 15-10 in a close-fought East Midlands Cup Final at Dillingham Park.

Ampthill: I. Campbell, W. Sneath, B. Venthem, J. Hurrel, A. Green, J. Offer, M. Troiano, A. Shindler, D. Barry, F. Newberry, A. Best, M. Cresswell, T. Stokes, S. Jones. M. Scott

Replacements: J. Rolls, D. Dexter, P. Saunders, J. Lothian, D. Mechem

Ampthill Colts celebrate their victory over Wellingborough in the East Midlands Cup Final

The Colts also were runners up in the East Midlands Colts seven a side competition, this season.

The Academy

Season 2017/18

The Academy was started this season out of a need to keep a very strong group of players, last season's U17s, playing rugby and, more importantly, playing at Ampthill Rugby Club. A group which had been very successful in the leagues and winners of the Bedfordshire Cup for a number of years. The age range is from 16 to 18 and the squad was to play in the East Midlands Colts League, The Bedfordshire and East Midlands Cups and the National Colts Cup. The aim of the Academy is to develop players coming up from youth rugby, preparing them for the senior game and potentially, a semi-professional contract with Ampthill's 1st XV squad.

Ex - London Scottish and Ampthill 1st XV forward, Tom Gray, was appointed Head Coach during the close season and he set about putting together a good group of coaches. Assistant coaches, Steve Everitt, Phil Donvaband, Giles Witheat and Leigh Clarke were joined by Craig Shelley the following season. Ailane Clarke became team manager. The aim was to establish a strong squad with the added assistance of some from last season's Under 16s. Pre-season fitness training was well attended and a good squad formed with increasing input from the younger age group.

The Academy won nearly all their games with only the very odd disappointment through the season and the stand-out result would be the Bedfordshire Cup victory over Bedford in a very hard-fought final. In mid-January, the team travelled to Sedgley Park, Manchester and had a convincing win. Visits to various parts of Warwickshire and Leicestershire have also seen some good wins for this well-travelled side.

A number of players have also played representative rugby for the East Midlands with hooker Charlie Fleckney going on to play for England Counties and receiving a cap against Italy.

Towards the second-half of each season a number of players who are ready to move up will start training and mixing with the senior squads gaining valuable experience. If the Academy has no Saturday fixture players gain time experience with the 1881s, Jets, Extras, or 5th XVs. It is thought this arrangement is unique among Championship-level clubs

As the older players now move on into the full adult sides this year's U/16s will all join the Academy and a few have already had some training and one game, a win up at Barkers Butts.

The Academy won the Bedfordshire Cup and were East Midlands league winners. The progression of players; 7 regulars in the 1881s, 5 playing regular university rugby.

2017-18	played	won	drawn	lost
	22	19	0	3

Season 2018/19

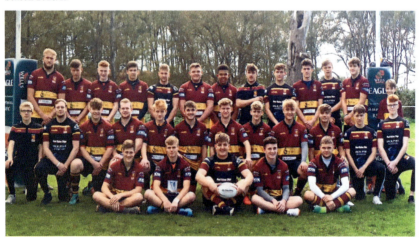

The Academy Squad 2018/19

The new intake of players for the season saw the Academy with a strong looking squad for the new season. It was decided to run two squads; a Saturday (1st XV) and Sunday (development), though this proved difficult with injuries and availability issues.

The test came very early with Bedford away in an East Midlands League game in September. An early try conceded but a brilliant fight-back saw Ampthill return home with a 12-43 victory.

Following league games saw Ampthill travel to Old Northamptonians and return with an EML defeat, followed with a very healthy win over Peterborough. The League season continued with the lads putting in some good and hard-fought performances to finish the season well.

Early season wins in the National Cup over Lutterworth and Ashby saw the Academy then go out to Kettering in a close game at Dillingham Park and after early victories in the East Midlands Cup were followed by a semi-final defeat to Old Northamptonians.

A cracking Beds Cup Final ended with the runners-up spot after losing to Bedford.

The squad enjoyed a good weekend tour to Sedgley Park and a victory.

Next season looks very promising with a good group of players joining the squad for a Championship season. Player progression; 6 regulars in 1881í and Jets, 4 playing university rugby.

2018-19	played	won	drawn	lost
	27	15	0	12

Season 2019/20 – Academy Results

A much bigger squad, but now just playing Saturday games but including development XV games on Saturday as well (which accounted for 5 losses against teams who played their 1st XVs).

The Academy were unbeaten in the East Midlands league and reached the final of the East Midlands Cup before the season was ended prematurely.

Date	Opponent	Comp	H/A	Result
Aug. 31	Syston	F	A	W 14-64
Sept. 7	Kettering	F	A	W 7-27
14	Luton	Beds Cup R1	H	postponed
21	Northampton Old Scouts	F	A	W 10-24
28	Towcestrians	EML	A	W 0-57
Oct 5	Hinckley	F	H	W 60-5
5	Bedford	F	H	L 19-52
12	Old Laurentians	EML	A	W 7-10
19	Kettering	NCC R1	H	D 31-31
26	Oadby Wyggestonians	F	A	cancelled
Nov. 1	Market Harborough	F	A	L 7-5
9	Luton	EMC R1	A	walkover
9	Olney	F	A	W 0-46
16	Leicester Forest	F	A	L 48-10
23	Huntingdon	EML	H	postponed
30	Pinley	F	A	W 0-46
Dec. 7				
14	Kenilworth	F	A	cancelled
21	Bedford Athletic	Beds Cup R2	H	L 7-20
Jan. 4	Ashby	F	A	W 50-21
11	Olney	F	H	W 38-17
18	Towcestrians	EMC QF	H	W 75-0
25	Barkers Butts	F	A	cancelled
Feb. 1	Leicester Forest	F	A	cancelled
8	Nuneaton	F	H	L 14-15
22	Old Northamptonians	EMSF	A	W 10-22

29 March	Northampton Old Scouts	F	A	cancelled
	Old Northamptonians	EMSF	A	W 0-58

Tom Gray - Head Coach & Alaine Clark – Team Manager

Girls Squads U13, U15, U18

2008/09 saw the Girls section of the club consolidate, in terms of numbers and we now have great group of players to springboard into 2009/10.

As with previous seasons, finding opposition has proved a little difficult and we have often joined forces with Bedford and Letchworth in putting out sides. The highlight of the season for the U18s was the 45-45 draw against Saracens when a pure Ampthill side was pitched against a team made up of mostly Herts county players. For the U15s strong performances in the 7s tournament at Saints showed the progress the team has made over the year.

We had excellent representation in the County side with 6 in both age groups. Alice Redman (U15) made it to the regional trials with Rachel Gibb (U18) going one step further and playing in the regional side after Christmas.

I summary, another good season where we have continued to develop and we can look forward to next season with confidence.

Paul Farthing & Richard Redman

Girls Under 15s

Ipswich Shield Winners 2016/2016, 5 girls selected for East Midlands 2018/19

2008/09

Season 2018/19

Under 13 Girls

This season has been a difficult season for the U13 Girls due to depleted numbers and experience. However, all the girls who have worn the Ampthill jersey dug deep and soldiered on to take part in lots of matches and festivals, sometimes having to join other teams. This is not necessarily a bad thing as the players get to be coached by other teams with different ideas and as such the rugby learning process increases.

The girls are a tight unit who play for each other and thrive when playing together. With silverware won to place in the ARUFC Cabinet, the U13 Girls have contributed to club success and have had many comments about them voiced by other teams throughout the season with invitations to play as guests at other clubs.

Coaches – Jules Gale, Richard Roberts, Shaun Wood, Craig Rolfe, Charlotte Saunders, Team Manager – Becky Kerr

Under 15 Girls

The season started with a real cracker. Playing Cambridge at home in wet and windy conditions, the girls played some excellent rugby, deservedly ending the first half leading 19-0. Cambridge mounted a second half fight back and we found ourselves 19-20 down. With only minutes left to play, Sian, our flying winger collected the ball deep in our half, and once she was off there was no catching her, sprinting the length of the pitch to score the winner in the corner to claim a well-deserved opening win for the girls.

Our next trip to the Sudbury 7s and Towcester XR7s were a stern test, winning and losing in equal numbers. Following these fixtures, the coaching team implemented a back to basics training regime concentrating on pace, aggression, and commitment. This handsomely paid off with success in our following fixtures, most markedly when we scored an incredible 236 points in an hour of rugby against Biggleswade! Surely a club record?

At the Royston 10s Festival, hosted by England Ladies, Hannah Gallagher and Tamara Taylor, the girls played 3 excellent matches, winning 3 and only narrowly losing out to an always strong and well organised Peterborough team.

Early in the year came the East Midlands trials. Five of our girls were selected for the regional team- Sophie, Chloe, Sasha, and Sian. An outstanding achievement for them and a great reflection on the club. During the short East Midlands' season, our girls made a massive contribution, showing superb commitment and work rate. Especially well done to Anwen who swapped her preferred number 10 jersey to play at number 15 and Sophie moving from scrum-half onto the wing. Both showing the all-round skill, work rate and commitment that lead them to multiple tries in both the 7s and 15s.

While some of our girls were away with the East Midlands, our others performed equally well, clustering with Aylesbury for a fine 57-19 win over Bletchley. Here we saw outstanding performances from Ashley, running in two great tries and Abby kicking 6 out of 9 conversions.

Coaches – Jules Gale, Richard Roberts, Shaun Wood, Craig Rolfe, Charlotte Saunders, Team Manager – Becky Kerr

Under 18 Girls

11 girls selected for East Midlands in 2018/19, Sian Mills selected for England Deaf, RFU Regional Plate winners 2017/18,

This season started with a few bumps as the new U15 graduates and the existing group got to know each other. An early defeat by an excellent Gosford side was followed by a really good performances at the Sudbury 7s and Towcester XR7s in September.

This was followed by two defeats to Old Albanians and High Wycombe, as the girls prepared for the RFU Cup in Norwich against Crusaders in early November.

Now, this game will go down in folklore. The girls travelled with only 13 players due to injuries and unavailability. The game started with Crusaders running in 3 tries and Ampthill were 19-5 down at half-time. After a Churchillian speech by Ian Scarr and Gloria Mills the girls set about Crusaders with a vigour not witnessed before. Not only did they score 4 unanswered tries, they also kept Crusaders out with only 12 players winning the game 19-25, in probably the best rugby any of them has ever played.

The above win spurred the team on to defeat Aylesbury/Fullerians by cricket scores in December, coming back down to earth with a bump against Tamworth just before Christmas. A return to winning ways against Letchworth in January, was followed by the East Midlands trials where 11 girls were selected for the squad.

By fortune of the comeback win against Crusaders, the girls were crowned champions of the RFU Area 4 Pool 2 and were matched against their bogey side of Old Northamptonians in the RFU Area 4 semi. Losing this would mean they would be in the Bowl against Market Harborough. Lose it, they did as the ON's hoodoo returned (ON's had 17 girls selected for the East Midlands). Harborough ran out 20-15 winners in the best game they had played all season. Funny old game rugby. So, a runners-up bit of silverware and the highest ranked placing for the girls, firmly cementing themselves in the top 20 teams in the country.

The final tournament of the season at Bletchley XR7s just before Easter, saw the girls enter two sides, playing Rochford, Buckingham, and High Wycombe. Ampthill lost only one game and were runners-up.

As the season drew to a close, Hanna, Kiera, Megan, and Bethan were all selected to participate in the East Midlands ladies squad making their debuts against NLD and Warwickshire with Hannah being selected for the first Gill Burns Cup game against Sussex in April. The girls will feature in matches played against Surrey and also Kent in May. A special mention to Bethan who was retained by the Saracens Centre of Excellence during the season and participated at an RFU selection camp at Camberley with 100 other top players in the country.

Finally, we now have two international members of the squad. Last year Gloria Mills, coach of the squad was selected for England Deaf, this year her daughter Sian made her debut on the wing, playing with mum in the same team.

Mini & Youth – Hall of Fame

Season	Coach/Chairperson – Mini Section	Coach/Chairperson – Youth Section
1971/72	Dave Williams	
1973/79	Bill Edward	
1980/81	Bruce Hart	Norman Brown
1981/82	Bruce Hart	Norman Brown
1982/83	Roger Phillips	Bert Sheard
1983/84	Roger Phillips	Bert Sheard
1984/85	Roger Phillips	Larry Grant
1985/86	Roger Phillips	Larry Grant
1986/87	Roger Phillips	Larry Grant
1987/88	Frank Henry	Frank Henry
1988/89	Frank Henry	Frank Henry
1989/90	Frank Henry	Frank Henry
1990/91	Colin Copperwheat	Colin Copperwheat
1990/91	Jack Wilkinson	Jack Wilkinson
1992/93	Jack Wilkinson	Jack Wilkinson
1993/94	Brian Clark	Brian Clark
1994/95	Brian Clark	Brian Clark
1995/96	Brian Clark	Brian Clark
1996/97	Ian Cooper	Ian Cooper
1997/98	Jack Wilkinson	Jack Wilkinson
1998/99	Ian Cooper	Ian Cooper
1999/20	Ian Cooper	Ian Cooper
2000/01	Ian Cooper	Ian Cooper
2001/02	Ian Cooper	John Wilkinson
2002/03	John Wilkinson	John Wilkinson
2003/04	Kevin Tonkin	Nigel Macklin
2004/05	John Cresswell	Nigel Macklin
2005/06	Yvonne Russon	Kevin Tonkin
2006/07	Nigel Macklin	Nigel Macklin
2007/08	John Cresswell	John Cresswell
2008/09	John Cresswell	John Cresswell
2009/10	John Cresswell	John Cresswell
2010/11	Bruce McTavish	Clive Stallwood
2011/12	Bruce McTavish	Clive Stallwood
2013/14	Bruce McTavish	Clive Stallwood
2014/15	Bruce McTavish	Clive Stallwood
2015/16	Bruce McTavish	Clive Stallwood
2016/17	Keith Garwood	Keith Garwood
2017/18	Keith Garwood	Keith Garwood
2018/19	James Wiggett	James Wiggett
2019/20	James Wiggett	James Wiggett

Author's note: In the Spring of 2021 the Mini & Youth section will be fifty years old.

Printed in Poland
by Amazon Fulfillment
Poland Sp. z o.o., Wrocław

64609572R00193